2004

W9-AEP-499

We, the People of Europe?

TRANSLATION / TRANSNATION

SERIES EDITOR EMILY APTER

Writing Outside the Nation
BY AZADE SEYHAN

The Literary Channel: The Inter-National Invention of the Novel
EDITED BY MARGARET COHEN AND CAROLYN DEVER

Ambassadors of Culture: The Transamerican Origins of Latino Writing
BY KIRSTEN SILVA GRUESZ

Experimental Nations. Or, the Invention of the Maghreb
BY RÉDA BENSMAÏA

What Is World Literature?
BY DAVID DAMROSCH

The Portable Bunyan: A Transnational History of The Pilgrim's Progress
BY ISABEL HOFMEYR

We, the People of Europe? Reflections on Transnational Citizenship
BY ÉTIENNE BALIBAR

ÉTIENNE BALIBAR

We, the People of Europe?

Reflections on Transnational Citizenship

TRANSLATED BY **JAMES SWENSON**

PRINCETON UNIVERSITY PRESS

PRINCETON AND OXFORD

Copyright © 2004 by Étienne Balibar

The French edition of this book, *Nous, citoyens d'Europe: Les Frontières, l'État, le peuple*, was
published by Editions la Découverte in 2001. Some essays have been dropped and others added
for the English edition.
Published by Princeton University Press, 41 William Street, Princeton, New Jersey 08540
In the United Kingdom: Princeton University Press, 3 Market Place, Woodstock,
Oxfordshire OX20 1SY

All Rights Reserved.

Library of Congress Cataloging-in-Publication Data

Balibar, Etienne, 1942–
  [Nous, citoyens d'Europe. English]
  We, the people of Europe? : reflections on transnational citizenship / Étienne Balibar ;
translated by James Swenson.
    p. cm. — (Translation/transnation)
  Includes bibliographical references and index.
  ISBN 0-691-08989-2 (cl : alk. paper) — ISBN 0-691-08990-6 (pb. : alk. paper)
  1. Citizenship—Europe. 2. Political rights—Europe. I. Title. II. Series.

JN40.B3513 2004
323.6′094—dc22   2003055450

British Library Cataloging-in-Publication Data is available

Publication of this book has been aided by the French Ministry of Culture—Centre National du
Livre

Cover photo by Liesl Ponger, courtesy of Charim Galerie

This book has been composed in Minion with Gill Sans display

Printed on acid-free paper. ∞

www.pupress.princeton.edu

Printed in the United States of America

10 9 8 7 6 5 4 3 2 1

333.6
B186

CONTENTS

PREFACE   vii

1

At the Borders of Europe   1

2

Homo nationalis: An Anthropological Sketch of the
        Nation-Form   11

3

Droit de cité or Apartheid?   31

4

Citizenship without Community?   51

5

Europe after Communism   78

6

World Borders, Political Borders   101

7

Outline of a Topography of Cruelty: Citizenship and Civility in the
        Era of Global Violence   115

8

Prolegomena to Sovereignty   133

9

Difficult Europe: Democracy under Construction   155

10

Democratic Citizenship or Popular Sovereignty? Reflections on
        Constitutional Debates in Europe   180

▌▌
Europe: Vanishing Mediator? *203*

NOTES *237*

INDEX *283*

This book is the American equivalent to the volume published in France with the title *Nous, citoyens d'Europe? Les Frontières, l'État, le peuple.*[1] But although there is much similarity of content between the two volumes, I should make clear immediately that it is as much an adaptation as a translation.[2] First, some of the chapters were originally written in English and, although they needed some editing and rewriting, are now basically returning to their original form. Second, some texts included in the French volume have been removed because they had already appeared in recent collections in England or the United States, were less significant for an English-speaking readership, or were partially redundant with other essays in the volume, and we wanted to make room for more recent essays that updated the ideas and descriptions of the earlier texts.[3] Third, two substantial essays included in this volume have no equivalent in the French volume because they were written after its completion. They now form my last two chapters: "Democratic Citizenship or Popular Sovereignty?" and "Europe: Vanishing Mediator?"

As a consequence, the organization of the book has been reconsidered: it is no longer made of separate parts with specific summaries and introductions. Instead, the chapters are presented in continuous succession, with an Ouverture (my address to the University of Thessaloníki in 1999) and a Finale (my George L. Mosse Lecture from November 2002, also originally addressed to a European audience but as a public reply to what I perceived as an interpellation to "Europe" coming from American intellectuals). In this manner, I hope that the goals of the volume have gained clarity. As will become clear from a progressive reading, many of the peculiarities of my arguments are dependent on the circumstances, dates, places, kinds of audiences that specified each of the essays. This results from my conviction, now firmly rooted, that political matters cannot be examined from a deductive point of view (be it moral, legal, philosophical, sociological, or some combination of these), but can only be theorized *under the constraints* imposed by the situation and the changes in the situation that one observes or tries to anticipate. This is not to say that the discourse remains purely *descriptive or empirical*, but that—precisely in order to be "theoretical" in the way that the political matter requires—it has to *incorporate as much as possible a reflection on its immediate conditions*, which determine the understanding and use of concepts. This "method" could be called "clinical": it combines the epistemological interrogation of the speculative categories that we use in political philosophy (such as borders and territories, state, community and "public" structures, citizenship and sovereignty, rights and norms, violence and civility) with a consistent affirmation that only singular forces, unpredictable events, and dialectical evolutions actually shape history. Far from preventing us from concentrating on fundamental issues, it does—so I believe—actually allow the progressive clarification of a central *problem* and its logical and practical implications.

The central problem throughout these essays is what I call "transnational citizenship," which I try to distinguish carefully from the idea of both "supranational" and "postnational" citizenship. I would not deny that this problem is raised precisely by the way in which European unification (certainly not reducible to a mere effect of "globalization," which would tend to create political units larger than the traditional nations) has progressively divorced the two concepts of *citizenship* and *nationhood* that the classical state practically identified. But I think that what has emerged is neither a reproduction of the same "constitution of citizenship" (my equivalent for the classical Greek term *politeia*) at a *supranational* level (not even in the form of a "federal citizenship" in a "federal state"), nor a dissolution of the notions of "community" and "people" in a postnational "cosmopolitical society." There are indeed *supranational structures* (above all in the form of administrations and representative bodies) and there are *postnational cosmopolitical anticipations* (in particular, the attempt to create a political identity that is open to continuous admission of new peoples and cultures) in the construction of Europe. But the basic problems result from an open process of immanent transformation of national identity, national sovereignty, and national membership, which I tentatively call the transnationalization of the political, whose results are not really predictable.

In the following essays, I have put considerable insistence on the idea that this process, albeit *necessary* (if only because European unification has reached a point of irreversibility, where it becomes a condition for the very continuation of the different "nations" and "states" that it transcends), meets with considerable *obstacles*. I have even used the terms *crisis* and *critical point*. This can give the impression that I look at the current processes with a skeptical or pessimistic eye. In fact, I am neither pessimistic nor optimistic, but I try to understand what the elements of the historical dialectic in this critical conjuncture have become.

From a theoretical point of view, the obstacles are concentrated around the fact that a "European Constitution" sharpens the classical debate between the different ways of laying the "foundations" for a democratic state (by referring either to the existence of *a people* within its territorial limits and with its own history or to the "basic rights" and "constitutional rules" that organize the distribution of powers and legitimize the form of government) but, more important, *radically reopens the discussion on the notion of sovereignty*. For historical and structural reasons, *a European "constitution of citizenship"* can only emerge on the condition of being *more democratic* than the traditional constitutions of the "national" states—or it will be deprived of any legitimacy, any capacity to "represent" the populations and solve (or mediate) their social conflicts (be they conflicts of economic interests or cultural-religious loyalties). In a sense therefore, a European "constitution of citizenship" has to take decisive steps *beyond the concept of sovereignty* as it was progressively elaborated throughout the history of nation-states (where it amounted to concentrating the "representation of the people" within the "public powers" of the state). But in another sense it must deepen and rearticulate the notion of "popular sovereignty" in the sense of effective responsibility of the political leadership before the constituency and direct representation of the population and its social interests in political terms—not "ethnic" or "cultural" ones—whereas the current system is one of uncontrolled bureaucracy and hidden compromises among national politicians. It is my suggestion that this dilemma, affecting the very concept of the political, will lead not only to a debate concerning the particular articles or even principles of the constitution but also to a transformation of the very *notion* of "constitution," or a new era of juridical-political science.

But the theoretical problems are only one way to approach the dialectic of the construction of "Europe" as a new type of political entity. In a sense, it is much more urgent to discuss it from the point of view of concrete issues, which directly affect the future of democracy in this part of the world. Europe has certainly no privilege in this respect. It has, undoubtedly, a democratic inheritance (with national nuances), which I see in particular in the field of *social policy* (where Europe has invented a "social-democratic" model—I prefer to speak of "conflictual democracy"—that allows the recognition of individuals as bearers of collective rights and protections) and in the field of *religious policy* (where it has invented an intermediary path between the official recognition of certain cults and the absolute freedom for religious groups to compete in the offer of "spiritual goods"). Whether this is a foundation to be built on, or an inhibiting system of past achievements that prevents new institutions from being invented, is sometimes hard to decide. Perhaps it is both, which amounts to explaining that the core of the process is a tension or an unresolved dilemma. As in previous books, I have laid considerable insistence, in this respect, on the emergence, alongside with the formal aspects of "European citizenship" (that is, a system of institutions, rights, and obligations common to the various peoples associated in the European construction), of a virtual *European apartheid.* I use this intentionally provocative expression to signal the critical nature of the contradiction between the opposite movements of inclusion and exclusion, reduplication of external borders in the form of "internal borders," stigmatization and repression of populations whose presence within European societies is nonetheless increasingly massive and legitimate. In this sense I try to describe Europe as a "democratic laboratory," a juxtaposition of "worksites" where new aspects of democracy are needed, and perhaps likely to be developed, something that could be meaningful not only locally but also generally, or globally.

As I was completing this volume, writing the final chapter (for which I took advantage of the invitation of the Humboldt-Universität for the Mosse Lecture), the political situation in the world (and particularly in the Near East and the Mediterranean area) was becoming increasingly tense and dangerous. Not only because of the continuous aggravation of the Palestinian-Israeli conflict, which has an immediate impact on "identity politics" in Europe (including the rise of new forms of "generalized" anti-Semitism, both "judeophobic" and "arabophobic"), but also because of the prospects of war in Iraq (which may have taken place, or will be continuing, when this book comes out). I was led to ask the question of the extent to which the democratic potential involved in the construction of Europe, supposing that it proves able to "resolve" its intrinsic contradictions, could be considered a *challenge* (as some Europeans believe or dream) or, much better, an *alternative* to the model of "global power" now represented by the United States, especially since the collapse of the socialist bloc and the evolution of its former members to either "wild" capitalist societies (the case of Russia) or nationalist combinations of political authoritarianism and economic liberalism (the case of China). This was also the result of my becoming aware of the growing interrogations of American intellectuals about the European political process, an interest that is testified to by the very commissioning of this book for a new series at Princeton University Press. I realized that the title that I had chosen ("We, the People of Europe?") as a way to refer to the democratic tradition and quest that is common to Europe and America, in order to show its open and unfinished character, had acquired an additional meaning, perhaps a more conflictual one. There should be no misunderstanding on this point, however. Apart from specific political (and strategic) issues, which are likely to evolve according to the changing orientations of governments, there is—at least as far as I am aware—no thought in this book of "teaching America a lesson." I think that lessons are always taught reciprocally or, better said, are drawn from the confrontation and subsequent relativization of one's own experience with the diversity of the world. Not only the United States and Europe (that part of Europe already involved in the construction of the transnational ensemble) are included in this comparison but also all the other "civilizations" emerging from the twentieth century, the century of colonization and decolonization, revolutions and imperialisms, "world wars" and civil wars. My own hypotheses on transnational citizenship are thus offered to a multilateral confrontation "from a European point of view."

I express my deepest thanks to the friends and colleagues who have acted for the good realization of our project, in particular Emily Apter of New York University, the editor of the series "Translation/Transnation," Mary Murrell and Fred Appel of Princeton University Press, and my good friend and accurate translator James Swenson.

Paris
December 22, 2002

I

At the Borders of Europe

I am speaking of the "borders of Europe" in Greece, one of the "peripheral" countries of Europe in its traditional configuration—a configuration that reflects powerful myths and a long-lived series of historical events. Thessaloníki is itself at the edge of this border country, one of those places where the dialectic between confrontation with the foreigner (transformed into a hereditary enemy) and communication between civilizations (without which humanity cannot progress) is periodically played out. I thus find myself, it seems, right in the middle of my object of study, with all the resultant difficulties.

The term *border* is extremely rich in significations. One of my hypotheses is that it is undergoing a profound change in meaning. The borders of new sociopolitical entities, in which an attempt is being made to preserve all the functions of the sovereignty of the state, are no longer entirely situated at the outer limit of territories; they are dispersed a little everywhere, wherever the movement of information, people, and things is happening and is controlled—for example, in cosmopolitan cities. But it is also one of my hypotheses that the zones called peripheral, where secular and religious cultures confront one another, where differences in economic prosperity become more pronounced and strained, constitute the melting pot for the formation of a people (*dēmos*), without which

Lecture delivered October 4, 1999, on the invitation of the Institut français de Thessalonique and the Department of Philosophy of Aristotle University of Thessaloníki. French text first published in *Transeuropéennes* 17 (1999–2000): 9–17. The translation of this essay, by Erin M. Williams, originally appeared under the title World Borders, Political Borders, *PMLA* 117 (2002): 71–78.

there is no citizenship (*politeia*) in the sense that this term has acquired since antiquity in the democratic tradition.

In this sense, border areas—zones, countries, and cities—are not marginal to the constitution of a public sphere but rather are at the center. If Europe is for us first of all the name of an *unresolved political problem*, Greece is one of its centers, not because of the mythical origins of our civilization, symbolized by the Acropolis of Athens, but because of the current problems concentrated there.

Or, more exactly, the notion of a center confronts us with a choice. In connection with states, it means the concentration of power, the localization of virtual or real governing authorities. In this sense, the center of Europe is in Brussels, Strasbourg, or in the City of London and the Frankfurt stock exchange, or will soon be in Berlin, the capital of the most powerful of the states that dominate the construction of Europe, and secondarily in Paris, London, and so on. But this notion has another, more essential and elusive meaning, which points to the sites where a people is constituted through the creation of civic consciousness and the collective resolution of the contradictions that run through it. Is there then a "European people," even an emergent one? Nothing is less certain. And if there is not a European people, a new type of people yet to be defined, then there is no public sphere or European state beyond technocratic appearances. This is what I meant when I imitated one of Hegel's famous phrases: *Es gibt keinen Staat in Europa.*[1] But the question must remain open, and in a particularly "central" way at the border points.

There are more difficult issues. We are meeting in the aftermath of the war in Kosovo, the Balkans, or Yugoslavia, at a moment when the protectorate established at Priština by the Western powers is being put into place with difficulty and for dubious ends, while in Belgrade uncertain maneuvers are unfolding for or against the future of the current regime. It is not certain that we all have the same judgment about these events, from which we will not emerge for quite some time. It is even probable that we have profoundly divergent opinions on the subject. The fact that we do not use the same names for the war that just took place is an unequivocal sign of this. It is possible—it is probable—that some of you condemned the intervention of NATO for various reasons, and that still others, also for various reasons, found it impossible to take sides. It is possible—it is probable—that certain of us saw striking proof of the subordination of Europe to the exterior, hegemonic power of the United States, whereas others saw a mercenary utilization of American power by the European states in the service of continental objectives. And so on.

I do not presume to resolve these dilemmas. But I want to state here my conviction that these events mercilessly reveal the fundamental contradictions plaguing European unification. It was not by chance that they occurred when Europe was set to cross an irreversible threshold, by instituting a unitary currency and thus communal control of economic and social policy and by implementing formal elements of "European citizenship," whose military and police counterparts are quickly perceived.

In reality, what is at stake here is the definition of the *modes of inclusion and exclusion* in the European sphere, as a "public sphere" of bureaucracy and of relations of force but also of communication and cooperation between peoples. Consequently, in the strongest sense of the term, it is *the possibility or the impossibility of European unification*. In the establishment of a protectorate in Kosovo and, indirectly, other regions of the Balkans, as in the blockade of Slobodan Milošević's Serbia, the elements of *impossibility* prevailed obviously and lastingly—even if one thinks, as is my case, that an intervention one way or another to block the ongoing "ethnic cleansing" could no longer be avoided and even if one is skeptical, as is my case, of self-righteous positions concerning a people's right to self-determination in the history of political institutions. The unacceptable impasse that we had reached on the eve of the war in the whole of ex-Yugoslavia was fundamentally the result of the powerlessness, inability, and refusal of the "European community" to propose political solutions of association, to open possibilities of development for the peoples of the Balkans (and more generally of the East), and to assume *everywhere* its responsibilities in an effective struggle against human rights violations. It is thus Europe, particularly the primary European powers, that is responsible for the catastrophic developments that subsequently took place and for the consequences they now may have.

But, on the other hand, if it is true that the Balkan War manifests the impasse and the *impossibility* of European unification, it is necessary to have the courage (or the madness) to ask in today's conditions: *under what conditions might it become possible again?* Where are the potentialities for a different future? How can they be released by assigning responsibility for the past but avoiding the fruitless exercise of repeating it? An effort of this kind alone can give meaning to a project of active European citizenship, disengaged from all myths of identity, from all illusions about the necessary course of history, and a fortiori from all belief in the infallibility of governments. It is this effort that I would like to call on and contribute to. We must privilege the issue of the border when discussing the questions of the European people and of the state in Europe because it crystallizes the stakes of politico-economic power and the symbolic stakes at work in the collective imagination: relations of force and material interest on one side, representations of identity on the other.

I see a striking indicator of this in the fact that during the new Balkan War that has just taken place the *name of Europe* functioned in two contradictory ways, which cruelly highlighted the ambiguity of the notions of *interior* and *exterior*. On one hand, Yugoslavia (as well as to varying degrees the whole Balkan area, including Albania, Macedonia, Bulgaria . . .) was considered *an exterior space*, in which, in the name of a "principle of intervention" that I will not discuss here but that clearly marked a reciprocal exteriority, an entity called *Europe* felt compelled to intervene to block a crime against humanity, with the aid of its powerful American allies if necessary. On the other had, to take up themes proposed by the Albanian national writer Ismail Kadaré,[2] for example, it was explained that this intervention was occurring on Europe's soil, within its historical limits, and in defense of the principles of Western civilization. Thus, this time the Balkans found themselves fully inscribed *within the borders of Europe*. The idea was that Europe could not accept genocidal population deportation *on its own soil*, not only for moral reasons but above all to preserve its political future.

However, this theme, which I do not by any means consider pure propaganda, did not correspond to any attempt to anticipate or accelerate the integration of the Balkan regions referred to in this way into the European public sphere. The failure of the stillborn "Balkan conference" testifies eloquently to this. There was no economic plan of reparations and development involving all the countries concerned and the European community as such. Nor was the notion of "European citizenship" adapted—for example, by the issuing of "European identity cards" to the Kosovo refugees whose identification papers had been destroyed by the Serbian army and militias, along the lines of the excellent suggestion by the French writer Jean Chesneaux.[3] Nor were the steps and criteria for entrance into the "union" redefined.

Thus, on the one hand, the Balkans are a part of Europe and, on the other, they are not. Apparently, we are not ready to leave this contradiction behind, for it has equivalents in the eastern part of the continent, beginning with Turkey, Russia, and the Caucasus regions, and everywhere takes on a more and more dramatic significance. This fact results in profoundly paradoxical situations. First of all, the colonization of Kosovo (if one wants to designate the current regime this way, as Régis Debray, with whom I otherwise totally disagree, suggested by his comparisons with the Algerian War) is an "interior colonization" of Europe (with the help of a sort of American foreign legion). But I am also thinking of other situations, such as the fact that Greece could wonder if it was interior or exterior to the domain of European sovereignty, because its soil served as a point of entry for land-occupation forces in which it did not want to take part. I can even imagine that when Turkish participation in the operation was discussed, certain Greek "patriots" asked themselves which of the two "hereditary enemies" was more interior to political Europe, on its way to becoming a military Europe.

All this proves that the notions of interiority and exteriority, which form the basis of the representation of the border, are undergoing a veritable earthquake. The representations of the border, territory, and sovereignty, and the *very possibility of representing* the border and territory, have become the object of an irreversible historical "forcing." At present these representations constitute a certain conception of the political sphere as a sphere of sovereignty, both the imposition of law and the distribution of land, dating from the beginning of the European modern age and later exported to the whole world—what Carl Schmitt in his great book from 1950, *The* Nomos *of the Earth*, called the *Jus Publicum Europaeum*.[4]

But, as we also know, this representation of the border, essential as it is for state institutions, is nevertheless profoundly inadequate for an account of the complexity of real situations, of the topology underlying the sometimes peaceful and sometimes violent mutual relations between the identities constitutive of European history. I suggested in the past that (particularly in *Mitteleuropa* but more generally in all Europe), without even considering the question of "minorities," we are dealing with "triple points" or mobile "overlapping zones" of contradictory civilizations rather than with juxtapositions of monolithic entities. In all its points, Europe is multiple; it is always home to tensions between numerous religious, cultural, linguistic, and political affiliations, numerous readings of history, numerous modes of relations with the rest of the world, whether it is Americanism or Orientalism, the possessive individualism of "Nordic" legal systems or the "tribalism" of Mediterranean familial traditions. This is why I have suggested that in reality the Yugoslavian situation is not atypical but rather constitutes a *local projection* of forms of confrontation and conflict characteristic of all of Europe, which I did not hesitate to call *European race relations*, with the implicit understanding that the notion of race has no other content than that of the historical accumulation of religious, linguistic, and genealogical identity references.[5]

The fate of European identity as a whole is being played out in Yugoslavia and more generally in the Balkans (even if this is not the only site of its trial). Either Europe will recognize in the Balkan situation not a monstrosity grafted to its breast, a pathological "aftereffect" of underdevelopment or of communism, but rather an image and effect of its own history and will undertake to confront it and resolve it and thus to put itself into question and transform itself. Only then will Europe probably begin to become *possible* again. Or else it will refuse to come to face-to-face with itself and will continue to treat the problem as an exterior obstacle to be overcome through exterior means, including colonization. That is, it will impose in advance on its own citizenship an insurmountable border for its *own* populations, whom it will place indefinitely in the situation of metics, and it will reproduce its own impossibility.

I would now like to broaden this question of European citizenship as a "citizenship of borders" or confines, a condensation of impossibility and potentials that we must try to activate—without fearing to take things up again at a distance, from the point of view of plurisecular history.

Let us remember how the question of sovereignty is historically bound up with the questions of borders, as much political as cultural and "spiritual," from the classical age to the crisis of imperialism in the mid-twentieth century, and which we have inherited after the dissolution of the "blocs." We know that one of the origins of the *political* significance of the name of Europe, possibily the most decisive, was the constitution in the seventeenth and eighteenth centuries of a "balance of powers" among nation-states, for the most part organized in monarchies.[6] Contrary to what one often reads in history books, this did not occur exactly with the Treaty of Westphalia (1648), signed to put an end to the Thirty Years' War, which had ravaged the continent by opposing Protestant and Catholic forces against the background of the "Turkish menace." Rather, it happened a little later, when two conceptions of this European order confronted each other: the hegemonic conception, represented by the French monarchy, and the republican conception, in the sense of a regime of formal equality among the states, which coincided with the recognition of certain civil rights in the interior order, embodied by the coalition put in place by the English and the Dutch.[7]

It was then, in the propagandistic writings commissioned by William of Orange, that the term *Europe* replaced *Christendom* in diplomatic language as a designation of the whole of the relations of force and trade among nations or sovereign states, whose balance of power was materialized in the negotiated establishment of borders. We also know that this notion never ceased fluctuating, sometimes toward a democratic and cosmopolitan ideal (theorized by Kant), sometimes toward surveillance of the movement of peoples and cultural minorities by the most powerful states (which would triumph at the Congress of Vienna, after the defeat of Napoleon). But I would like rather to direct attention to two evolving trends, which affect this system more and more deeply as we approach the present moment.

The first of these comes from the fact that the European balance of power and the corresponding national sovereignty are closely tied to the hegemonic position of Europe in the world between the seventeenth and mid-twentieth centuries—the imperialist division of the world by colonialist European powers, including of course "small nations" like Holland and Belgium and peripheral nations like Russia, later the USSR. This point has been insisted on in various ways by Marxist and non-Marxist theoreticians such as Carl Schmitt, who saw in it the origins of the crisis of "European public law," but before him Lenin and Rosa Luxemburg, later Hannah Arendt, and closer to us, the historians Fernand Braudel and Immanuel Wallerstein.

Drawing "political" borders in the European sphere, which considered itself and attempted to appoint itself the *center of the world*, was also originally and principally a way to *divide up the earth*; thus, it was a way at once to organize the world's exploitation and to export the "border form" to the periphery, in an attempt to transform the whole universe into an extension of Europe, later into "another Europe," built on the same political model. This process continued until decolonization and thus also until the construction of the current international order. But one could say that in a certain sense it was never completely achieved—that is, the formation of independent, sovereign, unified, or homogeneous nation-states at the same time *failed* in a very large part of the world, or it was *thrown into question*, not only outside Europe but in certain parts of Europe itself.

This probably occurred for very profound reasons that we need to consider. It is possible that that form of "absolute" sovereignty of nation-states is not *universalizable* and that in some sense a "world of nations," or even "united nations," is a contradiction in terms. Above all, this connection among the construction of European nations, their stable or unstable "balance of power," their internal and external conflicts, and the global history of imperialism resulted not only in the perpetuation of border conflicts but also in the demographic and cultural structure typical of European populations today, which are all *postcolonial* communities or, if you will, projections of global diversity within the European sphere—as a result of immigration but for other causes as well, like the repatriation of displaced peoples.

The second development that I would like to discuss concerns the evolution of the notion of a people, and it goes in the opposite direction from that of the preceding one, creating a strong tension that may become very violent on occasion. The historical insertion of populations and peoples in the system of nation-states and of their permanent rivalry affects *from the inside* the representation of these peoples, their consciousness of their "identity."

In the work that I published in 1988 with Immanuel Wallerstein, *Race, Nation, Class*,[8] I used the expression "constitution of a *fictive ethnicity*" to designate this characteristic nationalization of societies and peoples and thus of cultures, languages, genealogies. This process is the very site of the confrontation, as well as of the reciprocal interaction, between the *two* notions of the people: that which the Greek language and following it all political philosophy calls *ethnos*, the "people" as an imagined community of membership and filiation, and *dēmos*, the "people" as the collective subject of representation, decision making, and rights. It is absolutely crucial to understand the power of this double-faced construction—its historical necessity, to some degree—and to understand its contingency, its existence relative to certain conditions.[9]

This construction resulted in the subjective interiorization of the idea of the border—the way individuals represent their place in the world to themselves (let us call it, with Hannah Arendt, their right *to be in the world*) by tracing in their imaginations impenetrable borders between groups to which they belong or by subjectively appropriating borders assigned to them from on high, peacefully or otherwise. That is, they develop cultural or spiritual nationalism (what is sometimes called "patriotism," the "civic religion").

But this construction also closely associates the democratic *universality* of human rights—including the right to education, the right to political expression and assembly, the right to security and at least relative social protections—with particular *national belonging*. This is why the democratic composition of people in the form of the nation led inevitably to systems of *exclusion*: the divide between "majorities" and "minorities" and, more profoundly still, between populations considered native and those considered foreign, heterogeneous, who are racially or culturally stigmatized.

It is obvious that these divisions were reinforced by the history of colonization and decolonization and that in this time of globalization they become the seed of violent tensions. Already dramatic within each nationality, they are reproduced and multiplied at the level of the postnational or supranational community that the European Union aspires to be. During the interminable discussion over the situation of immigrants and "undocumented aliens" in France and in Europe, I evoked the specter of an apartheid being formed at the same time as European citizenship itself. This barely hidden apartheid concerns the populations of the "South" as well as the "East."

Does Europe as a future political, economic, and cultural entity, possible and impossible, need a fictive identity? Through this kind of construction, can Europe give meaning and reality to its own citizenship—that is, to the new system of rights that it must confer on the individuals and social groups that it includes? Probably yes, in the sense that it must construct a representation of its "identity" capable of becoming part of both objective institutions and individuals' imaginations. Not, however (this is my conviction, at least) in the sense that the *closure* characteristic of national identity or of the fictive ethnicity whose origin I have just described is as profoundly incompatible with the social, economic, technological, and communicational realities of globalization as it is with the idea of a "European right to citizenship" understood as a "right to citizenship in Europe"—that is, an expansion of democracy by means of European unification.

The heart of the aporia seems to me to lie precisely in the necessity we face, and the impossibility we struggle against, of collectively inventing a *new* image of a people, a new image of the relation between membership in historical communities (*ethnos*) and the continued creation of citizenship (*dēmos*) through collective action and the acquisition of fundamental rights to existence, work, and expression, as well as civic equality and the equal dignity of languages, classes, and sexes. Today every possibility of giving a concrete meaning to the idea of a European people and thus of giving content to the project of a democratic European state runs up against two major obstacles: the emptiness of every European social movement and of all social politics and the authoritarian establishment of a border of exclusion for membership in Europe. Unless these two obstacles are confronted together and resolved one by the other, this project will never happen.

The persistence of names is the condition of every "identity." We fight for certain names and against others, to appropriate names (Europe, Yugoslavia, Kosovo, Macedonia but also France, Great Britain, Germany). All these battles leave traces, in the form of nostalgic longings and borders or utopias and transformational programs. Thus, the name of Europe— derived from distant antiquity and first designating a little region of Asia or Asia Minor—has been connected to cosmopolitan projects, to claims of imperial hegemony or to the resistance that they provoked, to programs dividing up the world and expanding "civilization" that the colonial powers believed themselves the guardians of, to the rivalry of "blocs" that disputed legitimate possession of it, to the creation of a "zone of prosperity" north of the Mediterranean, of a "great power in the twenty-first century."

The difficulty for democratic politics is to avoid becoming enclosed in representations that have historically been associated with emancipatory projects and struggles for citizenship and have now become obstacles to their revival, to their permanent reinvention. Every identification is subject to the double constraint of the structures of the capitalist world economy and of ideology (feelings of belonging to cultural and political units). What is currently at stake does not consist in a struggle for or against European identity in itself. After the end of "real communism" and the taking of sides, the stakes revolve instead around the invention of a citizenship that allows us to democratize the borders of Europe, to overcome its interior divisions, and to reconsider completely the role of European nations in the world. The issue is not principally to know whether the European Union, too, will become a great military power, charged with guaranteeing a "regional order" or with "projecting" itself outward in humanitarian or neocolonial interventions; rather, it is whether a project of democratization and economic construction common to the East and West, the North and South, of the Euro-Mediterranean sphere will be elaborated and will gain the support of its peoples— a project that depends first on them. Europe impossible: Europe possible.

2

Homo nationalis: An Anthropological Sketch of the Nation-Form

I had thought of two different titles for this presentation: "Ambiguity of the Universal," or "Anthropology of the Nation-Form." Either of these titles would have been too ambitious, since in the first case I would have announced the development of a hermeneutic thesis with all its consequences, and in the second, a complete explanatory model. I will therefore limit myself to trying to put a bit of order into the set of questions raised by the theoretical discourses that have been proposed (and that we sometimes hazard ourselves) concerning the nation. But at the same time, I will intersect with both the hermeneutic theme of the ambiguities of the universal and the project of an anthropological study of the questions posed by the history, the social functions, and the evolution of the nation-form. At the end, it will be up to you to determine whether these insights can be brought together in a single problematic.

More specifically, I would like to conduct a critical examination of the relation between nation, "nation-form" (or national social formation), and "nationalism" with respect to three major questions: that of the historicity of nations and of nationalism, that of national identities, and that of structural violence. These three aspects of a single problem are not identical, but they constantly interfere with one another. I am bringing them together because I am convinced that a critical situation is

Lecture originally delivered at the Colloquium on Faces of Nationalism/ Gesichter des Nationalismus, organized by the Zentrum zur Erforschung der Frühen Neuzeit of the Johann Wolfgang Goethe Universität and the Hamburger Institut für Sozialforschung, Frankfurt am Main, September 27–29, 1995.

currently developing throughout the world that affects both the stability of the institutions of the nation-state and the hegemony of the nation-form over major social structures, from education to economic policy. This situation obliges us to rethink our concepts of nationality and nationalism, our conception of collective identities and the subjective processes that support them, and finally the possibilities of violence (especially warfare but other forms as well) they imply and the constraints they impose on political life. In an even more significant way, this situation, in its very uncertainty, obliges us to ask to what extent the categories of historicity, identity, violence, and political action depend on a national perspective. To put it another way, it obliges each of us to ask to what extent he or she is not only a "sociable being" (*animal sociale*) or an "economic subject" (*homo œconomicus*), but also a "national being" (*homo nationalis*). Certainly this is not all we are, but we cannot of our own accord escape this determination, which penetrates our categories of thought and action, in order to adopt an opposite point of view, an "internationalist" or "cosmopolitan" worldview for example (these very terms show just how inescapable the national reference is). We must begin our examination of the limits and particularities of our universal ideas of history, identity, violence, and politics, which, even in our efforts to sketch out alternatives, are still oriented by their relation to the nation.

In the paper that she presented in this same forum, Aleida Assmann tried to situate herself at an equal distance from the refusal of the idea of a national community and from its transformation into an absolute: she pleaded brilliantly for what she called a *reflexive* concept of the nation and of nationality.[1] In turn, I would also like to adopt a reflexive, that is, critical point of view, with respect to not only the *value* of the national community but also its *signification*. We are henceforth in a situation in which the question of knowing what the terms "nation," "national," and "nationalism" mean, and the idea of inscribing the relations between the individual and society in a national model, have become distinctly more obscure.

Critical distance is all the more necessary insofar as, here in Europe (but this is doubtless true in a much more general way), the question of whether certain nations, or even the nation-form as such, are undergoing a phase of refoundation and regeneration or have irreversibly entered a process of withering away and transition toward a "postnational" society has become more and more insistent. Personally, I am convinced that the problem is poorly posed. Not only do such alternatives turn out to be insoluble, but they do not contribute to clarifying the problems with which we are dealing. The situation is thus far from comfortable. It refuses us any recourse to simple, universal watchwords, whether they be those of *defending the nation* (national citizenship, national culture, social policy within the national framework if not for "nationals" alone),[2] or of *going beyond the nation* (for supranational institutions or transnational procedures), formulated on the basis of such diverse tendencies as the globalized "new economy," ecological consciousness, or the internationalization of cultural models. But while this complexity may be discomforting on the practical and ideological levels, it may also represent an opportunity for theorization: the occasion to think without simplifying the problems that must be grasped.

The "End of Nations"

Since the end of the Cold War and the division of the world into ideologically and militarily adverse blocs (which, we must never forget, left a large remainder, usually called the Third World, which was in many respects the primary stake of the conflict), we have seen the emergence and the legitimization of a discourse on the "end of the nation-state" or the "end of the hegemony of the national form" in social life. According to this discourse, we are about to enter a postnational era whose needs include the organization of modalities of economic development and the regulation of problems of law and security. For some, this would be an essentially positive phenomenon, a progress of humanity in its self-affirmation as such to the detriment of national particularism, bringing the great universalist project of modernity to a fitting conclusion,[3] whereas for others it would represent a grave peril, a symptom of regression and crisis—a position that is not necessarily "romantic" or antimodernist precisely because modernity and the nation have such a strong historical affiliation.

It would seem that if we are justified in speaking of an end of the nation or a decline in its importance, this phenomenon would have to be illustrated in specific, concrete situations. Particular nations or groups of nations, for example, would have to be crossing the "threshold" of postnationality together; certain societies would have to be becoming progressively "denationalized" or "transnationalized." Particular traditional nations would have to be dissolving in a more or less dramatic way— once again, as a consequence, a choice between progress and regression, expansion and decline. The first alternative can perhaps be observed in the case of Western Europe, prefigured in the project of the European Union. The second alternative can be feared in the case of Britain[4] or in that of Italy.[5] Can the processes of division of the political unities of Eastern Europe (the Soviet Union, Czechoslovakia, Yugoslavia), whether peaceful or violent, be interpreted in this perspective? This is a somewhat embarrassing question: the answer would be yes if these were indeed "nations," but many commentators doubt that this was the case, albeit after the fact.[6] I am not sure that a simple yes or no answer is meaningful; I prefer to ask which model or concept of the nation founds such a judgment in each case. A simple decision will never get us out of this logical circle.

There is, however, no lack of objections to the discourse of the end of nations and its presuppositions. I will only discuss one of them to begin with: this is in essence a discourse situated *in the North*, and it translates certain interests and preoccupations of the "North." It is not difficult to hear in this discourse a more or less veiled warning for the "nations in the course of formation" of the South, which can be summarized as follows: if you insist upon becoming sovereign nations in the full sense, on bringing to a conclusion the process of autonomization and "national" development that formed the heart of the programs of decolonization, even as the developed societies, cultures, and economies of the North have entered a postnational era, you are running the risk of insurmountable difficulties for yourselves and for the community of nations. The great division of the world and the domination of world politics by this division into two blocs, institutionalized in the very organization of the "United Nations" (Security Council) had a profoundly ambiguous effect. At the same time as it *preserved* the form of national institutions, it in fact prepared their decline. The blocs conceived of themselves as *alliances of nations* "with different social systems." But the fall of the Wall with all its consequences opened up paths for the emergence of a de-ideologized world in which, sooner or later, supranational interests and cosmopolitan sentiments will impose themselves. Thus, this discourse concludes that, if the peoples and the states of the "South" insist on believing that their future depends on programs of development and national independence, not to speak of "delinking,"[7] they will contribute to the emergence of new antagonisms and a new division between "blocs." The consequences could be all the more dramatic in that the line of demarcation between "North" and "South," between zones of prosperity and power and zones of "development of underdevelopment," is not actually drawn in a stable way. The North itself contains much "South," and the South has not given up on becoming part of the "North."[8] Where would a country like China be situated? Or Brazil?

The existence of such a discourse, even implicit, and even if it does not necessarily accompany the thematic of the "postnational," is significant enough to put us on guard against any feeling that these questions are *self-evident,* and particularly against lending any credence to schemas of linear evolution, advance, and delay. It encourages us to pay greater attention to the intrinsic ambiguity of universalism. It is a pretty safe bet that criticism of other people's nationalism, in the name of our own capacity to transcend it or the idea that we have already moved beyond it, is only another figure of nationalism. Once again we can see an illustration of the essentially *projective* character, as the psychoanalysts say, of nationalist ideology.

Let us thus return to the question of the end of nations. It is possible to try to respond in a first degree, to carry on a discussion of whether it is true that nations are coming to an end, whether the effects of this development are beneficial, and how fast it might be occurring in particular cases. It would then be possible to "take sides." But would it not also be appropriate for intellectuals such as we are, trained in critical philology, to begin to analyze the form of the statement itself? "The end of nations" is a sort of phrase that has many analogues and precedents, all of which refer to a certain tradition of philosophy of history and imply a certain concept of evolution or historicity. For example: "the end of empires," "the end of religions" or "the sacred," "the end of civilization" (Paul Valéry wrote in 1919: "We later civilizations . . . we too now know that we are mortal").[9] What all of these phrases have in common is an explicit or implicit reference to the idea of *origin:* the origin of empires, of civilizations, of religions, and finally the *origin of the world* as a "human world," the world of culture or particular cultures. In an admittedly brutal formulation, I would like to suggest that if there is now a new discourse (but is it so new after all?) on the *end of nations,* it is because there is already and more than ever a discourse on the *origin of nations.* The statement that "nations are coming to an end" (or losing their preeminence) does not have an essentially cognitive function. It is not a statement that adds something to our knowledge of the world, that can be verified or refuted. It is first of all a statement that repeats, in an inverted form, a prior statement: "Nations have an origin"; they stem from that origin and maintain a permanent relation to it. This is an inversion (whether optimistic or pessimistic) of the discourse individuals and groups carry on about their original identity and the (supposed) origins of their identity.

Once this thesis has been admitted, we can disentangle a number of aspects of current debates. The fact that, in the same conjuncture, we produce and receive discourses announcing the end of nations and the advent of the postnational, even as we witness an outburst of debates on the diversity of national models of citizenship and the instability of combinations of nationality and citizenship, should no longer seem quite so paradoxical. These recurrent considerations on the difference between national models represent in the first place a way to approach the problem of origins, a way of proposing a more or less idealized image of origins.[10] Thus Franco-German debates constantly come back to a comparison between two models of national citizenship (and of the state) that would supposedly illustrate a "French path" and "German path," each of which wants and believes itself to be *exceptional* in its own way, following the idea of a *Sonderweg*: on one side we have *the model of the political nation*, on the other *the model of the cultural nation*. But this is clearly an imaginary representation of two symbolic types of origin of political institutions—one that refers to "will," "consciousness," and a "revolutionary" moment, the other to "tradition" and an unconscious "nature"—and a projection of this representation onto history (whether one's own or that of the other).

Nations and the Nation-Form

In order to get out of the circle implied by such confrontations, it is necessary to posit that history or historical development is not, properly speaking, to be situated between an "origin" and an "end"—whether the end is conceived as an indefinite distance from the origin or as still showing its domination. These processes are characterized by contingency, reversals of direction, and ruptures, which put into question two quite distinct realities: on the one hand, *individual nationalities* that exist, have existed, or even will exist in the world; on the other, the *nation-form* (or the form of nationality) as such. I will take a moment to elaborate this distinction since it seems to me necessary in order to dissipate the confusions and projections to which the sentiment of collective identity gives rise.

Nations or nationalities are institutions that last a certain time, that span at least several generations (I will return to the concept of "generation," which seems to me to play a determinant role: it is an essential aspect of nations that they configure time by instituting the connection between generations). They are more or less effectively unified by sentiments, collective memories, political ideologies and structures, the administration, economic interests, and other elements that have their own "historicity." It seems to me that the general rule is that historical nations at a given moment put to work *one of the existing possibilities* for uniting populations in the framework of the same institution. But it is never the only possibility, and other possibilities that seem to open new historical and political perspectives or to correspond to other relations of power can always recover their credibility—whence the frequency of "divisions" or "separations" and "fusions" or "federations." To put it in terms of a concept borrowed from Marx (and are we not here in Frankfurt?), insofar as nations are sets of codified relations between state and society, political community and individuals, social groups and public sphere, they can certainly acquire in the course of history a singular collective "identity" (what Rousseau went so far as to call a "common self" endowed with life and will)[11] but only *on the condition of being reproduced* as such. The continuous reproduction of a system of institutions is never something natural; it is not the result of mechanical inertia or organic life, but neither it is a pure effect of will (the "daily plebiscite" that Renan spoke of in his 1882 lecture "What Is a Nation?" although he was careful to correct this programmatic formula with considerations on institutional memory and forgetting).[12] Such reproduction has both internal and external conditions that can change and be easily broken. The key point to which we must pay attention here is precisely *the ambivalence of circumstances*, the role of "fortune" in Machiavelli's sense. In particular, it is well known that, depending on circumstances, war can either be the most efficient way to reproduce the nation and assure its continuity, or the determining cause of its collapse, whether immediately or through its long-term consequences. This is why history, understood as a history of national "individualities," has so often represented war as a sort of divine judgment or universal immanent justice (*Weltgericht*).

But this is not exactly what the *nation-form* is. The nation-form is not an individuality but a type of "social formation," that is, a mode of combination of economic and ideological structures. It is thus also, in particular, a model for the articulation of the administrative and symbolic functions of the state, capable of taking on a central role as what Luhmann would call a "reduction of complexity" for the groups and forces acting within a society.[13] It is apparent that there are other models for administering the economy and managing the symbolic in history that have followed one another or competed with one another at a given moment (the city-state, the empire). Taking into consideration *all levels* of social practice and *all regions* of the world (in particular the "core" and the "periphery" or the "North" and the "South"), one can form the hypothesis that there has never been a time when the nation-form has been the *only* existing form, or even the only *dominant* form, at work everywhere to the same degree. Yet another reminiscence of Marx: let us say that the hegemony of the nation-form only occurs historically in the form of *uneven development*, which makes it either a dominant or dominated structure according to circumstances of time and place.

Obviously I should be asked to be more precise in my definitions and descriptions, which is clearly necessary but not possible a priori. At this level, all we can do is to sketch out an ideal type, taking as our guiding thread the idea of the necessary articulation between economic and symbolic (that is, ideological) forms.

With respect to questions of economics (in the broad sense, including all processes of production, exchange, and consumption of both material and immaterial goods), I am here following the presentation made by Immanuel Wallerstein on the basis of a generalization of Fernand Braudel's ideas that permitted a decisive inflection of the Marxist tradition: a "world-economy" that has developed in the form of a universal market cannot (contrary to the liberal myth) form a *homogeneous* whole without boundaries; it must be divided into a plurality of *political unities* that allow for a concentration of economic power and the defense of positions of unearned income (*rente*) or "monopoly" by extraeconomic means.[14] There is no market without monopolies, no monopoly without instruments of political (or juridical) compulsion, which in practice means national states. But if this is the case, we must go a step further, for the condition required for the convergence of economic and political forces is *the political control of class struggles in and by the state.* To put it better: there must *be class struggles*, capable of repressing or absorbing other forms of social conflict (such as tribalisms, illegalisms, regionalisms), but *at the same time* these class struggles must be controlled or regulated by force and, even more important by means of a specific political representation.[15] It is thus necessary to invent institutions and discourses that allow class conflict to be subordinated to a relatively effective, durable, and "equitable" "general interest." This allows us to understand in particular why projects of national construction, and consequently nationalist ideologies in the modern age, have such difficulty presenting themselves as something other than either *imperialist* or *anti-imperialist* programs, a way to establish or tear down hegemony. If there is no monopoly to defend or conquer, there can be no state; and if there is no state, there can be no nation.

But the economic and administrative functions of nation-states, as they are defined in the framework of an unequal world market, only represent half of what is necessary for understanding the nation as social "form" or "formation." But understanding halfway is the same as not understanding at all, if it is true, as I would like to suggest here, that the "law" of history is indirect action or action at a distance. The determining factor, the cause, is always at work *on the other scene*—that is, it intervenes through the mediation of its opposite.[16] Such is the general form of the "ruse of reason" (which is every bit as much the ruse of unreason): economic effects never themselves have economic causes, no more than symbolic effects have symbolic or ideological causes. But the cause, or the determination of the efficacity of ideological causes, on account of the fact that a given ideological force, a given symbolic structure does not remain without historical effects, can only be economic, just as only ideological "causes" or "structures" can account for the fact that economic forces or interests have a given social effect. Louis Althusser used to say that the cause as such is essentially "absent" from the scene where its effects are produced. If the effects are necessary, they are neither predetermined nor predictable, but subject to an essentially indirect, and thus "aleatory," determination.[17]

Nation-Form and Anthropological Differences

What then are the symbolic structures of the nation-form that command its ideological processes? And how can we escape from tautological formulations such as, national ideology is an ideology that organizes the individual and collective imaginary around the state in a typically "national" or "nationalist" form? In my contributions to *Race, Nation, Class*,[18] I concentrated on two sets of particularly strong constraints: those of the *genealogical* form (or, if one prefers, the "symbolic order" insofar as it articulates conscious and unconscious relations, transmitted from generation to generation in the framework of the family, with state institutions, in particular juridical norms and schemas of authority of a "paternal" type),[19] and those of *language* (insofar as language is not merely an instrument of communication, or even a "cultural form," but a transindividual "bond" that produces its own forms of identification or counteridentification).[20] Their importance lies in the fact that each of them allows an internal control or regulation of certain fundamental *anthropological differences* that intervene as soon as it is a matter of inserting subjects into discourse and relations of power. To put it another way, these are apparently "eternal" divisions of the human species that can be metaphorically described as articulating "nature" and "culture" in that they *divide* human subjects both among themselves (that is, from one another), and in themselves or from themselves, in a more or less violent and oppressive fashion.[21] Such differences obviously have an intrinsic relation with what the sociological tradition (in particular the Durkheimian tradition) calls "the sacred."

States cannot become *nation-states* if they do not appropriate the sacred, not only at the level of representations of a more or less secularized "sovereignty,"[22] but also at the day-to-day level of legitimation, implying the control of births and deaths, marriages or their substitutes, inheritance, and the like. States thus tend to withdraw control of these functions from clans, families, and, above all, churches or religious sects. In the same way, the state must deprive families, professions and other corporate bodies, and (once again) churches of the administrative control of "communication," the definition of culture and national language, the regulation of hierarchies and relations between different sorts of "qualifications," the legitimation of academic diplomas (even if they do not take over—or do not do so equally everywhere—the control of teaching establishments themselves and the formation of teachers). It can certainly be thought that the nation-state never reaches the end of this double process of appropriation. But it becomes the supreme instance that controls the play of anthropological differences or, to use Ernest Gellner's term, the "Supreme Court of Appeal" in matters of normalization of fundamental cultural processes.[23] Let us note that it is precisely when this process has become irreversible in the West (at the cost of recurrent and violent conflicts), at the beginning of the nineteenth century, and in order to interpret its signification, that anthropology constituted itself as a comparative discipline, measuring with respect to the development of the nation-form (the "Western" model) the efficacity of nonnational social structures (generally perceived as "prenational") in the symbolic and institutional regulation of anthropological differences.

Finally, let us insist on the fact that *the nation-form is not itself a community*, it is not even the ideal type of a community, but *the concept of a structure capable of producing determinate "community effects," which* is obviously something quite different. It is (individual) nations or what I called "nationalities" that are communities, more or less coherent, capable of replacing other communities, swallowing them, or combining with them. The nation-form cannot be defined simply as an abstraction of the national community (that is, in the way that it perceives itself); it needs to designate the concept of the constraints that are exerted together, that is, a causality exercised according to a certain model, a way for the absent cause to move from one scene to the other, *a way for economic forces to determine symbolic effects and vice versa.* Forces are exerted and battles fought under these structural constraints. The result of this can be either a reinforcement or a weakening of a given individual nationality. And in this framework social groups and particularly *classes* meet as actors upon the social stage and their members meet as subjects—that is, citizens identified with their convergent or antagonistic roles (for example, as bearers of mutually incompatible conceptions of the "national interest"). I am purposely using a terminology derived from the "structuralism" of the 1960s and 1970s, for it allows us to understand how the nation-form does not fall on either side of the classical opposition between "community" (*Gemeinschaft*) and "society" (*Gesellschaft*) but needs to be thought in a way that is both more abstract and more historical, as a structure or type of structural causality.

We need to guard here against an always possible misunderstanding: the concept of structure does not imply eternity or immutability. To the contrary, we have every reason to think that any structure *has never stopped transforming itself,* differentiating itself from what it was at the moment it began to produce its effects (a moment difficult to situate in history and, in any case, probably neither simple nor unique). If the conditions of reproduction of the nation-form change, the form itself must change, for in a sense it is nothing more than the set of its own conditions of existence. It is absurd to imagine that the conquest of monopolistic positions within the world-economy occurs in the same way and with the same results in the period of small-scale manufacturing and merchant capital as it does in the period of "virtual" financial markets; or that the political control of class struggles passes through the same institutions in an age of international migrations of labor as in the age of the Canuts, the Chartists, or the Paris Commune; or that the "nationalization" of the genealogical order before and after the so-called sexual revolution, before and after the development of "biotechnologies," requires the same juridical instruments and the same moral discourses.

Structures that did not constantly change in form could quite simply not exist.

I believe that such working hypotheses can clarify at least some of the difficulties contained in the discourses currently circulating about the "origins" and "ends" of nations, or help us to dissipate the mystifications they produce. Nationalities, whether they have continued to exist over long time spans or only had an ephemeral existence (something that is only ever known after the fact), have necessarily traversed critical circumstances in which their reproduction was by no means assured. It may have happened that they disappeared and then were resuscitated, which means that a *new* individual nationality has appeared where another one disappeared. The *name* symbolically attached to national existence, to a territory that remains the same in whole or in part, or which was that of a neighboring territory (thus "Germany," "Russia," "Serbia"), often contributes to allowing the nation to forge a continuous identity by means of a set of "national" stories in which it plays a prevalent imaginary role. But, as a result of technical, economic, cultural, and religious processes and their interactions with heterogeneous social forces, *the nation-form itself has never stopped being transformed* through these vicissitudes. In the end, a given nation (for example, France, Germany, China) is no doubt always a relatively individualized nationality, but *it is certainly no longer a "nation" in the same sense of the word* as it was two hundred years or even two generations ago—not to speak of what it might have been a thousand years ago (a period given great symbolic importance by national "consciousness," that is, by myth). This does not prevent nationalities from being presented as so many expressions of *the nation in itself* (that is, as the ideal of an invariable national community) or *the nation-form*—or at least the privileged, "traditional," or "contractual" social bond between the state and the citizens, "the people" (that is, the easiest part of it to see)—from being supposed to have endured *sub eternitatis specie*, precisely since it has been incarnated in the same nationality, the same historical individual: France as an "old man exhausted by ordeal," as General de Gaulle wrote in his *War Memoirs*.[24]

Nations and Nationalism

Perhaps you will think that I have spent much time on generalities. These foundations nonetheless seem to me necessary if we want to understand what, in various situations, makes the idea of national construction (or reconstruction) acquire a normative content and express itself in the form of a genuine *imperative* (unless it be confronted with the opposing imperative: yesterday internationalism, today the ideal of a supranational or postnational construction). They are necessary if we want to get away from *moralizing* attitudes with respect to nationalism and its characteristic ambivalence. For if it is true that the history of individual nationalities throughout the world has been determined by the emergence and transformations of the nation-form as much as they have determined it in return, it would be derisory—indeed, a contradiction in terms—to claim that nations can form without the development of a nationalist ideology. *Everywhere that nations exist nationalism reigns.* Any structural combination of state institutions and social forces presupposes an organic ideology, whatever variety there may be in its realizations. I would thus gladly admit that two given national ideologies never coincide (the "German ideology," the "French ideology"). Every national ideology produces its own symbols, fictions, and myths in its own way and has a "unique" mode of investing in the "sites of memory" that help it to become an "imagined community" capable of developing its own model for the regulation of social conflicts.[25] This does not in the least alter the fact that what is at stake is always the construction of a "national identity" that will win out over all others and arrive at a point where national belonging intersects with and integrates all other forms of belonging. But this, by definition, *is precisely what nationalism is.*

The question of whether nationalism is in itself an ideology of domination or exclusion is thus (at least in my eyes) a pointless one. Nationalism is the organic ideology that corresponds to the national institution, and this institution rests upon the formulation of a *rule of exclusion, of visible or invisible "borders,"* materialized in laws and practices. Exclusion—or at least unequal ("preferential") access to particular goods and rights depending on whether one is a national or a foreigner, or belongs to the community or not—is thus the very essence of the nation-form. As a structure, the nation-form produces and perpetuates a differentiation that it must defend. One could say that the nation-form resists the suppression or indefinite extension of borders. It constitutes an institutional means of preserving the rule of exclusion or insisting upon its necessity. This is true with the proviso that there are indeed fundamental historical, political, and moral differences between institutions that practice the rule of exclusion in ways that are rigid or supple, restrictive or expansive (lands closed to immigration and asylum or countries of immigration, *Einwanderungsländer*), universalist or discriminatory, considering it as a fact of nature or as a negotiable convention (for example, *jus sanguinis* and *jus soli*). Sometimes it is a way of pushing foreigners out, sometimes a way of admitting them and "integrating" or "assimilating" them in a more or less compulsory way, and sometimes a way of expelling certain nationals by imaginarily representing them as "foreigners."[26] Finally there are many cases where the line of demarcation between nationals and foreigners, "us" and "them," does not appear in a "natural" way and therefore constitutes a political issue. This is in particular the case in all postcolonial situations and states. *But Europe as such is postcolonial.* The decisive question then is how nation-states and their populations (or certain elements of their populations) define themselves in circumstances in which a rule of exclusion becomes historically inoperative, in which it turns out to be impossible to maintain it or to adapt it to a change of borders.

In the final analysis all these questions draw our attention to the way in which the nation-form and nationalist ideology are articulated with a *structural violence*, both institutional and spontaneous, visible and invisible. And in order to discuss this we need to pause on the question of the formation of collective *identities*. Precisely to the extent that we refuse to conflate all degrees of violence, to erase the thresholds that separate the lived feeling of belonging to a group from xenophobia and racism, the idea of an "us" (*Wir-Gruppe*) and "normal" national identity from programs of genocide or "ethnic purification" (but without thinking that there is an essential incompatibility between them), we must understand how the fluctuation of identities is articulated with the universality of nationalism.

These questions involve political choices. For my part, I consider the demarcation between democratic or liberal policies and conservative or reactionary policies today to depend essentially (if not exclusively) on attitudes toward ethnic discriminations and differences of nationality, on whether pride of place is given to national belonging or emancipatory goals (the rights of man and the citizen). This is why, more and more, the modalities in which political programs of *struggle against exclusions and discriminations* are defined and put to work constitute the touchstone of democracy in a world in which self-sufficient nationality has disappeared, even in the case of the dominant nations of the world-economy.[27] This is precisely why we should resist the illusion of believing that the nation-state could exist without nationalism or, with respect to the acceptance or rejection of foreigners, that some national traditions are open, tolerant, and "universalist" by "nature" or on account of their "exceptionality," whereas others, still by virtue of their nature or historical specificity, are intolerant and "particularist." This idea is nothing but a nationalist prejudice. For the same reason I refuse the idea that it is possible to distinguish between a "good" and progressive nationalism and a "bad" and reactionary one by essential properties. The heart of the problem is always the difficulty of *creating political programs and movements* not only from economic interests, diplomatic and military balances, and social conflicts, but *with ideologies*, and in the first place in the field of *our own ideological determinations*. The difficulty does not reside in the good or bad, advanced or backward character of nationalism, but in the combined economy of identities and structural violence, in the subtle differences between forms of violence combined with beliefs, ideals, and institutional norms, and in the way these forms crystallize on a mass scale.

In the end this is once again an anthropological question, or one that requires an anthropological point of view. The processes of identification and the economy of violence, and therefore the existing possibilities for converting violence into symbols or relations of domination and power, just like the conditions that lead to the inverse transformation of domination and power into destruction and cruelty, are more characteristic of *degrees of civilization* than of specific "cultures." And this is indeed the difficulty at stake: because the nation-form appears as the "ultimate" or "sovereign" community and thus the only one that is truly real, whereas the others seem conventional or transitory, and because humanity never seems to form anything more than an ideal community, would the nation-form express a determinate *civilization*? And is this civilization "mortal," even already dying?

"Primary" and "Secondary" Identities

To conclude, let us thus spend a moment looking at the closely connected notions of identity and belonging. Aleida Assmann insisted on the distinction between *primary* and *secondary* identities.[28] I am in complete agreement with the idea that national identity as such, reflected simultaneously in discourses and stories, beliefs or affects, and institutional practices, is a *secondary* identity that presupposes primary identities, so as to distinguish itself from them, stand above them, and legitimate them for its own ends. I use the term "hegemony," in a sense derived from Gramsci, to designate such relations.[29] Nonetheless I am not sure that *ethnicity*, considered as a signifier and horizon of the collective imaginary, is distributed in as simple a way between the two ends of the scale, whether at the bottom or the top, as Assmann seems to maintain. To the contrary, I think that ethnicity, which indeed forms a powerful model of identification—combining cultural characteristics with characteristics that are claimed to be racial but in fact are always fictive elaborations founded on the representation of genealogies and religious or linguistic affinities—is by nature an ambivalent configuration, circulating between the top and the bottom, between "primary" and "secondary" identities.[30] But this is only one aspect of the question of identities and identification. The other aspect, or other side of the first, is the construction of the individual—the "individual personality," if you will. Here we would have to have recourse to more elaborated concepts; I will limit myself to the idea that *every identity as such is transindividual* (in psychoanalytic terms one would say "transferential"). Nothing like the predeterminate models of *collective* identity that *Völkerpsychologie* and more generally "organicist" or "culturalist" theories of social psychology use to represent national characters and group identities actually exists. But neither does anything allow us to think that the individual "self" constitutes an autonomous and self-sufficient reality whose identity could be formed independently of social processes and a collective imaginary.[31]

Every individual must construct an identity for himself or herself: but he or she can only do it by accepting or rejecting the roles imposed on him or her in the framework of transferential relations that he or she must participate in, that is, by adopting the positive or negative identifications they imply. Individuals are always already implicated in a multiplicity of practices that put them in relation with "objects" in the Freudian sense, which was also the sense given to the term by the classical age (Descartes, Spinoza, Hume), that is, other individuals who are sources of dependency, love and hate, fear and hope, and it is thus that they become subjects. Each individual has a multiplicity of competing identities or "personalities" constructed since childhood. An individual is never (we are never) "one" but "many in one."[32] This is why each of us is confronted with the same problem: how to proceed in order to orient oneself—to "find oneself"—among one's multiple personalities, with the help of others (who can be *abstract or ideal others*: memories, stories, symbols or institutional emblems, "maps" in the most general sense of the term). My hypothesis is that the two extreme situations turn out to be unlivable, if not absolutely impossible, in practice, which means that they mark permeable, fluctuating borders between the normal and the pathological.[33] One of these extremes is represented by the absolute univocality of identities, their forcible reduction to a unique social role from which we cannot deviate, whether it be a *private* role, such as "good" or "bad" child, father or mother, servant, or boss (mostly a masculine category), or a *public* role, or at least a role exhibited in public, such as activist, soldier, or civil servant. On the other extreme we find infinite multiplicity, the continual passage from one identity to another, which has become an ideal for a certain postmodern ideology of liberation from authoritarian figures of the construction of personality, at the risk of lending itself to another form of subjection: that imposed by the model of the universality of "exchanges," that is, the market and its own "libidinal flows."[34]

I would thus like to formulate the hypothesis that the power or *effectivity* (*Wirklichkeit*, in the Hegelian sense) of the nation-form and of the hegemonic normalization that takes place within the framework of the nation-form, just like that of other historical universalisms (in particular, religious ones), stems from its capacity to resolve both problems at once, and in some sense to resolve each by means of the other, giving *a single response* to the question of secondary identities and to the question of the construction of individual personalities (of the subject), or their regulation between the two "impossibilities" of absolute unity and absolute multiplicity. All the fundamental institutions of the nation-form— "national" familial structures, the national market (in particular the national organization of the labor market with its codified hierarchies of professional qualifications), "national" churches or confessions, national armies whether standing or temporary[35]—operate simultaneously in both directions. To put it another way, they create *double* belongings, at two levels: primary identities that are also secondary forms of "recognition" of and by the supreme instance (the "Supreme Court of Appeal"). On account of this fact, no individual is a man or woman "without qualities" but always a particular individual with social and moral properties: worker or boss, "Herr Doktor," "housewife," "amateur musician," "good Christian" or "good Muslim," "anarchist," "green," "family man" or "skirt chaser." And by this very fact they create norms or models of life for individuals, in some sense "subjective trajectories" that can be followed with varying degrees of success and suffering, in an attempt to find satisfaction (Hegel) or *jouissance* (Freud) and avoid ending up either desperately alone or irreversibly shattered in public view.

The term Hegel used to designate this double-faced effectivity is generally reputed to be untranslatable in other languages: *Sittlichkeit* (derived from *Sitten*, the German equivalent of *mores*, customs or manners, and generally rendered as "ethical life" in English). Why not use it here? The risk it carries of introducing into the analysis a statist point of view, a primacy of the state over the individual, is not really a risk, because what we seek to explain is in fact the secret power of the state, including with a view to understanding how the collapse or withering away of the state (and, in particular, of the nation-state) produces such destructive effects on individual personalities and lives.[36] Even the class struggle can become in this sense a way to construct national identities, even a privileged means, with the help of professional and political organizations that legitimize social and individual revolt and thus normalize it.

Of all "ethical" institutions (in this sense), the most interesting is probably the *national system of education*, because it displays the totality of the mechanism of the process of identification inherent in the construction of hegemony. The educational process as it has been generalized and reorganized by modern nations (*Erziehung* and *Bildung*, "instruction" and "formation") clearly shows that *primary identifications* of all sorts (class, regional, linguistic, religious, familial, sexual) cannot be immediately transformed into *secondary* (national, civic) identifications (which would imply, were it possible, that *in order to be* a boy or girl, an intellectual or a manual laborer, a Catholic or a Jew, *one must first recognize oneself as French, American, or German*—as for recognizing oneself as European, that is still far off). Primary identities as such have an ability to resist integration, even when individuals accept integration "intellectually," that is, in the abstract. They can constitute kernels of resistance to integration. The heart of this conscious or unconscious ability would seem to be the body or body image (whether one's own or that of others, between which currents of identification and rejection flow). This can be clearly seen in "symbolic" episodes charged with emotion, such as the conflicts in the schools over the presence of religious or political symbols in the classroom: crosses on the schoolhouse wall in Bavaria or "Islamic veils" on the heads of young women in French schools. Primary identities, in order to be incorporated into national identity, must be worked on for a long time and in some sense "deconstructed": the "subjects" must spend long hours sitting in the classroom for years in order for things to work well (although they may turn out badly, even disastrously). The interest of the example of the educational system (but we should also think about the family, religious practice, professional orien-

tation—in short, everything that Althusser had proposed calling "ideological state apparatuses" and Foucault "disciplines") is that it shows us
and even makes us feel the level of structural violence (or "symbolic
violence") inherent in this process of deconstruction and reconstruction.
We can be helped here (for, however visible they may be, these mechanisms are nonetheless the object of powerful denial and most of us, as
adults, have repressed these ambivalent memories) by those who have
made it the very substance of their writing: James Joyce, Louis Guilloux,
Robert Musil, Thomas Bernhard.

Several types of violence are virtually at work here. A permanent
but diffuse violence is an intrinsic part of the *Bildungsprozeß* and more
generally of any process of identification controlled by national or religious hegemony. A violence that can be more immediately recognized as
political refers us to the "multicultural" problem that has arisen in most
contemporary nationalities, which stems from the fact that a given linguistic, religious, geographical, or historical identity is not officially considered to be one of the "legitimate mediations" of secondary national
identity (or at least as not having the same legitimacy as others). We
speak of *exclusion* in this case because the logic of hegemony ought to be
able to use *all primary identities* in order to integrate them into the national community, or to construct a "fictive ethnicity." But the point is
that this is not always possible; sometimes it is actively rejected, for there
exist forces that work to render the primary identities in question mutually incompatible. Thus in the postcolonial states of Western Europe, Islam is not always accepted without conflict as one religious mediation of
national identity among others (just as, in the preceding generation, Jewish identity was excluded from the system of national mediations, at the
cost of horrifying tragedies). The violence exercised in this way generally
stems from the "majority" and takes the "minority" as its target. Often it
is the action of minority groups within the "national community" upon
other groups that are equally minorities but that are excluded from this
community or whose access to it is rejected as part of a reconstruction of
imaginary integrity.

Finally, a third type of violence develops when key institutions of
the nation-form have lost their coherence and their ability to work together in the direction of ideological integration: for example, the labor
market and the educational system in times of "unemployment crises,"
or the urban environment and structures of parental authority, which
makes individuals find it increasingly difficult to inscribe themselves in
subjective trajectories of formation of the personality and social integra-

tion. The risk then is that the mediating function of primary identities within a hegemonic culture or historical *Sittlichkeit* will fall into what the sociologists call "anomie" or "negative individuality,"[37] even into what the psychoanalysts call "borderline" syndrome—in other words, the direct expression, in social relations, of the ambivalence of identities, of the "primary process" of affective displacement between love and hate. Not only "civilization's discontent," but its decomposition.

I am convinced that in many regions of the world today, *including Europe*, the task and challenge of politics as such is to confront these different forms of mutually overdetermining structural violence. This is why, even while reiterating my skepticism with respect to the undifferentiated idea of the end of nations, I recognize that we cannot escape the question of the shaking of the foundations and existence of the nation-form and its historical and social function.

3

Droit de cité or Apartheid?

The questions of right raised by the way successive governments have envisaged the status of foreigners in France and the social questions posed by immigration policies and their repercussions in public opinion lead to a fundamental interrogation concerning republican citizenship. It might be thought that recent developments in the immigration debate, marked by laws sponsored by former interior ministers Charles Pasqua and Jean-Louis Debré, followed by its "adjustment" by Interior Minister Jean-Pierre Chevènement, under the authority and with the active support of Prime Minister Lionel Jospin, constitute a regression to an increasingly limited set of issues that, in the end, repress the previously debated question of principle concerning the articulation of citizenship and nationality. But some commentators have also thought that the confrontations and political divisions over residency, the administration's treatment of demands for regularization on the part of the "undocumented" (*sans-papiers*), or the growing interference between situations of asylum and work add fundamental dimensions to the problematic of citizenship. The way in which the "diverse left," after the elections of 1997, decided to adopt the essential core of the framework and methods inherited from its predecessors, and the resistances that this policy (which was also, we should not forget, a complete about-face at the level of discourse) encountered and continues to encounter, makes clear the centrality of a *droit de cité*[1] for foreign workers in the process of

This chapter was originally published in Étienne Balibar, Jacqueline Costa-Lascoux, Monique Chemillier-Gendreau, and Emmanuel Terray, *Sans-papiers: L'Archaïsme fatal* (Paris: La Découverte, 1999), pp. 89–116.

transformation of citizenship, which appears to be the major political issue for our societies in the coming decades.

It is not up to us to decide whether we will be implicated in this process, but only—and this is already a great deal—how we might be able to influence its direction. What is at stake here is the very possibility of preserving a meaning for the principles of collective emancipation, popular sovereignty, and universality of the public sphere, principles that our tradition calls "democratic," through this profound displacement of the borders of the political. Or, to put it in the terms proposed by Jacques Rancière, it is the possibility of redrawing between "police" and "politics," in the most general sense of the words, a line of demarcation that we can never be sure leaves no remainder, but that we can be certain is never established once and for all.[2]

We recall that the social movements of the end of the 1970s and beginning of the 1980s, in reaction to the first massive effects of deindustrialization (such as the strikes in the steelworks in Lorraine, at Citroën and Talbot), in which immigrant workers played an important role, then the explosion of demands for recognition and equality on the part of the children of immigrants (the "Marche des Beurs" and "Convergence 84")—occurring against the backdrop of the long-awaited return to power of the left, an acceleration of the process of European integration, and a rise in the power of xenophobic organizations such as the National Front—had provoked a debate on the modalities of acquisition of nationality (with the respective parts of *jus soli* and *jus sanguinis*), on voting rights for immigrants, and on the relations between citizenship and nationality in general.[3] All political groups and many movements within civil society had to take positions. It was generally admitted (even if the conclusions drawn could be diametrically opposed) that the revolution in territorial scales and distributions of population could not remain without consequences upon the symbolic and institutional bond that we call "citizenship." Fifteen years later, if this question has not been totally forgotten (we will return to this point), it seems to have given way to dilemmas that are no more the object of consensus but which do not imply such fundamental choices.

Still, during this same period there has been a continual transformation of the socioeconomic structures and strategic states of affairs upon which the future function of the nation-state depends; the relations between xenophobic reaction and projects of republican refoundation have become extremely tense; and the gap between the violence of administrative practices and the elementary requirements of the lives of foreigners installed within the polity as workers, consumers, and users of public services has grown ever greater. This gap exposes an intimate imbrication of apparently abstract questions concerning political status (who forms the "universality of citizens," the "people" or the "sovereign nation" referred to by the founding texts of our constitutional order?),[4] and more quotidian questions concerning visas, residency permits, the parallel economy, and the controlled or spontaneous organization of population movements and "private" life choices.

Foreigners, whether with or without papers—this distinction, as we have seen, is far from stable—are directly concerned by each of the directions that the evolution of the status of "citizen" can take on the national or transnational scale. Their presence and conditions of existence in public space also make clear that citizenship is at a crossroads. It is thus of prime importance to delineate the choice between a political archaism of either the "right" or the "left" that can have fatal effects on democracy, and the alternative possibilities that come into being in the very heart of these conflicts, not without confusion and risks, but in the name of civic principles that are indisputably more progressive.

We will attempt to do this by sketching out four aspects of the question: the drift of republican ideology, the heritage of colonial discriminations in a new "hierarchical order" of world populations, the European implications of the national blockage of social citizenship, and the militant responses to state practices of repression and integration. We will conclude with a discussion of the criterion that the inclusion of immigrant workers in an enlarged and reinvented citizenship represents for democracy.

The Officialization of "National Republicanism"

In order to understand the political complex encountered by every attempt to break with the authoritarian management of the "immigration problem," we need to take into account both collective practices (particularly those of the administration) and discourses (whose fluctuation across time gives rise to astonishing ideological short-circuits), and compare them with one another. For reasons that will become clear when we have identified the factors that today inscribe the exclusion of immigrants at the heart of what is wrong with citizenship, we will concentrate our attention on repressive practices and the discourses that seek to legitimate them.

We do not mean to claim that the condition of immigrants in France, irrespective of differences in personal status and modalities of work and residence, can be reduced to exclusion, or that exclusion subsumes all its aspects.[5] Nevertheless the long and often dramatic debate over whether undocumented foreigners should be sent back to their countries of origin or more or less completely regularized—stretching from the legislation proposed by Debré in 1993 to the application of the Chevènement law "on the entry and residence of foreigners in France" in the fall of 1998 and passing through the violent procedures of expulsions on chartered airlines and the hunger strikes (Saint-Ambroise, Saint-Bernard, and the Temple des Batignolles in Paris, but also in Créteil, Le Havre, Lille), with the reactions these events provoked in France and in Africa—had the virtue of putting three essential facts into clear light:

1. The repressive and humiliating methods that are given free reign whenever the state believes that its authority is being "defied" by those whose presence in France it considers equivalent to organized delinquency, form the visible face of a vast set of practices contrary to the fundamental rights inscribed in our constitutional texts, to which all foreigners cataloged as "immigrants" are subjected on a daily basis.

2. Alternations between "left" and "right" governments have no notable effect on the content of these policies, whose essence remains unchanged and even becomes the object of a sort of competition around the themes of combating insecurity and defending the national interest. The way in which the Jospin government decided to put into effect the essential dispositions of the Pasqua and Debré laws, against which one of the great mobilizations of the "people of the left" had been held during the previous administration, and whose abrogation Jospin himself had promised during his electoral campaign, is particularly revelatory in this respect. All the more so since it was accompanied by an intense production of the "rhetoric of reaction" (in Albert Hirschmann's sense) aiming at a stigmatization of the "moral" (or "angelic") left and its "abstract claims of the rights of man,"[6] in this case the militants who had the weakness to believe—in the light of past experience—that fidelity to engagements is an essential component of a politician's credibility.

3. The continuity of the repressive point of view in the way the status of foreigners is instituted in France, which translates the convergence of the political class and serves as a ground of agreement between

the parties of the left and the right during periods of "cohabitation," is legitimized by a particular discourse. This discourse is organized around the idea of a menace threatening the republican state, stemming from the economic forces of "globalization," "criminal" immigration networks, religious or cultural "communitarianism," and finally cosmopolitan intellectuals and nongovernmental organizations that allow themselves to be seduced by a "postnational" ideology.

The moment this discourse crystallized was doubtless when the prime minister (Lionel Jospin), forced to take affairs into hand by the dramatic turn of events resulting from the hunger strike of the "third collective" of undocumented immigrants in the summer of 1998, stopped trying to present his choices as representing a "balance" between extremes and decided to raise the political stakes of the "Chevènement regularization" to the level of a conflict for or against respect for the law and the authority of the administration, a conflict brought together under the name of the *rule of law*. From that point on, a link was forged with the "defense of the republic" generically combating all threats to national sovereignty from abroad and from "foreign agents," promoted both on the right (Charles Pasqua) and on the left (Jean-Pierre Chevènement).

This complex of practices and discourses is what I call national republicanism.[7] It is striking to see it gain ground not only in politico-literary circles, or, which is more serious, among corporate bodies such as teachers, public transit workers, or the police, who are subjected to the full force of the phenomena of destructuration of society and the crisis of civil service, but also in the attitude of spokesmen for the parties of the left. The same Lionel Jospin, who, as minister of national education in 1989, at the time of the "affair of Islamic veils" in Creil, had managed to defuse the maneuvers of dramatization and mobilization of teachers in the name of the defense of "republican secularism" by refusing any measure of exclusion of the young women or religious discrimination, seems to have joined this camp, at least as far as immigration policy is concerned.[8]

We can note several domains in which the effects of national republicanism are directly felt. This is particularly the case in the functioning of justice where, despite the protests it has raised, there has come to be a practice of *double jeopardy*, consisting in the addition of measures of expulsion or interdiction from French territory to penal condemnations falling upon individuals of foreign nationality, regardless of the biographical or familial links that they might have established there (that is, adding banishment to any criminal punishment concerning a foreigner).

Double jeopardy is particularly revelatory of the way that fundamental rights that are supposedly "inalienable" are modulated as a function of national membership, in a law-and-order perspective.[9] It institutes a retroactive effect of privation of civic rights upon the enjoyment of personal rights.[10] We shall see that this is equally the case with respect to social rights, which have gradually and increasingly been incorporated into the notion of the rights of man in industrial democracies over the past fifty years.

This revelatory example needs to be complemented by a full description of the forms of institutional racism on the part of the bureaucracy to which foreigners (or rather *certain* foreigners, "swarthy" ones from the "South") are exposed to once they try to claim the benefit of a right or are suspected of wanting to attribute it to themselves. They include racial profiling in police identity checks, modalities of detention that resemble concentration camps, and expulsion from the territory.[11] In these sordid realities, which are now fairly well known but continue to be obstinately denied by governmental and administrative spokesmen even when evidence for them has been repeatedly furnished, a profound tendency of the state and those who identify with it completely is expressed. The maniacal obsession with authority is not sufficient to explain it completely: it is overdetermined by two other ideological and passional complexes.

The first revolves around state sovereignty, which seems to be demonstrated with all the more ostentation to the detriment of individuals who are practically defenseless (that is, as an *excess of power*), as it is less assured of its own perennity and has even become frankly doubtful at the level of the great issues of economic policy, collective security, and information technology, over which the nation-state by itself no longer has any power today. What we have elsewhere called the syndrome of the "impotence of the omnipotent" signifies the appearance of both a multiplication of harassment of foreigners by the state's servants and a "demand" for such discriminatory practices on the part of some citizens, disoriented by the contrast between the imaginary power that the state upon which their existence depends attributes to itself, and the daily spectacle of the state's impotence to master the phenomena of deindustrialization and speculative movements of capital accelerated by "globalization." Thus, in order to reconstitute in the imaginary a sovereignty that is in fact mythical, there develops an *institutional* racism, much more decisive for the evolution of collective attitudes than the system of prejudices or ideologies of rejection of the Other.[12] The state *demonstrates* (at low cost) the force that it claims to hold and at the same time *reassures* those who suspect its destitution.

This still does not account for everything, because nationalism also demands a specific stigmatization of the foreigner. The "republican" self-evidence, according to which the status of citizenship ought to confer rights that noncitizens do not possess, then furnishes it with an impregnable justification that works through substitution: national citizens can be persuaded that their rights do in fact exist if they see that the rights of foreigners are inferior, precarious, or conditioned on repeated manifestations of allegiance (often baptized "signs of integration"). We thus see the development of an abstract communitarianism, centered on the state and its exclusive claim to incarnate the universal. This public communitarianism continually affirms itself by denouncing the danger of rival communitarianisms or real or imaginary differentialisms that reflect the irreducibility of contemporary societies to a single model of national assimilation. It allows the permanent stigmatization of any foreigner who does not consider his presence on national soil to be simply a revocable concession. The great equation instituted by modern states between *citizenship* and *nationality* (which is what gives the idea of "popular sovereignty" its content) then begins to function against the grain of its democratic signification: nationality no longer appears as the historical form in which collective liberty and equality are constructed but is made into the very essence of citizenship, the absolute community that all others must reflect.

Can we say that what we encounter here is something like the notion of "national preference," which has become the watchword of far right or frankly fascist organizations in France such as the National Front? We must be prudent here, because linguistic thresholds also translate dividing lines in public opinion on which the future of our political freedoms depends.

What "national preference"[13] means today is that immigrants, beginning with foreigners in irregular situations or who can easily be rendered illegal, are deprived of fundamental social rights (such as unemployment insurance, health care, familial allocations, housing, and schooling) and can be expelled as a function of "thresholds of tolerance" or "capacities of reception and integration" that are arbitrarily established according to criteria of "cultural distance"—that is, race in the sense the notion has taken on today. Republican nationalism cannot simply be conflated with such a discourse, as was seen at the time of debates on the reform of nationality law, or the insistence of many republicans that French citizenship has a broad capacity to integrate immigrants. But given the way it sacralizes nationality, identified with a process of assimilation to the dominant culture of political and intellectual notables ("republican elitism"), or projected onto the multiplicity of cultures existing in France by a demagogic populism,[14] the least that can be said is that it does not pose much resistance to those who would invert its criteria of inclusion and assimilation into criteria of exclusion and purification. This is how we can end up with a situation in which a project of "universal social protection" (the Couverture médicale universelle, "Universal Medical Coverage") can also function as a means of triage among nationals and nonnationals, requiring the cooperation of civil servants in the registry of public identity documents, the national education system, social security agencies, and everywhere.

Immigration Recolonialized?

It then becomes clear that the absolutization of nationality and national values, inherited from a long statist tradition but exacerbated by a conjuncture of social crisis and uncertainty with respect to coming limitations of the sovereignty of nation-states, no longer constitutes a principle of unity but instead a factor of dissolution of the system of personal rights, social rights, and political rights that is the heart of modern citizenship, the result of several centuries of adjustments and battles (since the French Revolution at least). We will verify this hypothesis by examining the way in which the civic status of immigrants is affected by the processes of globalization and European unification, which are commonly agreed to form the horizon of coming debates.

In order to introduce a bit of clarity into discussions of the "racialization" of processes of globalization, it seems to me indispensable to begin once again with the question of the colonial heritage and its permanence, which obviously does not exclude displacements that will have to be taken into account. Two antithetical theses are often affirmed in this domain: the first sees the phenomena of "closure" of national identity and exclusion of foreign populations as a prolonged effect of the archaic character of the state; the second, to the contrary, sees them as a by-product of the imperialism of the market and the new economic order, in which the weakening of national and fundamentally "political" communities goes hand in hand with an exacerbation of feelings of ethnic or ethnocultural belonging. But both of these theses occlude the crucial question of the colonial heritage.

The "recolonialization" of immigration in the recent period is a general phenomenon of which the French case gives a flagrant illustration, both marking important effects of repetition and occurring in a new context.

The part of the colonial heritage that interests us here involves primarily three mutually reinforcing aspects. The first is the persistence of administrative methods and habits acquired during contact with "indigenous" populations, which, after having been "projected" into colonial space during the decisive period of the formation of the republican state apparatus,[15] were reintroduced and "naturalized" in the metropole. These methods are applied in a privileged way to people coming from former colonial territories or territories that stayed in a semicolonial state (DOM-TOM)[16] and, by extension, to populations coming from a "South" generically perceived as a world exterior to the values of civilization and ways of life of the "developed" West (but this world begins on the Mediterranean margins of Europe, as is shown by the cases of Portuguese immigration in the past or Maghrebin or Turkish immigration today). Next there is the continuity of currents of migration of labor, which follow paths established during the colonial period and, generally, the period of French imperialist influence. As is well known, things in this domain are very complicated, on the one hand because France is the European country in which immigrant labor is both the longest established and most widespread phenomenon, drawing, beginning in the middle of the nineteenth century, on sources ever farther removed from bordering areas and the initial "underdeveloped regions," and on the other because colonial recruitment properly speaking, in both sub-Saharan Africa and the Maghreb, required the direct establishment by industry of specialized networks, whose most important development took place after the process of independence had begun.[17] Finally there is the significance of a discourse of imperial unification in which, quite to the contrary of what an abstract theorization might lead us to imagine, the notions of assimilation and differentiation do not exclude one another but rather form a hierarchy analogous to that of the universal and the particular, or the public and the private. This hierarchy bears the profound trace of the way in which the colonizing nation, imbued with its civilizing mission, categorized "cultures" and "ethnicities" in order to delimit and control the possibilities of moving from the status of an indigene to that of a newly "emancipated" citizen—whence today's extreme sensibility to symbolic conflicts concerning customs, family structures, religion, and education, since this is where a questioning of old Francocentric and Eurocentric classifications is, somewhat belatedly, now appearing (as can be seen in the whole question of the status of Islam in France).

The colonial heritage, constituted by both human and economic relations, and by schemas of knowledge (or, more frequently, ignorance parading as knowledge) of the Other, thus institutes a "pragmatic anthropology" of populations introduced onto national territory from the outside. This territory always tends to see itself as a metropole, minimizing its differentiations and internal conflicts in order to represent its unity by opposition. To put it in a word, the colonial heritage is the persistence of the empty place of the *subject*, forming the shadow cast by the *citizen* in the space of sovereignty. This place has been preserved beyond the process of decolonization (whose limits and illusions, moreover, need to be examined). But it has also undergone a reversal of its politico-juridical criteria: whereas the colonial subject, at the cost of some acrobatics in the references to the founding texts of the republican philosophy of the rights of man, was considered as a "national" who did not enjoy the plenitude of the rights of the citizen, the immigrant worker is considered to be a nonnational (an *alien*, as we say in English) more or less integrated into French society, and partially incorporated on this account into the system of the rights and duties of citizenship, but in some sense kept in a status of legal tutelage. In exchange for his work he can receive a formation and a protection that assimilate him with the citizen, but only on the condition of respecting the terms of a "contract" whose terms he can never negotiate for himself (as is shown by the way in which questions of naturalization and residency rights are handled).

It can easily be understood that, from the beginning, this hierarchization had to raise difficulties affecting the very conception of the republican constitution. This is particularly the case when the "social citizenship" characteristic of capitalist societies such as ours, in which class struggles are the object of a negotiated regulation passing through the state's oversight of contracts and working conditions, social security, and public services available to the entire population, is founded on a reference to *both* national cohesion and salaried employment with the "rights" it confers on individuals.[18] But immigrants are situated at precisely the point where the gap between these two references appears: there is nothing surprising about the fact that this should be a point of particular tension, which can give rise to totally divergent evolutions, whether toward the adjustment or relativization of the criterion of nationality (which amounts to finding, for the totality of individuals forming the active population of a given territory and their families, a means of joining the "political body" on which the institution and negotiation of the social rights they possess depend), or of a regression of citizenship toward a purely formal framework (which amounts not only to an exclusion from all or part of social rights on the basis of nationality but, little by little, to an increased vulnerability of all workers). This is why the rights of immigrant workers—their protection against excessive exploitation and discrimination, the organization of their access to citizenship through procedures of naturalization or dual nationality or, more fundamentally still, by a development of social rights in the direction of political rights (which, in return, would constitute a true guarantee against the violation of individual rights), in a word the abolition of the condition of subjection or tutelage—constitute a privileged index of the degree of vigor of citizenship and its dynamic, even if they do not exhaust it.

But this process, if it was ever really underway (although it certainly was on the horizon of a certain number of social and cultural movements of the post-1968 period), has been brutally counteracted by the effects of economic globalization and the new inequalities it has created on both the global scale and at the local (that is, national) level.[19] A veritable process of recolonialization of social relations had begun by the beginning of the 1980s. If it does not purely and simply abolish anterior dynamics, it makes their success all the more difficult.

Such a recolonialization can be read both at the level of daily realities and at that of great effects of representation on the scale of humanity as a whole, the link between the two being more and more assured by the system of communications that reflects for each human group a stereotyped image of its hierarchical "place" in the order of the world by "virtually" projecting it onto the place it lives. It is occasionally transformed into naked violence, particularly in the urban or suburban ghettos where the public services tend to function as if on conquered territory, under siege from the hostility of the new barbarians (when they do not simply withdraw).

We then have, on the one hand, the pressure exerted on groups of displaced individuals on account of their origin, their culture, or their type of employment. In the places they live and work, they experience a systematic confusion—characteristic of the condition of subjects in opposition to that of citizens—of administrative and juridical powers, of police and political authorities. This fact explodes the myth of a status of foreigners whose dignity is equal to that of nationals and whose privation of the rights and duties of the citizen in a given political framework would be compensated for by the possibility of exercising those same rights elsewhere, "in their own land." What corresponds to this absence of civic rights (as well as, in variable proportion, freedoms of enterprise, association, and opinion, and right to dissidence), is not a reciprocity of protected status—contrary to what occurs for nationals of other dominant nations or members of the international bourgeoisie—but the constant and unpredictable exercise of arbitrary power.

On the other hand we also have—following the old model of *ethnic classification* invented by colonialism in order to divide and hierarchize the dominated—the racial, administrative, and cultural categorizations of immigrants of different origins and different generations that serve, as Immanuel Wallerstein in particular has demonstrated,[20] to divide a global labor force that must be made to compete on a world scale. And this division itself includes complementary social aspects. Some of them are economic, such as the "outsourcing on site" studied by Emmanuel Terray,[21] by means of which the countries of the "North" avoid or delay the effects of competition from countries of "low wages and low technological capabilities."[22] Others are directly political, such as the maintenance of ethnic divisions between foreign and national workers, and among foreigners themselves, creating an obstacle to their participation in the traditional forms of the class struggle, or to the invention of new forms in a context of transnationalization of social relations. It is clear that the ethnicization of human groups and the correlative representation of unbridgeable "cultural differences" between individuals, maintained against the logic of the work situation itself by the accumulation of discriminatory practices, is much more the doing of the societies of the North that organize the movement of immigrants than that of the immigrants themselves. It is also clear that the prohibition of access to the public sphere and to rights of free expression and the possibilities for struggle they offer, and confinement in ghettos and in some cases in an "underground" seek to prevent *both* the individualization and the socialization of foreigners, the conquest of individual and collective freedoms, exactly as occurs in colonial situations, since that would threaten dominant positions and the possibilities of exploitation offered by the rule of *nonright.* But what is a threat from one point of view could also be an opportunity from the point of view of a rebirth of civic life, which presupposes the inclusion of all components of society and the recognition of conflicts within common space.

Toward a European "Apartheid"?

It is widely recognized that the configuration of this common space has already begun to change with the displacement to the European level of a certain number of powers of decision and oversight in economic and financial, cultural, juridical, diplomatic, and, soon too no doubt, military matters. And many participants in the political debate have concluded that the emergence of a European public space, whatever detours and conflicts it may have to pass through, will inevitably pose the problem of a transcendence of atavisms inherited from a political history marked as much by exploitation and colonialism as by democratic conquests and movements of social emancipation.

It seems in particular that the concretization of "European citizenship" as the watchword of a political program, inscribed in founding texts or treaties having a quasi-constitutional value, will eventually imply the crossing of a double threshold, concerning both the articulation of social and political rights and the opening of citizenship to the diverse components of the "European people" on some basis other than the simple inheritance of nationality in a country that is a member of the European Union. As far as the first point is concerned, it is difficult to conceive of supranational institutions being recognized as legitimate if they do not procure for the individuals they bring together an at least equal (and in fact greater) level of security and degree of democratic participation than existed in the framework of traditional nation-states, even when weakened by the crisis of governability and mass unemployment. As far as the second point is concerned, unless *jus soli* is generalized and extended in the direction of a veritable *citizenship of residence in Europe*,[23] the addition of the exclusions proper to each of the national citizenships united in the European Union will inevitably produce an explosive effect of apartheid, in flagrant contradiction with the ambition of constituting a democratic model on the continental and world scale.

Such hypotheses are not equivalent to a pure dissolution of national citizenship, even though they challenge the absolutist and exclusivist conception of it. On the one hand, they indeed pluralize and displace the link between social citizenship and national belonging that, for more than a century, has allowed national unity to survive sometimes extremely violent crises, particularly during European and world wars. On the other, they set it within a wider framework of rights of representation and participation in public life acquired by birth or by naturalization: that of a "community of fate"[24] whose limits cannot be determined in advance but are elaborated pragmatically in confrontations between different historically constituted groups whose interests and modes of thought do not converge spontaneously but that are indeed obliged by history to live together and invent the rules of their coexistence.

These perspectives are not absurd, but they are not being directly realized, and even seem to pass by way of their opposites. European unification, far from counteracting tendencies toward the recolonialization of labor power resulting from the globalization of competition, seems rather to be the instrument of their intensification. The Maastricht Treaty prescribes the attribution of European citizenship—implying the right to vote in local elections in the country of residence and the right of petition or appeal before European tribunals—only for nationals of member countries, to the exclusion of people coming from other countries (who are, in the majority, immigrant workers, including Turks in Gemany, Indians in Great Britain, Algerians or Chinese in France, and Moroccans in Spain). It thus creates a new discrimination that did not exist within each national space. The 13 million nationals of "third" countries (who have been accurately compared with a "sixteenth European nation"),[25] installed for one or several generations on the soil of the various European countries, and who as a whole have become indispensable to European well-being, culture, and civility, become a mass of second-class citizens or subject residents "at the service" of Europeans by full right, even when they enjoy long-term or permanent rights of residency.

As can be expected, such a situation favors the development of forms of a specifically "European" racism, which a number of international inquiries have tried to study. The construction of the European Union generates discriminations on the basis of national origin by radically separating nationals of member countries from those of nonmember countries. "It seems that the constitution of a permanently inferior position in the hierarchical structure of Europe cannot be excluded. . . . The different modes of designation of the 'foreign foreigner' in each national context—*ethnic minorities, immigrés, extracommunatari, Ausländer*—designate the 'other' nationals. In the process of constitution of European identity, all these terms come together to qualify the 'others' who are not European. . . . They constitute the category of 'less than white [*sous-Blanc*],' the *outsiders*, those who are neither white, nor secular, nor Christian."[26] This distinction becomes ipso facto a presumption of illegitimacy in questions of residency and cultural or social rights, not to speak of political rights, and forms a natural background for the legitimation of repressive turns in the national policies of limitation of rights of residency and travel.[27]

In these conditions, the half regularization of "clandestine" immigrants in France in 1997–98 takes on another signification than the one that could be attributed to it at the time, in the firestorm of controversy over the criteria. As is well known, the government had in principle prepared these criteria on the basis of an expert report that reflected the latest research on the modalities and functions of immigration in France,[28] but it ended up combining the ill will of the prefectoral administrations (which it refrained from forcing into line with official policy) with various "softenings" conceded along the way to arrive roughly at the symbolic proportion of 50 percent regularizations and 50 percent expulsions that had been announced in advance. This clever maneuver was precisely interpreted as a sign of the fact that the government was unwilling to proclaim in the social space of France either the priority of struggle against exclusion or an end to the manipulation of nationality status as a means of rendering parts of the working class ever more insecure. But insufficient attention seems to have been paid to the fact that it was also inscribed within a particularly tense European context, at a time when several countries of the union (Italy, Spain, Belgium) were conducting much more massive regularizations, whereas others (Austria, Switzerland) were accentuating repressive legislation, and when intergovernmental negotiations were underway concerning border controls and the linking of data bases on the entry and exit of foreigners (in the framework laid down by the Schengen agreements). It was therefore a matter of sending a signal of "firmness" to neighboring countries, which, like France, oscillate between measures of "integration of legal immigration" and "repression of illegal immigration," and of a contribution to the development of European apartheid. And no doubt, in the longer term, the government was hoping to see a reinforcement of its own "republican nationalist" conception of citizenship, which precisely assumes that the insertion of states into supranational groups will not be allowed to destabilize the way in which those states have long organized the control of popular participation in decision making and the debates that bear upon the very definition of political representation.

The *Sans-Papiers* as Active Citizens

The fact remains that apartheid leads to untenable contradictions and conflicts, for several interconnected reasons.

The first is that it constitutes a focal point for repeated forms of violence. The most massive forms: institutional violence, profoundly destructive of public order, exercised at the margins of legality by the representatives of "legitimate force." The most comprehensible forms, even if they are not necessarily proportionate: the reactive violence of victims of discrimination (it is well known that such violence seldom comes from undocumented workers, who are totally vulnerable to repression, but primarily from young men of the second or third generation who are constantly confronted with social exclusion and professional and administrative racism). The most disturbing forms: ideological violence, often quite bloody, perpetrated by nationalist groups or marginal figures influenced by them against non-European residents. All of these forms of violence are inscribed within a general context of degradation of social relations and "disaffiliation" of those left behind by globalization.[29] The law-and-order discourse that states spontaneously oppose to such violence, highlighting some forms and minimizing or camouflaging others, creating a priori categories of suspects and scapegoats, is even more difficult to legitimize on the European level than in the national framework, since it would put at the heart of the construction of the community a police order that is synonymous with a perpetual attempt of national repressive apparatuses to outdo one another (as well, no doubt, as mutual suspicion between them).

The second reason is that the promotion of the social component of European unification cannot be indefinitely deferred. But its effectuation can only be accomplished in a contractual way, not only between the governments, central banks, and financial groups who for the time being have invested sites of decision making, but by negotiating and coming to accords with representatives of the world of labor (and of more or less forced nonlabor). This means, to put it clearly, that the reconstitution and development of a powerful trade-union and associative movement constitute a political requirement for the progressive emergence of a true transnational public sphere, or, if you prefer, of a new sort of decentralized state, and must go hand in hand with it. But these popular components of the institution of the social and the political cannot in turn acquire the representativity and universality they need without an intensification of struggle against the quasi-colonial forms of modern exploitation (as they have moreover begun to do, unevenly in different countries).

The last (and not least) reason has to do with the flagrant contradiction that will continue to develop between the inclusive and exclusive aspects of the construction of a European political entity. Since the collapse of the Soviet system, the European Union, which at the beginning represented only half the nations of the continent, has begun to present itself as an organizing and civilizing power at the regional level, engaging various processes of integration, association, or reciprocity with what was the "East" (or the "other Europe"). It is clear that this evolution cannot occur without concomitant population movements, both on account of the reestablishment of a long-forbidden freedom of movement (which was one of the major demands of the peoples of Eastern Europe) as well as by the accentuation of the mobility of labor. This is even truer since dramatic conflicts, generative of exoduses and asylum requests, have begun to arise from postcommunism, activated by nationalist frenzy and pauperization. But one cannot imagine either that the "dominant" European nations will extend to East Europeans the closing of borders and hunt for illegals currently directed against streams of immigration coming from the Third World, or that they will reinforce their discriminatory procedures by constructing a supplementary level in the hierarchy of rights of travel. At the time of the ethnic purification of Kosovo, with massive population displacements looming in Serbia, Albania, or Macedonia, Lionel Jospin's unfortunate phrase about those unsuccessful in seeking regularization, that "their calling is to return home,"[30] with the practices of "cleansing" of French territory of its undesirable elements that it covers in practice (or whose perpetuation it justifies), cannot fail to appear as an unbearable provocation.

What is the alternative? It is what we call a *droit de cité*, a right of entry and residency of foreigners and, in particular, of "immigrants," in the diversity of collective situations and individual trajectories covered by this term. *Droit de cité* subtends and prepares citizenship, without prejudging the juridical modalities in which it might be instituted and transformed in adapting to the requirements of the modern world, either through the modification of criteria of nationality (for example, the generalization of dual nationality, which has just been abandoned in Germany under the pressure of the extreme right and which, despite colonization and decolonization, has never been seriously considered in France), or through a progressive extension of the political rights of all residents independent of nationality, at the local, national, and community-wide levels. It does not correspond to a triumph of liberalism but to something entirely different: a resolute liberation of the rights of residency and labor. Its indispensable regulations can only result from *negotiation* and from the recognition of those concerned as legitimate interlocutors who have the right to explain their situation, formulate demands, and propose solutions.

We can then understand why *droit de cité* and, beyond it, citizenship are not primarily granted or conceded from above but are, in an essential respect, constructed from below. Paradoxically the struggles of the *sans-papiers*, perceived by the government as disturbances of the public order, desperate forms of blackmail or products of a conspiracy whose manipulators should be sought among "criminal networks," have been and are privileged moments in the development of *active citizenship* (or, if you prefer, direct participation in public affairs) without which there exists no polity (*cité*) but only a state form cut off from society and petrified in its own abstraction.

Taking up in their own way the requirement for a "manifestation of will" that had been so much in question at the time of the debate on the reform of the nationality code, in order to displace it onto a more immediate and more concrete ground, the *sans-papiers*, many of whom had been *illegalized* in the course of the preceding months and years by the effect of the Pasqua and Debré laws, manifested their will to *leave behind obligatory clandestinity* and to obtain a status in conformity with the function that they fill (and often have filled for many years) in French society. Having carefully studied the list of criteria of admission stated by the government, having assumed that the government was acting in good faith, and having taken the advice of associations that work in the field and which themselves are officially recognized (in the framework of the National Consultative Commission on the Rights of Man), they filled out the administrative questionnaires and thus placed their personal security as well as their future in the hands of the administration. It is not too much to say that they anticipated a rationality of the state that they also contributed to making possible, by giving it concrete information and establishing a difference between authority and arbitrary power.

But the *sans-papiers* also made their contribution to the development of active citizenship by arousing, through the forms and content of their action, an activist solidarity that has shown a remarkable long-term continuity, beyond the understandable alternations of mobilization and discouragement. In all essential respects this solidarity has been free from both utopian naiveté and political cynicism. It has respected the autonomy of struggling workers and families while putting the skills in analysis and negotiation of both experienced and beginning activists at their service. It has assembled significant numbers of demonstrators who wanted both to signal their allegiance to the left and to judge the government on the basis of its actions. It has overcome organizational sectarianism and contributed to the progress in reflection of at least part of the "official" left.[31] Finally, at the moment when the Debré proposal crossed the red line of an attack on fundamental rights by trying to institute forms of individual denunciation that recall the darkest periods of collapse of public freedom, the struggle of the *sans-papiers* led a portion of the intellectuals and of public opinion to reactivate the idea of *civil disobedience*, recalling to us that, with all the risks it carries, it forms an essential component of citizenship and contributes to its refoundation in moments of crisis, when its principles have been put into question.

In conclusion, let us signal an aspect whose importance should not escape us in this period of vacillation of the old forms of national sovereignty (which is not the disappearance of nation-states, far from it): the struggle of the *sans-papiers* and their defenders has made a contribution to the progress of the *democratization of borders* and of the freedom of movement, which states tend to treat as passive objects of a discretionary power. This was clearly seen when the use of chartered flights for expulsion had to be stopped on account of the reactions it provoked among passengers and in public opinion in the countries of destination, and the demonstrations it gave rise to. The democratization of borders, institutions that are essential to the existence of states but that are themselves profoundly antidemocratic, can only come from the development of *reciprocity* in the organization of their crossing and their protection. It has today become a determining criterion of the distinction between police and politics to the extent that the circulation of capital, goods, persons, and information becomes generalized, even as it is the object of profoundly inegalitarian control on the part of the most powerful public and private apparatuses of domination.[32]

In fact, two conceptions of citizenship are opposed here. One is both authoritarian and abstract. It can claim to advance objectives of social transformation and equality, but in the final analysis it always limits itself to the statist axiom, "the law is the law," which presumes the omniscience of the administration and the illegitimacy of conflict. The other attempts to form a concrete articulation of the rights of man and the rights of the citizen, of responsibility and militant commitment. It knows that the historical advances of citizenship, which have never stopped making its concept more precise, have always passed by way of struggles, that in the past it has not only been necessary to make "a part of those who have no part,"[33] but truly to force open the gates of the city, and thus to redefine it in a dialectic of conflicts and solidarities. What was the case for the ancient and medieval plebs, for the third estate, for workers, for women, and what is not ended, is every bit as much the case today for foreigners—more precisely, for the quite particular foreigners who, even as they are "from elsewhere," are also completely "from here." Immigrants, today's proletarians.

In her magisterial book, *Community of Citizens*, Dominique Schnapper wrote: "It is currently fashionable to condemn the closing of the nation, defined as a system of exclusion of non-nationals. This is to emphasize one dimension and to neglect the relation of inclusion/exclusion which characterizes any political organization. It is clear that by including and by integrating some, the nation, at the same time, excludes others. . . . The collective identity of nationals is defined against the otherness of foreigners. This property distinguishes any group and even, more generally, any identity which is affirmed by opposing itself to others. . . . This discrimination is not however necessarily 'discriminatory,' that is to say, founded upon a pejorative motivation judged illegitimate."[34]

But when, by a structural necessity, the criteria of distinction and triage become violently discriminatory, when the exclusion of the "others" is no longer simply the logical corollary of the inclusion of "some" but what threatens to make it impossible or illusory, and when political identity can only conceive of itself or reassure itself by adopting the forms of national communitarianism it claims to combat, then we must change methods. We must set the idea of a "community of citizens" back into motion, in such a way that it should be the result of the contribution of all those who are present and active in the social space.

Français, encore un effort si vous voulez être républicains!

4

Citizenship without Community?

In order to avoid any ambiguity, I would like to make clear right away that I do not wish to attack such notions as *res publica*, "public space," "public property," or "public service," which in one way or another imply a reference to community or to commonality. But I do intend to try to deconstruct them, as the philosopher says—that is, critique some of the fairly inveterate self-evidences they carry with them, with a view toward preparing their mutation. For it may be the case that this is the condition of their survival. It may also be the case that such a deconstruction implies *separating* the reference to the "good" from the reference to the "common"—in other words, conceptualizing a political citizenship in which space, action, interest, in short everything that should be *put in common*, is not put in common in the univocal, substantial, and normative mode of the *good* (or even of the just), and that conversely does not exclusively attach ethics, the evaluation of conduct, to the modality of the "common" or of being-in-common. Not to leap to the opposite point of view, that of absolute individualism, but to preserve the possibility of a retreat and a dissidence, even of a "resistance" and thus of a refoundation.[1] This necessity became apparent to us when the *national*

Expanded version of a presentation at the colloquium on Le Bien commun, March 2, 2000, at the USTL-Culture of the Université des Sciences et Technologies de Lille, under the direction of Jean-François Rey. Other presentations included Myriam Revault d'Allonnes, "La Question du bien commun relève-t-elle du politique?"; Alain Le Guyader, "L'Éthique et le bien commun"; Françoise Collin, "Le Commun et l'excentrique"; as well as interventions by discussion groups (students from the Lycée Faidherbe in Lille, the École nationale de la Santé publique, and the Ateliers de pédagogie participative in Roubaix).

form of the political community began, in a sense, to vacillate in its function as the ultimate, if not exclusive institutional reference.

I

In order to anchor this discussion concerning the difficulties that arise in the relation between "citizenship" and "community" (or belonging) once the reference to the nation as the historical framework and form in which citizenship is instituted ceases to be evident and perhaps even acceptable, we will take our point of departure from the formulations proposed by Dominique Schnapper in her *Community of Citizens: On the Modern Idea of Nationality*.[2] I want to make clear that I have not chosen this book in order to attack caricatured formulations but precisely on account of its pertinence. Schnapper's book, which has served as a point of reference for a broad current of thought, going beyond boundaries of party and country (which can be called "neorepublican"),[3] is no doubt the most interesting attempt in France in recent years to *dissociate the idea of the nation, considered as a political unity, from any "ethnic" reference* (following an intellectual tradition considered, rightly or wrongly, as typically "French," that is, postrevolutionary or, better, post-Jacobin),[4] and on this basis to give a "civic" framework to the set of rights and obligations that bind democratic practices to the form of the state.

To the question of whether citizenship, understood as the active participation of individuals in political life (ranging from the exercise of universal suffrage to the collective management of conflicts with a view toward creating or recreating consensus),[5] could exist *without a community* "integrating" citizens into a valorized (and even "consecrated")[6] whole, Schnapper responds with a clear no. Still, in relation to other, analogous positions taken by figures associated with the "national republican" current,[7] she has the immense merit of not believing that the opposition between ethnic belonging and belonging to the civic nation is self-evident, that it is in some sense given *by definition* (or by the institutions whose goal is to impose it, notably the republican school). She shows that this opposition—if and where it exists—is rather the result of a labor within *culture* (in the double sense of *Kultur* and *Bildung*), which must be torn away from its "genealogical" or "mythical" roots in order to raise it to a "rational" and "political" content, without depriving it of all subjective signification for individuals or its value of *adhesion* to a common "fate." The most appropriate designation for this value (in the same way that Kant poses the problem of creating a *counteraffect* inspired by the sense of duty to be opposed to "pathological" affectivity) is the classical term *patriotism*.

Schnapper is thus conscious of the fact that the line of demarcation between patriotism and nationalism is never established once and for all but must be continually redrawn by means of civic education. And even though she is convinced that the civic nation has triumphed historically (notably in Western Europe since the nineteenth century), she also sees that this "singular institution" includes elements of fragility, if not impossibility, in the current situation. Her objective is at bottom to *pose the problem* of knowing on what conditions a "national solution" can still be given to the problems of democratization and modernization of European societies. She is nonetheless persuaded that this solution is the only effective one, so that were it to turn out to be impossible (that is, if *adherence to the nation* as the horizon of the political community were revealed to be impossible today), we would have to fear the death of the political institution itself.[8]

What retains our attention here are the formulas by means of which—not without difficulty—Schnapper tries to show that the nation (on the condition, we should not forget, that it is a matter of the "civic nation," that is, the authentic nation, the one that corresponds to its ideal type) is, as a "group," an absolutely singular form, in which the particularity of belonging *does not contradict the universal* and even constitutes the necessary channel for its historical institution:

> The democratic nation became concrete insofar as it serves as the source of identity, morals, emotions, and collective behaviors: the national integration created, according to Norbert Elias's terms, a socially specific *habitus*. The internalization of the norms of national society means that the dignity of individuals is no longer linked solely to their particular place in a familial or statutory group, but to their character as universal man and citizen. By mobilizing and shaping collective memory and its transmission from one generation to the next, statist institutions indissolubly maintain the individual and collective identity of the nationals. Patriotism in old nations might arouse the same emotions as belonging in ethnies, as demonstrated by the war of 1914–1918. This holds true even if the objective and sentimental relation between the individual and family or his

particular community, religious community, or historical communities and the State is not the same according to the history of the nation.

It is currently fashionable to condemn the closing of the nation, defined as a system of exclusion of non-nationals. This is to emphasize one dimension and to neglect the relation of inclusion/exclusion which characterizes any political organization. It is clear that by including and by integrating some, the nation, at the same time, excludes others. The inclusion of the first implies the exclusion of the second, as the collective identity of nationals is defined against the otherness of foreigners. This property distinguishes any group and even, more generally, any identity which is affirmed by opposing itself to others. Any characterization has as its function the separation and the classification of individuals. This discrimination is not however necessarily "discriminatory," that is to say, founded upon a pejorative motivation judged illegitimate. In order to appreciate the uniqueness of the nation, it is necessary to compare it to other modes of political organization.

The nation is by its very essence more open to others than any form of ethnies, and it is even more so that it is, in its concrete forms, closer to the idea of the nation.[9]

As can be seen, what Schnapper wants to make explicit is a universalism inherent in the *national political form,* for which this form would not be a historical contingency, still less an obstacle, but a necessity and a point of arrival. Next comes the movement typical of her argumentation, rejecting *simultaneously* two antithetical positions: a "substantialism" for which the community can only be founded on the citizens' participation in a single traditional culture, a single language, or ethnic heritage, inaccessible to all those who have not inherited them by birth or been entirely assimilated into them; and a "formalism" for which citizenship would stem entirely from individual adherence to certain moral values (the rights of man), from the respect for certain juridical (constitutional) rules, and for the "contract" implicit in republican institutions. The nation must both escape from exclusive nationalism and create a singular identity. The nation must both integrate or welcome the foreigner and bring forth a belonging that is experienced in common and transmitted from generation to generation, for which individuals are on occasion willing to die (that is, a belonging whose "time" or "fate" transcends and appropriates their own).

This middle position can be clarified by comparison with the grand figures of contemporary political philosophy. By paradoxically speaking of a "nondiscriminatory discrimination" (*discriminant non-discriminatoire*), Schnapper seems to want to avoid the foreigner being necessarily considered as an enemy, being declared to be unassimilatable and dangerous for "our" identity. In a comparable way, the political scientist Pierre Hassner recently wrote, "If it is false to see, as Carl Schmitt does, the essence of politics in the opposition between friend and enemy, it seems incontestable that the distinction between 'us' and 'the others' is inseparable from any human community."[10] Opposed to a nationalist position of the Schmittian type that sees an at least potential enemy in every foreigner, we have the sort of position that Jürgen Habermas has defended for the past several years. He indeed concedes that "any political community that wants to understand itself as a democracy must at least distinguish between members and non-members,"[11] and observes that "this ethical-political self-understanding of citizens of a particular democratic life is missing in the inclusive community of world citizens."[12] But he sees no necessary link between the nation-form and the "logical space" that is the collectivity of citizens, and he thinks that it is in a postnational framework (such as the one the current European Union seems to be becoming) that, by means of a federal-type constitution, an essentially inclusive "consciousness of cosmopolitan solidarity" instituting "procedures for creating, generalizing, and coordinating global interests" could be concretely realized.[13] Combative communitarianism and humanitarian cosmopolitanism thus appear as the two terms of a historical antinomy for which, for theoreticians such as Schnapper, a third term, the *civic nation* or community of citizens, would make possible a solution.

Without being able to enter into these confrontations in detail here, we should still note that things are not as simple as they first seem on either side. In fact, the tendency of Carl Schmitt and his "sovereigntist" successors is not to impose the distinction between "friend" and "enemy" in an undifferentiated way. To the contrary, they consider it essential to distinguish between the foreigner as legitimate collective enemy (*hostis*), with whom power relations are established on the basis of equality or competition within the framework of a "division of the world" that is also an international juridical order, and the *illegitimate interior enemy* (the "bandit" or "revolutionary," who brings subversion and civil war), who must be eliminated by any means necessary in order to preserve order and the state.[14] Thus the specter of "total war" that has ravaged the twentieth century, mixing interests and ideology, can be set aside theoretically. As for Habermas, by founding the political institution on democratic *rules*, on *procedures* of debate and openness, his intention was not simply to make each civic space a "logical" one, that is, a space existing in complete abstraction of the realization of a juridical and moral ideal, but to designate a set of concrete practices of communication and mediation of particular interests that would be capable of founding a *legitimacy* and engendering among the citizens a "constitutional patriotism" that would reinforce legal belonging and root civic spirit in social life (the *Lebenswelt* or "life world"). But for him it is true that the "nation," however democratic or universalist it may be, constitutes at this point an obstacle to rather than a means of realization of this goal. For Habermas, the framework of constitutional patriotism by definition must be *as large as possible*, or approach as closely as possible "the normative model for a community that exists without any possible exclusions," that is, humanity.[15] All this confirms that the logical space situated *between communitarianism and cosmopolitanism*, within which the "civic nation" would be situated, is highly paradoxical; or yet that the mode in which the nation institutes belonging and engenders a form of *identification through the universal*, by understanding itself as the historical incarnation of the universal, hides profound antinomies.

Rather than posing in a general way the question of the "common good" (in which one "has a part," in contrast to those who are excluded on account of their "nonbelonging," whether provisional or definitive), I would like to insist upon the particular acuity that the relation of inclusion-exclusion Schnapper describes takes on in the framework of the *modern nation, precisely on account of its universalist content*. Thus, contrary to what she herself most likely believes, the contradiction between "exclusive identity" and "political form" or "universal citizenship" has been tending not toward attenuation but toward exacerbation.[16] We can schematically give the reasons for this by referring in turn to two aspects of classical universalism that are correlative of one another: the *extensive* (or expansionist) aspect and the *intensive* (egalitarian) aspect, and then by showing that, far from attenuating this tension, the contemporary construction of the "social state" has accentuated certain of its aspects.

We do not contest here the idea that the Western nation-state represents a decisive moment in the historical advance of universalism. Quite to the contrary. It is precisely because universalism finds in the framework of the nation-state, by means of the *national* (or *national-popular*) *citizenship* that emerged from the series of revolutions of the classical age (including the Dutch, English, American, and French), a more complete and more effective formulation than it had ever had before (in particular, a secular formulation that allows it to escape cosmic and theological classifications and hierarchies) that the dialectic of its contradictions can be more broadly developed.

The first form that we must mention concerns the relation between the *national state* and *colonization*, and thus *colonialism*. One could try to show that—ever since the "discovery" of the Americas, followed immediately by what Las Casas called "the destruction of the West Indies"[17]—there is a material correlation between the development of the nation-form, its progressive triumph as a specifically "bourgeois" form of political life (thus a form of institution of "bourgeoisie" or citizenship) over other competing forms (urban republicanism, dynastic empire, and so forth), and the *dominant position occupied in the world-economy* by the nations in the course of formation. In other terms, the juridical and political armature of nation-states (in particular, their conception of *sovereignty*, which presents them as opposed to one another as rival powers forever in search of equilibrium, each one of which has "its" territory, "its" population, "its" money, "its" language, even "its" religion), constitutes the counterpart of a division of the world or what the same Carl Schmitt called a "law of partition of the entire earth."[18] In this sense I have in the past put forth the position that, in the end, the trajectory of the modern nation is entirely circumscribed by the history of colonization and decolonization (which we are far from being completely done with).[19] But what is of more interest to us here is the way in which this historical correlation is translated into the very formulation of universalism: first in religious language, as a mission of evangelization, then in secular terms through the discourse of the Enlightenment, as a mission of civilization of the whole of humanity with which, each on its own account and all together, "European" nations, bearers of a certain idea of Man, the *polis*, Culture, and so forth, would have been invested on behalf of the rest of the world. This represents an *extensive* (or assimilationist) universalism whose relation to an imperialist politics (in the double sense of economic-political imperialism and cultural imperialism, formation of an "Empire of Truth") cannot seriously be denied.[20]

It is essential to understand that the idea of this "mission" was deeply interiorized by the nations themselves—that is, it became an effective part of the way individuals and professional groupings such as merchants, engineers, soldiers, and intellectuals, in Europe and in the West more generally, understood the universal contents (scientific, technological, juridical, economic) of their participation in public life and the way in which they contributed to the development of universalism in return. But it is even more important to understand (and to problematize) the way in which a sharp contradiction between the two movements of *assimilation* and *subjection* was installed in universalism and the "nation-form" that constituted its institutional framework. The status of colonized populations, both incorporated into dominant nationalities and excluded from the rights of citizens, even though public law associated citizenship rights with those nationalities, is only the most flagrant expression of this contradiction.[21] It is well known that the functioning of typically "national" and "republican" institutions such as the *public school*, with its contents, its methods of selection, its own unequal development, has been at the heart of this contradiction for more than a century.

But this point brings us into contact with another, even more determinative aspect, which refers not only to the extensive aspects of universalism, but to what I call, symmetrically, *intensive universalism*. The core of the representations of the universal that give the movement of domination of the world by nation-states (and later to the movement of generalization of the nation-form, beyond the vicissitudes of "national liberation," decolonization, and claims for economic and political sovereignty) its self-consciousness and its language is not, in fact, a *particular cultural model* that was abusively generalized: to the contrary, it is the idea of the unity of the human species and the rights that it confers on all its members—even if this idea is interpreted in a historically determinate code, the national code.[22] In the revolutionary "declarations of rights" that found the modern institution of citizenship, within the framework of the democratic nation-state oriented toward "universal suffrage" and representative government, this idea typically took the form of a "proposition of equal liberty."[23] Such a proposition is not content to posit the unity of the human race and the originally equal value of all the individuals who compose it, but states that the purpose of the political institution is to guarantee the effective respect of the rights of man that are its immanent norm. In this sense founding declarations, just like the constitutional texts that follow them, fundamentally identify the notions of "society," "people," and "nation." They open onto the idea that, at least potentially, all men are citizens (wherever, historically, they can be).

One might therefore expect the construction of modern nation-states to correspond purely and simply to a progressive abolition of exclusions from citizenship. This emancipatory tendency exists, naturally: it is the guiding thread of the movement of generalization of rights and participation in citizenship that can be seen in the history of democratic nations (which is a tautology insofar as the democratic character of a political regime is measured precisely by its realization of these emancipatory objectives). But we also know that emancipation never occurs spontaneously and must always be actively conquered in struggle by the different categories of human beings who have been the object of historical discriminations, who live or have lived under regimes of subjection. And we also know that the obstacles this struggle encounters themselves can be formulated in the language of the universal, the very language of the conditions of citizenship, of the rights of man and the citizen.

This would be something like a "perverse effect" of abstract, "symbolic" universalism (which is, however, the only one that, to date, has given an *institutional translation* to the idea of the unity of the human species beyond all "differences" it involves and makes it appear as *unsurpassable*).[24] But this seemingly "self-contradictory" effect of universalism is in reality inherent in the double conditional proposition on which universalism rests: *if* men are free (and must be treated as such by political institutions), *it is because* they are equal, and *if* they are equal (and must be recognized as such), *it is because* they are all free. When such a maxim is inscribed in political and social reality, its immediate consequence is that *exclusions from citizenship* (and, first and foremost, from "active" citizenship, characterized by the full exercise of political rights) *can no longer be interpreted and justified as exclusions of what is outside humanity* or does not meet human norms: whether in an apparently benign form (such as the case of "minor" children), or in a manifestly atrocious form (such as the case of "inferior races").[25] More precisely, the potential identity between "men" and "citizens," between the conditions for recognition as a human being and the conditions for civic participation, opens a universal right to politics for humans, but it also implies that foreigners, outside the *polis*, have no defense *as humans unless* they are represented by a sovereign state of equivalent power,[26] and that those nationals who are "incapable" of active citizenship (depending on the period: women, minor children, the sick or "abnormal," criminals) are generically considered as "deficient" or "diminished" humans. This can be reformulated more theoretically by saying that the fundamental *anthropological differences*[27]—the difference between the sexes (and sexualities), the difference between the normal and the pathological (and between the pathological and asociality), differences between cultures (and within culture)—are systematically interpreted as inequalities and inscribed as such in the constitution of citizenship. This is why modern citizenship, working through institutions characteristic of national sovereignty whose function is, in a sense, to administer the universal by subjecting individuals to it (the school, judiciary, public health and other systems), has gone hand in hand with a vast system of social exclusions that appear as the counterpart of the normalization and socialization of anthropological differences.

But henceforth the question of exclusion bears another aspect. In the conclusion to her book, Schnapper poses the question of whether there is not a contradiction between the requirements of democracy and those of the nation-form: "The political project," she writes, "is also weakened internally by the democratic age's own evolution, whose characteristics in and of themselves pose a challenge to the nation."[28] This question is both pertinent and iconoclastic, and we might think that the author has not thought its implications all the way through. Certainly she has once again avoided the simplistic opposition—as widespread today in "neoliberal" as in "neorepublican" circles—between universal rights and social rights.[29] But she has not gone on to ask in what sense and to what extent citizenship itself in some countries (and ours in particular) has been transformed into a true "social citizenship," incorporating guarantees against certain risks and the recognition of certain material, individual, and collective rights tied to status as a salaried worker (what Robert Castel calls "social property")[30] into the very definition of the citizen. She has taken care not to raise the question of how the mutually dependent relationship between the national and republican form of the state, on the one hand, and the benefits of social rights, on the other, is established today.

As I have tried to show elsewhere, only this correlation—whose realization in institutions and practices is uneven, but which is present everywhere and has become a sort of universal model over the past century—has made possible the perpetuation of the nation-form (or, as classical philosophers would have said, its "continuous creation") possible and has given it its current content. The question of whether "the political character of common life [is withering away] to the advantage of its economic and social dimension"[31] is thus poorly posed. What must be said is that *without* an "economic and social dimension" and more precisely without a dimension (however precarious and conflictual it may be) of economic and social *democracy*, consisting in rights of redistribution and participation in "public services," supported by institutions and practices of negotiation and conflict, the representation of a "community of citizens" of the national form could never have been maintained (just as, moreover, without reference to the nation, social problems could never have been the object of a constitutional solution).

But what then inevitably happens is that citizenship comes to be charged with a substance, the *"common good" of nationals* as workers or as having the rights of workers in a broad sense: a substance that is also *the "common good" of workers* as nationals.[32] As a consequence, we can say that the passage from citizenship to social citizenship, and from the national state to the national social state, considerably *accentuates* the tension between the logic of universality and the interior exclusions that are its counterpart. This can be clearly seen in the situation of "immigrant workers." Following the logic of "social property" and the rights attached to their status as workers, they participate in a *universalization* of the "community of citizens" that concerns all workers and confers on them, in modern society, a dignity they had never before enjoyed, and which is not purely theoretical. But these same rights imply an affiliation with a social and historical group, a condition of solidarity (when it is not a condition of preference) that is never acquired "naturally." They thus are situated at the very point where the two inverse movements of inclusion and exclusion meet and contradict one another.

II

We now see that this question of the interior exclusion of "immigrants" constitutes a genuine test of truth for the nation-form and for the "community of citizens" to which it gives a name. To use philosphical language momentarily, we can say that it is entirely placed under the sign of the *negative* and of *negativity*. But this negativity has a dual face and lends itself to two interpretations. On the one hand, we are dealing with a gigantic denial, in practice, of the idea of a community of citizens, in which the state and citizenship are set in contradiction with themselves. But this is not merely a matter of the general and almost fictive contradiction between the moral and juridical principles, the ideals of the republic, and the more or less satisfactory realities that in fact correspond to them, given the imperfection of human institutions. More fundamentally, institutions are turned against themselves; practices incompatible with both the spirit and the letter of institutions arise at the very center of their daily functioning, completely mixing up the limits of normality and exceptionality (even of *constitutionality* and the *state of emergency* [*l'état d'exception*]). With this return of the repressed, betraying the true meaning of the institutions of the "rule of law," the other face of the negative shows itself. Such a situation is in fact profoundly unstable and can become unbearable for those who suffer from it in their flesh and in their dignity, and for all those among the citizens themselves who want to see politics as a movement of universal emancipation. On such a basis we will try to take up once again the questions of community at their root. But let us first describe the effects engendered by the discriminatory status of immigrant (and a few other) populations within the contemporary state.

In the first place, the state, as a system of institutions invested with popular sovereignty and the guarantor of fundamental rights, is set in contradiction with itself. It is clearly demonstrated now, not only by experience but by the declarations of governments themselves (showing a remarkable continuity on this point), that the goal of "policies of immigration control" is not to put an end to so-called underground employment, or to the trade in man-power that supplies it, or to the situations of illegality that result from it. As was shown particularly eloquently by the most recent episode in France (the "Chevènement regularization," followed by the passage of the so-called RESEDA law [*loi relatif à l'entrée et au séjour des étrangers en France et au droit d'asile,* "relating to the entry and residence of foreigners in France and to the right of asylum"]), the goal is rather to *reproduce an illegality* that in return justifies the necessity of repressive measures. Indeed, the goal is first of all to *produce* this illegality by blocking the efforts of migrants—recruited by "national" enterprises on account of their low labor cost—to acquire legal status for themselves. The illegality that is supposedly to be eradicated then becomes the raison d'être of the security apparatus and enters into the production of the "insecurity syndrome" that affects the entire state. I have elsewhere had the occasion to reflect on the strange mechanism of this "impotence of the omnipotent," which is surely one of the institutional mainsprings of the current production of racism.[33] Seen in its place within this continuity, the absurd decision of the French socialist government to limit a priori the regularization of undocumented immigrants to 50 percent of those requesting it—whose result could only be to maintain an interminable administrative imbroglio and to poison relations between nationals and foreigners on French soil—is in fact not at all surprising. Just like the policies and laws that preceded it, it puts the state at the service of a social and economic program of discrimination and hierarchization of populations; it ensures that the condition of immigrants will remain marked by insecurity, even when one has crossed the threshold of legality or even naturalization, so that in sum, *once an immigrant always an immigrant*, with the unlimited possibilities of exploitation that status allows. But this goal can only be achieved at the cost of a flagrant contradiction with the state's own rationality insofar as it claims to "administer" and "pacify" the polity.

We must go further, for this contradiction is not limited to juridical and administrative aspects. It is also translated by permanent violations, often quite serious, of what is called the "rule of law" in the treatment of persons. Little by little, the rule of institutional racism, contempt, and excessive power is extended to all "immigrants" or those considered as such. And since here we are discussing not only the European framework, where questions of borders, residency and travel rights, personal guarantees, and individual fundamental rights are in the process of displacement, but specifically *France*, we are obliged to observe that, at the very moment that the entry into the Austrian government of an openly xenophobic party (Jörg Haider's FPÖ) has led the community of European states (with France playing a leading role here) to raise the specter of an aggravation of discriminatory laws and practices against foreigners, nothing concrete has been done—to say the least—that would put an end to the slippage of the French administration, of public opinion, and of the law itself toward a regime of persecution based on national, cultural, and racial origin. An endless spiral links the refusal to consider residency rights as a *democratic norm*, the repression of "illegals," the amalgamation of different phenomena of illegality and criminality (it is particularly serious that "unlawful residency" is designated and punished as a *crime*), the syndrome of collective insecurity, the stigmatization of foreigners in general (or, rather, of those "foreigners among foreigners" who come from the South including Africans, Arabs, and Turks), and the normalization of violence against them.

The result is the invasion of public space by practices of nonright or what the philosopher Gilles Deleuze called "microfascisms."[34] A further result, and this may be no less serious for the evolution of political institutions, is the rendering *invisible* of growing parts of public space and a correlative *denial* by the authorities of the realities hidden by this invisibility, a new version of "reason of state" and its *arcana imperii*: control of the social body by the police, arbitrary power of the administration over "second-class citizens," loss of legitimacy of representative organs (such as the municipal governments of cities that contain a large population of residents without citizenship),[35] transformation of civil servants into petty tyrants convinced that they "are the law" over an inferior population (just as was the case in the colonial empire).[36] To put it plainly, something is rotten in the *res publica*.

Here we have reached a deeper dimension of the contradiction, which affects the very idea of citizenship in its current realizations. Why should we be astonished at the perverse effects of a representation of the "community of citizens" that is not only differential ("there is us and then there are the others") but actually discriminatory (not every entry into the community, not every adhesion is equally possible, desirable, accepted, not every permanent subjection to the law has as its counterpart participation in the elaboration of the law, that is, citizenship)? This representation is shadowed by a definition and by practices that continue to make citizenship into a privilege, a title to enjoy a surplus of rights within a given territory. In this respect, the fact that, by historical tradition and despite periodic attempts to reverse its meaning, the French republican state has remained attached to *jus soli* in opposition to *jus sanguinis* as far as naturalization law is concerned, does not fundamentally change the results.[37]

Personally I am convinced that if the problem is not posed in this way, there is no chance of understanding the flagrant paradox that has struck French politics for several years now.[38] "Republican communitarianism" has made the cultural, scholastic, and administrative *nonrecognition* of "particular identities" (be they linguistic, religious, national) within the nation into the mark of purity that allows one to recognize the character of one's own political universality. Thus, by a term-for-term reversal that does not fail to produce some strange mimetic phenomena, the struggle against communitarianisms of various degrees of reality, perceived as threats, is turned into the construction of an exclusive identity that, while defined in an "abstract" and "political" way (in particular through the sacralization of the state, the institutions and symbols of French republican history), is nonetheless used in a very concrete way to draw lines of ethnic demarcation (because there is the people of the republic, with its history, its symbols, and its traditions—and the others).

But this quite French paradox is the symptom of a more general crisis. In my opinion it cannot be correctly analyzed if it is seen simply as the proof that the nation-form and the classic equation of citizenship and nationality have "reached their limits" or find that their signification has been turned upside down (so that expressions of universalism become expressions of particularism). What we must consider in reality, as I have tried to show elsewhere (particularly in my analysis of the constitution of a *European apartheid* as forming the other face of the development of the European union and its quest of identity), is that we are dealing with *a simultaneous crisis of the "national" and the "postnational"* that is presented as going beyond it. The old can no longer benefit from the self-evidence and legitimacy it had acquired in the framework of a particular hegemony, but the new remains impossible, or appears as a regression. It is thus that, in European politics and in particular in the constitution of a "European citizenship," archaism and modernity are inextricably mixed: the coupling of an identitarian self-consciousness and practices of exclusion and discrimination stems both from the persistence and exacerbation of national heritages ("Frenchness," "Germanness," and the like) and from attempts to transfer marks of sovereignty, belonging, and subscription to common "values" to the European level.

The question we are dealing with is not only that of *which community* should be instituted as a priority and form the overall horizon of citizenship but that of knowing *what the speculative concept of community means* and how we should understand it in an age of crisis of nation-states.

III

A complete discussion of what a "community" is or should be is obviously out of the question here, whether in the form of a history or evolutionary schema of political communities and their ideal models (*polis*, "people," "nation"), or in the form of a deduction of the major oppositions that have always structured political sociology (natural and artificial, egalitarian and hierarchical, contractual and organic communities, and so forth). What I would like to do, in the deconstructive perspective announced at the beginning, is to use some contemporary philosophical investigations in order to put into question the overly simple (but also firmly established by institutional ideologies) representations that support the idea that every community (and in particular every civic community) is defined, *in fact*, by the opposition between an "inside" and an "outside"—even when the exposition of this idea is as scrupulous as it is in Schnapper's work. This idea even haunts its reversal, the regulative ideal of an "inclusive community" of all humanity found in the modern cosmopolitan tradition, from Kant to Habermas. Rather than repeating the initial choices (nationalism and cosmopolitanism, sovereigntism and federalism, and so on), we will then broach the problem of a "citizenship without community" or a "citizenship beyond community" and try to assess the political pertinence of such a notion.

Beginning from Habermas's formulation cited earlier ("The self-referential concept of collective self-determination demarcates a logical space for democratically united citizens who are members of a particular political community"), we can raise two sorts of preliminary—that is, metaphysical (or metapolitical)—problems. First, there is the question of whether there exists, properly speaking, a *generic notion* of the "common," in other words, following a classic paradox, a "common common," or if the different notions and institutions of the common instead present a dispersion, a radical *disjunction*. This would make the very *name* of the "common" equivocal as such (which does not, we should note, do away with the question of why it is nonetheless used to designate absolutely heterogeneous realities). Next, we have the question of whether the logical schema of this supreme "genre" (even and particularly if it is equivocal) is the *One*, the *reduction of multiplicity to unity*.[39] This is what seems to be presupposed by most of the discussion we have previously referred to, even if, depending on the context, the notion of Unity is substituted for various other categories that (as the scholastics would have said) can be converted into one another: *being-in-common*, the common *good*, the common *interest*, common *values*, the "general" *will* or *subjectivity*, the collective *body*, *identity*. It is not very difficult to identify in this series and in the thesis that underlies it a metaphysics of politics that we have every reason to think perpetuates hierarchical or traditionalist conceptions of the government of men. It is well known that a major part of contemporary philosophy has sought to promote alternative categories: *multiplicity, conflict, difference* (or *différance*), "*paradoxical grouping.*" Without wanting to force all these notions to be gathered together in a single point of view, we should emphasize that, precisely on account of the long "companionship" of the idea of the common and the community with the logic of unity and of the gathering of particularities in unity, they all run up against the same question—namely, whether a thought of multiplicity, difference, conflict, and so forth, in politics and in an ethical viewpoint, authorizes anything other than absolute individualism and selfishness. *Can difference and sharing, conflict and the general interest be thought together?* Let us keep sight of this horizon of questions as we move toward a more specific problematic, that of *exclusions from citizenship.*

As long as we are working from an exclusively logical point of view, it seems difficult to escape the dilemma: *either* the emergence of a particular community that "gathers" a multiplicity of individuals or groups under a common denominator or by the relation they all maintain with a given set of institutions must *exclude* from its unity for one reason or another all those who do not "participate" as full-fledged members, *or else* multiplicity, differences, even conflict remain irreducible, placing us before the paradox of a community that could not clearly distinguish the inside from the outside or unity from division. But this logic, precisely, is only a logic, founded on the formal schema of all or nothing (*either belonging, or else nonbelonging*). It is by no means certain that it applies in an absolute way to social and political realities. In any case, it calls for a close discussion of the modalities of its application.

In the first place we must ask *at what level the principle of exclusion* from the "community of citizens" is to be situated. It could be *in citizenship itself* as a model of collective emancipation, that is, a system of rights and duties ascribed to individuals with a view to their participation in public affairs. This would give us the model of an essentially *statutory* citizenship, in which the citizens form a *body.* But it could be limited to the particular modality of such a model of emancipation being *instituted by the state,* which by this very fact limits its reach, because the state must control the expansive, even socially explosive ("insurrectional") power that is in fact characteristic of models of civic emancipation. It is certainly very difficult for the state—in any case *for the state by itself,* relying on its own strength and recognizing no legitimate power outside itself, and thus considering itself as the incarnation of the community—to allow for limitless democracy, for the element of infinity inscribed in the notion of citizenship at its origin and periodically reinscribed in terms of "unlimited magistracy,"[40] "popular sovereignty," "equal liberty," the "right to have rights," and so forth. But what would citizenship without a state be? Whence comes a third and final hypothesis: the principle of exclusion could reside in a sort of anticipatory response on the part of the state—or more generally on the part of the institution that traverses history under the name of *res publica*—to the fact of exclusion itself: in the absence of an ability to construct a community and confer real political rights and a recognized status to citizens while maintaining an unlimited openness, it would have to find a compromise representing the lesser of evils and a sort of transition between statutory closure, belonging as a privilege, and indiscriminate openness, the dissolution of the polity in a "universal republic." It is fairly common to hear these days, in the name of "realism" when not in that of the republican tradition, that the closure of national or communal (that is, those of the European Union) borders is the condition of the progressive integration and equality of rights of "inside foreigners."[41]

In the second place we must ask whether all the forms of instituting the *cité*, the different historical types of state that rest on a *politeia*, a "constitution of citizenship," and subordinate their criteria of belonging to it, imply exactly *the same kinds of exclusion*. We have reason to think that this is not the case, and that, even if the historical sequences in question are not linear (not only because the Hegelian and Proudhonian hypothesis of a "progress of freedom" through different forms of citizenship is unverified but also because forms such as the "nation" or "federation" each belong to a variety of historical periods), the logic of exclusion has changed in method as often as it has changed in historical space. But this logic is no less important for the characterization of a social and political formation than, for example, the form of sovereignty or domination (*Herrschaft*, the term Max Weber used to designate the forms of institution of political power), from which it is probably inseparable.

The ancient city-state (and in particular the Greek *polis*, whence comes our very notion of the "political") fundamentally *excluded by including* and ultimately by *enclosing* in "domestic" space the women, children, and slaves who, to different degrees, were rejected from the space of equality (in particular equality of speech, of participation in deliberations on the common interest, on the collective "ends" that are presumed to be theirs as well).

The modern democratic nation (resulting from the great "bourgeois revolutions," which we should not forget also means, following the etymology, *revolutions in citizenship*), whose principles gave rise to "declarations of the rights of man and the citizen" or their equivalent, fundamentally excludes by *denaturing* those reputed to be incapable of autonomous judgment, that is, by inventing *anthropological alterity*, whose major variables are sex, race, morality, health, and physical or mental age.

Finally, the contemporary national-social state excludes by *disaffiliating* all or part of those who, in the development of class struggles and social movements more generally, had been progressively included in the network of social rights and social citizenship (which recreates a form of inner exclusion, this time not in the framework of a territorially limited city-state but in that of a competition that, because it is virtually global, has no outside and thus no possibility of flight).[42] This is why we cannot be content simply to reiterate the sort of generic discourse on inclusion and exclusion, inside and outside, belonging and nonbelonging that underlies the invocation of a "community of citizens." In a conjuncture marked by both the appearance of new practices of exclusion and by a vacillation of the borders of the community (or by a profound and durable uncertainty as to the type of political institution that will be able to serve as a guarantor of universal access to citizenship), we need to rethink the antinomies that are at the base of the very notion of "community."

I will here base my reflections on recent elaborations proposed by two French philosophers broadly open to a space of cosmopolitan thinking: Jean-Luc Nancy and Jacques Rancière.

In his book *The Inoperative Community*[43] (originally conceived as a dialogue with Maurice Blanchot about certain themes in the thought of Georges Bataille), as well as in a series of later texts centered on the relations between liberty and individuality (or more properly, singularity),[44] Nancy introduced the paradoxical expression of a "community without community," or community without "a communal work," to designate the modality of *sharing* that forms the horizon of a politics of freedom, distinguishing it from both a utilitarian individualism and communitarianism. Nancy wants to introduce the idea that it is not exclusion that forms the deepest level of social alienation but, in a certain way, inclusion itself insofar as it goes hand in hand with a normative fetishization of being-in-common. This is even more clearly the case when there develops a myth of communion that would bring about the equivalent of a bond of love or mystical fusion among its members. But does not such a myth haunt every communal construction, even when there is no totalitarian politics to attempt to "produce" the community on the base of its own myth? Nancy responds to this problem with an attempt to distinguish rigorously between the etymologically related notions of "communication" and "communion." He sees Rousseau—paradoxically given the readings that make him a precursor of totalitarianism—as the thinker par excellence of the finitude (and fragility) of the community, which can never totally absorb the singularities that make it up:

In the place of such a communion, there is communication. Which is to say, in very precise terms, that finitude itself *is* nothing; it is neither a ground, nor an essence, nor a substance. But it appears, it presents itself, it exposes itself, and thus it *exists* as communication. . . . Communication consists before all else in this sharing and in this compearance [*com-parution*] of finitude: that is, in the dislocation and in the interpellation that reveal themselves to be constitutive of being-in-common—precisely inasmuch as being-in-common is not a common being. . . . Finitude compears, that is to say it is exposed: such is the essence of community. Under these conditions, communication is not a bond. The metaphor of the "social bond" unhappily superimposes upon "subjects" (that is to say, objects) a hypothetical reality (that of the bond) upon which some have attempted to confer a dubious "intersubjective" nature that would have the virtue of attaching these objects to one another. This could just as easily be the economic link as the bond of recognition. . . . Rousseau was the first to conceive of this: in his thinking, society comes about as the bond *and* as the separation between those who, in "the state of nature," being without any bond, are nonetheless not separated or isolated. The "societal" state exposes them to separation, but this is how it exposes "man," and how it exposes him to the judgment of his fellows.[45]

In order to think more deeply of the paradoxical modality of this relation of communication between singularities, both more originary and more conflictual than the "social bond" that is supposedly the basis of the community of citizens (or that such a community is supposed to produce as its continuous historical work), Nancy relies on a reading of Marx. Not the Marx of the class struggle as the motor of history, but the Marx of "communism" understood as the dissolution of social categorizations in which the organization of the division of labor and religious or patriotic myths alienate freedom. Such a communism will always still be "to come" in any historical community, and nevertheless it would already form its condition of existence:

It is here, in this suspension, that the communionless communism of singular beings takes place. . . . Community means here the socially exposed particularity, in opposition to the socially imploded generality characteristic of capitalist community. If there has been an event in Marxist thought, one that is not yet over for us, it takes place in what is opened up by this thought. Capital negates community because it places above it the identity and the generality of production and products. . . . It is the work of death of both capitalist communism (including when it goes under the name of "advanced liberal society") and of communist capitalism (called "real communism"). Standing opposite and to the side of both of these—and resisting them both, in every society—there is what Marx designates as community: a division of tasks that does not divide up a pre-existing generality. . . . but rather articulates singularities among themselves. This is "sociality" as a sharing, and not as a fusion; as an exposure, not as an immanence.[46]

For Nancy, this sharing without "wealth" to be shared (without *commonwealth*), which is only the exposition that follows from exposure to the same fate, from the fact of being thrown together, in the same place, by history, has as its model less the distribution of *tasks* than that of *voices* in a dialogue to be pursued, and this is what makes it close to literature (as opposed to myth):

Organic totality means the totality of the operation as means and of the work as end. But the totality of community—by which I understand the totality of community resisting its own setting to work [*mise en oeuvre*]—is a whole of articulated singularities. Articulation does not mean organization. . . . Dialogue, this articulation of speech, or rather this sharing of voices—which is also the articulated being (being articulated) of speech itself. . . . It is not an exaggeration to say that Marx's community is, in this sense, a community of literature—or at least it opens on to such a community.[47]

As a consequence, not only is such a community not truly totalizable (for it refers to no organic or ideal unity subsuming its constitutive singularities), but its only end is to *expose* (in both senses: to exhibit and to endanger, to endanger in order to exhibit) the irreducible human project of being "through one another" or "in common." This is why it finds its truth in limit situations (which are also situations of political urgency), where the most exterior, the most *foreign* must be admitted to the sharing of public space as such. Which amounts to saying that the community experiences its greatest capacity to represent the common in the inclusion of the widest difference.[48]

Such an idea is carried forward by the recent work of Roberto Esposito (whose debt to Nancy is open), for whom *community* is, as the etymology shows, the exact opposite of any institution of *immunity*, in the sense of a protection of propriety and belonging that might think it could indefinitely assure itself against the risks of difference and conflict, and thus death, by pushing them back beyond its borders (even by establishing borders to protect itself against them, and ipso facto creating points where conflict and death accumulate under the sign of "difference").[49]

Jacques Rancière is every bit as radical in his own way when, in *Disagreement*, he puts the very idea of sharing or distribution (of the Good or of public service) as the foundation of the political phenomenon into question. What is essentially "political" for him (in opposition to any "police" in the classical sense of the term, that is, prudent administration of the interests of the governed by rational governors) is thus neither *given* nor to be *conferred* (as a status, be it the status of freedom). And thus it cannot truly be considered as something to be *claimed* either. Insofar as it expresses the movement of collective emancipation, the criterion of political citizenship is the ability of a "polity" to free itself from the forms of distribution and redistribution ("accounting"). It does not take as its objective the "balance of profits and losses" among those who *already possess something*, be it only a "symbolic portion" of the common good, but the constitution of a "people" (or *dēmos*) that begins as nonexistent on account of the exclusion of those who are considered unworthy of the status of citizen (depending on the epoch and the circumstances: slaves or servants, workers or paupers, women, foreigners, and so on). Consequently, far from being a question of granting the excluded a status as victims or extending them compensatory rights within a given social order, what must be done is to reconstitute the community's universal by making "a part of those who have no part," or by giving an unconditional right to the discourse of equality whose bearers they are historically. On account of this fact, the notion of *political right(s)* is in principle disassociated from any preexisting "quality," which obviously cannot occur without a conflict with the social order (the "police"), which necessarily sees in such qualities the correlate of a property or a capacity:

> Not only does freedom as what is "proper" to the *dēmos* not allow itself to be determined by any positive property; it is not proper to the *dēmos* at all. The people are nothing more than the undifferentiated mass of those who have no positive quali-

fication—no wealth, no virtue—but who are nonetheless acknowledged to enjoy the same freedom as those who do. The people who make up the people are in fact simply free *like* the rest. Now it is this simple identity with those who are otherwise superior to them in all things that gives them a specific qualification. The *dēmos* attributes to itself as its proper lot the equality that belongs to all citizens. In so doing, this party that is not one identifies its improper property with the exclusive principle of community and identifies its name—the name of the indistinct mass of men of no position—with the name of the community itself. . . . [T]he Ancients, much more than the Moderns, acknowledged that the whole basis of politics is the struggle between the poor and the rich. But that's just it: what they acknowledged was a strictly political reality—even if it meant trying to overcome it. The struggle between the rich and the poor is not social reality, which politics then has to deal with. It is the actual institution of politics itself. There is politics when there is a part of those who have no part, a part or party of the poor. Politics does not happen just because the poor oppose the rich. . . . Politics exists when the natural order of domination is interrupted by the institution of a part of those who have no part. This institution is the whole of politics as a specific form of connection. It defines the common of the community as a political community, in other words, as divided, as based on a wrong that escapes the arithmetic of exchange and reparation. Beyond this set-up there is no politics. There is only the order of domination or the disorder of revolt.[50]

The institution of politics is thus indissociable, in any given situation, from a *forcing of political participation*, since participation began by being monopolized or "privatized" (and perhaps inevitably becomes so once again, as in the institution of national closure).

Does this mean that politics necessarily appears in the form of *revolutionary violence?* Rancière seems instead to be trying to loosen the alternative between police domination and anarchic violence. This is why he attaches so much importance to the discourse and the movement of "mass" political subjectification, which is precisely what the tradition of political philosophy (from Aristotle to Hobbes or to the contemporary debates between "communitarians" and "liberals"—Michael Walzer,

Habermas) has tried so hard to repress out of the political, which it identifies with preventive order, rationality, and *constituted* right:

> Politics is a matter of subjects or, rather, modes of subjectification. By *subjectification* I mean the production, through a series of actions, of a body and a capacity for enunciation not previously identifiable within a given field of experience, whose identification is thus part of the reconfiguration of the field of experience. Descartes's *ego sum, ego existo* is the prototype of such indissoluble subjects of a series of operations implying the production of a new field of experience. Any political subjectification holds to this formula. It is a *nos sumus, nos existimus.* . . . Political subjectification produces a multiple that was not given in the police constitution of the community, a multiple whose count poses itself as contradictory in terms of police logic. . . . A political subjectification is the product of these multiple fracture lines by which individuals and networks of individuals subjectify the gap between their condition as animals endowed with a voice and the violent encounter with the equality of the logos.[51]

We should thus not be surprised to see that Rancière ends up opposing the notions of *democracy* and *consensus*, which permits him (among other things) to characterize the "new racism of advanced societies," that is, liberal, republican, postcolonial societies, posterior to the "end of myths" or ideologies (which implies the radical delegitimization of the class struggle and other forms of contestation):

> The new racism of advanced societies thus owes its singularity to being the point of intersection for all forms of the community's identity with itself that go to define the consensus model—as well as all forms of defection from this identity and of compensation for such defection. So it is only normal that the law should now round off this coherence, in other words, turn its unity into the mode of reflection of a community separating itself from its Other. In dealing with the problem of immigrants, the law, of course, proposes to act for justice and peace. By defining rules of assimilation and exclusion until now left to the luck of the draw and to disparities in the regulations, it claims to be bringing the particular into the sphere of its universality. By separating good foreigners from undesirables, it is meant to be disarming racism, which feeds off lumping ev-

eryone together. The problem is that this distinction itself can only be made at the cost of putting a face to this indefinable Other who excites feelings of fear and rejection. The law, which is supposed to sort out the confusion of "feeling," does so only at the cost of borrowing its object, its way of uniting, without any underlying concept, heterogeneous cases of the other's unacceptability, and of handing it back subsumed in a conceptual unity. The law decreed by the consensus system is also confirmation of the kind of relationship with oneself that the consensus system itself constitutes. Its principle is to establish continual convertibility from the *one* of the law to the *one* of feeling that defines being-together. The work of consensual law is thus first to devise the schema that transforms the felt but indefinable *one* of rejection into *one* of common law. It is this schema that constitutes the untraceable object "immigrant" by unifying heterogeneous cases. . . . Consensus is a circular relationship between nature and the law that leaves to the latter the problem of determining the antinature experienced by the former as intolerable.[52]

Of course, the "consensus" in question here is a representation, and even an anticipated representation. It makes no real judgment about the actual neutralization of differences and conflicts within a social order submitted to a single law (or a single constitution). On the other hand, it forms the "subjective" counterpart (on the side of opinion, of what Rancière calls feelings, or what could also be called passions) to what is "objectively" gathered under the name of culture: a certain number of marks of identity proposed to the "people" considered as a "nation" by the history of its dominant understanding.

I would like, for my own part, to retain a crucial element of this radically democratic elaboration (in which the movement of conquest of equality, beginning from a "wrong" that has the function of discriminating between police and politics, takes primacy over the positive "constitution"), while drawing the lesson of the critique, by Jean-Luc Nancy, of the myth of communion (even revolutionary communion). No doubt the path between consensus and universality, between common being and sharing, exposition of the community and dissolution of the social bond, is very narrow. This is the price of the *admission of negativity* into the field of political practices, in opposition to the *normativity* and *normality* toward which both juridical positivism and the dominant culture tend—

at least until historical circumstances make the partial and arbitrary character of these norms apparent. What I hypothetically called a "citizenship without community" is another way to name this element of negativity, that is, to underline that in some circumstances the *traditions*, the more or less fictive "memories," in short, all the admitted representations of a common—historical and, even more so, natural—identity must be put in question.[53] This is in fact the condition for *some to become active citizens once again* ("authors" of or "responsible" for the political institution) while *others become active citizens on both sides of a border* (not only a geographical or geopolitical border but a political and anthropological one, because it tends to divide humanity into unequal species with respect to the status of citizenship). But the converse is also true: some can only *become* active citizens for the first time (collective bearers of personal rights to speech, participation, and decision making in the public sphere) if others become active citizens *again*, or exercise once again their capacities in some way other than in a nominal fashion, by heritage and delegation. This provides a model for what Jean-Claude Milner, in a book that is decisive for our purposes, calls "paradoxical groupings," which join together, in order to construct their own equality or parity of rights, classes of individuals whose identities are "contrary," whose mutual recognition is capable of extending or refounding citizenship: masters and servants, men and women, nationals and foreigners, but also "educated" and "ignorant," "healthy" and "sick," even "honest folk" and "delinquents" or criminals.[54]

The idea that I would like to defend is that *it is always the practical confrontation with the different modalities of exclusion* (social, and thus political, for the two notions have never truly been separate) *that constitutes the founding moment of citizenship*, and thus of its periodic test of truth.[55] This is where "republicanism" finds itself backed into a corner. As we have seen, every institution of citizenship involves the institutionalization of exclusions, following different historical modalities. But the constitutive movement that gives it its democratic power is the same movement that carries an institutional schema of inclusion and exclusion (the institution of a "border" of citizenship) *beyond itself* once the status quo turns out to be untenable, except at the cost of a reinforcement of police practices, and thus of violence, or cycles of violence and counterviolence, at first on the "margins" of public space, and finally in its center. It can thus be presented neither as a simple demand for inclusion (admission to the "club") on the part of those who, for one reason or another, have been excluded, nor as a humanitarian initiative on the part of those who see civic universalism as the source of legitimacy of their own rights. It must be the *common operation* or, if you prefer, the *"shared" act* of both—for example, those "with" and those "without" (papers, citizenship qualifications)—in such a way as to democratize citizenship beginning from its borders, thus "making right" and civilizing the state and politics.

The question of the community of citizens, raised on the occasion of debates on nationality, residency rights, and electoral participation by Dominique Schnapper and others, thus has no *definite* or ultimately *definable* solution, whether in the form of an *empirical community* (such-and-such a society, culture, or state), or in the form of an *ideal community* (for example, the "republican nation," but also the "postnational" federation). Nor does it have an unequivocal "logical space," contrary to what Habermas seems to think, but rather a moving historical site that is both sociological and symbolic: a meeting point between processes of transformation of the division of labor, of population movements, of revolutions in manners, and dynamics of emancipation or solidarity.[56] Its domain—not that of its solution but that of its permanent reopening—is a dialectics and not a constitution, a sociology, or a logic (even if all these aspects can emerge in it in turn). A dialectic of "constituent" and "constituted" citizenship (close to what I elsewhere called "insurrection" and "constitution"):[57] it is a contradictory process, fed by permanent conflicts between several types of subjectifications or identities, some cultural or prepolitical, others political (and, from this point of view, divided into several degrees of civic consciousness, ranging from patriotism or the spirit of "resistance" to "class consciousness" or engagement in feminism, movements of struggle against racism, etc.)—whence subjects always come to inscribe themselves, historically, between the figures of tragedy and those of the epic.

5

Europe after Communism

Before beginning what can more properly be called a course of investigation than an analysis, at best a set of hypotheses, I should like to make a
confession, reflect upon an experience, and make an observation.

The confession is that, although I am well aware of the enormity
of that event known as the collapse of "real socialism" in Europe over the
space of few months, I am not all that distressed by it. At least not as
much as I might have expected to be. Perhaps simply because we are not
"on site" in Eastern Europe, or even in the "reunified" Germany that is
only a few kilometers away. But also because I feel a certain sense of déjà
vu, as if I had already attended the dress rehearsal of the play. Having
belonged to the French Communist Party for twenty years (from 1961 to
1981), I believe I have already lived, even if in an attenuated form less
heavy with consequences, the "implosion" of the apparatus that was
called communist and that claimed to be based on Marxist theory. The
"end of communism," in one form or another, has seemed to me inevitable since the late 1970s or early 1980s. Others felt it much earlier (but I
will return to this).

At the same time, I would like to discuss an ambiguous experience, which is not my own. In the second half of the 1980s, several

Paper presented at the seminar on Géophilosophie de l'Europe, directed by
Jean-Luc Nancy and Philippe Lacoue-Labarthe at the Université des sciences
humaines de Strasbourg, November 8–9, 1991. First published in *Les Temps
modernes* 547 (February 1992): 56–89; reprinted in Étienne Balibar, *Les Frontières de
la démocratie* (Paris: La Découverte, 1992), pp. 206–37. This translation, by Erika
Thomas, originally appeared in *Rethinking Marxism* 5, no. 3 (fall 1992): 29–49, and
has been revised for this publication.

among us had seen and heard, in Prague and elsewhere, Western intellectuals and politicians "selling" (against the recognition of anticipated debt) the "bright future" to dissidents, to resisters who were preparing, morally and politically, the end of dictatorship. The bright future was contained in three words: market, democracy, Europe. Of course, this was not new, but it was more and more effective, more and more "credible." We ourselves doubtless contributed modestly to supporting this perverse exchange, because it was the very condition of our communication, whatever precautions of language we imposed on ourselves for fear of future disappointments and out of respect for our interlocutors, many of whom demonstrated a particularly acute and prescient lucidity ("optimism of the will, pessimism of the intellect," once again).

Finally, allow me an observation that will lead us directly into the matter. Scarcely two years have elapsed since the fall of the Berlin Wall, two years that have seen the "revolutions" of Hungary, Romania, and Czechoslovakia, among others (all very different in their unfolding), and finally the "putsch" (or the pseudo-putsch—someday we will know the final word) in Moscow and the disintegration of the Soviet state, and so forth. But already—we read, we hear—the diagnosis of the collapse of communism, the evaluation of its consequences and (allow me the expression) of its "cost," is in the process of changing tonality. Is this because of the Yugoslavian civil war? Because of the rise of neo-Nazism in Germany? Because of the "apathy" of Polish voters, or the "special powers" demanded by Boris Yeltsin? Or from a proper understanding of our own interests? No one, it will be said, thinks any longer of spontaneous democracy. And from admiration for the antitotalitarian revolutions that return "Europe" to us, among other things, we pass imperceptibly into anxiety, if not distrust. The evidence—for example, that of the *irreversibility* of the historical mutation we are living through—persists, but the *sense* of that mutation begins to appear for what it is: totally problematic.

Revolution? Restoration?

These words, along with a few near synonyms, are in wide circulation. Let us not be mistaken: their usage is not distributed in a clear or simple way between those who are for and those who are against the "end of communism." There are some fierce adversaries of communism who are in favor of describing the changes of regime in the East as a turning back ("capitalist transition" or "reestablishment of capitalism"), if not as a pure and simple restoration. There are militants and intellectuals faithful to communism who prefer to describe the changes as "revolutionary," not only in a descriptive sense but in the same sense in which Marx spoke of "breaking the chains" that bind the future.[1]

Everything obviously depends on one's notion of the regime that collapsed before our eyes and on the manner in which history is analyzed. In the genesis of an event from which we have not yet attained any distance, everything depends on the importance attributed respectively to external factors (notably to the military, economic, and political pressure of the "West"), to the factors of the internal crisis, and above all to the role played by popular movements. This last point is the most decisive for anyone attached to a strong democratic tradition, since it raises the question of whether the peoples of the East, dispossessed of their political rights for decades, have at least virtually reappropriated the means of self-government.

No one could claim that these "revolutionary" elements, which go well beyond the actions of some dissidents and symbolic personalities, played no role in the preparation and unfolding of events. This extends from the long resistance of the Poles who backed Solidarity or the Czechs behind Charter 77, to the mass demonstrations organized in East Germany in 1989 by the *Neues Forum* or the defeat of the "putsch" of 1991 by the population of Moscow.

But neither should the amplitude of the phenomena that properly belong to the counterrevolutionary tradition be masked: at stake are the purges and settling of accounts (often demanded by former members of the communist apparatus), the "return of the former proprietors" (indeed the former autocrats, or their descendants taken out of formaldehyde), or the "return of the religious," whose immediate practical consequences are sharply regressive, notably in their effects on the freedoms won by women and on the secularism of the state (not to mention anti-Semitism). It would be a mistake to allow the forms under which the liquidation of a dictatorship was effected to obscure the *primary meaning* of this liquidation: dismantling of the repressive apparatus, reestablishment of the liberties of opinion and expression, and so on. But the general hesitation about the choice of political categories that ought to be applied to the process underway indicates, at least, the impossibility of classifying it in the framework of reigning representations, whether they are produced by socialists, liberals, or conservatives.

Would it not then be appropriate to adopt the position outlined by François Furet, a good reader of Marx who knows that all radically new events are first grasped in an archaic imaginary?[2] The "end of communism" in the East is also, fundamentally, the end of the political "modernity" opened by the French Revolution and dominated by the notions that it produced (among which are precisely those of revolution, counterrevolution, and restoration); but paradoxically it must first be thought in the very language that it radically deprives of meaning.

This point of view would be undeniable if a still more hazardous postulate did not underlie it: that the "revolutions/restorations" that we have witnessed constitute an entrance into a political, if not social, *normality*, the end of an "exception" (explained as utopianism, Machiavellianism, Jacobinism, or something else). But what we see is nothing of the kind, and we can only suppose that this postulate could be merely the reflection of the purely ideological view of the nature of communist societies adopted by the majority of Western political scientists (and, to a large extent, elaborated as the inverted image of the official ideology of the communist regimes themselves). It is thus necessary to return to the prior question: what is currently "collapsing" in the East?

The Two Circles

A first observation: what disappeared in a few months from the historical scene were, fundamentally, *states*. As these states had communism as their official ideology, descended from the Marxist tradition as revised by Lenin, Stalin, and their successors, and invested first in the "construction of socialism," then in the management of "actually existing socialism," another result is the collapse of *state communism*. This is the strict sense in which it is most appropriate to understand the expression, "the end of communism." But because state communism, for half or even three-quarters of a century, had reorganized within itself or polarized around itself most of the movements that called themselves communist, it was also the end of "communism" as a socially autonomous movement.[3] Once again, in short, the experimental proof of the fragility of "strong states" was carried out before our eyes—even if we had to wait seventy years for this proof in the case of the USSR. We must consequently acknowledge the prescient lucidity of Antonio Gramsci, who, at the very center of the communist movement, without allowing himself to be deceived by the Marxist ideology of the "end of the state," diagnosed this weakness by showing that the type of state constructed by the Bolsheviks on the ruins of the Russian Empire was incapable of hegemonizing "civil society," that is (in the paradoxical sense in which he used the term), stimulating its self-organization.[4] This analysis is, even today, manifestly more pertinent than those inspired by the theory of totalitarianism, from which is derived the thesis of the quasi-supernatural immutability of communist regimes.

In any case, if the evidence of the statist character of this communism in the course of collapse cannot be challenged, it leaves to the side two problems that manifestly preoccupy many of our contemporaries, and which may in fact constitute a single problem. One is the *communist idea* (or ideal, or doctrine); the other is the future of communist *movements* in the noncommunist world (for which it will doubtless be necessary to find new designations, now that it is formally "the only one").

As far as the communist idea is concerned, striking divergences of appreciation can once again be observed. Next to those who affirm that it is definitively "dead," in all camps voices can be found to affirm, with hope, nostalgia, or anxiety, that the dissolution of a regime is not the death of an idea. Some liberal intellectuals have taken up the pen to say that we must not forget the contribution of its followers to struggles for liberty and equality.[5] Others, less magnanimous, have responded that it was not necessary to "grant to communism *post mortem* [what one] had always refused it during its life."[6] Many communists, whether or not they belong to the party of that name, are moved to explain that a radical critique of capitalism is indestructible as long as capitalism continues to develop its own contradictions. Some speak in the name of *truth* (which does not necessarily coincide with certainty), others in the name of *utopia* (or, if you will, hope). Some, finally, go so far as to maintain that, with the death of state communism—an inverted and perverted form of the communist ideal—the ground is finally cleared for an authentic communism and, on the theoretical level, an authentic Marxism.[7]

This argument, the motivations of which I understand (even that of resisting a new intellectual conformism, which often hides fairly poorly its complicity with social conformism), nevertheless seems to me politically as well as theoretically weak. Because *historical* communism has not found in its heart the strengths that would have permitted a correction of its perversions, or Marxism the theoretical means to explain its causes with veracity, the call to a truth, a utopia, or to an immortal ideal today can contain only the very emptiness of the desire that it transmits. It is fundamentally a way of saying *no* (and it is often important to say *no* but, as Bertolt Brecht suggested, it is still more important to say *how*). There is more: this position is particularly untenable in the case of a theory and a movement that aspire to be inseparable from one another, and inseparable from their own *realization* in history, from their own "becoming-a-world." Communism is, in a sense, the only theory that cannot hope to save itself from a historical catastrophe by taking refuge in its high ideals or in the intemporality of utopia (it owes it to itself to exist). And if Marxism is to continue to exist, as a program and as an instrument for the knowledge of the real, it will have to be based on other grounds: proving its capacity for analysis and attaining the intelligibility of its own history.

The distinction between real and ideal, specifically founded on the premise that the "real" on which the ideal foundered was the institutionalization of communism by the state, is pretty much the position that Louis Althusser had already taken in 1978, when he proclaimed a henceforth irreversible "crisis of Marxism" and proposed the necessity of "a communism outside of the state."[8] In reality this formulation, in its related forms, has been a historical constant of socialism and communism at least since the October Revolution: it constitutes the point of departure for all *critical Marxisms* and all "communist oppositions" to orthodoxy and to the dominant apparatuses within states and parties of the Soviet type. Which brings us fairly directly to the second question raised.

In reality what is lacking in any description of the end of communism in terms of a collapsed state apparatus, as well as in terms of the unveiling of an imposture, is not the residue of the ideal but an understanding of the duality of institutional realizations of communism and the intrinsically conflictual nature of their articulation. This duality has been completely masked (including, and perhaps even especially, in the discourse and conception of "Western" communist parties) by the representation of the struggle between the two "blocs" and its simplistic logic.[9] We mean by this that "real communism" in fact consisted of the intersection of *two circles*: the system of communist *states* (called "socialist"), and the system of communist *parties* and *social movements* in the "capitalist" world. Perhaps it would even be necessary, in all rigor, to speak of *three* distinct circles, adding the circle of critical dissidences and oppositions to the first two. This duality, more or less denied depending on the place and period, appears in retrospect to be a decisive phenomenon.

It is clearly not a question of two independent realities (and this is why, among other reasons, communist parties today have fallen together with the communist states, and critical currents are frittering away together with the parties they opposed). The *state-parties'* mimicry of the *party-states* is self-evident, a sort of trademark that has resisted every crisis and every attempt to achieve autonomy. But this mimicry should not occlude the real contradiction, due in the last analysis to the "contingent" fact that the parties and communist movements, which were thought and lived from the base to the leadership as a "countersociety," in reality operated within the framework of "bourgeois" societies and participated completely in their political and social history, whereas the *party-states* of the East were more or less completely isolated from them. The "conveyor belt" was constantly at work, but it actually functioned in both directions.[10] More fundamentally, the importance of this articulation stems from the fact that, within the world communist movement (with all the latent or overt divisions that threatened to tear it apart), the organizations of the "second circle," exterior to the system of socialist states, in practice represented contact with a class struggle that was recognized as such, however badly analyzed and practiced it may have been. In 1968 Sartre and many others were able to think and write, "the communists are afraid of the revolution."[11] This state of affairs could be explained by the properly conservative (and not subversive, no matter what Western propaganda may have said) function of the system of socialist states in regard to the "equilibria" and thus to class relations in the world, and by the fact that most communist parties (Bolshevized, Stalinized, and then de-Stalinized) had placed all of their hopes in the long-term "victory" (technological, economic, political, even military) of the "socialist bloc." But this did not mean that the communist parties on the outside could ever avoid being constantly implicated in class struggles, which thus indirectly affected the whole "communist system." At a certain moment class struggles, or analogous social conflicts, themselves began to be produced within the communist states as well, further disrupting the monolithic character of the communist movement as a whole, already disturbed by the divergence of national interests.

These overlapping effects draw our attention to one of the greatest paradoxes of the period that is coming to an end: the existence of an "internal communism" and an "external communism," at once indivisible and practically dissociated, leaves us with the memory of a mechanism of paralysis of political action and thought, steadily suffocated by the weight of the "center" represented de facto or de jure by the Soviet party and state. But in reality the point of conflictual articulation between the two "communisms" and the innumerable replications of that articulation in all the nations of the world were *also* sites of intense production of political meaning, arenas for the confrontation of programs, strategies, and ideas during fifty years and more, if only, once again, on account of the dissatisfaction and criticism they provoked. In the vicinity of this articulation, meaning and its absence were improbably close to one another and were unceasingly transformed into one another.[12] Today their dissolution leaves an emptiness in politics: it is empty of errors, crimes, and manipulations, empty of organizations, disciplines, and revolts, but also empty of stakes and problems. To me this nihilistic situation does not seem foreign to the dull anxiety that makes a number of our contemporaries jump from the "end of communism" to the "end of ideologies," and from there to the "end of politics," and finally to the "end of history."

Two Histories in One

We must now concentrate our attention on *one* dimension of the history of communism, in which the unity and tension of what I have called the "two circles" take on a particular importance for us: the specifically European dimension. We are, in effect, all the more called upon to address the question of what effect the "end of communism" will have on the evolution of Europe, or what is called "European unification," in that this unification has been one of the principal ideological motifs accompanying the course of events. A bit more than a year ago I undertook to show that its effect would be primarily one of blockage, in any case of redirection.[13] But I think today it is necessary to take things up closer to the root.

We must begin by asking, in all the universality of the question, that is to say, in terms of the philosophy of history, what is the place of communism (as idea, movement, and political system) *in the history of Europe?* What is the relationship between the history of communism and the history of Europe—indeed, what is the relationship between the history of communism and the fact that *there has been history in Europe?* It is necessary to pose this question (or to begin to pose it, because it is not going to be settled by a few theses) *against the current* of the dominant orientations of political science, not only because political science approaches the question with an unfavorable bias, but especially because it is entirely dominated by ahistorical, neoliberal problematics. It consequently practices an active denial of "speculations about history" and limits itself to the comparison of "systems."[14] As a consequence of this bias and denial (fair requital, in a sense, for the concrete certitudes of "historical and dialectical materialism"), we are exposed today to the risk of a great repression of the history of communism and the very *concept* of that history. Perhaps it would be better to say: the risk that communism's great repression of its own history (political, social, and intellectual), with the active aid of anticommunism, might never be lifted.

This question, it seems to me, has a double aspect. On one hand, it concerns the relation of communism to *European political thought*. On the other, it concerns the role played by communism, particularly in the modern era, in *the very existence or emergence of a European social and institutional reality*.

It is not possible to deny that communism as an idea or ideology is at the heart of European social thought as the thought of the social "bond" or "relation," one of whose poles of reference it represents. There are some who claim that it occupies almost entirely by itself the place of *utopia* (which we rediscover here as a mode of thought), to such an extent that many definitions of utopia are presented quite simply as definitions of communism. I prefer, for my part, to insist on the fact that communism has presented itself at three moments as an alternative universalist critique of the great statist constructions of the social bond: expressing, in the face of the state or the ideologies of its legitimation and constitution, the "insurrectional" (which does not necessarily mean violent) viewpoint of the dominated.[15] From these moments came three successive "layers" of representations of society and history, three points of view on the social antagonisms whose pregnancy made itself felt, each time, throughout the totality of the intellectual field.

The first manifestation of communism in this sense is not Plato.[16] But it does appear in medieval thought, where it is perhaps the determining agent of the first "modernization" of *Christian* theology and politics. It is the philosophy of *poverty* (not to be confused with destitution) as a condition of justice in the world and the health of the community, such as the radical wing of Franciscanism developed it and attempted to put it into practice in the thirteenth and fourteenth centuries, opposed equally to mystical or monkish asceticism and the sovereignty of private property.[17]

The second attempt, some centuries later, was "egalitarian" communism, an essential component of the "bourgeois revolutions" of the seventeenth and eighteenth centuries, notably in England and France, whose great theoreticians were Gerrard Winstanley and Gracchus Babeuf: a fundamentally *secular* ideology this time, which sought to construct the polity by means of the realization of liberty and equality, not denying property (which precisely distinguishes it from contemporary "utopias") but *subordinating it to equality* (or regulating the conflict between "individual" property and "collective" property in an egalitarian fashion).[18] This second form of communist thought is at the origin of the representation, renewed throughout the nineteenth century, of the *proletariat* as an incarnation of the authentic reality of a people in the face of "bourgeois" egoism.

But, in the meantime, a third conception of communism arose, no less "organically" linked to the general history of European society, a conception formed in the framework of labor socialism, that is to say, linked to an economic representation of the contradictions of society and an anthropology of labor provided by Charles Fourier and Marx and Engels. It places at the center of its problematic of community the struggle against the subjection of labor to industrial and financial capital, the latent conflict at the core of the modern organization of production between two types of productivity or "development" of human "productive forces": one founded on the division of labor, the other on cooperation and the reunification of manual and intellectual capacities.

There is no need to enter further into the details to grasp that the place occupied by communism (or rather, *communisms* in their successive layers) in the history of political thought is such that the very idea of Europe directly depends on it. This includes its ambivalent relations to universality, because in "exporting" communism to the entire world (after the Bible and cannons), Europe has been placed outside of itself in such a way that it is no longer able to exist as a *closed* unity. It is as much our representation of European civilization as of European political unification that is affected by the "end of communism." (Perhaps it ought to be said, by the *new end* of "communism," but this time it is not a question of repressing a revolt or a confrontation, at least at first glance; it is a question of the failure of an institution. This is also why a resurgence is difficult to imagine.) This observation is in no way nostalgic; it merely seeks to explain a fact. But even in this we are obliged to ask about the material role that communism will have played in the emergence of the European entity.

This role, by all evidence, is extraordinarily contradictory, and this contradiction reached its peak after 1945. We will not gain anything, after the fact, by reducing it to only one of its aspects.

On one side figures the long trail of "proletarian internationalism," still perceptible even in the worst paralysis of the "two communist circles" (the states and the parties).[19] This is all the more true insofar as this internationalism had in fact more of a European than a global reality. Europe as such, with all its fissures, was present in a certain way with the International Brigades in the Spanish Republic, or in the peace movement; where is the "global" equivalent? Marxism and "proletarian culture," within narrow enough limits but in an effective way, functioned as languages common to intellectuals, artists, workers, and peasants over the whole continent: it remains to be proven that liberalism, parliamentary democracy, and "supranationality" can do as much and more.

But on another side communism has played a decisive role in the institution of impassable borders, cutting the continent in half and subdividing each region. It is not by chance that the signal for the destruction of the "socialist system" was given by a gigantic revolt, beginning in Germany and spreading to Poland, Hungary, and Czechoslovakia, against the "Iron Curtain," enclosure, and the prohibition of movement. In this revolt, the attraction of the Western world's consumerism played a well-known role, but so did claustrophobia and the affirmation of the right of movement as a fundamental *political* right. State communism or "real" communism, theoretically internationalist, was in fact constructed as a society of closure and fetishism of boundaries, a society of border guards.[20] Rather than entering into the discussion of the respective roles played by the hostility of the "free" or capitalist world and the police apparatus of the "dictatorship of the proletariat" in the generalized partitioning of Europe, a debate that remains open to historians,[21] I prefer to be content with this hypothesis: from the time of "war communism" in response to the counterrevolutionary intervention of the English, French, Japanese, and Czechoslovakian armies, until Yalta and the Berlin Wall—which is probably its most tragic symbol—communism could only ever respond to Western "containment" through what must be called "self-containment," an internalization and organization of isolation. This strategy consistuted a veritable schema of thought and intervention in history, operative at every level, from the "cells" that constitute the party's base to the partitioning of the "socialist bloc" itself. This is why, beyond the horror that it represented in itself, the Soviet gulag could symbolize the whole system: real communism was the society of the enclosed encloser (whereas liberal capitalism, for the most part, excludes and massacres only on the *outside*). But if we pursue this indication to the end, strange consequences come into view. No doubt Soviet expansionism (more political and military than economic) occurred in Europe and throughout the world, alternating latent and aggressive phases, responding to attacks from outside or initiating conflict. But in a sense this expansionism was never more than a way for communism to fortify itself, to regroup, an intrinsically contradictory project of conquering the world by folding back upon itself.[22]

A Phantom Europe

This is perhaps, for what directly concerns us today, the most infernal logic binding together the history of communism and the history of Europe, of which "real" communism, of both state and party, is at once victim and perpetrator. Inscribed in the institutions of Europe, it weighs heavily upon their current "deconstruction" and "reconstruction." It makes Europe at once an obsession and a phantom, still in need of blood for nourishment, which we do not know whether to exorcize or to bring to life, in a great collective *nekuia*, now that the Trojan War of our time is over.

This phantom is first of all the illusory Europe, the *Europe of contradictory illusions* maintained since 1920, and most particularly since 1945, by the very way that each of the two "blocs" laid exclusive claim to the idea of Europe in its confrontation with the other. It is enough to have traveled a little in the East, or simply to have heard its language, to know that Soviet communism claimed, no less than the "West," to be the representative of the European idea, the bearer of its heritage and future. In this claim there is even (reappropriating an old Russian dream of the alternating "tides" of history—see the last chapter of Tolstoy's *War and Peace*) an idea of revenge for the hegemony and appropriation of European civilization by the West. This began with the symbolic "transfer" of the Jacobin Revolution and the Paris Commune to Petrograd and Moscow and continued with each of the two "Europes" claiming to be the only authentic incarnation of the spirit of antifascist resistance, because the other was stigmatized by its impure collusion with Nazism (whether on account of Munich, or the German-Soviet Pact, or imperialism and monopoly capitalism, or totalitarianism, or the *Berufsverbot*, or else the gulag). The project of "people's democracies" constructed by "fraternal parties," as dreamed by Dimitrov, responded to the "European federalism" of the successors of Aristide Briand, Gustav Stresemann, and

Edvard Beneš. The liberal and democratic Europe of the Helsinki treaties was a reply, thirty years later, to the socialist and pacifist Europe of the Stockholm Appeal. Even the practice of "sister cities" flourished on both sides. The question here is not whether the balance is equal (it isn't, at that), but how, in this merciless dispute, comes to be constituted the dream of an "end of the division" and, consequently, the imagination of Europe as a *unified body* that has been *cut up* and needs to be sewn back together. Following the disappearance of one of the two blocs, the struggle itself is vanishing, which in fact constitutes a great trial of truth: now or never is the moment for the dream to materialize, for Europe to rise up, renewed or revitalized. This is also the moment when the dream risks being smashed into pieces.[23]

These symbolic considerations are hazardous by definition. But they suggest to us another line of approach. Communism was desired, then imposed, then refused, defended, and combated over three-quarters of a century following a war of mutual extermination that marked the height of European nationalism. Can it be said that its whole history is in truth that of the *blockage* of European unification, insofar as it concerns in principle *all European peoples*, a blockage resulting from the very incompatibility of the conceptions that it proposes?[24] This hypothesis deserves investigation, now that it is an urgent question whether the end of communism indeed represents the lifting of the obstacle that was blocking the progress of European unity (in a federal or any other form), or whether it will instead mark the opening of a new era of exclusive nationalisms. From this point of view, the history of the twentieth century will appear to us as a process in which each *defeat* of communism (and its history has involved defeats above all else—I would be tempted to say, at the risk of pathos, that the process represents more a defeat long-deferred than a progress suddenly halted) has also marked a defeat of European unification. Shared defeats cannot be completely without posterity.

One could thus begin this history at the "beginning," after the failure of the Hungarian, German, and Italian revolutions between 1918 and 1920, which opened the way to fascism and the triumph of Stalinism in the USSR. This was in a sense still the model of 1848: revolution and counterrevolution in Europe. But I prefer to insist on two other conjunctures, nearer to us and less often mentioned from this angle.

First that of 1933–45, the rise and fall of Nazism. In what way, in the final count, was this a defeat of communism? People of my generation were hardly prepared to comprehend it. To various degrees, we were raised on the conviction that communism represented, if not *the* single force victorious over Nazism, at least *the* working-class and more generally populist component of the democratic camp's victory over Hitlerism. This is why the power of Marxist socialism and the communist parties arose from the defeat of Hitler. But, after the fact, we are obliged to acknowledge that this vision of things was at best an illusion, in reality a mystification and an imposture. It provided the communist parties of both East and West with a borrowed legitimacy with which they were themselves intoxicated. Not that communists throughout Europe and Soviet citizens by the millions did not fall in battle against the "brown plague." No current or future revisionism can erase this from history. But what is important here is that communism was powerless to oppose Nazism, and Marxism incapable of analyzing it and understanding the reasons for its power, on *their basis of their own identity and resources* as a "proletarian" movement and a theory of "class struggle." European communism (including Soviet communism) combated Nazism by becoming one component among others—an indispensable one, on account of its size, its organization, its spirit of sacrifice—in a front of democratic and patriotic forces. Marxism was able to interpret fascism and Nazism only as new forms of imperialism and "instruments" of capitalist politics in a period of crisis and did not in the least understand the ambivalence of mass ideologies in the historical phases of state collapse.[25] Failing to comprehend nationalism, it found itself "nationalized," from one end of the continent to the other. One could say as much, naturally, of the other branch of socialism and European Marxism that emerged from the split of 1914–20, social democracy. But this, far from relativizing it, brings an additional dimension to the historical defeat of communism: the struggle against Nazism, which could and should have resulted in a reunification of European socialism and thus a revival of the interpretation and application of Marxism (and a return to the thesis of the *Communist Manifesto*: "The Communists do not form a separate party. . . . [They are] the most advanced and resolute section of the working-class parties of every country"),[26] instead brought about their irreversible antagonism, their instrumentalization by the politics of blocs, and the radical impossibility of combining the idea of European unification with a politics of class, even a simple social politics.

Equally significant and full of consequences was the defeat of the 1970s, from the revolutionary movements of 1968 to the coup d'état in Poland of 1981. Probably the negative and even very disturbing aspects of the current "revolutions-restorations" for the future of Europe are to a great extent the result of these developments. The consideration of the two circles of communism and their articulation is particularly important here. Let us not forget that the movements of 1968, in both East and West, were at the origin of what is called "Eurocommunism": a significant term, which goes well beyond its official use and the theorizations of intellectuals, denoting not so much the search for a "third way" between Stalinism and social democracy or liberalism[27] as the momentary *convergence* of social and political struggles and critical revolutionary tendencies in the East and in the West.

The formidable social effect of 1968, its lasting intellectual trace in the East (especially in Poland) and in the West (especially in Italy), is the first expression of this convergence.[28] There is more than an analogy and a common reminiscence of the mythical formulations of the labor movement between the "workers' councils" in Prague during the spring and the "factory councils" throughout the Italian "creeping May"; there is a historical initiative linking the autonomy of labor to the search for new political forms, occurring at the very edges of the "bourgeois" or "socialist" democracy and circulating throughout the entire continent. Similarly, the history of labor struggles in Poland (Solidarność, and before that the KOR [Worker's Defense Committee]) and their interpretations in Western Europe bear witness to a virtual unification of the two camps. In both cases, it is necessary to take up the idea—today nearly inconceivable but not long ago more or less self-evident in the eyes of many—that the innovations and advanced models that "bourgeois democracy" itself needs will be due to the renewed movement, critical development, and contradictions of "socialist democracy."[29] Before disappearing completely, this idea was to take on another paradoxical but certainly recognizable form, which consisted of seeking the most advanced form of democratic politics in the *class anticommunism* (labor or popular) and forms of self-management of "civil society" against the state of a movement like Solidarność.[30]

However, we know what was finally to come of it. The Italian "creeping May" suffocated under terrorism on the extreme left, terrorism on the extreme right, and the counterterrorism of the state (which were perhaps all one and the same); the labor struggles in Poland failed under the military coup d'état. Due in particular to the lack of similar movements in the USSR itself, as well as the absence of a truly internationalist dimension in the movements of Western Europe (often masked by an abstract "Third Worldism" over which the Chinese Revolution had no small influence), the East and West of Europe remain irredeemably cut off from one another. In the final count, and this is its tragic side, 1968 (with its continuation in the following years) profoundly unsettled the division of Europe, only to implacably sanction it anew. This fact was heavy with consequences, which were felt with particularly strength in the West's passivity in the face of Brezhnev's "normalizations" and in the isolation of pacifist movements on both sides of the Iron Curtain in the 1970s and 1980s. Can we truly consider 1968 as independent of another fact that is directly responsible for the forms taken by the "end of communism" today, namely the definitive exhaustion of the capacity for critical contestation *at the heart* of the socialist regimes and "real communism"? We mean by this that after the "1968 decade" there were no longer any programs of political reform of communism, nor forces capable of conceiving and defending it, nor, a fortiori, masses who might imagine their future in it. This probably represents the moment when the verdict whose execution we see today was silently pronounced, as was clearly attested by the failures (each in its own way: one by the "summit," the other by the "base") of both Gorbachev (in whom Alexander Dubcek believed he could pay homage to his spiritual heritage) and the *Neues Forum* in East Germany.

Communism or Nationalism

These are the conditions in which the problem of nationalism reemerges: the explosion of federal states, "ethnic" or ethnoreligious conflicts, and finally the atrocious Yugoslavian civil war are in the process of placing it at the center of the postcommunist "transition"—to the point that, as I recalled earlier, its dominant representation is in the process of evolving from an optimistic vision (return to democracy, reentry into the market) toward a pessimistic and even fatalistic one (slipping into barbarism, transformation from one "totalitarianism" to another).[31]

Two principal observations seem immediately necessary to me.

First, the categories that we use to interpret and, more simply, to perceive the history of the peoples of Eastern Europe, beginning with that of "nationalism," are themselves strongly charged with ethnocentrism. They draw their signification, the associations of ideas that they carry, from a hierarchical vision of European history that was constructed at the same time as the political divisions of continental space and that willingly suggests an absolute heterogeneity of East and West (Germany oscillating from one side to the other, at the mercy of conjunctures). More clearly, this means that the temptation is stronger than ever to describe "nationalism" as a phenomenon of which Eastern Europe had the monopoly, or that it carried to the extreme by a natural disposition. In thinking this way we create a straw man and forget that nationalism also exists in the West. It is even in the West that some of the most extreme forms of nationalism *began* to appear during the recent period. The same is true for autonomist or secessionist movements in the historical nation-states, for the ideologization of conflicts of interest in the European Economic Community, and especially for the development of populism and of xenophobia toward "extracommunal" populations. Not only have we not been outdone, but it is possible that we have provided the model and that, *seen from the East*, Western Europe appears not as the example of cosmopolitanism it claims to be, but as a conglomeration of national egoisms—which would simply demonstrate that "nationalism" is a *relative* notion, and its manifestation and effects depend on the conjuncture.

This leads to a second observation. The most widespread idea at the moment, fed by all sorts of memories from history textbooks, is that the end of state communism is a pure and simple "liberation"—as if from Pandora's box, a metaphor that crops up frequently—of a mass of border disputes and ethnic and religious conflicts *from out of the past* of Eastern "empires" (Austria-Hungary, the Balkans, Russia, the Caucasus), fundamentally linked to the absence of true nation-states or a delay in their construction. At this point certain "realist" minds begin to miss the Soviet order, which was at least capable of keeping these conflicts in awe, if not of controlling them. Perhaps it is necessary to complicate this vision of things a little. Whether these ethnic and linguistic-religious "identities" come from the bottom of ages or more simply from the nineteenth century, it is impossible to deny that they are appearing everywhere, from Prague to Baku and from Vilnius to Belgrade. The question is why they have once again so polarized collective movements. The notion of a "revenge of the past"[32] seems insufficient to me; the role of communism itself in this affair, both active and passive, must be taken into consideration. As has been noticed by excellent experts on Eastern Europe—E. J. Hobsbawm and, particularly, Pierre Hassner[33]—there is no pure and simple continuum from the "nationalisms" of the past century to current "nationalisms," in the Caucasus as in the Balkans, even if the latter do seek a legitimacy and self-consciousness in the properly "fictive" reconstitution of past history. Rather than seeing the decomposition of communism as having provided the chance for a *resurgence* of what, fundamentally, has never ceased to exist, it is more realistic to see it as the *cause* of the fact that, among available ideals, entire populations should seek their vision of the future in the nation or micronation, transforming every communal difference into a dream of autonomy and provoking contrary identifications in reaction.

But we can go further. One of the fundamental reasons for this "nationalist explosion" (which goes to the point of raising up entirely fictive nations, for example, the Belarussian nation) clearly resides in the intensely national and nationalistic character of the communist state itself. This is what, paradoxically, has never been emphasized in the comparisons between Nazism and communism that are so prevalent in political science, obsessed as they are with the ideological antithesis of class and race. Like all others and more than most in the twentieth century, the "class" state of the Soviet type was a national-social state. The rapidity with which leaders of the communist apparatus in Russia, Armenia, Azerbaijan, Serbia, Croatia, and so on have been transformed into nationalist leaders could serve as an indication of this.[34] What we witness today, rather than a resurgence or an appearance *ex nihilo*, is, on a sliding scale, a gradation of nationalism: from federal nationalism, or imperial nationalism, to regional and from there to local nationalism. In this sense, there is no doubt that Slobodan Milošević, Boris Yeltsin, Franjo Tudjman, and Zviad Gamsakhurdia still proceed from Stalin and Tito.

The Semiperipheral State and Its Disaggregation

It is thus impossible to avoid the question of the external constraints that have conferred to *nationalism within communism* its continuity and, at the same time, its capacity for displacement.

The form in which the Soviet "model" was propagated in the Third World after World War II (in the course of which Stalin had brought about the complete fusion of proletarian ideology and Russian nationalism) is in this light greatly clarified. It was not the idea of a world revolution that won out (even if it periodically attempted to make itself heard, as in Che Guevara's "tricontinental" enterprise) but rather the example of "socialism in one country," that is, a practice of national construction that reflected upon itself and presented itself in an inverted form, in the universalist language of the class struggle. An explanation in terms of caste interests (intellectual, bureaucratic, and military) would be insufficient, however real they were. A more profound explanation doubtless resides in the fact that all "national socialisms" of the Third World find themselves by turns in the same situation as the USSR and a large part of Eastern Europe, which, borrowing Immanuel Wallerstein's terminology, I characterize as *semiperipheral* in the world-economy.[35]

Politically, communist regimes were implanted by mass democratic movements or coups d'etat, even by foreign conquest, which profoundly differentiated the modalities of their ideological underpinnings. But structurally they have corresponded (especially the Soviet regime) to the prolonged attempt to *constitute a semiperiphery*, that is, to relax the constraint of the world market (what Samir Amin calls "delinking"),[36] and thus to find an autonomous place between the two permanent poles of the world economy, the financially, industrially, and culturally dominant pole and the dominated pole, used as a reservoir of labor and raw materials—the pole of the concentration of wealth and that of the concentration of poverty. This other structure, perhaps more decisive in the long term, was completely masked by the dualist representation of world history in the twentieth century as a confrontation between two "blocs," East and West, characterized by the difference between their regimes and their ideologies, a representation totally assumed by the communist regimes themselves and reinforced by Western crusades against the "evil empire." If we set aside the ideological understanding of East-West confrontations over political and military hegemony, which reached their peak in the context of the Cold War and the arms race, we can formulate the hypothesis that in the twentieth century it was the socialist bloc that constituted the true "third way," the true Third World, that is, one that attempted to gain an autonomy *between* the world of wealth and the world of poverty (most often referred to today as the North and the South).

Here we discover another dimension, another determination of the phenomenon of the internalization of autarky mentioned earlier, which is best characterized by the combination of nationalism and planning (including nonmonetary planning, which in its very form escapes the influences of the world market). But we also understand that the end of communism, a provisional attempt to delay capitalist polarization in the name of an ideology of equality and at the price of dictatorial constraint, was in preparation within its own modalities on both sides of this combination: planned industrialization led back to dependence with respect to the more advanced technologies and financial credits of capitalism, while nationalism implied the acceptance of the strategy of blocs, and thus militarization if not imperialism. The history of the USSR symbolizes both the impossibility of economic autarky and the blockage of national construction in the "imperial" form.[37]

If this hypothesis can be confirmed (and it would certainly require further discussion and specificity), it casts a discouraging light, it must be said, on the national and nationalist conflicts that are in the process of developing in Eastern Europe. There has been much talk in recent years about the displacement of the axis of East-West confrontation in favor of that of North-South conflicts, which we can translate as a regression of ideological determinations of world politics under the effect of a growing burden of economic inequalities. The idea of a regression of ideological determinations is dubious, if only because there is no less ideology in economics than in the form of the state. But the other part is significant. To say that the East has passed into the South is to say that "Third Worldization" and relegation to the periphery are the order of the day in all of Eastern Europe.[38] The "liberal revolutions" were made in part in the name of a universalist and formal conception of the market: a return to economic efficiency by means of competition and the dismantling of state planning, an end to state enterprise contaminated by bureaucracy, routine, parasitism, and corruption. But the reality of the relationship of forces, those structural inequalities that organize commodity circulation on the global scale, is imposing itself much more rapidly than any constitutional reform. The "liberalization" of economic planning begins by taking the form of a gigantic liquidation, in which a division is made between what is to be "auctioned off" and what must be purely and simply destroyed to make room for merchandise from the "developed" core, at the price of dramatically accentuating the inherited penuries of the socialist economy. Paradoxically, it is now *in the West* that an important public and private *planning* continues to exist (concerning the control of capital movement, the improvement of the territory, or the preservation of a certain correlation between economic and social policies, despite deindustrialization and the decline of trade-unionism), while in the East they are passing without transition from bureaucratic centralism to the most savage deregulation.[39]

Thus the ethnic conflicts in Eastern Europe also appear as byproducts of a formidable economic constraint, already latent for some years, but whose field is suddenly opened by the collapse of the national or multinational socialist *states*. It is sometimes asked why the "rich" nations of the West do not seek to create a "Marshall Plan" for Eastern

Europe. Even if they had the political will and the financial means, which seems doubtful, there would remain a quasi-insurmountable obstacle: such a plan supposes the conservation and even reinforcement of the links among the old socialist states. But such links have been totally destroyed, just as each state is riven by the disintegrating effects of incorporation into the market. The Yugoslavian civil war, if it was not only that, is also a ferocious confrontation whose stake is either incorporation into the developed "core" of capitalist Europe or collapse into a "periphery" henceforth stripped of any possibility of protecting its labor and valorizing its resources. *Who will be poor? Who will be rich* (or at least incorporated into the institutions of the community of the rich)? The same question is posed, in terms hardly less violent, in the Baltic states, in Georgia, in Slovakia. It was formally solved in the case of the former German Democratic Republic, but only in order to give rise to another reality test: that there are poor in the universe of the rich, an internal as well as an external exclusion.

What Happens When the State Collapses in Europe?

The "real" nationalism ignited by the embers of communism thus assumes a final aspect, in the most disquieting sense of all: not only product and prolongation of the history of "real socialism," not only by-product of world economic constraint, but reaction and compensation for a veritable collapse of the state. Lilly Marcou was not mistaken in speaking of an "almost supernatural resemblance to the syndrome that gave birth to fascism in the 1920s."[40] This is what neoliberal ideology, accustomed to imagining that market society is organized democratically by virtue of its own logic, independently of power relations, is least prepared to comprehend and explain. We said earlier that the end of communism is above all the end of state communism, but the "fusion" of the two terms was so close that it seems impossible, in reality, to eliminate the one and preserve the other. It is thus also a matter of the end or *collapse of the state as such*, of one of the variants—however "pathological" it may have been—of the European state-form, including its administrative and cultural structures. This phenomenon is certainly comparable, in its amplitude and that of the catastrophes that it is able to bring about, with what occurred in Germany and Central Europe after World War I and the economic crisis (and perhaps also in Russia after the civil war: it might be very useful to reexamine the interpretation of the origins of Stalinism from this angle). Since the state today has become the very condition of individual existence, the collapse of the state (even the most repressive state) inevitably implies the launching of a mass "panic" over questions of identity. Even as it seeks to save itself from itself, this panic is maintained by a blind flight forward into the imagination of absolute community. It thus has only to seek its modalities in the historical past or in the image its neighbors offer. The neo-Nazi immigrant hunters of the former East Germany, subjected to an intense process of eradication of memory, seek models in the memory of a Hitlerism that had itself been suppressed in an authoritarian way.[41] But they are also imitating a "European" xenophobia whose manifestations, for ten years now, have not ceased to multiply throughout the West.

Without doubt it is necessary to acknowledge, with sadness and anxiety, that after the failure of the critical movements and social struggles that attempted to democratize Soviet-style socialism from the 1950s to the 1970s, after the ebb of the euphoria that arose last year (1990) from the end of single-party dictatorships, the liquidation of the political police, the establishment of freedom of speech, and the rediscovery of European peoples, authoritarianism and xenophobia are now the order of the day in the former "socialist bloc." The reestablishment of parliamentary democracy seems like a very weak recipe for combating them, to judge by its health in our countries.

More than ever, Eastern Europe thus appears as a *border* of democracy, where the stakes are all or nothing. But it would once again be a mistake to conceive of this border as a separation. In today's world, it has not the slightest chance of being maintained, and no one would want to rebuild the Wall a little further east. The true question is whether we in the West are seeking to invent new forms of European solidarity, of communication between peoples with the aim of formulating common objectives, or whether we will continue to treat the problems of "European equilibrium" by means of force, market logic, propaganda, and formal diplomacy. Most recently it was the Albanian "boat people" we threw back into the sea. We ignored Gorbachev's proposals for economic and political cooperation, leading to the collapse of the federal Soviet structure that he was trying to preserve.[42] Today it is the states of the European Economic Community that are consulting together, not only to rethink the political structures of Europe but to guarantee the impermeability of the communal borders (I should say, borders protecting identities) against the influx of refugees from the East. Helsinki is nothing but a vague memory. The idea of European citizenship is carefully left on paper. The Serbs and the Croats, who speak the same language, give or take a few words, kill each other for our benefit, for our tourist currency, and for our offers of employment a few kilometers from Vienna and Venice, and we have absolutely nothing to offer them but economic sanctions and "blue helmets"!

If the proclamation of this collective responsibility is not sufficient to influence the course of events, it is at least necessary. Over decades and, in a sense, centuries, the relation to communism has contributed, both positively and negatively, to the formation of solidarities in Europe. Today the very existence of Europe is at stake in our collective approach to the "end of communism."

6

World Borders, Political Borders

Any reflection on the relation between politics and globalization confronts us with the possibility of a play on words based on two different meanings of the word "border." A few years ago the economist Georg Vobruba, a specialist in *Wohlstandgefälle*—differences in economic prosperity—between neighboring countries such as Germany and Poland, the United States and Mexico, or France and North Africa, published an article with the title, "The Limits of Borders."[1] His idea was to show that state borders have reached a historical limit beyond which their internal and external functions are filled less and less well. But Vobruba still dismissed the hypothesis of a pure and simple disappearance of borders in the world that is taking shape today.[2] This perspective, he said, is neither plausible nor desirable, and I think he was right. But the whole question is to know whether current tendencies sketch out a univocal evolution. I do not think this is the case, and to show why, I want to open the debate to other aspects of what is called globalization (*Globalisierung* in German, *mondialisation* in French).

Let us begin with the problem of the relations between the concept of politics and what we call the "world." I will pose the following question in order to keep the discussion from becoming too abstract and make the issue more precise: what criteria are most often used to affirm

Paper presented on May 16, 1998, at a round table organized by the Centre de philosophie politique, économique et sociale (CNRS ERS 0596), directed by Mireille Delbraccio, Liliane Maury, and Bernard Peloille. An earlier version had been delivered as the opening lecture of the workshop Politik in der Globalisierung, Globalisierung der Politik, Hamburger Institut für Sozialforschung, September 25, 1997.

that the world has entered an era of globalization, or that the process of globalization of the world has irreversibly crossed a decisive threshold? In the overwhelming majority of cases it seems that the determining criterion is that of economic transformations. The economists were the first to begin using the terminology of "globalization" and "globalized" processes.[3] The implicit idea is that the globalization of agents and processes leads to an even stronger determination of politics by economic structure than ever before. But this asymmetrical situation can allow for two interpretations: either it is the pure and simple withering away of politics to the benefit of the economy,[4] or this means that all politics at bottom has now become economic policy and that the field of social tensions is polarized by economic constraints and strategic choices. If what we call the "world" is nothing more than the "market" or the "process of accumulation on a global scale," need we conclude that regulatory mechanisms or conflicts between economic interests will continue to reduce the field of what can properly be called politics, or even tend to render politics superfluous? Or should we rather conclude that henceforth the falsely "natural" domain of production and circulation will be entirely shot through and infected with conflicts, alternatives, and properly political reversals in the conjuncture, implying that economic agents become virtual *subjects* of strategic choices and ideological passions and not merely subjects calculating interests? Before returning to this question, I would like to show that our initial hypothesis needs to be filled out.

Any description of globalization as a purely economic process, even when its goal is to account for the dominant usage of the term, its rapid diffusion and extension to all sorts of contexts and disciplines, is insufficient on its own ground. By definition a process of economic development is a continuous phenomenon and does not require that thresholds be set at any particular moment. It will always be possible to explain, and for good reasons, that what Immanuel Wallerstein calls the modern "world-system"[5] was "globalized" or in the course of "globalization" *from the beginning*, or that the portrait of the expansion of capital drawn by Marx in the *Communist Manifesto* represents the first general theory of globalization. Inversely, one can always adduce arguments to show that globalization today is still largely a utopia on account of ongoing resistances to the homogenization of territories and social regimes and the development of new processes of polarization and separation.[6] This leads us to think that the astonishing generalization of talk of "globalization" and "globalism" should be understood as a symptom, referring to an *overdetermination of phenomena*. The economic process seems unprecedented only to the extent that it has been combined with other processes. At the risk of a dangerous simplification, I would suggest that globalization has appeared with such striking obviousness as a structurally irreversible process *only in a determinate political conjuncture.* This conjuncture is itself the result of heterogenous events that have seemed to reinforce one another and radically to reverse the previous course of social life, whence the impression of a turning point in the history of civilization. I would like to signal three such events in particular.

The first is in fact an economic event: the appearance of multinational corporations whose financial power exceeds that of most states and which have thus gained the ability to delocalize and transport their activities toward whatever region offers the lowest production costs. The counterpart to this mobility is the constitution of a single system of capital and monetary exchange, operating in real time and tying together all financial markets. As a consequence, monetary policy (both national and supranational) and, with it, economic development policy have become totally dependent upon the fluctuations of financial markets, which themselves are determined by the anticipated profitability of stocks and bonds.[7] I leave it to the economists to fill out or correct the description of this stage in the development of capitalism and the new institutions it implies. It is incontestable, however, that these institutions and the economic role of institutions generally can no longer be identified to the extent they could in the past with the construction and functioning of a national state. This puts into question the generally admitted equation between the framework of the state and that of politics.

The second event without which we could have never seen "globalization" used in its current sense is the collapse of the Soviet socialist system, bringing with it the end of the "division of the world" into two antagonistic "blocs." This event is *both* political and ideological: the widely held representation of its origins and consequences is an integral part of its meaning and its power to overdetermine other processes. The widely invoked date of 1989 would seem primarily conventional in this respect, for it can be argued the decisive steps in the "reintegration" of socialist societies into the capitalist world had been taken well beforehand. It remains the case that, in retrospect, it appears as the culmination of a major cycle of conflicts and transformations that concern humanity as a whole, stretching over an entire century but whose origins go even further back.[8] This event includes two aspects that concern us here.

First, it appears as the end of a struggle or competition between *radically different social systems,* each of which claimed in its way to sketch the future of humanity. This conflict was crystallized in the form of a confrontation between "superpowers," that is, imperial states seeking to conquer ideological and territorial hegemony in their respective spheres of influence. The end of this antagonism in the collapse of one of the two protagonists does not seem to have been immediately followed by the appearance of a new *polarization* of the world dividing humanity politically in a comparable way.

Second, we can observe that the *other demarcation* of the world, the division between North and South (which had to some extent required a relativization of the importance of the East-West antagonism), has not succeeded, notwithstanding a few tendencies and many predictions, in occupying the "empty place" of the conflict between Socialism and Capitalism as a cosmological and cosmopolitical conflict. This "end of ideologies," as it is sometimes called, would seem to be explained by the fact that the diversification of situations and the growth of social inequalities are occurring even more rapidly *within the North* and *within the South* than they are *between North and South*—whence a general redistribution of wealth and power, and whence also the fact that none of the ideologies that might "unite the poor against the rich" seems able to keep up with the rhythm of the process constantly displacing the borders between spheres and making them permeable to one another. This is why, even if some have foreseen a "clash of civilizations,"[9] there are no signs of a tendency for simple and global front lines to be drawn that would be able, even at the level of ideology, to "polarize the world" or reduce its complexity.

I would interpret all this in the following way: "globalization" would never have become the issue it is, or in any case it would never have become an issue in such a "global" way, had there not *already* existed "global" faultlines (or *global superborders*), as well as a "global" antagonism, and had these lines not then been erased. In this respect globalization is nothing more than the transcendence of the division of the world, the end of the antagonism, apparently forever. In other words, it is always already a *second globalization*, the first one having been that of the antagonism between blocs. This dialectic, as we will see, also carries decisive consequences for the representation of politics. But first we must take a third factor into account.

I constitute this third factor by taking together all the processes that have *both a technical and a natural aspect* that prove that the *earth*, with its immediate environment and the life it supports, has become a single "system" in which flows of information, energy, and matter influence one another. It might be said that, from a purely physical point of view, such a natural and technical system has always existed. This is true, but with the qualification that since the "technical" processes now exist on the same scale as the "natural" ones, there exist cumulative effects of technical interventions that, in a way perceptible to all, alter the life environment of the human species or transform its natural conditions of existence. Likewise there are biotechnological processes that have an influence on the life of the human species (and other species). This is why I would include in this third source of the idea of "globalization" not only the existence of a system of electronic communication on the scale of the entire earth,[10] by means of which every individual is virtually in contact with every other individual through a whole variety of channels, whether open or closed, but also the growing consciousness of the seriousness of ecological problems, and finally the transformations of the biosphere itself. What all these processes have in common is a combination of or reciprocity between the *virtual and real* aspects of the action. "Virtual" does not mean the same thing as the "imaginary" described in our old psychological and phenomenological analyses, and in a sense it means exactly the opposite. From the point of view of the imagination and the imaginary, virtual processes and events appear "more real than reality," that is, they have a quasi-hallucinatory consistency. What we must take into account, and what becomes an irreducible component of the very idea of a "world" or a "globalized world," incorporating its own limits or boundaries, is this inner doubling that allows it to represent itself to itself according to various interdependent systems of signals, images, codes, and models. Each local individuality is thus associated with the image of the place it occupies in the "whole."

In short, my hypothesis is that the discourses of globalization and the generalization of "global" (or "locally global," sometimes expressed by the portemanteau word *glocal*) explanatory models are the conjunctural result of three factors overdetermining one another: a new stage in the development of the capitalist market, the end of the global antagonism that formerly appeared as the ultimate horizon of political practice, and the constitution of a system of both real and virtual planetary interdependencies erasing the border between nature and technology and associating each locality with the image of its place in the whole. It is their superimposition in a single present that gives the appearance of a unique, irreversible event that is itself of global importance. The central economic process turns out to be modified by two essential "supplements," one of which is *politico-ideological* and the other *technico-natural* in character. It is particularly important to emphasize the multiplicity of these criteria, *none of which can be logically deduced from the others*, for only this overdetermination can account for the dominant representation of the effects of globalization on politics, namely an oscillation between the *globalization of politics* (sometimes interpreted as its passing into a "postnational" or "cosmopolitical"—in the literal sense—era) and the *end of politics* (at least in the traditional sense of the term).[11]

Has globalization then destroyed politics, or is it politics that has invaded the field of the globalized economy? Taking the various aspects of the tableau we sketched here into account suggests the first answer. Let us then examine how "the end of politics" should be understood in the current situation.

We will call the first current acceptation *positivist.* It refers in fact to what nineteenth-century theorists (John Stuart Mill, Antoine Augustin Cournot) called the *stationary state,* or the state of generalized social equilibrium, due to the automatic character toward which market decisions—"rational" decisions—tend.[12] The result of this is not, of course, to render any further transformation impossible; cultural and technological changes can, in fact, go on and even accelerate. But transformation would henceforth occur *without essential conflictuality* between classes, social groups, powers and counterpowers, "systemic" and "antisystemic" forces. It thus never leads to *radical alternatives,* to the formation of mutually incompatible cultures, irreconcilable ideologies and subjectivities, nor would it open up the perspective of evolution in a contrary direction or "bifurcation" of the system. At the most it would have to count with perturbations, oscillations around the equilibrium, and individual revolts against the general norm, which are not to be confused with *resistance,* if it is true that resistance is always connected with a vision of a reversal in the course of things. This impression, as we know, stems largely from the way that the opposition between politico-ideological "blocs" was able to appear as the horizon, if not the model, of all forms of social struggle and conflicts between values inherited from past history, opposing between them adverse conceptions of the community of citizens and of the political. With the end of the East-West conflict and the absence of any new comparable configuration, Marx's prediction of the "end of the political state"[13] would have come true, but against the grain of his vision—that is, not as the consequence of the overthrow of capitalism but of its triumph and generalization.

A particular importance can be attributed in this respect to the fact that, by definition, a *globalized market* has no "outside" in either a geographical or sociological sense. Once all human activity takes the form of commodity exchange, or occurs under the constraint of the law of value, there is no place available for alternative practices and modes of life. There exist only forms of *inner exclusion,* synonymous with extreme precariousness and verging on elimination.[14] Likewise, if the allocation of resources is more and more regulated on the global level "in real time," it is difficult to see where there could be space for individual and collective adventures, for economic challenges or projects for autonomous development. The only question would be how quickly and easily one can adapt to changing technological conditions. To conclude, if the reality of interactions between individuals and groups is shadowed by an omnipresent virtual interaction, are we not led to imagine that all the possible conflicts and alternatives that have traditionally been identified with the domain of the *political* will also be projected into a virtual world, that is to say, "simulated"? All of them being simultaneously realized and tested, none of them will really be put into action. "Adaptive" general rationality would pass by way of the simulation of alternatives and the elimination of disturbances (and thus of disturbers).[15]

Such is the positivist or objectivist configuration of the end of politics. Some of the neoliberal prophecies of the end of history that received so much media attention at the time of the fall of the Berlin Wall and the collapse of the Soviet bloc are in the end not very different: they simply add a dimension of moral normalization to the techno-economic description.[16] On the other hand, we should draw a clear distinction between these viewpoints and the discourses that I would call apocalyptic or messianic. We can think here about the way in which references have been made recently to the role and the propositions coming to us from Chiapas and the resistance movement of Indian communities under the direction of subcommandant Marcos and the possibility of its worldwide contagion.[17] But there are other messianic statements of politics and its end. Some passages of Jacques Derrida's *Specters of Marx* describing the "ten plagues" of the current world that as a whole constitute the economic horror of our "out of joint" time are clearly oriented in this direction, although we should never lose sight of the ironic element in Derrida's writing, which constantly plays with the contemporary return of archetypes.[18]

I have intentionally chosen these examples among many others precisely because they are not vulgar and contain elements of explicit criticism of the eschatological myths of the end of history and the ideological functions these myths fulfill. But are not eschatology and myth in fact simply racheted up a notch, passing from a belief or religious hope to a hypothesis or an ethical injunction? The guiding thread remains the idea that, if we look at the *facts*, there is no more distinction between globalization and the absolute alienation of human existence and freedom, including phenomena of expropriation and massive social exclusion, and ending in the quasi normalization of exterminations and ethnocides resulting from famine and war, as well as those of cultural dispossession (or "*dispropriation*"), the domination of communication by depersonalized networks that allow the daily conditioning of thoughts and feelings. But is not such a situation, which takes the human condition to *extremes* (*ta eschata* in the Greek of the church fathers), in reality *unbearable*, tending to destroy human desire itself, the mainspring of personal life and of the construction of any "social bond"? From such a point one arrives at the idea that we are approaching an inseparably material and moral (or spiritual) "watershed" (or point of bifurcation) where the choices confronting both individual and collective existence will be posed in terms of all or nothing[19]—which also means that politics could be reborn from its own death, be it in unheard of and unforeseeable forms.

There is no lack of reasons for seeing this opposition of positivism and the apocalypse—which, as one might suspect, is by no means completely new in the history of ideas—as the two sides of a single vision.

In order to get out of such a nihilistic dichotomy, rather than proposing a new global discourse, I would like to return to the specific question I posed at the beginning, namely the current status of borders. All of the paradoxes we have just evoked will reappear, but in a much more concrete fashion, once we pose the following simple problem: what can be done, in today's world, to *democratize the institution of the border*, that is, to put it at the service of men and submit it to their collective control, make it an object of their "sovereignty," rather than allowing it to subject them to powers over which they have no control (when it does not purely and simply serve to repress them)? As I have tried to show elsewhere in greater detail,[20] borders are historical institutions: their juridical definition and political function, which determine the way in which they are drawn, recognized, and crossed (with the rituals and formalities prescribed for particular points of passage), have already been transformed several times in the course of history. The question of their transformation *in a democratic direction*, giving the citizens they serve to control both a de jure and de facto power over them, is on the agenda today everywhere. This is true in Europe as in Africa and the Americas. But this does not mean that we can adopt the idea of a universal process of weakening and eventual disappearance without further examination.

When we say that borders are institutions, we are pointing out that there have never existed, anywhere, "natural borders," that great myth of the foreign policy of nation-states. Everything here is historical, down to the *linear* character of borders as they appear on maps and, to the extent possible, are marked on the ground. This is the culmination of a construction of and by the state that identified the exercise of sovereign power with the reciprocal determination of territories, and thus with the attribution to the state of a right of eminent domain over populations and their movements, before making populations themselves the ultimate reference of the constitution of political powers in the framework of recognized territorial limits. But we must go one step further. If borders are instituted, they must also be considered as *limit institutions*, that is, they represent an extreme and essentially antinomical case of institutions. For, at least in principle, they must be able to remain stable while all other institutions are transformed; they must give the state the possibility of controlling the movements and activities of citizens without themselves being subject to any control. They are, in sum, the point where, even in the most democratic of states, the status of citizen returns to the condition of a "subject," where political participation gives way to the rule of police. They are the *absolutely nondemocratic*, or "discretionary," *condition of democratic institutions*. And it is as such that they are, most often, accepted, sanctified, and interiorized.

Democratizing the border would thus mean democratizing some of the nondemocratic conditions of democracy itself that always come between the people and its theoretical sovereignty. It could be thought that this objective is simply absurd were it not so clearly on the agenda everywhere in our "globalized" world. This has to do with the fact that, sometimes noisily and sometimes sneakily, *borders have changed place.* Whereas traditionally, and in conformity with both their juridical definition and "cartographical" representation as incorporated in national memory, they should be *at the edge of the territory*, marking the point where it ends, it seems that borders and the institutional practices corresponding to them have been transported *into the middle of political space.* They can no longer function as simple edges, external limits of democracy that the mass of citizens can see as a *barrier protecting* their rights and lives without ever really interfering with them. More and more, however, borders are creating problems in the heart of civic space where they generate conflicts, hopes, and frustrations for all sorts of people, as well as inextricable administrative and ideological difficulties for states (just as, on another level, the question of the "nationality" and "citizenship" of successive generations of immigrants has become an inextricable difficulty)—whence proceed contradictory political strategies whose results are totally unpredictable.

These difficulties seem to stem from a growing gap between the level—transnational or "across borders"—on which a large number of private practices and social relations are now organized, in the cultural as well as economic field, and the framework of the majority of public institutions (and in any case the state), which remains fundamentally national. I do not think that this means that the solution lies in a simple *adaptation* of the institution to this new social framework, whether this be imagined as a progressive weakening of borders or as a limitation of the role, matching the "relativization of the nation-state." There are a number of reasons for this. First of all, psychological reasons: even as the usefulness of borders in civic space is becoming more problematic, one can observe a tendency for collective identities to crystallize around the functions of imaginary protection they fill, a fetishism of their lines and their role in separating "pure" identities. Next, geopolitical reasons: beside the weakening or erasure of (often very old) separations as a consequence of free-trade or "common market" agreements and the disappearance of the strategic "blocs," one can also observe a multiplication of new borders and in particular an insistence on the function of borders in controlling populations. Finally, and most important, these difficulties, which date from the very origin of the modern state, cannot be overcome without a radical recasting of the relations between people and sovereignty, citizenship and community: in short, without a new conception of the state. The reference to these symbolic entities proves that what is necessary here is an *institutional creation,* the invention of new institutions (or new "laws," as Montesquieu would have said) for the public sphere. There are relatively few precedents for this in history, other than, precisely, the transition from city-states to empires, and from empires to nations (if one assumes that these transitions were ever in fact fully accomplished).

It seems to me that such a process can only be long and conflict-ridden; by its nature it is an unequal development. But it is also *political* in the strongest sense: this is why I call it a "border of politics," emblematic of the horizons that globalization itself has raised, even if it not the only one. And this leads me to hold the position that, far from determining an "end of politics," in either a technocratic or apocalyptic sense, globalization in fact carries with it a need to recreate politics. Perhaps it even produces the conditions for entry into a new age of politics.

In conclusion, I would like to give a schematic account of what I previously called the paradox of the movement of borders from the "edge" to the "center" of public space.

To begin with, this displacement takes on quite concrete and perceptible forms. They include the phenomena of reproduction of "ethnic borders" within the urban neighborhoods of the great "world cities" that accompany the migration and concentration of populations from the whole world, and whose complexity explodes the far-too-reductive idea of "communitarianism" or "ghettos."[21] We would have to accompany them with a typology of today's "divided cities," each of which fundamentally represents a singular case that can only be measured by its own history: Jerusalem, Hong Kong, Berlin still and always, Frankfurt, Paris.[22] But there is another aspect that has been forced on our attention by the problems relative to the treatment of asylum seekers and the modalities of control of so-called clandestine immigrants in Western Europe, which pose serious problems of the protection and institution of human rights: the system of identity verifications (generally occurring within the territory) allowing a triage of travelers admitted to and rejected from a given national territory. For the mass of humans today, these are the most decisive borders, but they are no longer "lines": instead they are *detention zones* and *filtering systems* such as those located in the center or on the periphery of major international airports. It is well known that these transit zones are zones of "nonright" in which guarantees of individual freedom are suspended for a variable length of time, and where foreigners again become noncitizens and pariahs—a clear illustration of what I said above regarding the nondemocratic conditions of democracy.[23]

These phenomena of multicultural urbanization and internal control of migrations affect millions of people today. They have become banal, even if not universally well known. But there are also more abstract, more structural aspects, which are of particular concern to us here because they affect civic space in the totality of its dimensions: not only as the geographical space in which the life of citizens unfolds, but also symbolic, and thus institutional space. I will briefly evoke two of these aspects in conclusion.

The first consists in the fact that, as sociologists and anthropologists have observed (for example, in the case of relations between North

Africa and France, or more generally Europe), the permanent installation of migrants, the division of families between several national territories, the emergence of "new ethnicities"[24] in the "second generation," lead to a veritable "genealogical interruption": links of descent are, so to speak, interrupted, or have to be perpetuated "straddling borders" and with increasing difficulty.[25] We should not be surprised that such situations (which a few, but only a few, communities of migrants manage to resist through a strict communal surveillance of education, socialization, and marriages, etc.)[26] tend to crystallize internal and external violence. Nor should we forget, however, that they are also a focal point of intense cultural and artistic creativity. These situations are particularly significant if we put them in relation with the distribution of age categories between the populations of the "North" and the "South," which seems to interest economists more and more: not only do distinct regimes of population growth correspond with class conditions and inequalities of income, skills, rates of exploitation, and the like, but there is also now appearing a conflict of interests between *older* populations benefiting from guarantees of income, social security, and medical protection, and *younger* populations among whom the highest rates of unemployment are concentrated and who are subject to the most savage competition on the labor market.[27]

Such observations suggest that there is now an interference between border lines and the separation between "private" and "public" spheres, which can either reinforce or confuse this separation. Now, this separation, at least in the framework of the traditional nation-state, was always considered to be constitutive of the *political*, even if we were not always conscious of it (although it only required a little attention to the intensity of the ideological discourse about the protection of "family values" and "family policy" that has accompanied its entire history). There is no doubt that the nation-state was a mode of the institution of genealogies and regulation of latent conflicts between generations just like other structures studied by anthropology, such as lineage or the feudal bond. This character became particularly strong when the state became a "state of social protection" or "welfare state," in other words, a *national (and) social state*. This leads me to suggest here that, when the location and social function of borders moves toward the center of the political community, the contradictions and tensions affecting its use pose more and more clearly the problem of a new civility, that is, new relations between *belongings*: from belonging to a family, to a generation, to more or less hereditary "primary" communities, on the one hand, and to "secondary" communities (which require an apprenticeship, an adaptation to the social environment and to the "meaning" of history, and which can be experienced as a choice and a liberation) and the political community, on the other.

But all of these problems of belonging are overdetermined by another phenomenon: a progressive disjunction in the way the state controls different flows—material or immaterial—whereas traditionally everything was concentrated on the same border lines and was the domain of a single administration. What is more, we can see that in practice there is now a separation between the control of goods, funds, and information, on the one hand, and the control of migratory flows and displacements of human persons, on the other.[28] Nothing could be more wrong than the idea that globalization would be accompanied by a parallel growth of material, immaterial, and human circulatory flows. Whereas information has become practically "ubiquitous," and whereas the circulation of goods and currency conversions have been almost entirely "liberalized," the movements of men are the object of heavier and heavier limitations. This difference of status appears essential to the defense of state "sovereignty" in the international political and diplomatic field; it goes together with an intensification of the *socially discriminatory function* of borders (in other times we would have called this their "class function"). A world that is now broadly unified from the point of view of economic exchange and communication needs borders more than ever to segregate, at least in tendency, wealth and poverty in distinct territorial zones (as well as, to a certain extent, health and sickness, which go together with wealth and poverty but pose more difficult problems from a technical point of view). The poor, at least, need to be systematically triaged and regulated at points of entry to the wealthiest territories. Borders have thus become essential institutions in the constitution of social conditions on a global scale where the passport or identity card functions as a systematic criterion.[29] It was for this reason that I found it appropriate to speak of a *global apartheid* being put in place after the disappearance of the old colonial and postcolonial apartheids.[30] But there is a flagrant contradiction between apartheid and the "democratic" and "social" forms of the modern national state, which is why the situation is heading toward an unavoidable crossroads. Either the social state and social citizenship will have to be completely dismantled, or citizenship will have to be detached from its purely national definition so that social rights with a transnational character can be guaranteed.

The task of democratizing borders—which implies that their representation be desacralized, that the way the state and administration use them with respect to individuals becomes the object of a multilateral control, and that the rites and formalities of crossing them become more respectful of fundamental rights—is at the heart of the difficulties, and perhaps, at present, the aporias, of a reinvention of politics in the context of "globalization." It is a task that can only be taken on simultaneously "from above" and "from below," both as a function of principles of right and of popular interests. It is a "global-local" problem. It might also be a privileged point for globalization to become a subjectification, where universal individuality could be constructed.

7

Outline of a Topography of Cruelty: Citizenship and Civility in the Era of Global Violence

With this pretentious title, I want to continue investigating a nexus of problems, both theoretical and philosophical, that I have already touched upon several times. The term "cruelty" is chosen by convention (but with some literary references in mind) to indicate those forms of extreme violence, whether intentional or systemic, physical or moral—although such distinctions become questionable precisely when we cross the lines of extremity—that seem to be, as is said, "worse than death." It is my hypothesis, generally speaking, that the actual or virtual menace of cruelty represents for politics, and particularly for politics today in the context of "globalization," a crucial experiment in which the very possibility of politics is at stake. I use the term "civility" (which indeed has many other uses) to designate the speculative idea of a politics of politics, or a politics in the second degree, which aims at creating, recreating, and conserving the set of conditions within which politics as a collective participation in public affairs is possible, or at least is not made absolutely impossible. "Civility" is certainly an ambiguous term, but I think that its

This essay, rewritten in English by the author for publication in *Constellations* 8 (2001): 15–29, is based on a lecture delivered at the Université de Genève, November 8, 1999, for the inauguration of the Diplôme de formation continue en Action humanitaire. The text published here, which has been edited for this collection, differs in significant respects from the French version. For previous approaches to the questions treated here, see in particular the 1996 Wellek Lectures at the University of California at Irvine, to be published as Étienne Balibar, *Extreme Violence and the Problem of Civility* (New York: Columbia University Press, forthcoming).

connotations are preferable to others, such as civilization, socialization, police and policing, politeness, and the like. In particular, "civility" does not necessarily involve the idea of a suppression of "conflicts" and "antagonisms" in society, as if they were always the harbingers of violence and not the opposite.[1] Much, if not most, of the extreme violence we are led to discuss in fact results from a blind political preference for "consensus" and "peace," not to speak of the implementation of law-and-order policies on a global scale. This, among other reasons, is what leads me to discuss these issues in terms of "topography," by which I understand at the same time a concrete, spatial, geographical, or geopolitical perspective—for instance taking into account such shifting distinctions as "North and South," "core and periphery," "this side of the border or across the border," "global and local"—and an abstract, speculative perspective, which implies that the causes and effects of extreme violence are not produced on one and the same stage, but on different "scenes" or "stages," which can be pictured as either "real," "virtual," or "imaginary" (but the imaginary and the virtual are probably no less material, no less determining than the real).

This chapter is based on a talk that I was asked to deliver in November 1999 for the opening of the Graduate Course in Humanitarian Action at the University of Geneva. This explains why the issues of citizenship and segregation, asylum and migration, and mass poverty and genocides in the globalized world order play a central role in this discussion. These are to me the crucial "cosmopolitical" issues that we should try to locate and connect if we want to understand how and why democratic citizenship in today's world cannot be separated from an invention of concrete forms and strategies of civility.

I focus on two sets of problems. The first, typically European, concerns the negative repercussions of postnational integration and introduction of "European citizenship," which is not only a revival of "communitarian" demands and "identity politics," but above all a development of quasi-apartheid social structures and institutions. This forms a contradictory pattern, which in many respects is now becoming highly unstable. The second set of problems is global: it appears as a systematic use of various forms of extreme violence and mass insecurity to prevent collective movements of emancipation that aim at transforming the structures of domination. For this reason—and also with the pattern of state construction that Thomas Hobbes once described in the *Leviathan* as preventive counterviolence in mind—I do not hesitate to speak of a politics of global preventive counterrevolution or counterinsurrection. But from another angle this "politics" is really antipolitical, because in a ni-hilistic way it leads to the suppression of the very conditions necessary to build a polity. Instead, we witness the joint development of various sorts of wars and a kind of "humanitarian" action or intervention, which in many cases functions as an instrument in the service of precisely the powers that created the distress. Not by chance, in these two sets of problems, the traditional institution of borders, which I think can be defined in the modern era as a "sovereign" or nondemocratic condition of democracy itself, mainly works as an instrument of security control, social segregation, and unequal access to the means of existence, and sometimes as an institutional distribution of survival and death: it becomes a cornerstone of institutional violence. This explains in advance why I insist on the democratization of borders, not only as their opening (and not as their generalized abolition, which in many cases would simply lead to a renewed war of all against all in the form of savage competition among economic forces), but above all as a multilateral, negotiated control of their working by the populations themselves (including, of course, migrant populations). Perhaps new representative institutions should be set up in this regard that are not merely "territorial" and certainly not purely national. This is part of what I would call a "cosmopolitics of human rights," where citizenship and civility are closely associated.

Citizenship and Civility: The Question of the "Right to Have Rights"

Before giving more detail about the two sets of concrete problems I want to deal with here, I think that we need some philosophical instruments to place them in the broader perspective of a reflection on the relationship between human rights and politics. It is widely accepted—and I share this view to a large extent—that Hannah Arendt's work provides a necessary starting point here. Allow me a few considerations on what we can draw from her. In her discussion of imperialism in *The Origins of Totalitarianism* she addresses the question of "stateless" populations, deprived of all civil and civic rights, which had been immensely increased in Europe (and elsewhere) after the two world wars.[2] In so doing, she inverts the perspective of political philosophy in a double manner.

First, she brings forms of exclusion and situations of extreme violence that threaten the survival of humans, as mere representatives of the species, back into the center of debates concerning citizenship and political regimes. Her goal was not only to assert a humanistic criterion with a view to doing justice, but to show that it is only through the discovery of a solution for such situations that we can find a new foundation for the public sphere, one in which not only the management of population movements and policing of social conflicts but also collective political *action* (or *praxis*) takes place. In a very similar way, the French philosopher Jacques Rancière has recently argued that, since the very origins of democracy, the measure of equal liberty for all in the political realm was based on the "part of those who have no part," that is, giving a fair share to those who hold no share in the commonwealth, or the political recognition of the have-nots. In other words, this would mean an active transformation of processes of exclusion into processes of inclusion of the discriminated categories into the "city" or "polity."[3] This is exactly what *isonomia* in Greek cities was about. In this respect, "politics" in the strong sense becomes inseparable from "permanent revolution," a notion that Arendt might have inherited from Rosa Luxemburg.

From this perspective, the juridical form of equal liberty is clearly not eliminated, but it has to be completely reworked. With respect to the principles of modern humanism and universalism, a notion of "persons without rights" is a contradiction in terms, because de jure nobody is without rights, not even children or the handicapped. But if we view positively, for instance, such claims as those of propertyless peasants in Brazil, whose motto is "justice for the rightless," when they demand that paramilitary forces who kill and terrorize the poor be tried and condemned,[4] or those of migrant workers in France who protest against their being denied official documents by demanding a *droit de cité pour les sans-papiers* (legal residence for the undocumented),[5] we can view these demands based on resistance and the refusal of violence as partial but direct expressions of the process of creation of rights, a dynamic that allows the political constitution to be recognized as "popular sovereignty" or democracy.

This is one aspect of the lessons we can draw from Arendt's reflections on citizenship, but another perspective is even more relevant today. I am thinking of the famous argument showing that the history of nation-states, from the age of democratic national revolutions through the generalization of international conflicts and the development of imperialism, has produced a reversal of the traditional relationship between "human rights" and "political rights" (or *droits de l'homme* and *droits du citoyen*). *Human rights* in general can no longer be considered a mere prerequisite and an abstract foundation for political rights that are set up and preserved within the limits of a given national and sovereign state, nor as a limit to the domination of the political over the juridical. The tragic experiences of imperialism and totalitarianism in the twentieth century have made manifest that the opposite has become true: political rights, the actual granting and conditions of equal citizenship, were the true basis for a recognition and definition of "human rights," to begin with the most elementary ones concerning survival, bare life. By giving a new, "unpolitical" meaning to the *zōon politikon* itself, those who were not citizens of some state, who were "citizens of nowhere in the world," were in practice no longer recognized and treated as humans. When the *positive* institutional rights of the citizen are destroyed—when, for example, in a given historical context where citizenship and nationhood are closely associated, individuals and groups are chased out of their national belonging or simply put in the situation of an oppressed national "minority"—the basic rights that are supposed to be "natural" or "universally human" are threatened and destroyed: we witness forms of extreme violence, setting a distinction between so-called *Untermenschen* (subhumans) and "humans" believed to be supermen, *Übermenschen*. This is by no means a contingent phenomenon; it results from an irreversible process that has become common in contemporary politics. It imposes upon democracy the immediate task of a renewed foundation. The very essence of politics is at stake here, because politics is not a mere "superstructure" above the social and natural conditions of life, communication, and culture. The *true* concept of politics already concerns the very possibility of a *community* among humans, establishing a space for encounter, for the expression and dialectical resolution of antagonisms among its various constitutive parts and groups.

Seen from this angle, the crucial notion suggested by Arendt, that of a "right to have rights," does not feature a *minimal* remainder of the political, made of juridical and moral claims to be protected by a constitution; it is much more the idea of a *maximum*. Or, better said, it refers to the continuous process in which a minimal recognition of the belonging of human beings to the "common" sphere of existence (and therefore also work, culture, public and private speech) *already* involves—and makes possible—a totality of rights. I call this the "insurrectional" element of democracy, which plays a determinant role in every constitution of a democratic or republican state. Such a state, by definition, cannot consist (or cannot only consist) of statuses and rights ascribed from above; it requires the direct participation of the *dēmos*.

Arendt's argument clearly recognizes the importance of the egalitarian or insurrectional element constitutive of democratic citizenship, but she also conceptualizes it in a dialectical relationship with the politics of civility. This stems from the fact that the radically excluded, those who, being denied citizenship, are also automatically denied the material conditions of life and the recognition of their human dignity, do not provide only a theoretical criterion to evaluate historical institutions against the model of the ideal constitution. They force us to address the reality of extreme violence in contemporary political societies—nay, in the very heart of their everyday life. This is only apparently a paradox: the limit or "state of exception," to use Carl Schmitt's term, is nothing exceptional. On the contrary, it is "banal": it permeates the functioning of social and political systems that claim or believe themselves to be "democratic." It is both an instrument for the continuity of their vested interests in power and a permanent threat to their vitality. This is why we should not consider the choice between access to and denial of the rights of citizenship—more generally, between the possibility and impossibility of an inclusive political order—as a speculative issue. It is a concrete challenge. The (democratic) political order is intrinsically *fragile* or *precarious*; if it is not continuously recreated in a politics of civility, it becomes again a "state of war," within or across borders.

European Apartheid: The Violence of Borders

We know that Arendt's argument was based on the experience of a "catastrophe" in European history: Nazism, World War II, and the racist extermination of European Jews, Gypsies, and other groups. She tried to trace back its "origins" in the evolution of the nation-form toward imperialism, while at the same time carefully remaining aware of its uniqueness. We might summarize her idea by speaking of a deadly circle in which the national constitution of the state had trapped us. It was at the same time the sole positive or institutional horizon for the recognition of human rights and an "impossible" one, producing the destruction of the universal values it had supported. Now we must ask ourselves whether we are still living and acting in the same conditions. If not, we should ask what the claim of "a right to have rights" could become in today's politics. This question becomes acute when we observe that, although the nation-form has not simply been withering away, the conditions of politics, the economy, and culture, the material distribution of power and the possibilities of controlling it, have become increasingly transnational. "Postnational" state or quasi-state institutions have emerged in the general framework of globalization, of which the "European community" is a privileged case. Let us first reflect on some of the contradictory and worrying aspects of this process, which, from another side, holds much promise.

I take it to be a crucial issue to acknowledge that, along with the development of a formal "European citizenship," a real "European apartheid" has emerged. In the long or even the short run, it could obstruct or *block* the construction of a democratic European community. Therefore it could block European unification altogether, since there is no real possibility of the supranational community being achieved in an authoritarian way, à la Bismarck, even for the sake of accumulating power or creating a regional power that would be able to match the world's economic, political, and military superpower. A supranational European community will exist only if, compared with existing national constitutions, it creates a *democratic surplus* for the majority. Let me clarify the issue by asking two symmetrical questions: Why speak of a *European* apartheid? Why speak of *apartheid* in Europe?

Why Speak of a European "Apartheid"?

This cannot be simply the case because foreigners are granted lesser rights (more precisely: some categories of foreigners, mainly immigrant workers and asylum seekers from the East and the South who legally or illegally crossed the frontiers protecting the wealthy "civilization" of Europe, the Balkan region featuring in this respect a kind of combination of both forms of exteriority). For the term to be justified, there must be something qualitatively new. This is indeed the case with the new developments of the construction of Europe since the 1993 Treaty of Maastricht. In each and every one of the European nation-states, there exist structures of discrimination that command uneven access to citizenship or nationality, particularly those inherited from the colonial past. But the additional fact with the birth of the European Union (coming after a mere European Economic Community) is that a status of *civis europeanus* progressively acquires a specific content: *new* individual and collective rights, which progressively become effective (for example, possibilities to appeal to European Courts against one's own national administration and justice).

Now the crucial question becomes: new rights *for whom?* It could be, abstractly speaking, either for the whole *population of Europe,* or simply for a more limited *European people* (I am expanding here the dilemma which is now taking place in Germany about the distinction between *Volk* and *Bevölkerung,* since this dilemma actually concerns all of Europe and the German controversy is paradigmatic). It proves very difficult and embarrassing to "define" the *European people* as the symbolic, legal, and material basis for the European constituency. Maastricht solved the problem by simply stating that those and only those who already possess citizenship (that is, are nationals) in *one* of the constituent national states will automatically be granted European citizenship. But this definition—which may remind us of debates among the Founding Fathers of the United States—already determines an orientation. Given the quantitative and qualitative importance of the immigrant population permanently residing in Europe (what French political scientist Catherine Wihtol de Wenden has called "the sixteenth member-state"),[6] it immediately transforms a project of inclusion into a program of exclusion, which could be summarized by three metamorphoses:

1. From *foreigners* to *aliens* (meaning second-class residents who are deemed to be of a different kind).

2. From *protection* to *discrimination* (this is a very sensitive issue, as shown by the Austrian case, but again, with some differences in degree and language, it is a general European problem: since some of the immigrant workers who are deprived of political citizenship enjoy some social rights, that is, are included in "social citizenship," it becomes a crucial political issue and an obsession for conservative forces to have them expelled from welfare, social protection, and the like—what the French National Front has called "national preference," but precisely because a degree of *preference* already exists in the national institutions, it is likely to become a "European preference").

3. From *cultural difference* to *racial stigmatization,* which is the heart of the process of creation of the "new racism," postcolonial and postnational.

Why Suggest a Parallel with South African "Apartheid"? This Could Only Be a Useless Provocation . . .

Should we really suggest that, while apartheid has officially disappeared in Africa, it is now reappearing in Europe (and perhaps also elsewhere)—a further development in the process of "the Empire striking back"?[7] Also, we could think of other comparisons with historical cases of institutional racism, for example, the United States, which we know has never completely forgotten the "Jim Crow" system and periodically seems to be on the way to recreate it when conservative policy is on the agenda. My German colleague Helmut Dietrich, who has long worked on refugees and migrants on the "Eastern Border" of Europe, particularly the Balkans, has spoken of the *Hinterland* of the new European *Reich*, etc.

Leaving aside the question of how to measure the amount of suffering created by one or another system and focusing instead on the structures, I suggest two complementary reasons to at least borrow lessons from the historical example of apartheid, in terms of a comparison between the situation of the regions whence most of the migrants come, in Africa, Asia, or other parts of Europe, with *homelands* in the South African sense. One is that the position of the important group of workers who "reproduce" their lives on one side of the border and "produce" on the other side, and thus more precisely are *neither insiders nor outsiders*, or (for many of us) are *insiders officially considered outsiders*, produces a steady increase in the amount and the violence of "security" controls, which spread everywhere in the society and ramify the borderline throughout the "European" territory, combining modern techniques of identification and recording with good old "racial profiling." This in particular is what the Schengen agreement was about. The second complementary reason is that the existence of migrant *families* (and their composition, their way of life) has become a true obsession for migration policies and public opinion. Should the alien families be separated or united (that is, reunited)? If so, *on which side of the border*, which kind of families (traditional, modern), which kind of relatives (parents, children), with what kind of rights? As I have argued elsewhere, the interference of family politics, more generally a politics of genealogy, with the definition of the national "community" is a crucial structural mode of production of historical racism. Of course, this is also true when the national becomes a multinational community.

From all this we might draw the conclusion that a *desegregated Europe*, that is, a democratic Europe, is far from being on the agenda. Indeed, the situation is much more contradictory, since tendencies exist in both directions; we are in the middle of a historical crossroads, only partially and reluctantly acknowledged. But I prefer to insist on another idea, which provides me with the necessary transition to the next point, namely the fact that these issues typically illustrate a *global-local* ("glocal") problem. The contradictory and evolutionary pattern of "European citizenship-*cum-apartheid*" (or statutory, ascriptive citizenship)[8] in a sense is a *reaction* to real and imaginary effects of globalization. In another sense it is a mere *projection*, albeit with historical specificities, of such effects.

Global Preventive Counterinsurrection: "Violence without Borders"

I now directly address the main issue that I announced, that of the "global counterinsurrection": not the violence of the border but violence *without borders, or beyond borders.*

Allow me to quote from a recent study of humanitarian action, published by a Swiss expert, Pierre de Senarclens of the University of Lausanne, who rightly insists on the importance of *official definitions of contemporary violence* and also on the problematic aspects of the justifications they provide for an extension of the scope and meaning of "humanitarian interventions":

> In 1981, the United Nations General Assembly adopted a reso-
> lution dedicated to a *New International Humanitarian Or-
> der.* . . . Shortly thereafter, the Assembly gave its support to the
> creation of an independent commission on international hu-
> manitarian questions, which brought together eminent peo-
> ple. . . . The Commission's 1986 report placed within the
> humanitarian project the principal political and social chal-
> lenges of the age, such as environmental degradation, demo-
> graphic transition, population movements, human rights
> violations, weapons of mass destruction, North-South polariza-
> tion, terrorism, and drugs.[9]

He concludes: "We consider humanitarianism as a frame of reference for the identification of important contemporary problems and a formula for their solution." Later the author shows how, after 1989, the collapse of the Cold War system of "two blocs" suppressed the limits that the confrontation between the superpowers had set to political violence and blurred the borderlines between "war" and "peace":

> No one foresaw the destruction of the Berlin Wall, the prelude
> to the swift end of the Cold War. Nor did anyone anticipate the

transformations in international structures and the violence that followed. Toward the mid-1990s, we count more than fifty new armed conflicts, essentially civil wars. Certain of these conflicts—in Rwanda, Yugoslavia, Chechnya, or Algeria—are shocking in their violence and cruelty, the extent of the destruction and the population movements they provoke. International society has never been confronted with so many wars making so many victims in such a short time.[10]

In such conditions, we can incline toward divergent conclusions. Either we can think that the multifaceted phenomenon of mass violence and extreme violence has generally replaced politics, including internal and external relationships of forces among states, or we fully take into account the fact that the fields of politics and violence—a violence that seems to lack rational organization, not excepting self-destruction—are no longer separated. They have progressively permeated one another. It is precisely in such conditions that something called "humanitarian action" or "intervention," both "private" and "public," has become the necessary supplement of politics. I cannot discuss all the aspects of this mutation, but I would like briefly to address three questions that seem to me to have an importance for the concept of politics itself.

Are We Facing an "Unprecedented" Spread of Extreme Violence (or Violence of the Extremes)?

I should like to be very careful on this point, which raises a number of discussions ranging from the issue of "old and new wars"[11] to the highly sensitive moral questions of why and how to "compare genocides" in history. Perhaps what is unprecedented is basically the *new visibility of extreme violence*, particularly in the sense that modern techniques of media coverage and broadcasting and the transformation of images—in the end, as we could see for the first time on a grand scale during the Gulf War, of the production of "virtual reality"—transform extreme violence into a *show*, and display this show simultaneously before a world audience. We also know that the effect of such techniques is, at the same time, to *uncover some violent processes, or scenes of horror* (truly horrifying, such as hundreds of mutilated children in Angola or Sierra Leone), and to *cover up others* (equally horrifying, such as babies starving in Baghdad). We suspect that powerful ideological biases are at work when the coverage of extreme violence gives credit to such simplistic ideas as the political transition from the "equilibrium of terror" during the Cold

War to the "competition among victims," by way of the undifferentiated uses of the legal and moral but hardly political notion of "crimes against humanity." In the end, we become aware of the fact that talking about and showing the images of everyday horror produces, particularly in the relatively wealthy and protected regions of humanity, a very ambivalent effect: raising compassion but also disgust, reinforcing the idea that humankind as such is really divided into qualitatively different cultures or civilization, which, according to one political scientist, could only produce a "clash" among them.[12]

I am aware of all these difficulties, but I would maintain that a reality lies behind the notion of something "unprecedented." Perhaps it is simply the fact that a number of *heterogeneous methods or processes of extermination* (by which I mean eliminating masses of individuals inasmuch as they belong to objective or subjective groups) have themselves become "globalized," that is, operate in a similar manner everywhere in the world at the same time, and so progressively form a "chain," giving full reality to what E. P. Thompson anticipated twenty years ago with the name "exterminism."[13] In this series of connected processes, we must include, *precisely because they are heterogeneous—they do not have one and the same "cause," but they produce cumulative effects*:

1. Wars (both "civil" and "foreign," a distinction that is not easy to draw in many cases, such as Yugoslavia or Chechnya).
2. Communal rioting, with ethnic and/or religious ideologies of "cleansing."
3. Famines and other kinds of "absolute" poverty produced by the ruin of traditional or nontraditional economies.
4. Seemingly "natural" catastrophes, which in fact are killing on a mass scale because they are overdetermined by social, economic, and political structures, such as pandemics (for example, the difference in the distribution of AIDS and the possibilities of treatment between Europe and North America on one side, Africa and some parts of Asia on the other), drought, floods, or earthquakes in the absence of developed civil protection.

In the end it would be my suggestion that the "globalization" of various kinds of extreme violence has produced a growing division of the "globalized" world into *life zones and death zones*. Between these zones (which indeed are intricate and frequently reproduced within the boundaries of a single country or city) there exists a decisive and fragile *superborder*, which raises fears and concerns about the unity and division of mankind—something like a global and local "enmity line," like the "amity line" that existed in the beginning of the modern European seizure of the world.[14] It is this superborder, this enmity line, that becomes at the same time an object of permanent show and a hot place for intervention but also for nonintervention. We might discuss whether the most worrying aspect of present international politics is "humanitarian intervention" or "generalized nonintervention," or one coming after the other.

Should We Consider Extreme Violence to Be "Rational" or "Functional" from the Point of View of Market Capitalism (the "Liberal Economy")?

This is a very difficult question—in fact, I think it is the most difficult question—but it cannot be avoided; hence it is also the most intellectually challenging. Again, we should warn against a paralogism that is only too obvious but nonetheless frequent: that of mistaking consequences for goals or purposes. (But is it really possible to discuss social systems in terms of purposes? On the other hand, can we avoid reflecting on the immanent ends, or "logic," of a structure such as capitalism?) It seems to me, very schematically, that the difficulty arises from the two opposite "global effects" that derive from the emergence of a chain of mass violence—as compared, for example, with what Marx called *primitive accumulation* when he described the creation of the preconditions for capitalist accumulation in terms of the violent suppression of the poor.

One kind of effect is simply to generalize material and moral insecurity for millions of potential workers, that is, to induce a massive proletarianization or reproletarianization (a new phase of proletarianization that crucially involves a return of many to the proletarian condition from which they had more or less escaped, given that insecurity is precisely the heart of the "proletarian condition"). This process is contemporary with an increased mobility of capital and also humans, and so it takes place across borders. But, seen historically, it can also be distributed among several *political* varieties:

1. In the "North," it involves a partial or deep dismantling of the social policies and the institutions of social citizenship created by the welfare state, what I call the "national social state," and therefore also a violent transition from welfare to workfare, from the social state to the penal state (the United States showing the way in this respect, as was convincingly argued in a recent essay by Loïc Wacquant).[15]

2. In the "South," it involves destroying and inverting the "developmental" programs and policies, which admittedly did not suffice to produce the desired "takeoff" but indicated a way to resist impoverishment.

3. In the "semiperiphery," to borrow Immanuel Wallerstein's category, it was connected with the collapse of the dictatorial structure called "real existing socialism," which was based on scarcity and corruption, but again kept the polarization of riches and poverty within certain limits.

Let me suggest that a common formal feature of all these processes resulting in the reproletarianization of the labor force is the fact that they suppress or minimize the forms and possibilities of *representation of the subaltern* within the state apparatus itself, or, if you prefer, the possibilities of more or less effective *counterpower*. With this remark I want to emphasize the political aspect of processes that, in the first instance, seem to be mainly "economic."

This political aspect, I think, is even more decisive when we turn to the *other scene,* the other kind of result produced by massive violence, although the mechanism here is extremely mysterious. Mysterious but real, unquestionably. I am thinking of a much more destructive tendency, destructive not of welfare or traditional ways of life, but of the social bond itself and, in the end, of "bare life."[16] Let us think of Michel Foucault, who used to oppose two kinds of politics: "Let live" and "let die."[17] In the face of the cumulative effects of different forms of extreme violence or cruelty that are displayed in what I called the "death zones" of humanity, we are led to admit that the current mode of production and reproduction has become a mode of *production for elimination,* a reproduction of populations that are not likely to be productively used or exploited but are always already *superfluous,* and therefore can be only eliminated either through "political" or "natural" means—what some Latin American sociologists provocatively call *poblacion chatarra,* "garbage humans," to be "thrown" away, out of the global city.[18] If this is the case, the question arises once again: what is the rationality of that? Or do we face an absolute triumph of *irrationality*?

My suggestion would be: it is economically irrational (because it amounts to a limitation of the scale of accumulation), but it is politically rational—or, better said, it can be interpreted in political terms. The fact is that history does not move simply in a circle, the circular pattern of successive phases of accumulation. Economic and political class struggles have already taken place in the nineteenth and twentieth centuries with the result of *limiting* the possibilities of exploitation, creating a balance of forces, and this event remains, so to speak, in the "memory" of the system. The system (and probably also some of its theoreticians and politicians) "knows" that there is no exploitation without class struggles, no class struggles without organization and representation of the exploited, no representation and organization without a tendency toward political and social citizenship. This is precisely what current capitalism cannot afford: there is no possibility of a "global social state" corresponding to the "national social states" in some parts of the world during the last century. I mean, there is no *political* possibility. Therefore there is *political resistance*, very violent indeed, to every move in that direction. Technological revolutions provide a positive but insufficient condition for the *deproletarianization* of the actual or potential labor force. This time, direct political repression may also be insufficient. Elimination or extermination has to take place, "passive" if possible, "active" if necessary; *mutual elimination is "best,"* but it has to be encouraged from outside.

This is what allows me to suggest (and it already takes me to my third question) that if the "economy of global violence" is not functional (because its immanent goals are indeed contradictory), it remains in a sense *teleological*: the "same" populations are massively targeted (or the reverse: those populations that are targeted become progressively assimilated, they look "the same"). They are *qualitatively* "deterritorialized," as Gilles Deleuze would say, in an intensive rather than extensive sense: they "live" on the edge of the city, under permanent threat of elimination; but also, conversely, they live and are perceived as "nomads," even when they are fixed in their homelands, that is, their mere existence, their quantity, their movements, their virtual claims of rights and citizenship are perceived as a threat for "civilization."

In the End, Does "Extreme Violence" Form a "Global System"?

Violence can be highly "unpolitical"—this is what I wanted to suggest—but still form a system or be considered "systematic" if its various forms reinforce each other, if they contribute to creating the conditions for their succession and encroachment, if in the end they build a chain of "human(itarian) catastrophes" where actions to prevent the spread of cruelty and extermination, or simply limit their effects, are systematically obstructed. This teleology without an end is exactly what I suggested calling, in the most objective manner, "preventive counterrevolution" or, better perhaps, "preventive counterinsurrection." It is only seemingly "Hobbesian," since the weapon used against a "war of all against all" is another kind of war (*Le Monde* recently spoke about Colombia in terms of "a war against society" waged by the state and the Mafiosi together).[19] It is politics as antipolitics, but it appears as a system because of the many connections between the heterogeneous forms of violence (arms trade indispensable to state budgets with corruption; corruption with criminality; drug, organ, and modern slave trade with dictatorships; dictatorships with civil wars and terror); and perhaps also, last but not least, because there is a politics of extreme violence that *confuses all the forms* to erect the figure of "evil" (humanitarian intervention sometimes participates in that), and because there is an economics of extreme violence, which makes both coverage and intervention sources of profitable business. I spoke of a division between zones of life and zones of death, with a fragile line of demarcation. It was tantamount to speaking of the "totalitarian" aspects of globalization. But globalization is clearly not only that. At the moment at which humankind becomes economically and, to some extent, culturally "united," it is violently divided "biopolitically." A politics of civility (or a politics of human rights) can be either the imaginary substitute of the destroyed unity, or the set of initiatives that reintroduce everywhere, and particularly on the borderlines themselves, the issue of equality, the horizon of political action.

Conclusion

There will be no "real" conclusion, only an attempt to direct reflection and discussion toward some sensitive issues: the issue of "counterviolence," the issue of international law, the issue of access to "citizenship," and what I called "insurrection." We might think of different kinds of "strategies of civility." To discuss their possible foundation and implementation would be a matter for another, different essay. Let me simply suggest the following. Since the *real* and *virtual* aspects are so closely interwoven in the nexus of extreme violence or cruelty, it is very difficult to escape an attitude that privileges either one or the other. This is, in a sense, what classical concepts of political action have always done: they were mainly directed at either building *communities* and communal feelings (and I would certainly agree with Benedict Anderson that all historical communities are primarily "imagined communities"),[20] or at changing "the world," that is, in a more materialist way, transforming *social structures*, particularly structures of domination and exploitation (classical Marxism being in this respect a paradigmatic example). I think that the central character of the issue of extreme violence in today's politics makes it even more urgent to look for and invent an *Aufhebung* of this dualism, not by ignoring its dual aspects but by trying, practically and concretely, to combine their demands and constraints in a critical manner.

This might explain why, for instance, I would not feel satisfied with the idea that the foundation of a politics of civility is an insistence on *international law*, although I admit that it is a decisive element of democracy on a world scale. Jürgen Habermas, for instance, has consistently moved in this direction, adding an insistence on the underlying ethics of *communication*.[21] But Habermas neglects the fact that the gates of "communication" sometimes have to be opened by force, sometimes in a violent manner, or they will remain locked forever. International law is necessary here, but not sufficient. From the opposite angle, we might suggest, there is certainly a good case to be made that the looming counterrevolutionary or counterinsurrectional character of massive violence calls for a "counter-counterinsurrection," a renewal of the idea of revolution—this time, perhaps, a true "world revolution" directed against the very global structures that connect violence with capitalism, imperialism, and what Antonio Negri and Michael Hardt now call "empire."[22] But, again, there is a difficulty here: that of falling back into the very *symmetry* of political methods and goals that, since the first socialist and anti-imperialist revolutions attempted to seize power in the name of "the dictatorship of the proletariat," has helped extreme violence become built into the very heart of emancipatory politics and helped the twentieth century become what Eric Hobsbawm called the "Age of Extremes."[23] It is not only the *state* or the *economy* that needs to be "civilized" or to become "civil," but also *revolution itself.* I am convinced that the solution for that historical puzzle is actively searched for in many places today, but it is not clearly found or shown.

In the end, in a more cautious and perhaps aporetic manner, I would consider seriously some suggestions recently made by the Dutch political scientist Herman van Gunsteren.[24] I think that van Gunsteren is right to suggest that *all* political communities—including virtual communities, from neighborhoods to cities to nation-states to continents to the globe itself (Gayatri Chakravorty Spivak would prefer the term *planet* in this context),[25] from "territories" to "networks"—are *communities of fate* (as opposed to "destiny"). They are communities that already include difference and conflict, where heterogeneous people and groups have been "thrown together" by history and economy, in situations where their interests or cultural ideals cannot spontaneously converge, but also cannot completely diverge without risking *mutual destruction* (or *common elimination* by external forces). Taking inspiration from Hannah Arendt's critique of human rights (and also from Kant's formulation in his 1796 essay "Toward Perpetual Peace," "they . . . must finally put up with being near one another"),[26] van Gunsteren sets the admittedly metapolitical *principle that for every individual in every group there must be at least one "place" in the world where he or she is recognized as a "citizen,"* and hence given the chance to enjoy human rights. But, moving just one step beyond that principle (which in another sense is but a question that interpellates us), we may simply ask: *where is that place?* If communities are "communities of fate," the only possible answer is the radical one: *any place where individuals and groups belong,* wherever they "happen" to live and therefore work, bear children, support relatives, find partners for every sort of "intercourse." Given what I have suggested concerning the "topography" of today's globalized and cruel world, I think we could even say more precisely: the recognition and institution of citizens' rights, which practically command the development of human rights, have to be organized beyond the *exclusive* membership to one community; they should be located, so to speak, "on the borders," where so many of our contemporaries actually live. Of necessity, this means an unstable situation but also very precise demands. Van Gunsteren is right in this respect to stress the idea that, from what I would call a point of view of "civility," the important question is permanent *access to* rather than simply *entitlement to* citizenship, and therefore humanity (or, as he writes, citizenship "in the making"). It is an active and collective civil *process,* rather than a simple legal status.

8

Prolegomena to Sovereignty

It has become common to associate the uncertainties of European unification, in the context of a new phase of globalization, with the idea of a
crisis of sovereignty. But most often this formulation is taken in a re-
stricted sense because the notion of sovereignty is identified a priori with
its national form, and, at the same time, an equivalence is suggested
between the crisis of sovereignty and the development of surpranational,
transnational, or postnational political spaces. In my view, this restriction
has three drawbacks.

In taking the form of a binary opposition, it occludes the fact
that the *alternatives to sovereignty* currently at work in Europe cannot be
reduced to a single type. To begin the discussion, we can evoke at least
three: *subsidiarity, federalism,* and *empire.* Obviously these alternatives are
not "the same age" as far as their origins are concerned. The idea of
subsidiarity refers to premodern institutions that are contemporary with
feudalism: medieval franchises and hierarchies of imperial or ecclesiasti-
cal competencies.[1] Federalism in its various conceptions (see, for example, the work of Charles-Irénée Castel de Saint-Pierre, Immanuel Kant,
Pierre-Joseph Proudhon, Richard Coudenhove-Kalergi) constitutes a sort
of reverse side of modern national sovereignties, which comes to the fore
during the moments of mutation or crisis they have undergone during
the past four centuries.[2] Finally, empire—the term proposed by Michael
Hardt and Antonio Negri, designating the new political, economic, and
communicational order resulting from decolonization, the end of the

First published in *Les Temps modernes* 610 (September–November 2000):
47–75, special issue on *La Souveraineté: Horizons et figures de la politique,* ed.
Michel Kail and Emmanuel Wallon.

conflict between the Cold War blocs, and the information revolution—even if it is still seeking its institutions through conflicts whose outcome remains unpredictable, represents nonetheless a postmodern innovation.[3] The differences in "age" of these alternatives do not prescribe their future or prevent them from influencing one another, but it is clear that giving a privilege to any particular form will imply different perspectives on the nature and historical capabilities of the "sovereign" nation-state. The confusion of current discussions on postnationality provides an eloquent illustration of this point.

Second, the idea that the essential cause of the regression of sovereignty is a disintegration of nations, abolishing borders or putting their political function into question, obscures the question of the relation between the two notions of *state sovereignty* and *popular sovereignty*. It seems that even though they are conceptually distinct, their reality is either confirmed or denied simultaneously. Whence the difficulty in discussing the pertinence of the idea of *democratic sovereignty* in supranational institutions without amalgamating it with a defense of the centralized state and nationalism (as do generally speaking those today called "sovereigntists"). The warning contained in Nietzsche's allegory—"I, the state, am the people!"[4]—seems more timely than ever. Whenever the people is invoked, most often it is state interest that is speaking. But inversely, the idea of a popular sovereignty (collective decision making, representation of the interests of the mass of citizens, and control of the rulers by the ruled) that could be dissociated from its statist forms remains enigmatic, if not inconceivable. Its genealogy is masked more than it is illuminated by the current opposition between national sovereignty and the "postnational constellation."[5]

Whence the third difficulty. It would doubtless be important, in the current stage of events, to be able to give a clear and operational content to the notion of a "people of Europe." It would be even more important to be able to give this "people of Europe" a political existence (without which the idea of European citizenship will remain a mystification), whether from the point of view of belonging and borders or from the point of view of its social implications. At this level the founding question of modern philosophy, that of the political representation of the people and of the incarnation of the state in the power of the multitude, arises once again in an insoluble way. From the fact that there is still no truly constituent, democratic power on the European scale, or beyond, must we conclude, as I did several years ago, parodying Hegel: "There is no state in Europe" (*Es gibt keinen Staat in Europa*)?[6] Here it seems we are running into a strange aporia: the typically European notion of sovereignty, a long-term product of European history in which the constitution of the people and the constitution of the state come together, turns out to be inapplicable to Europe itself.

The first conclusion I would draw from these difficulties is that we need to avoid simplistic dichotomies between national and postnational eras, between sovereignty and the withering away of the state. Next, we need to ask not only what *happens* to sovereignty in circumstances of crisis or mutation of the political institution but also how its concept is *formed*, that is, what tensions and oppositions it contains. Such an inquiry takes the form of a genealogy in which different institutions, ages, and discourses are framed and analyzed in the light of the present. There is no question of being able to accomplish this all at once. Here I have set myself a more limited, preliminary goal: taking a few classic texts as a point of departure, I will attempt to disengage typical articulations of the European concept of sovereignty, which we have reason to think are still determining the forms of its supersession.

In this perspective, I examine in turn the following points: What knot of political questions should be retained from Carl Schmitt's formulations, which today haunt the defenses as well as the critiques of national state sovereignty? How have these formulations displaced the axis of theorization in which the typically modern definition of "state power" is broadly recognized? How does "popular sovereignty" lead to a characteristic double bind—*the impotence of the omnipotent*—one of whose symptoms is the blockage of the political in European unification?

What Does the Schmittian "Exception" Mean?

The unevenness that has marked the introduction of Carl Schmitt's work in France[7] has not made it—or the reasons that it appears at the end of all the avenues in which debate on the limits of the applicability of the concept of sovereignty is engaged—any easier to understand. After a long period where nothing more than a simple residue of romantic irrationality was seen in his work, Schmitt's theorization of sovereignty, elaborated in the midst of the "European civil war" of the first half of the century, now appears indispensable, not only to understand the sources of "sovereigntist" or "national-republican" discourses, but also to illuminate attempts to reconstruct constitutional law (Olivier Beaud),[8] deconstructions of the "mystical foundations of authority" (Jacques Derrida),[9] utopian projections of the "constitutive power" (Antonio Negri),[10] or—*a contrario*—attempts to put "cosmopolitical right" into effect (Jürgen Habermas).[11]

The definition of sovereignty as the power to "decide on the exception" has become a commonplace. Going as quickly as possible, I will put forth the following thesis: in order to understand its importance for contemporary discussions, this definition needs to be put in the context of Schmitt's later theorization of European equilibrium and the domestication of war in his *The* Nomos *of the Earth*.[12] This book, by associating the institution of sovereignty with the conditions of the division of the world between European (or quasi-European, including the United States and Japan) imperialist powers, elucidates the concrete signification of the state of exception. At the same time, the way that the idea of *nation* itself as an intuitive synthesis of "people" and "state" plays the role of a *black box* in Schmitt's work appears clearly.

Political Theology (1922) begins by posing the fundamental characteristic that prohibits us from conceptualizing a "sovereignty without a subject": *Souverän ist, wer über den Ausnahmezustand entscheidet*, "Sovereign is he who decides on the exception."[13] This sovereign is necessarily personified, even if historically it is a fictive person, the state itself, that is in question. What the sovereign decides is the necessity of public safety and order: where and when it is in danger, and what means are to be used to preserve it. The exception thus cannot be identified with the state of siege or some other particular moment of distress; it has a more general application. Now, the *constitution* cannot determine the exception that suspends it. Conversely, the forms and limits of the juridical order can be characterized from the perspective of the exception. At its center is thus an antinomic reality: the unlimited and purely self-referential competence to suspend the laws in order to reestablish the conditions of their effectiveness, the interior exception without which no historical normality could exist. This antinomy does nothing more than make explicit the primacy of the concrete point of view, that of the existence of the state, over the abstract point of view of the validity of right. The instituting process goes from the state to right, and not from right to the state. The state of exception designates both the extreme conditions in which "the state remains, whereas law recedes,"[14] and the material conditions, which must always be presupposed, of political decision making. It is the intersection of these two ideas.

At the heart of Schmitt's presentation we thus find the unity of three concepts: (political) *decision*, the *exception* (or "extreme" sphere), and the *subjectivity* (or personality) of the sovereign. It is the last that obviously poses the most difficult problems.[15] Schmitt insists both on the necessity of avoiding the confusion between the prince and the state (fostered by the baroque origins of modern politics), and on the impossibility of detaching the state from a personal unity capable of making a decision, and to whom decisions can be imputed. At this precise point we can see a bifurcation that structures the entirety of Schmitt's thought.

The dilemma of the personality or impersonality of the state can be developed in two directions. One of them exhibits the paradoxes of popular sovereignty (to which we shall return). It would appear that, for Schmitt, there is no simple resolution to the antithesis that leads us to think that the attribution of sovereign power to the people both *fulfills* the requirements of sovereignty and virtually *abolishes* them. In fact only a "perpetual" power, as Spinoza (invoked by Schmitt as inspiring the distinction between constituent and constituted power) would say, is truly *absolute*, or corresponds to the concept of a decision without appeal, absolutely just by definition. But is such a power still *personal*, and does it in fact *decide* according to the schema of the unity of the will? Or is it rather only an anonymous result? The fact that, ever since the English, American, and French revolutions, the history of the idea of democratic sovereignty has been practically indissociable from that of the separation of powers, and thus from an internal limitation on the power of decision, leads Schmitt to see the democratic constitutional form as representing the decomposition of sovereignty—except if the exigencies of the state of exception appear once again. Two solutions are then possible: that of popular dictatorship (by the intermediary of organs of permanent revolution, committees of public safety, or soviets), and that of the transfer of full powers of decision to a charismatic leader, "guardian of the constitution." Even leaving aside any reference to the course of contemporary history (it is well known that Schmitt always avoided explaining himself on this point), we must admit that each of these "solutions" has its own aporias, and that in reality they only reproduce the difficulty they are supposed to resolve, namely the necessary and impossible subjectification of the "whole." We should also admit that this illuminates, at least in part, the necessity of *another path*, defined by the articulation of the concept of sovereignty with that of the equilibrium between powers and the *Jus Publicum Europaeum*, the prototype in Schmitt's eyes of a rational system of international right.[16]

Although the notion of the *state of exception* as founding the absolutism of decision is apparently absent from the argument of *The Nomos of the Earth*, all its functions are actually displaced onto the *nomos* itself (the Greek word for law, but to which Schmitt attributes what he sees as a more originary meaning: the partition, distribution, and organization of the earth). In its *abstract* aspect, this refers to the principle of territorialization of the life of men and of right, incarnated in "original juridical acts" Schmitt calls *Landnahmen*: occupation of land, founding of cities and colonies, conquests and alliances, and the like. In its *concrete* aspect it refers to a certain centrality of Europe, from the sixteenth until the twentieth century, in the determination of the regions and borders that "map" the world. Passing over a number of complex transitions, we can say that territorialization allows the secularization of the state-form characteristic of modernity by subordinating religion (*cujus regio ejus religio*, the principle of the Treaty of Westphalia) and organizing the "domestication of war" (*Hegung des Krieges*, a term that is very difficult to translate since it means both that the state *limits* war to rational goals, that it "civilizes" its means and its modes of declaration and conclusion, and that it *protects* its existence in such a way as to protect itself from the devastating effects of an ideology of the suppression of conflicts).

But the territorialization of the sovereign state (*imperium*) is only possible within the framework of a *global order* imposed on the entire earth as an "equilibrium" whose content is shifting but whose form is permanent. Historically, from the conquest of the Americas to the Congress of Berlin on the Congo in 1885, this equilibrium took the form of a dual partition: on the one hand, between the continents, which can be appropriated by particular powers, and the oceans, which remain free for circulation and commerce (and for privateering and the spoils of war); on the other, between the "central" European region where the *Jus Publicum* of treaties reigns, and the "periphery," open to fairly savage colonial competition. At the center of the system is a singular power, Britain, whose position gives it the functions of guarantor of European equilibrium, protector of the freedom of the seas, and principal beneficiary of the partition of the world. The state manifests itself as a historical subject within the joint institution of war and the international order as determined by this fundamentally asymmetrical structure. The equality in right of states and the fluctuations of their power relations give sovereignty its content, which is nothing but the necessary relation between right and war. In a sense, what is sovereign is the impersonal *nomos* itself, distributing and redistributing places and fates. But on the other hand the *nomos* is nothing other than the reciprocal action of states, who, as subjects or historical individuals, hold the constituent power (following the allegory of the Leviathan favored by Schmitt).[17]

In Schmitt's view this organization, in which the exception was materialized as the collective domination of civilized European nations, and decision making was concentrated in the political management of foreign wars, came irreversibly to an end with the world war of 1914, posing the problem—with no evident solution—of the invention of a new principle of territorial order. This was partly the inevitable result of the "globalization" of political and juridical forms formerly confined to Europe, partly that of new technologies transforming the conduct of war (in particular its extension to the air, strategically dominated by the United States, which Schmitt seems to have seen as the retroaction on the center of the barbarous methods in principle reserved for the periphery). But it was above all the result of a spiritual process, an overturning of the values of public right and the equality of sovereign nations, that abolished the distinction between *enemy* and *criminal* by designating certain "aggressor" states as enemies of humanity and by rehabilitating against them the medieval notion of "just war," whether defensive or punitive. Ultimately, it was sovereignty itself that thenceforth appeared as a criminal principle, since it associates the right to make war with the unconditional affirmation of the national interest, whereas now humanitarian, pacifist, and cosmopolitical ideals reemerge. The danger of this evolution, according to Schmitt, is not only that it authorizes, under the heading of reprisals or sanctions, violences incommensurable with those of classical warfare, but also that it imposes upon politics the deadly lure of "perpetual peace," which is likely to be transformed into endless war. Classical sovereign states had in some sense inherited the theologico-political function of the *kathēkon*, the one who "holds back" or "holds off" the apocalypse, but the limitation of state power in the name of the rights of man, which will be promoted throughout a "global" society, will release its horrors.

In the final account, Schmitt's conception of sovereignty includes a central idea that remains constant as the framework is displaced from an internal to an international one: that of the exception or watershed where the political order *turns into its opposite* in such a way as to abolish or neutralize limitations that normally affect every law and every institution. This signification is traditionally designated by expressions such as *summum imperium* or *summa potestas*, "power above the law" (*ab legibus solutus*), and "subjected to no other and recognizing no superiority" (*qui nulli subest et superiorem non recognoscens*.[18] But for medieval theoreticians it had been necessary to supply a transcendent theological foundation or, what amounts in practice to the same thing, to model its interpretation on that of the divine power of creation and redemption. In Schmitt's interpretation of "secularization" (which he understands as the expression of a real process of autonomization of the political), transcendence is not abolished but it is brought back into the hollow of immanence: it coincides with the inner power of negation that allows the temporal order to be founded upon itself.

Transcendence can never be dissociated from radically antinomical figures of power (what juridical normativism or constitutionalism seeks above all to avoid). *Dictatorship* (and a fortiori "democratic dictatorship") is one of them, obviously, but Schmitt's need for historical realism led him finally to end up privileging another one: that of the *border*, the unity of opposites where war and treaties, order and disorder, the "internal" and "external" figures of politics come side by side and alternate with one another. It could be said that, for Schmitt, sovereignty is always established upon a border and is primarily exercised in the imposition of borders. Thus in the end, one can understand the link between the doctrine of sovereignty and the definition of politics in terms of the demarcation of friend and enemy (with its extensions: the criminalization of the internal enemy, which forms a pendant to the justification of the external enemy, *justus hostis*). The border is the preeminent site where the controls and guarantees of the "normal" juridical order are *suspended* (it is truly, in the modern constitutional state, the *antidemocratic condition of democracy*), the site where the "monopoly of legitimate violence" takes the form of a *preventive counterviolence*. The *nomos* of the earth is thus the very order of borders: a violence that is supposed to domesticate violence by putting it in the service of the rationality of the state.

But this is also what allows us to understand the aporia Schmitt never ceased to chase after, and whose figures, as we have seen, are concentrated around the people as subject of sovereignty. It must be admitted that, in the concrete existence of a people, the effectiveness of borders really does mark a delimitation of friend and enemy; but Schmitt keeps running up against the fact that while the state can be personified as a subject, the people cannot be. What reason is there for this asymmetry other than the fact that the very notion of the people implies a multiplicity (or even a conflictuality) that resists absolute unification (even, perhaps, by the methods of totalitarianism)? The ideal unity of the state and the people is also a way to designate the *nation*. The "sovereign individuals" that the doctrine of European equilibrium speaks of are virtually nations, but only on the condition that their internal history be placed between parentheses, in a black box, as it were. And Schmitt cannot keep himself from noticing that national questions and the popular demands or "guerrilla warfare" they bring with them poison the European order by insinuating the subversive idea that there is a difference between the people and the state. The individuality of the historico-political "subjects" postulated by sovereignty never stops putting sovereignty itself into question.

The "Marks of Sovereignty": Bodin, Hobbes, and the Primacy of the Political

The fact that they attributed sovereignty to peoples or states constituted as absolute individuals with a "natural" tendency toward self-preservation is the fundamental reason Schmitt privileges authors such as Jean Bodin or Hobbes (whereas he distrusts Machiavelli). An examination of their work should allow us to make an advance in the analysis of the genealogical problem. Emphasizing the significant *gap* between the content of their doctrine and Schmitt's reading of it, I will again isolate one crucial theme: that of the marks of sovereignty.

The expression, which no doubt comes from an entire theological and juridical history, is at the center of Bodin's theorization in the *Six Books of the Republic* (book 1, chapter 10: "On the True Marks of Sovereignty"). It is taken up by Hobbes at the end of the great chapter of the *Leviathan* on the "Rights of Soveraignes by Institution" ("These are the Rights, which make the Essence of Soveraignty; and which are the markes, whereby a man may discern in what Man, or Assembly of men, the Soveraign Power is placed, and resideth").[19] According to Schmitt, the modernity of Bodin, further developed by Hobbes, is located precisely in this doctrine, in opposition to everything else in his work that is a simple continuation of the medieval heritage.[20] But the interpretation he gives practically inverts the meaning of Bodin's exposition so as to find a primacy of the exception that the entire doctrine of the *Republic* belies.

Whether in *Die Diktatur*,[21] *Political Theology*, or *The* Nomos *of the Earth*, Schmitt will seek out the passage in which Bodin attributes to the prince the right to suspend his own legality (or to unbind himself from his promises) "if the need is urgent,"[22]—that is, when the preservation of the state is in danger—and he opposes this right to the more often cited formal definition, "Sovereignty is the absolute and perpetual power of a republic."[23] Thus he argues that Bodin "incorporated the decision into the concept of sovereignty."[24] This is a deformation of the sense of Bodin's construction, which precisely considers the state of exception as an exception, whose status and treatment depend on the constituted norm. The sovereignty Bodin speaks about cannot be dissociated from a political order in which a certain internal reason is realized. It appears in his work as the crowning element of a theory of the "just government" of the state and of the justice reigning between the parts of a "well-ordered republic." A correlate of the definition of the citizen as a "free subject depending upon another's sovereignty,"[25] it designates the form of supplementary command added to the *archai* cataloged by ancient political thought in the city and the family, so as to account for a "free condition" of dependency that is neither that of the foreigner, the servant, or the slave, but that of the bourgeois. This is the framework within which we must interpret the absolutism inherent in sovereignty according to Bodin, in particular the thesis that gives the sovereign the "power of laws" imposed on subjects "without their consent," and which unbinds the sovereign from the necessity to obey the laws of his predecessors, allowing him to change them (a thesis that will return in the modern doctrine of the "constituent power"). The discussion concerning the prince's promises, which he must always keep except in situations of extremity, allows us to establish its meaning. The bond that the sovereign thus imposes upon himself is a requirement for coherence inseparable from justice or "well-ordered" power, which excludes arbitrariness.[26] Only a power that keeps faith with itself can be effectively obeyed. Rather than a founding decision, antinomical as such, sovereignty is a *function of order* (moral, social, and cosmic).

This does not mean that the doctrine of the "marks of sovereignty" has only a secondary importance; on the contrary, it defines the very content of this function. Examination will allow us to understand what sort of state corresponds to the erection of a sovereign power situated at this point of origin whence an *unconditional* obedience to the law can be prescribed to citizens as subjects. Bodin enumerates five "marks of sovereignty" (which in Hobbes will become twelve "rights of soveraignes," some of which are concordant and others not). The first is "the power to give the law to all in general and to each in particular . . . without the consent of any other, whether greater, equal, or below him."[27]

The second is the right of "declaring war or making peace, . . . included . . . in the lawmaking power of the sovereign."[28] The third is to "to establish the principle officers, and is never questioned in so far as it applies to the highest magistracies" (which means that intermediary magistrates have the ability to name their subordinates, but that responsibility for the administration depends absolutely upon the sovereign, a principle illustrated by Roman elections).[29] The fourth, "the right of judging in the last instance . . . , which has always been one of the principal rights of sovereignty,"[30] in other words the fact that the sovereign (possibly the people: as always, the example is that of the Roman Republic) hears all appeals, but itself judges without appeal (this criterion in particular allows Bodin to explain why the princes of the Holy Roman Empire are not sovereign). The fifth is "the power of granting pardons to the condemned, ignoring verdicts and going against the rigor of the laws to save them from death, loss of goods, dishonor, or exile"[31] (which has as its corollary the institution of capital crime or crime of lese majesty). Let us try to understand the meaning of such an enumeration, which combines historical heritage with a desire for logic.

What Bodin calls "marks" form a system in which each term presupposes the others, so that the whole expresses an *indivisibility* of sovereignty (in opposition to the division of sovereignty into parts or concurrent powers).[32] In other words, the functions we are dealing with (legislation as the supreme mark, war and diplomacy or "external sovereignty," command of the administration, high justice) are only the faces of a single reality, and are always simultaneously present. It goes without saying that they can neither be shared nor delegated. The *subtraction* of one of them would put sovereignty as a whole into question, and conversely, we must suppose that they form a *totality* that lacks nothing (I will return to this point). Still, their analytic distinction does express a fundamental reality, namely, the organization of public power, and thereby its autonomy with respect to private forces, personalities, and interests (those of "free subjects"—*citizens* who are *bourgeois*). At the heart of the definition of sovereignty by a set of *marks* is thus a diagram of power, as Michel Foucault would say, articulating the division of public and private spheres with the construction of a state machine whose specific organs cover the whole of society (the "republic").[33]

This interpretation allows us to bring forward another characteristic. The fact that sovereignty is exerted over a determinate *territory* whence it excludes any other is implicit in Bodin's general propositions as well as in the examples he discusses (particularly when he opposes the power of absolute monarchs or the Roman Republic to the entanglement of functions of authority characteristic of the Holy Roman Empire). But what he sees in this is primarily the condition of a direct relation between sovereign and subjects, or a relation of power without mediation or differentiation, which I propose to call *disincorporation* (although in a different sense than that used by Claude Lefort).[34] Reversing Louis Althusser's famous formula, we can say that the essential character of the sovereign is to *interpellate subjects as individuals*,[35] that is, to ignore or neutralize the intermediate "bodies," the "belongings" that confer a particular identity upon individuals, and which could be claimed either against one another or against the law and the sovereign itself.[36]

Does this mean that the institution of an absolute sovereignty (a public power enjoying a monopoly of legislation and administration) excludes every mediation and has a totalitarian character? Certainly not, but what needs to be specified is that the mediations involved are *its* mediations, forming the system of channels through which the sovereign (the state) reaches individuals one by one (*omnes et singulatem*, the phrase cited by Foucault)[37] in order to make itself recognized by them and gain their obedience. Does it mean, on the other hand, that sovereignty excludes *statuses* differentiating individuals, classing them into conditions or orders whose particular "rights" would be heterogeneous and unequal? Here we are at the heart of a major difficulty where the relations between the law and justice, or again between equality and equity as abstract principles of government, are in question. By posing in famous formulations the universality of the law, made by all and for all, admitting neither distinctions nor exceptions except following general criteria, Rousseau and the revolutionaries in his wake continue Bodin's tendency and radicalize it. Sovereignty does not abolish statuses and belongings, but it does envisage them "as null" in the eyes of the law and, as a consequence, superimposes on them another belonging, which is personal rather than "corporative," egalitarian rather than equitable, and which alone is *political*. What is instituted by sovereignty is thus a reciprocal belonging of the mass of individuals (the *population* rather than the *people*) and the *territory* over which a certain apparatus of *power* is deployed. At bottom, there is an equivalence between the two descriptions we have given: the expression of indivisible sovereignty in a system of "marks" of power and the interpellation of subjects as individuals forming a "unique" population within the limits of the territory.[38]

Here, however, arises what Bodin's interpreters agree is the most difficult problem, namely that of the *limitations* of a power that is nonetheless presented as being "unlimited." The question has been remarkably elucidated by Julian Franklin, who takes his cue from the opposition between Bodin's absolutism and the contractualism of the monarch-omachs, and the transformation this conflict produced in the thought of the author of the *Republic*.[39] At bottom there are two major limitations, which are "internal" to sovereign power in the sense that they express the necessity, for its preservation, of a regulation or a rationality of its own rather than an encounter with adversarial principles to which concessions would have to be made, but whose immediate effect is to establish an outside of sovereignty, where the absoluteness of its power comes to an end. It is obviously here that the question of the extent to which the system of marks can be considered to be "complete" is posed most sharply. The first limitation concerns what the classical age called the *jus circa sacra* of sovereigns, that is, the control they exercise over manifesta-tions of religious faith so as to prevent a division of subjects' allegiances between temporal and spiritual powers (the "war of the gods" that haunted Hobbes). The second concerns the knot of questions related to money (particularly the monopoly of coinage) and tax collection (who can be taxed, how much, and above all whether their "consent" is re-quired), which we can call, taking up the old name for the administra-tion of finances, the *fiscus*. Now, these two limitations are both symmetri-cal and heterogeneous. In the last analysis, the way that they are handled forms the field in which the fate of sovereignty is played out. At stake is sovereignty's ability to survive or to reconstitute itself beyond the per-ilous leap of democratic revolutions, when it passes from a princely to a popular form, that is, to emerge as truly *state sovereignty*, if it is true—as Schmitt clearly saw—that this is what monarchical sovereignty and pop-ular sovereignty "have in common," or rather what neutralizes the differ-ence between them (particularly from the point of view of war and diplo-macy). I will presently try to formulate a working hypothesis regarding this point.

The way that Bodin treats the limits of sovereignty is awkward but very instructive. In religious matters he anticipates a doctrine of sec-ularism whose close link with the notion of the republic has continued to be reinforced throughout the history of modern states, although in dif-ferent ways in different countries. A partisan of tolerance and informed by the tragic experience of the wars of religion (the *Republic* was written shortly after the Saint Bartholomew's Day massacre of 1572), Bodin thinks that religious homogeneity between the population and the sovereign is politically preferable, but that violent repression of religious dissidence is a remedy worse than the disease since it exacerbates the desire to resist oppression. He thus sets a limit to the sovereign's powers in matters of opinion even as he radically excludes any "right" on the part of the subjects to rebellion or resistance, thereby approaching the position that Spinoza would later theorize in the *Theologico-Political Treatise*, founded upon the distinction between actions and opinions. This amounts to applying to the domain of faith the distinction between public and private interests, or making the religious community a more or less "private" affair, thereby contributing to the secularization of the state.

No less delicate is the question of consent to taxation (more specifically, to the introduction of new taxes), demanded in the name of "traditional liberties" or the "fundamental laws of the kingdom," in France as in England, implying a conception of limited sovereignty, which from Bodin's point of view is obviously a contradiction in terms. Now, even while affirming that the right of coinage (*nummus*) is of the same nature as the law (*nomos*)—which is to say that there cannot be any "private money"—and that the right to tax subjects (or exempt them from taxation) is an attribute of sovereignty (indeed, coming as an addition to the preceding "marks"), Bodin rallies to the idea that new taxes require a consent voted by a representation of the subjects or the people. He invokes a prudential rule: taxes imposed on the people against their will either are never collected or cause revolts capable of endangering the state itself.[40] But it is clear that this limitation has a fundamental character, affecting bit by bit the whole of sovereignty, because the *fiscus* forms a totality in which monetary policy and tax policy must balance, and because the mastery of finances is the condition of the autonomy of the political in all other domains (just as the mastery of beliefs is the condition of obedience to power and to the law in general).

I draw two conclusions from these analyses, which ought to be compared with the lessons of other theoreticians. The first is that the concept of sovereignty is affected by an internal limitation that is both inevitable and unacceptable. It is striking to find that it can be manifested as an ineradicable remainder of either communitarianism (the existence and diversity of religious communities) or corporatism (the necessary intervention of a "representation" of social estates in state fiscal policy), and thus as either an obstacle to the individualization of subjects or an excess of individual autonomy (freedom of conscience, interests of property and, later, labor) whose existence depends not on the state but on the "natural right" of each. Of course, what appears here as a defect or limitation of sovereignty will later become thinkable as a possible way to reconstitute or *constitute sovereignty*, on the condition that sovereignty be taken as developing within an "organic" structure of the entire society, incorporating its own limits or converting obstacles to the exercise of power into means of development, as can be seen in either Hegel or Tocqueville. But such a development will only become possible if the conception of the "subject" and the subject's legal obedience to the sovereign is deepened by passing from the order of *subjection* to that of *subjectivity*, by incorporating new kinds of loyalties and disciplines (such as patriotism or civic spirit, public education, health, good morals).

The second conclusion is that the doctrine of marks provides a guiding thread for understanding not only the absoluteness and indivisibility that is the point of pride of the classical notion of sovereignty, but also what it lacks and what thereby becomes the ideal objective of its realization. We can say that sovereignty will only be truly absolute if, by regular means (thinkable as the development of its own order, and thus excluding dictatorship or the state of exception), it manages to *interiorize its own limits*, that is, to incorporate in the field of the political what at first seemed to escape it, showing the persistence of a remainder: the regulation of beliefs (whose type is constituted by religious faith and its intellectual, moral, and cultural continuations) and the regulation of economic processes by way of the *fiscus* (monetary and fiscal policy, unified by taxation and the public debt).

To put it in other terms, to the extent that the notions of sovereignty and the autonomy of the political have been historically identified (around the ability of state power to represent "society as a whole"), sovereignty will in practice coincide with a dual primacy: *the primacy of the political over the theological* (thus of states over churches and their preferred "objects": births and deaths, matrimony, education, and the like) and *the primacy of the political over the economic* (or, in a later terminology, the "socioeconomic"). The conquest of the domain of conscience, its control and transformation (by the secularization of education, of familial and sexual morality, and of what will henceforth be called culture), along with the conquest, control, and transformation of the economic domain (the domain of labor and production, of property and commerce) through a variety of means, often contradictory (stemming from what will be called, in different languages *Nationalökonomie, économie politique*, etc.), then become the fields of realization of an autonomy of the political that cannot exist as a simple separation, but only as the politicization of extrapolitical domains by the state. In both cases it is a matter of creating a public sphere and public authority above spheres of private initiative, not to absorb them but to control them. Of course, to the extent that the institution of such a primacy of the political is an asymptotic process, essentially incomplete, running up against obstacles that prevent its full realization, we must admit that sovereignty itself is an unfinished task, even an "impossible" one. Or, what amounts to the same thing, that it fails to transform integrally individuals into subjects.

"Popular Sovereignty": The Perilous Leap

We are now in a position to formulate, even if in a still abstract and partial way, a hypothesis that should permit both an interpretation of the *perpetuation* of sovereignty beyond its classic forms, and an identification of a few of the reasons for its *crisis*. Sovereignty runs into two obstacles, each of which could provoke its disappearance (and it is certainly not by chance that, in the transitional period leading to the second modernity, that of the "bourgeois revolutions" in Marx's sense, different alternatives to sovereignty appear under the headings of cosmopolitanism and internationalism). The first resides in religious culture's resistence to state hegemony and in the progressive autonomization of "economic society" with respect to the political borders of states, in other words, in the affirmation of civil society in opposition to political society (although these two terms had at first been interchangeable). The second resides in the overturning of the very notions of law, citizenship, representation, and authority that is implied by the transfer of supreme power from a monarchical person to the collectivity ("mass," "multitude") of the *people*, whose personality is both much more concrete (by the power of the effects of its historical intervention) and much more abstract (by the impossibility of giving it a single name or face, except in allegory). *But could we not think that these two difficulties resolve one another?* The creation of state institutions of spiritual power and economic power is what makes possible the transference of sovereignty to the people, or the invention of political forms allowing the "people" to come to occupy the place of the sovereign and to exercise, even symbolically, absolute power. The state's socialization, if you will. But, conversely, what makes possible the incorporation of new functions of sovereignty in the field that had previously been dominated by theology, or the field that will henceforth be developed by economic activity (in practice, capitalism), is the emergence of popular sovereignty and the means proper to it, above all universal suffrage, access to public employment on the basis of merit, the progressive introduction of a universal and proportional income tax, and other advances. All of these features of the postrevolutionary state, working to support one another, are so many ways of characterizing a single process: the development of the *nation-form*, with its statist face and its democratic face.[41] But perhaps this would give us at the same time a way to understand some of the distant causes of the crisis of sovereignty that we are witnessing today, to the extent that the relativization of national autonomies and of the nation-form itself (including in those nations that seem best to illustrate the idea of internal and external sovereignty, which in practice means the nations of the imperialist core) is accompanied by a growing autonomization of the theological and the economic (or of what corresponds to them today) with respect to political regulation. This is how there occurs the sort of reversal of a situation that in another context—where I had in mind its effects on the subjectivity of citizens of European nations and their sense of collective identity—I tried to describe as the syndrome of the "impotence of the omnipotent."[42]

Let us try to illustrate these hypotheses. There are, it seems to me, two primary ways to analyze the perilous leap represented by the introduction of the idea of popular sovereignty and to link the crisis to the resulting tensions. We can say that the first is more speculative, "Rousseauist" and "Marxian" (in the sense of the 1843 Manuscript),[43] taking its point of departure in the contradiction in terms represented by the idea of collective or "moral body" that would be *both sovereign and subject*, exercising the power of governing and making law and unconditionally obeying the same laws and decrees whose author it is. The other, meanwhile, is more historical (as well as more materialist), "Hegelian" and "Keynesian,"[44] and takes its point of departure in the way that the "developed" states of the nineteenth and twentieth centuries have tried to integrate into an organic construction the universal representation of populations as well as the juridical or sociological instruments of mediation of the class struggle, walking the fine line separating corporatism from democratism. But in both cases the reference to the *nation*—or more precisely to the equation of *nationality* and *citizenship* as the substance of *sovereignty*—appears as the key to the problem. This is why it might be useful here to use the historical contradictions to elucidate the speculative aporia and vice versa, in such a way as to approach the content of the crisis.

The jurists have neither been able purely and simply to avoid or accept the provocation contained within Rousseau's definition of sovereignty as a "relation" that the body politic maintains "with itself," whose effect is to unbind it from any obligation with respect to the form of government it has itself chosen and to render useless any formal guarantee of the rights of subjects (that is, of citizens taken individually), since "it is impossible for the body to want to harm all of its members."[45] The legacy of this position is incontestable in certain founding propositions such as article 3 of the 1789 version of the *Declaration of the Rights of Man and the Citizen* ("The principle of all sovereignty resides essentially in the Nation; no body, no individual can exercise any authority that does not expressly emanate from it").[46] Particularly revelatory here is Carré de Malberg, who sets out from a definition of the personality of the state as a "personification of the national collectivity itself," begins by explaining that the nation cannot be considered as "alternatively governing and subject" without absurdity,[47] then ends up with what he presents as a recapitulation of Rousseau: "[It] is in this sense that Rousseau could say that citizens appear as both participating in sovereign authority and as subjects submitted to the laws of the state. . . . There is no alternation here between sovereignty and subjection in the same person, but in the last analysis there is a separation of sovereignty and subjection into two distinct sorts of juridical persons. At bottom all these observations come down to the notion of the indivisibility of the nation and its power."[48] This deduction had been preceded by a discussion of the tendency to dissociate the *person of the state* from the *person of the prince*, from which it was not hard to conclude that, in a juridical and institutional perspective, the sovereignty of the people—assimilable to what others will call the appearance of a "new prince"—forms a crossroads. It can just as easily lead to the refoundation of the state as to its permanent contradiction.[49] A choice must be made, and Malberg's choice consists in privileging the representation of the sovereign nation in the political and administrative power of the state, with the proviso that it be constituted according to the "rule of law." In these conditions, popular sovereignty is as symbolic ("absent" in person from the place of power) as the idea of the collectivity of citizens itself.

The consequences are not without interest. For example, in this reading of the *Social Contract*, the constraint exercised by the general will over the subjects becomes explicitly repressive: the difference between the "citizen," theoretical member of the sovereign, and the real "subject" whom public power is charged with forcing to obedience ("which means nothing other than that he shall be forced to be free," wrote Rousseau)[50] comes from the fact that *his disobedience is already assumed* ("the passive subject of this power is the individual inasmuch as he resists measures already decided"). Or yet the fact that the condition of a subject "in a state of resistance before the law" induces, for the national, "a position similar to that occupied before of the state by a foreign individual," that is, a *hostis*. And finally, the fact that, taken in its full rigor, the notion of subjection can only be properly applied to nationals who do not enjoy the plenitude of the rights of the citizen, that is, to colonial subjects.[51] The condition under which it is possible to bring the two terms of subject and citizen together in a single construction is thus civism on a background of nationalism. We begin to sense that the notions at work are bound together in a circular way: the duality of the people and the state is overcome in the ideal unity of the nation, but the nation itself always divides back up into antithetical terms. The question is to know what practical contradictions underlie these logical operations.

We must then return to Rousseau himself. The identity of opposites (citizenship and subjection) is not only not avoided but forms for Rousseau the essence of the "two-fold relation"[52] to the law instituted by the pact, and thus the secret of the *reduction of verticality* by means of which, without suppressing the idea, Rousseau brings sovereignty down into the immanence of the people, abolishes the distance between the people and "its" sovereign in order to identify them with one another. By this very fact, the people—on the condition of the "total alienation" of the individuals who compose it—invested with the character of a *causa sui*, capable of permanently creating, on its own, the conditions of its power and its unity (for which Rousseau uses the term republic rather than nation). This speculative doctrine revolutionizes the idea of the relation between the citizen and the law (since, for the first time, there is a proposal rigorously to conceive of the citizen as situated *at the same level as the law*). But it is unstable by definition. It can develop in the direction of a democratic foundation for the constitution of the state (with the doctrine of the "constituent power" exposed for the first time in 1789 by Emmanuel-Joseph Sieyes in his pamphlet *What Is the Third Estate?* demanding the transformation of the Estates General into a National Assembly).[53] Or it can develop in the direction of a critique of the constitution in which the principle of popular sovereignty forces a stark choice between the "political formalism" of bureaucracy and the "legislative power" of the *dēmos*, which has "brought forth great, organic, universal revolutions."[54] It is well known that this position leads to demanding that social antagonisms be represented as such in the political sphere and even form its matter—which is obviously impossible without an abolition of the state in the sense in which the French Revolution had instituted it. The idea of sovereignty is still preserved here, but its development leads to a disjunction of the two terms it ought to have united (people and state).

It is obviously possible to think that this sort of abstract antinomy has nothing to do with reality. Such is not my hypothesis; I am persuaded that it illuminates the core of the contradictions inherent in the history of popular sovereignty as national sovereignty. But this is true on the condition of seeing clearly that, rather than leading immediately to an impasse, it has constantly been *displaced* in the course of the nineteenth and twentieth centuries. Its very movement has nourished the successive forms of "limited democracy" or unstable equilibrium that permit a way of avoiding both a purely symbolic popular sovereignty and a situation of permanent revolution that would delegitimate all the substitutions of power by which the state controls mass movements through the "representation" of a part of their interests. As if the forces confronting one another had understood, after frequently bloody crises, the warning contained in the "forgotten sentence" of the *Communist Manifesto*: "the history of class struggles . . . each time ended, either in a revolutionary reconstitution of society at large, or in the common ruin of the contending classes [*der gemeinsame Untergang der kämpfenden Klassen*]."[55]

We can thus formulate the hypothesis that state sovereignty has simultaneously "protected" itself from and "founded" itself upon popular sovereignty to the extent that the political state has progressively been transformed into a "social state" (or better, as I have proposed elsewhere, into a "national-social state"),[56] passing through the progressive institution of a "representation of social forces" by the mechanism of universal suffrage and the institutions of social citizenship whose vicissitudes measure just how effectively the equation *citizenship* = *nationality* = *sovereignty* is working.[57] This is what my hypothesis called the "Hegelian" and "Keynesian" path in order to mark the way in which, at both the beginning and the end, it was reflected upon by theoreticians of organic sovereignty and the interventionist state, capable of seeking the idea of the nation and the regulation of social conflicts not only in the sacralization of the *name* of the nation-state but also in the construction of its historical mediations, that is, in the institutions by which civil society penetrates the state and the state "organizes" civil society in turn.[58] As I suggested earlier, these institutions are fundamentally cultural (in the sense in which "culture," *Bildung*, made up of morality and education, has taken over from religion) and financial (in the sense in which mastery of public finances allows the tendency toward "savage" capitalism to be checked, at least in internal space, by a combination of monetary and social policies). The continuation of state sovereignty has thus been concentrated in the possibility of reconstituting the political from the outside or, what amounts to the same thing, finding forms of cultural communication within the people and forms of social mediation of class antagonisms that are not pure show. This has only ever been the case under the pressure of events, but it has known an undeniable reality in certain regions of the world (including parts of Europe).

In order to conclude, we still need to add the following point. The crisis of sovereignty we are living through today, and whose results are still unforeseeable, is the proof of the fragility and perhaps of the expiration of the "organic" process of autonomization *and* socialization of politics we have just described. It is insufficient to see in it a crisis of the idea of the nation unless we also specify (along with Carl Schmitt, but also along with a Marxist tradition stretching from Lenin and Rosa Luxemburg to Immanuel Wallerstein) that the condition of the equivalence between *national constitution* and *political sovereignty* has been a historically determinate, transitory position at the dominant "core" of an imperialist world-system, and that, as a consequence, today's crisis affects *both* states that have never been able to constitute themselves as nation-states in the strong sense, others that cannot remain nation-states by themselves, and finally others still who think they may have found a way of overturning, to their advantage, the old *nomos* of the earth.

But it is also insufficient to refer this crisis to globalization and its regional effects in a general way, for two precisions need to be added. On the one hand, it must be said that the disintegrative effects of globalization on national sovereignty pass through the constitution of a transnational cultural space in which the "civic religions" developed by each state are irremediably *particularized* and thereby lose their indisputable ability to incarnate the universal on their own territory—as they pass through the ongoing reversal of the relation of power between the global capital market and the ability of states to regulate or intervene in them.[59] The gap with the classical *representation* of sovereignty thus is becoming ever greater, which is why I have spoken of the "impotence of the omnipotent" (and we can also see why this impotence is so difficult for subjects to live with). But it must also be said that the antagonisms that the nation-state, as a social state, sought to mediate institutionally within certain boundaries, have not ceased to exist on the transnational level (quite the contrary!). It is by no means evident that the dialectic of popular sovereignty and state sovereignty (or of democratic demands and the constitution of public power) in which these antagonism have been expressed and displaced for two centuries has lost its significance. And if it is true that this dialectic, without any uniform solution, is where the political signification of the idea of sovereignty has finally become concentrated, then the crisis of sovereignty announces not so much an ending as an opening or an unpredictable mutation.

9

Difficult Europe:
Democracy under Construction

Ladies and Gentlemen, esteemed colleagues,

It is a great and moving honor for me to find myself here among you, in one of the most ancient universities of Europe. I thank you for your invitation, and in particular thank your president, Professor Antonio Pedro Pita, whose friendship was able to overcome all the obstacles that stood in the way of this meeting. And I believe it is in this way, at least as far as what is in our power is concerned, that we will gradually be able to give the idea of European citizenship a content that is not merely bureaucratic.

Europe is precisely what I want to speak about in this closing address that you so graciously asked of me: its difficulty, its borders, and its announced citizenship. Not merely because these themes are imposed upon any encounter between intellectuals of different countries in this time and place (although I do not forget that Portugal is currently assuming the presidency of the European Union and that circumstances have given this responsibility a particular seriousness). More important for me today, the questions raised by European unification, and the tensions it serves to reveal, form a particularly privileged object for political philosophy. You decided to consecrate this last congress of the twentieth century to an examination of the "general trends in philosophy" in the

Closing lecture at the fourth Congress of the Association of Professors of Philosophy of Portugal, University of Coimbra, February 11, 2000. The themes of this lecture were developed in my seminar on L'Europa difficile, held at the Istituto Italiano per gli Studi Filosofici in Naples (cosponsored by the group Immaginare L'Europa), January 31–February 4, 2000.

years to come. In my field, I see no way to do this without seeking to analyze a few of the *problems* opened by the conjuncture we have entered, a conjuncture that requires us not to renounce the conceptual equipment we have inherited from a long past but to rethink it and to put it to the test.

The question of citizenship has been at the heart of political philosophy since its origins, and it is no accident that the renewal of debates concerning it, as they lead to reexaminations of categories such as community and sovereignty, the universality of rights, the relations between citizenship and nationality, and the political function of social conflict, should also lead to a renaissance of political philosophy—not in opposition to historical or sociological approaches, or to individual and collective ethics, but in a unity that truly reconstitutes the totality of practical philosophy. Politics virtually occupies there what Aristotle, in the *Nicomachean Ethics*, called an "architectonic" function.[1] My seminar this year in Paris is devoted to the theme "Europe: From Myth to Politics," and I have just held a seminar at the Istituto per gli Studi Filosofici in Naples on "L'Europa difficile," so today I will try to summarize for you some of the themes and provisional results worked out together with the students who participated in these meetings.

It seems to me that European citizenship constitutes neither an acquisition nor a simple idea, but a process strewn with obstacles, one that is both absolutely necessary and entirely uncertain: in short, a "long march" on which all of us, whether we will it or not, are engaged. I would like especially to emphasize the contradictions of this process, since I am convinced, even though their "dialectical resolution" is by no means guaranteed, that they constitute the motor of the entire process. I will do this by addressing four points in turn: first, some reflections on the relation between the current revival of the problem of citizenship and the aporias of the notion of sovereignty raised by European unification; second, in guise of a transition, two hypotheses on the conditions under which the problem of a new "constitution of citizenship" (which I will use as a single term, believing it to be the best translation for the *politeia* of the ancients) has come to be on the agenda; third, a necessarily abbreviated analysis of the principle *obstacles* that make *citizenship in Europe* today a "necessary impossible"; and, finally, an enumeration (which makes no claim to exhaustiveness) of a few of democracy's laboratories or "worksites," the places where it is "under construction." These sites constitute, in my view, domains of initiative and reflection with a view toward a new citizenship in Europe, in the sense of an intellectual matter that needs to be worked in order to give body to a true "European public space."

<hr>

I

As a preliminary, let us begin with the way in which the aporia of sovereignty is combined with the revival of the problem of citizenship. Several years ago, I relied on a famous formulation of Hegel's that later found a wide echo (*Deutschland ist kein Staat mehr*, "Germany is no longer a state," he wrote in the 1801 text on *The Constitution of Germany*),[2] in order to argue that, as the title of my essay put it, *Es gibt keinen Staat in Europa*, there is no state in Europe, only national and supranational forms of statism and bureaucracy, since today the state can only be democratic, and there is no "democracy" possible without "popular sovereignty."[3] But where can the European *dēmos* be found? The symptoms of the impasse in which the problematic of sovereignty in Europe is caught are encountered every day; in the final analysis they all refer to the absolute blockage of the question of the "people" understood not as *ethnos* or "communal identity" but as *dēmos* or "constituent political power."

What has just happened with respect to the "Haider case" and the "Austrian problem" gives a striking illustration. With the "warning" and symbolic measures of distrust fourteen European states announced with respect to the fifteenth, it was indeed acts of sovereignty (or transferal of *authority*, as Hobbes would have said) that were played out for the benefit of public opinion, but they were *acts of sovereignty without any definite sovereignty*, or if you prefer, acts of a "sovereignty without subject." The heads of state or government acted like the spokesmen, tutors, or regents of a people absent from the historical stage and, in the end, unnameable. At best, they presume the constitution of such a people (through expressions such as "community of values" or "European contract"), but one might legitimately wonder whether the means they use to invoke it do not much more imply its indefinite distancing from the political scene. And even if we share neither the objectives nor the premises of those who are now called "sovereigntists" in France (not only politicians, but also intellectuals such as Régis Debray), we must do them the credit of recognizing that they have correctly identified an unavoidable problem, situated on the ground of both the functioning of institutions and the symbolic effects of legitimacy.

In order to get back to the reasons for this aporia, we must examine in some detail the different aspects of the collapse of the classical schemas of state sovereignty. Some of them can be called external and others internal, but in reality it is precisely the correlation between inside and outside that makes sovereignty what it is (and, above all, that constitutes a "political community" submitted to a sovereign authority and in some sense "created" by it, or creating itself through the institution of sovereignty). A state that was not treated as an independent power by other states would never be recognized as having unshared power over its own territory, and vice versa. This reciprocity of perspectives constitutes at the same time one of the keys of the ambivalent relation—both heterogeneous and indissociable—that, in the modern era (that of "sovereign nation-states" and of "popular sovereignty" as "national sovereignty"), associates the two significations of the word "people," as *ethnos* in the broad sense, that is, identity or common historico-cultural character, and as *dēmos*, that is, egalitarian constituent power.[4]

In its external dimension, classical sovereignty coincided (at least ideally) with an "autonomy" guaranteed by the relative equilibrium (periodically destroyed and reestablished) between military and diplomatic powers. In his theory of the *Jus Publicum Europaeum*, Carl Schmitt showed that, in the history of the state, sovereignty realizes the primacy of the territorial dimension in the grouping and denomination of populations, and consequently the primacy of the *border* as a point of concentration of decision and power.[5] But this collective "right" is today in ruins on account of the events that have successively marked the history of the twentieth century: the crisis and end of imperialism, the constitution and collapse of the division of the world into "blocs," the erasure by globalization of differences between "police" operations and war and between the "internal" and "external" use of force.

In its internal dimension, sovereignty (at least ideally) was affirmed both as a *primacy of the political* over communal bonds and relations of mutual dependence in civil society (thus essentially as the subordination to the state of religious authorities and economic forces, both of which were relegated to the "private" sphere), and as the *constitution of the "subject" as citizen*. In his *Six Books of the Republic* of 1576, generally considered to be the founding text of the modern theory of sovereignty, Jean Bodin uses an astonishing unity of opposites to name this figure, the "free subject";[6] Rousseau would later try to think the unity of the two terms as the faces of a "two-fold relation."[7] It is precisely inasmuch as (and to the extent that) the citizen is in fact liberated by the state from his dependency upon the "absolute" religious community or pure "corporative" economic and professional status (which we know had remained the obligatory condition of citizenship—"bourgeoisie"—in medieval cities and towns) that he is subjected to the sovereign power of the state (including when this state is officially that of the nation, or of "the entire people"). But contemporary history has put everything back into question in this register as well, plunging sovereignty into an apparently endless crisis.

This is valid for the relation between the political and the religious. Here, to put it very schematically, beyond the vicissitudes of *jus circa sacra* and the various concordats, more or less beneficial to the church (some of which are still in force), the stabilization of the state's power "over souls" (and through souls over bodies themselves)[8] consisted in the *nationalization of mass education*, inseparable from its *secularization*, and thus in the institution of systems of national education (whether centralized or not), oscillating between the ideal of individual *Bildung* and that of patriotic "civil religion."[9] We can note that in no European country—including France, despite the fact that it is a sort of point of honor there—has this "solution" ever been complete, but it has at least functioned as a basis of consensus and recognition of the state during more than a century, after having been prepared by the Enlightenment and cultural policies. But national educational systems today are in full-fledged crisis, and no scheme for "postnational" or "supranational" education as a mass formation is in sight. It can be feared that, more and more, education is caught between the disciplinary imperatives of controlling the poor (confronting violence in the schools) and those of a simple "ongoing training" in the use of instruments of global communications and consumption.

What then is the situation with respect to the *politico-economic* relation? Here the historical solution (this is, of course, only true for the dominant powers, those responsible for and benefiting from European world expansion or what Wallerstein calls the "European world-economy")[10] resided in the system of "national debt," that is, in the combination of monetary policy (control of a national money whose currency was obligatory) and fiscal power (state monopoly on the raising of taxes, a more or less democratic way for the state to set their base and use).[11] No more than the politico-religious, the politico-economic relation (what was known in nineteenth-century Germany as *Nationalökonomie*) was never entirely submitted to the primacy of state sovereignty. But the current situation, as is well known, brings with it a reversal of the trend that affects even the most powerful imperialisms (which is to say, even the United States): this is what is called globalization (in fact, its most recent phase), one of whose characteristics is the creation of competition between territories on the world market through conflicts of interest rates and fiscal policies. The "national debt" of states then becomes an instrument of the market to develop competition between national groups seeking investments.[12]

Nonetheless, if the aspects featuring the role of the state are the most visible (they directly affect what Bodin and Hobbes following him called the "marks of sovereignty," the conception of which has remained fundamentally unchanged since the appearance of nation-states at the beginning of the modern period), the heart of the crisis of sovereignty is the *disappearance of the people*, both as an instance of symbolic legitimation and as an instance of real control (or intermittent countervailing power acting upon political apparatuses), *the disappearance of the dialectic of constituent and constituted power* (Emmanuel-Joseph Sieyes, Carl Schmitt, Antonio Negri).[13] This disappearance affects the political function of parliaments (whether national parliaments or the European Parliament, between whom the dispute of "subsidiarity" is played out) in a central way. It goes well beyond the classic phenomenon of bureaucratization and the professionalization of politics, whence political science (for which this is a sort of founding phenomenon) drew the thesis of the *political apathy of the masses*, transforming "active citizens" into "passive citizens." This disappearance implies the return to a technical, reglementary status of the *law*, whose symptomatic consequence can be seen in the absence of any genuine European legislation to which citizens can refer.[14] But with neither people nor law there can only exist a phantom public sphere, a *regression* and not a progress in relation to the history of democratic states.

One could then (this is the sovereigntist position) argue that *by nature* (or at least within the *historical period* to which we still belong) the constituent power of a people, together with—to borrow Rousseau's terminology—the "general will" from which the law proceeds, can only exist on the *national* level and that both are intrinsic attributes of the nation-form. Unfortunately this position is (or has become) untenable. The crisis of internal and external attributes of state sovereignty progressively deprives the popular "general will" of its object within the exclusive frame of the nation-state even as the absence of an effective political referent (or "community of citizens") at the supranational level (Jacques Delors once spoke of an "unidentified object") prohibits working on the reconstruction of a sovereign power at the European level. We seem to be caught in an impossible interregnum: *after the end* of classical national sovereignty (but not of national identities as historical residue), *before the beginning* of a postnational sovereignty (but need we not fear that globalization is already well underway to dissolving the notion of "sovereignty" as such?).[15]

II

How can we get out of this circle in which the decline of sovereignty is to be referred to the disappearance of the people, which implies in turn the loss of the meaning of "citizenship"?[16] In order to move quickly, I will present my argument in the form of two hypotheses, which will of course need to be verified later.

First hypothesis: the problem of a *constitution of citizenship*[17] is indeed (as Jürgen Habermas and other contemporary theorists have repeatedly stressed) on the European political agenda.[18] Nonetheless, what cannot work here is a unitary or federal *formal constitution* considered to be a "fundamental law" (*Grundgesetz*) or a catalog of democratic rules and principles that would have to be intellectually "recognized" by states (and which moreover already exist in the text of the treaties founding the European Union). Such a definition *presumes to be resolved* what is in fact in question: the nature and existence of the constituent power on the European level.[19] This is why, in particular, the adoption of a "European Charter of Fundamental Rights," however important its principles and content might be, would not in the least constitute the beginnings of a constitution or "constitutionalization." We could, however, speak of a *material constitution* as formed by a dynamic of powers and countervailing powers or antagonistic social "principles." A constitution in this sense is a social and political practice and not merely a form of right (which does not mean that it can bypass the juridical moment).[20]

Second hypothesis: the project of a "European citizenship," inscribed in the founding texts of the European Union,[21] is today blocked by enormous structural obstacles (behind which of course stand social interests), but also by the fact that the strategies that can be used against each obstacle seem to be mutually incompatible.[22] But such will in fact be my hypothesis, which could be called voluntarist but is very much a realist one as well: *these "obstacles" or "impossibilities" must be taken as the matter of the European constitution* as a political constitution, that is, as the object of the transformative movements that will give the new historical citizenship its content. This citizenship does not consist in the passive enjoyment of formal rights, whether old or new, conferred upon individuals because the "historical community" to which they belong (by right of birth or adoption) has been formally integrated into the new European whole, but rather in the fact that European citizens themselves produce, by removing the existing obstacles, the conditions of a new belonging—and no doubt, inevitably, the conditions of a nonexclusive belonging in a new sense of the word.

This is what I propose to call the worksites (*chantiers*) of democracy, some of which I will discuss later (but there are more). For European citizenship is "impossible" *except as a progress in fundamental democratic rights and powers* in the "European" framework. Progress must be made not only with respect to current blockages but also with respect to the level of democracy previously attained by *the most advanced national states* (which means that none of them can constitute a "model"). Once such a collective process (which itself is made up of a multiplicity of goals, practices, and movements) exists, European citizenship would again become at least *thinkable*.

This hypothesis is obviously even more hazardous than the first. I am nonetheless convinced that, in this form or another close to it, it represents the condition without which the first will remain merely a pious wish. But, I repeat, what I am talking about is neither the clauses of a treaty nor the program of a party or a government; it is rather a program to "think Europe," as Edgar Morin would have it,[23] through worksites constituted by transnational initiatives. I am talking, if you will, about a perspective of thought for intellectuals, but intellectuals who are sufficiently "organic" in Antonio Gramsci's sense,[24] that is, personally and institutionally implicated (including within the university) in the struggle to transform Europe. I am sometimes tempted to say, "to save Europe," but such pathos is better avoided.

III

We must then take our point of departure from what makes citizenship "impossible" in Europe (even while making it necessary). I evoke three major obstacles whose real mutual overdetermination is becoming apparent in certain critical situations: the crisis of the European social model, the political and social division of the continent, and the constitution of a status of apartheid for "extracommunal" immigrants. Outside of this knot of the impossible and the necessary, there is no history and thus no politics.

The Problem of Social Citizenship

The uneven regression of the "welfare state" in various countries since the 1970s is a fundamental aspect of the crisis of policies concerning European integration. For it puts into question the "model of social relations" that, in part of Europe (precisely the part that has assumed the function of a model and pole of attraction for the rest of the continent), tended toward the institution of a *social citizenship*. What can be considered typically "European" in this domain?

We know that the model that was developed in the course of the twentieth century in Western Europe did not remain that of a purely political citizenship, founded on the equality of individuals in rights (excepting for personal incapacities) and on the representation of currents of opinion and group interests on the national and local levels. It also incorporated, in theory (at the level of constitutional texts that speak of the right to existence and of a social republic)[25] and above all in practice (through structures of regulation of labor conflicts, participation or involvement of employees, and joint management of insurance systems, highly varied and unevenly developed between one country and the next), a certain number of fundamental rights that as a group make up what has been called a "social citizenship." It is, however, important to see clearly that this was only ever instituted within the perspective of a reinforcement of the equation between *citizenship* and *nationality*, and in the framework of an exclusively national conception of sovereignty (which does not necessarily mean "national preference," since we know that the exceptions on this point—consequences of the struggles of the workers' movement and the heritage of resistance movements against fascism— are far from negligible). Unevenly developed, social citizenship has in any case remained in a close solidarity with the emergence and reinforcement of a *national social state*. This is one of the major reasons that no *European social citizenship* corresponding to the extension of social rights and of possibilities for intervention in the regulation of the economy by the social movement is currently in sight, even though the conjuncture of globalization makes its necessity brutally clear. It is thus fundamental for us to grasp what constituted the originality, possibilities for expansion, and limits of the model that is today in crisis.

If there truly is (or was) something like a "European social model," it was a matter of a number of different formulas in which social rights could develop and be politically recognized as conditions and components of effective citizenship, under the condition of membership in the state. The status of such a model was thus ambivalent: simultaneously collectivizing and individualizing, liberating and protective (sometimes constraining, since there is no protection without control), inclusive and exclusive.[26] T. H. Marshall, "theorizing" the reforms undertaken after the Second World War in England in his classic essay "Citizenship and Social Class," saw a "third generation" of subjective rights coming to complete the constitution of modern citizenship by recreating the conditions of a "community" (or "loyalty," a sentiment of belonging to the fatherland) threatened by liberal individualism.[27] But Robert Castel, studying the French example in detail, has shown that it is every bit as much a question of a *production of individuality* (or, to return to the great category of classical liberalism, "self-ownership") on the basis of social policy. According to the terminology elaborated by turn-of-the-century "*solidarisme*," social rights, always negotiated collectively but acquired and guaranteed individually, constitute for those who benefit from them a true "social property."[28] But they cannot be enclosed within a definition based on ideas of membership in corporate bodies or neediness. The great debate in Western Europe during the postwar period concerned precisely the question of whether social rights (including workmen's compensation, unemployment insurance, the right to health, education, and retirement benefits) were to be reserved for the "poor," thereby contributing to their stigmatization or isolation from society, or if they were to be considered as *universal*, entering into the definition of a new historical figure of human individuality and giving "labor" the dignity of a title to public recognition[29]—whence the bitterness of debates over whether "social rights" are civic rights properly speaking or whether they are merely particular concessions and protections, means of assistance one part of society offers to another. The question concerns both facts and principles; it brings together a relation of political forces and an epoch-making constitutional invention in the history of democratic regimes.[30]

The question of social citizenship today is caught in the vise of the defense of acquired rights threatened by ultraliberalism ("protection of protection," in a sense, which can also be translated as "protectionism") and the struggle against exclusion (what Castel describes as a phenomenon of *disaffiliation* tied to the transformations of the world of salaried labor: both a regression of the public oversight that had allowed the edifice of social citizenship to be constructed and the individual to be both autonomized and freed from chronic insecurity, and a reproletarianization of whole social groups at the cost of extreme violence suffered and exercised, thus of a massive production of asociality or *negative individuality*).

We know that this question is what divides European "social democracy." It is significant that the debate is going on within social democracy rather than within European conservatism. But it does not seem ready to produce any results. A new regime of assistance to the poor backed up by coercion (a new *Speenhamland*),[31] organized on the European level, is neither culturally conceivable nor economically desirable. A complete dismantling of regimes of social security would be synonymous with unbearable exclusions and perhaps political explosions (and not necessarily on the left: this is what is at stake in European "populisms"). A revival of public initiatives tied to the institutional recognition of "popular movements" on a European scale, called Neo-Keynesianism or something else, is far from commanding unanimous support: its shape has barely been sketched out. This is why we must insist now more than ever on the necessity of initiatives from below: the crucial function of the unity of European trade unionism, the importance of communication between different movements seeking to defend or renovate social citizenship (which appeared in December 1995 and in other circumstances), convergences between claims for cultural rights, for the equality of the sexes, and for protections of the quality of life.

Even put into practice and juridically formalized, under the condition of certain relations of power, social citizenship was never fully incorporated into the constitution of the economically most highly developed and democratically most advanced nation-states, nor was it conceived in similar terms in different places. To say that European unification depends on the possibility of inscribing a progress of citizenship in a "constitution" means to emphasize the following radical dichotomy: either Europe will institute social citizenship on more solid and broader bases than ever before, or it will in the long term become impossible. It was in this perspective, and not in the hope of benefiting from the most advanced forms of liberalism, that the peoples of the East made the "revolution of 1989." And this leads me directly to the following point: that of the division of Europe.

The multiple aspects of this problem crystallize a long history of differences that are always ready to become antagonisms, and it could be said, in a sense, that the defining property of Europe (which is not proper to it) is that *each* of its historical regions contains as many causes of division as the continent as a whole. The Channel or the Pyrenees is no easier to "cross" than the Berezina or the Carpathians. But it is clear that in the current conjuncture and for a long time to come, the question that will dominate all the others is that of the consequences of the political division that cut the European continent in two for more than a half century, and of the way it came to an end (if it is indeed the case that it has come completely to an end). This is the problem of "Europe after communism." After *its* communism.

If I may be permitted to summarize what I wrote on this topic some time ago,[32] not only is "European unification" in its current institutional form, as all serious historians and analysts admit, the "child of the cold war,"[33] but the confrontation that occurred in the frame of the division into two "blocs" (the first contemporary form of globalization, we should not forget) was actually one between two adversary conceptions of the European project. There was an "Eastern Europe" and not only a "Europe in the West." And we are beginning to learn today that however dictatorial and regressive its political institutions and social forms may have been, Eastern Europe did have a culture and a "civil society." The paradox of the situation after 1990 in this respect is that the effects of the end of totalitarianism were handled as if there had never been more than *one single society* in Europe, as if the system of "real socialism" had not only been antidemocratic, contradictory, and a failure, but fundamentally *imaginary*. As a consequence, the collapse of the states of the Soviet bloc did not produce any project to unify the historical parts of the continent, any vision of cooperation between them working toward common development. It was rather translated by a long continuation of Cold War structures, reinforced by a competition and hierarchy between clienteles, as if it were a matter of a "total victory" of one empire over another. The extreme edge of this "postsocialist" domination, which in particular exploits the mutual hatred and desire for revenge against Russo-Soviet imperialism of East-European nations,[34] is formed by phenomena of semicolonization and "containment."

Ten years after the "revolution of 1989,"[35] not only has the East-West division in Europe not been abolished, but it has in a sense been reinforced. When Europe was cut in two by the geopolitics of the Cold War, it was possible to imagine that it was a provisional phenomenon that would come to an end with the settlement of the conflict. Now we can see that it is a part of the "settlement" itself. It manifests the profoundly inegalitarian and dangerously conflictual character of that settlement. Once the vision of a "common European home" evoked by Mikhail Gorbachev was buried together with any idea of a negotiated evolution of the continent's structures (regimes, alliances, borders, sovereignties), the question has never again been raised of *refounding Europe* on the basis of a "Congress of European Peoples," or at least a conference of their governments, that could draw up a balance sheet of the consequences of the Cold War and the problems it left behind or that its end allowed to reappear. This was a possible but not necessary consequence of the internal collapse of communism, to which was added the pressure of global power relations and power strategies, in particular those of the United States.

But these determining factors are not solely responsible for the way that the principal European nations, spontaneously rediscovering traditional imperialist postures (reminiscent of the policies of the victorious states in 1918, which were already calling themselves "the democracies"),[36] began to carve out clienteles for themselves in Central and Eastern Europe (Germany in Croatia and Slovenia, as well as in Poland, France in Serbia, at least for a while). Nor do they explain the fact that the European Union tacitly classified candidates for admission to the new space of prosperity it wanted to define into "possible," "doubtful" (at least in the short term), and "excluded," so as to preserve for as long as possible the advantages of a division of labor between unevenly developed zones, and to push the difficulties of a new definition of European identity outside of the frames of thought and action that had resulted from the successive episodes of the "European civil war."[37] A veritable fracture has thus arisen, a sort of cold war after the Cold War (upon which many episodes of "hot war" are superimposed), but one which is both plural and mobile, and which is hidden under a thick mythology about "clashes of civilizations" between Eastern and Western Europe, supposedly inherited from religious tradition or from the form of state building, when not simply from the ethnic character of the nations involved.[38]

Following 1989, some analysts of the "other Europe,"[39] whether more pessimistic than others or less convinced of the virtues of the extreme neoliberalism that the European Union had inscribed in its founding texts, had warned against the impasses of presenting democratization as the automatic consequence of integration into the structures of the Western market.[40] Their prognosis has in part been verified, not only in the countries of the former Yugoslavia, but particularly in Russia, which is now dominated by an alliance between the political police apparatus (directly descended from the old KGB) and one of the most powerful "Mafia-style" economic criminal organizations in the world. And even though the European Union could have tried to influence events at least indirectly by proposing, from the beginning, an open negotiation on the modalities of economic cooperation between the East and West of the continent, from development aid and integration to common political institutions (which remain entirely to be defined), it abandoned the people of Russia and their neighbors to their fate and allowed national rivalries to develop (when it did not exploit them). Then the European Union had to call on the intervention of American military power in order to prevent the announced genocide in Kosovo, considering that policies of an exterminist sort (Srebrenica) or even of massive deportations (as in Krajina and Bosnia) could not longer be tolerated within the geographical space of Europe without incurring unacceptable political costs. But these costs will have to be paid at the end of this intervention no matter what, since the way it happened precipitated the massacres of Albanians rather than preventing them, added one ethnic cleansing to another, bombed and materially ruined the Serbian population without ridding it of its dictator,[41] and set off a chain reaction that will probably include the acceptance of genocide in Chechnya and the political destabilization of Austria. This sort of concatenation of circumstances that I have schematically summarized here (in a way that could certainly be contested and is in any case provisional) seems to me to bear at least two lessons.

The first is that from the moment that the question of the borders of Europe is no longer a simply theoretical question but the stake of conflicts (since the point at which violence will stop is never predictable a priori, and the idea of cloistering it or allowing destruction "to do its work" turns out to be both criminal and dangerous), the pragmatic method for which European leaders have so often been praised—consisting in *never posing the political problem underlying the theme of "European identity,"* but rather allowing the vicissitudes of diplomacy and economics to decide upon inclusions and exclusions, and only ever establishing formal rules of negotiation[42]—no longer works.

The second is that the exclusion of Russia from European space (or the acceptance of its self-exclusion, which is not a fact of nature but a political program benefiting certain forces, not to say certain clans) bears dramatic risks for tomorrow's history, no doubt comparable to those brought along by the injustice and blindness of the settlement of the First World War (including the treaties of Versailles and Trianon). In any case, if we follow a whole historical tradition[44] in seeing the plurisecular question of European identity as having been rent by the pressures and repercussions of the evolution of the two great border powers, both "inside" and "outside" European space, that are Great Britain and Russia, it should be obvious that the apparently irreversible insertion of the first in the mechanism of European unification requires the question of the second to at least be posed. Unless it is the other way around: the exclusion or self-exclusion of Russia will contribute to perpetuating the semi-inclusion (which is also a semi-exclusion) of Britain.

What has thus been created is a system of concentric circles: the first posed as the "true" Europe in opposition to the "outer Europe" that is still asking to be "Europeanized."[44] The latter is in turn divided into a first zone of economic and partial political integration (countries that are "candidates for entry into the European Union," the goal being to preserve for as long as possible the difference in salary levels while managing the competition between the "leading" countries of the European Union and the integration of its political structures), a second zone of "inner colonization" (the Balkans: not only Kosovo but a broad surrounding zone including Albania and most of the former Yugoslavia), and finally a third zone of predatory capitalism (who profits from the Russian financial crisis? where do the diverted IMF credits go?). This subdivision would appear to result from the vicissitudes of recent history, but in a more insidious way it rests upon the idea that some peoples (always those that are a bit farther to the East), whether by nature or by history, are not "mature" enough for democracy. But how could this be determined if they are denied the essential conditions that would allow them to prove it?

We cannot but generalize to the whole of relations between the western and eastern parts of Europe the British historian Timothy Garton Ash's disappointment with respect to relations between the formally reunited "two Germanies": "I am amazed and concerned by the neo-colonialist attitude of West Germans toward their compatriots. It is a sort of internal colonialism."[45] The result of such a logic is precisely the search for an impossible normative "European" identity and the multiplication of security problems (police, army, borders: the militarization of Europe, so as to maintain order both within and on the constantly pushed back borders). We have the right to think, without being immediately accused of idealism, that the solution in fact moves in the opposite direction: that of a clearly announced project to integrate all the peoples and all the countries of European space within a single territory of citizenship, of egalitarian or "cosmopolitan" inspiration, with the decentralized means of modern administration. This right of entry, translating a desire to be done with the consequences of eighty years of "continental civil war" mixed up with two "world wars" and the division into "blocs," must be proclaimed unequivocally, leaving the modalities of its implementation to be progressively negotiated and put in place. We must leave behind the paradox constituted by the creation of a "subaltern imperialism" in Europe (which does not even master the means of its own policies), which, on a backdrop of humanitarian, social, and ecological disasters, both perpetuates dictatorial structures and paves the way for militarist adventures in the former Soviet Union.

Immigration and Right of Asylum: Citizenship or Apartheid in Europe

A final obstacle, and not the least (particularly sensitive in France, but the problem is general: the recent anti-Moroccan pogroms in Anadalusia have given a dramatic illustration), blocks the constitution of a "European people." European citizenship, within the limits of the currently existing union, is not conceived of as a recognition of the rights and contributions of *all* the communities present upon European soil, but as a postcolonial isolation of "native" and "nonnative" populations. This exposes the European community to the reactive development of all sorts of identitarian obsessions, following the model of mutual reinforcement of exclusions and communitarianisms (including "national," "secular," and "republican" communitarianisms) promoted by globalization. This is why I have attached a great importance for several years now to bringing into the full light of day, in order to combat it, the current development of a true *European apartheid*, advancing concurrently with the formal institutions of European citizenship and, in the long term, constituting an essential element of the *blockage* of European unification as a democratic construction.

I am not unaware of the problems that the use of such an expression can pose. Wouldn't it be better, it could be asked, simply to analyze the set of discriminatory structures subsisting in each country, particularly as regards access to citizenship, paying attention in each case to the specific historical and juridical tradition? My response (as in other circumstances where the question has been raised)[46] is that European unification has introduced a qualitative change both in the symbolic register and in institutional practice. The status of European citizen, which until this point had only constituted an imprecise reference, has begun to take on an effective content (voting rights, recourse to appellate courts that in some cases are superior to national tribunals, materialization of the status of *civis europeanus* by a common passport, access to social and cultural services such as scholarships). But the fact that, with respect to individuals, this "citizenship" is defined as the simple addition of the national citizenships of the member countries of the union, transforms the status of the foreigner.[47] In *each particular country* the foreigner is only the national of another sovereign state, enjoying an equivalent "belonging," which is the object of reciprocal recognition. But *at the level of the newly instituted union,* he or she becomes the object of an internal exclusion.

In being *totalized* on the scale of Europe, the objective signification of the exclusion changes: European citizenship is presented as the mechanism that includes some of the populations historically present in the space of the community while rejecting others, most of which are long established and contribute equally to the development of the civil society of the new organism. Foreigners have become metics or *second-class citizens* whose residence and activities are the object of particular surveillance. Now, this exclusion affects highly diverse populations: both those of the South who have been attached to Europe through long-standing circuits for the recruitment of labor, and those of the eastern and southeastern parts of Europe whose peoples are subjected to a selective admissions process for entry in the "community." As I said before, it has become clear that these different mechanisms for exclusion from citizenship but inclusion in the economy (in particular in order to exploit differences in quality of life and salary levels) constitute structural characteristics that are "managed" as the internal and external conjunctures evolve.

An implicit comparison with South-African apartheid is thus not devoid of meaning. Its function is not merely to provoke.[48] Must we go so far as to say that, in the same period that this regime disappeared in South Africa, it is being reconstituted in Europe? *Comparaison n'est pas raison,* and we could think of many other situations of institutional inequality (in particular the system that long survived the official abolition of slavery in the United States and that today persists in discrimination in schools, professions, and the application of justice). What the use of this term suggests is the constitution of a population that is "inferior" in rights and dignity, tends to be subjected to violent forms of security control, and must perpetually live "on the border," neither absolutely inside nor totally outside. The immigrants from the East and South have in some sense left behind them the equivalents of the former South African *homelands* (returning to them occasionally, or sending back the resources necessary to a "separate development," or to keep their families alive)—whence the extreme importance and sensitive character of the problem of family reunification and "social rights" for immigrant families, one of the favorite targets of xenophobic propaganda. Or, to put it in other terms, what Catherine Wihtol de Wenden justly called the "sixteenth European nation" remains desperately excluded from the construction of a citizenship in Europe. We have recreated the "metics," if not the "helots"![49]

It would be naive to think that the development of such an institutional racism in Europe has no relation to the ongoing process of globalization.[50] As I have indicated elsewhere,[51] I think it is more accurate to see a double effect of *projection* of the new global hierarchy of powers, opportunities for development, and personal rights, and of defensive *reaction* to globalization. This differential inclusion of European apartheid in the process of globalization no doubt explains why, more and more, the traditional figure of the external enemy is being replaced by that of the internal enemy. It also refers to an economy of global violence that, for a decade or two now, has been transformed to the point that there are no longer any regions that can absolutely be considered *refuges*. Once again, we must recognize that the "insides" and the "outsides" express the same structural dynamics, even in their most extreme figures.

IV

Let us then proceed, in modesty, to what I earlier called "worksites of democracy." They correspond, if not term by term, to the obstacles I have just laid out. In fact, I do not believe it is possible to think of transformations, social movements, and intellectual developments on the model of what Gramsci calls "war of position" or direct confrontation, but rather on that of "war of manœuvre" or gradual construction of a new historical hegemony, that is, both a new way of thinking, a new collective "common sense," and interactions between multiple interventions stemming from both civil society and the public sphere.[52] It is only as a function of the goal of these interventions that specific "forces" can come together. I will list four of them, which are obviously not completely disconnected, and to which I cannot devote detailed expositions (all the more so since in most cases they are simply working hypotheses).

The idea of "worksites of (and for) democracy" is not incompatible with that of "cosmopolitanism" put back into honor today by Habermas and his disciples,[53] except that democratic work requires *determinate matter* and not just an ethics and juridical norms, and this sort of *matter* is only given *in situation*. But the situation cannot be furnished by an institutional or state framework, more or less consecrated by religion, war, law, and morality, but—at least such is my dialectical hypothesis— can only come from the specific way politics is traversed by conflicts, rent between local cultures ("particularisms") and global universalities, old and new, identities and interests. Rather than the formalism of the "theory of communicative action," always at risk of falling back from the "normativity of *Sollen*" toward the "normality of *Sein*,"[54] I prefer the combination (however unstable it may be) of a post-Marxist, and more particularly Gramscian[56] inspiration, with one coming from Hannah Arendt, such as is to be found in Herman van Gunsteren's notion of a "community of fate," in which individuals and groups can *neither separate nor get along at will*. This is precisely what engenders—in the best of cases, and thus in a fragile, "aleatory" (as the Althusser of the last period would have said) way—collective political practice, *collective access to citizenship*, always "in the making."[56]

A first worksite of democracy, in my eyes, concerns the question of justice. This question is fundamental as far as the individual's status as a "political subject" is concerned. But it is also decisive for the transformation of the notion of sovereignty on the European scale, and it is not surprising that subject and sovereignty should form a pair.

Since Aristotle, we know (or ought to know) that participation in the activity of judgment is as essential a component of democratic citizenship as participation in decision making or in legislation,[57] and since Hegel we know or ought to know that one of the symbolic keys of belonging to the community is the possibility of being judged as a criminal even while remaining a citizen, or the possibility for the criminal to recognize himself in the instance that judges him.[58] From this point of view, Europe as a whole is today at a crossroads. On the one hand (particularly as a result of the public exposure of problems of political corruption), the tendency toward the autonomy of the judiciary with respect to political power has made itself felt ever more sharply. On the other hand, the legal process and juridical practice (depending somewhat on the country, with France hardly distinguishing itself) remain spheres in which social inequality is massive, expertise all-powerful, and countervailing powers generally underdeveloped, due to the lack of widespread basic education in the law (which is at least as fundamental as basic education in technology or economics), and to the lack of material resources (which themselves are dependent on political will).

It is not difficult to identify the most sensitive point of political blockage, beyond everything that can be said about the inertia of national legal systems and their incompatible juridical traditions (particularly as concerns the opposition between the Anglo-Saxon and continental traditions, which continues to replay the "clash of civilizations" between *common law* and *Roman law* traditions). Appellate jurisdictions and notably the European Court of Justice and the European Court of Human Rights are among the most "advanced" institutions of the community, which European citizens (and even foreigners residing in Europe) can address directly, even if under restrictive conditions and subject to long delays. In this sense, they operate a virtual rebalancing of what Blandine Kriegel quite correctly calls the "primacy of the administrative state over the state of justice," that is, they put the constantly evoked notion of the *rule of law* back on its feet.[59] But we can go yet a step further. When, as is the case in Europe, a transnational structure tends to replace the instance of the *law* as the "expression of the general will" or to relativize the weight of parliamentary will in favor of a "legislation without legislators" made up of arbitrations, contracts, regulations, and jurisprudence,[60] the democratic instance must take the form of a universal access to justice (including for both individuals and groups of citizens opposing the state) and an a posteriori control of the equity of decisions sanctioned "in the last resort" by the European Courts.[61]

The need for and the difficulty of the democratization of the legal system (which is to say, its direct or indirect control by those who delegate their "power to judge" to it) are as flagrant on the level of the European community as on that of each nation. A European program for the democratization of justice would be a typical illustration of the idea of a community of citizens that would be *more advanced* than the national communities themselves.

A second fundamental worksite of democracy concerns the convergence of trade-union struggles and the associative movement around projects to reor-

ganize "labor time" on the European scale. Pierre Bourdieu, following the strikes of 1995 in France, gave a particular emphasis to the importance of this goal.[62] But can it be attained without a reexamination of the foundations of the articulation between citizenship and "profession"? The turning point in European citizenship coincides, de facto, with the crisis of the national social state, in which the relatively effective resolution of the "social question" made possible the reproduction of the nation-form at the same time as the nation-state codified and gave its sanction to a certain definition of labor and the laborer.

The question posed by this problem is that of knowing what a *social activity* (or a "socially necessary" activity) is, in all its generality. This question had first been raised by feminists and ecologists *against* the centrality of productive labor and the exclusivism of classical conceptions of the class struggle. But it would seem that what is now coming to light does not present an either/or alternative. The "centrality of labor," which historically took the place of classical bourgeois notions of *independence* or *self-ownership*, and of *ability* as the basis of social property or collective rights "to existence," has been not abolished but rather displaced and enlarged.

Here we are at the heart of the European social model and its crisis. The impossibility of making *labor* (as a production of the social bond) *disappear* is demonstrated *a contrario* by the unacceptable consequences of mass unemployment and transgenerational exclusion: "negative individualism," "disaffiliation," and in the final accounting the reactive violence of the poor and the counterviolence of law-and-order policies. But if productive labor becomes at the same time a "production of sociality" then it is not only *poiēsis*, fabrication of the material means of existence, but potential political *praxis*. Such a hypothesis is different from both that of Marx (according to whom labor "reproduces social relations," that is, it produces the capital of which workers are the living instruments, up to the point when class domination is overturned) and that of Arendt, or rather those who would use her at low cost (according to whom labor is opposed to *action* as the private sphere is to the public sphere). Negri and Michael Hardt's suggestion that transindividual intellectual activity as well as "caring and affective labor" be included in an enlarged concept of labor is particularly interesting here.[63] The *reproduction of social life in general* has also become the object of labor, which means that every worker has become a "social worker." He or she produces "sociality" or "social connectedness" at the same time as goods or services (just as, as has been explained to us for some time now, the remaining peasants produce both alimentary goods and environment, and all the more so to the extent that they resist agribusiness methods). The principle that can be formulated here, once again, reverses the traditional relation between activity and hegemony: not working in order to produce (goods, value), but producing (goods, services, information, knowledge) in order to work, that is, in order to exercise a fundamental civic right. *Work for all* (in multiple forms and statuses that do not necessarily reproduce the classical form of employment for wages, but which can include *no fewer* guarantees of recognition and solidarity) is thus another "constitutional" goal for a Europe that would be *more democratic* than the nations it comprises.

And thus is opened before the citizens of Europe a worksite for the renovation of the forms of collective struggle and the institutions of social *conflict*. As essential as it seems to refer to a concept of the polity and of citizenship that is not "integrationist" or "consensual" (as is the case, it must be said, for Habermas and a fortiori for the "national republicans"), it is equally unavoidable that we rethink its forms and its objects—or that we rethink the articulation of the *citizen* and the *militant* (precisely because the militant has been one of the great modern figures of active citizenship). At the same time, we shift from a national to a transnational point of view (since global space today is both that in which social labor time is redistributed as a function of the contrary policies of the profitability of capital and the satisfaction of social needs, and that in which the collective dimensions of militant citizenship or a solidarity irreducible to the form of the historical compromises between capital and labor can appear). This leads us to envisage a third worksite, which is intrinsically transnational—or which aims at transnationality as such.

The third worksite of democracy: the democratization of borders. I do not conflate it with an absolute opening or suppression of borders, which would only give rise to the extension of a savage capitalism in which men are definitively brought to and tossed out of production sites like commodities, even like simple useful or useless raw materials.[64] Rather, what is at stake is a *negotiation of the crossing of borders* on the level of the movements of circulation and migration of populations on the planet, one of whose poles is Europe, rather than allowing it to be the object of unilateral political decisions backed up by the development of reinforced security practices and ideologies, or what has been called "fortress Europe."[65] And thus we might begin to carve out a universal right of *circula-*

tion and *residency,* including reciprocity of cultural contributions and contacts between civilizations.

This is the material basis of a citizenship open to immigrants: not "European citizenship" but "citizenship in Europe," that is, the shared construction of citizenship by the diverse inhabitants of Europe considered as an effective progress in the history of the rights of man (and thus as a component of a veritable "politics of the rights of man," which is not the same as "humanitarian intervention"). This amounts to saying that we must think of the means to change the historical relation between territory and population in order to free it from schemas of property (including state property), just as the relations between territory and flows of commodities, capital and information have already changed under the pressure of globalization. And we must attack the obsessive question of collective *insecurity* by beginning precisely with the situation of the most "insecure," the nomadic populations who are the source and target of the obsession with law and order that is so closely intertwined with the obsession with identity.

Finally, a fourth worksite of democracy concerns culture, but above all the "language of Europe," which is the condition under which not only can we speak of a public sphere but can respond to the questions, "Whence does this sphere proceed?" and "For whom is it being built?" My hypothesis, which echoes that of Umberto Eco,[66] is that we must put into question, in both theory and practice, *and particularly at the level of educational practices,* the romantic ("Humboldtian") concept of language as a closed totality, the expression of a community equally closed upon itself (at the same time as it is universal in itself alone), which has lasted until our day (including in structuralist guises).[67] We must set forth from multicultural practices and not merely from the law that organizes both the hierarchy of state languages (including "languages of integration," primary and secondary "languages of work") and the protection of unofficial idioms (the Charter of Regional or Minority Languages of 1992, whatever its usefulness may be).[68] This means that we must set forth from a singular *usagē,* perhaps unique in the world, produced by the history of the European continent and its interaction with all the world's regions (there are other regions in the world whose civilization is built on a plurisecular colinguism, such as the far East, but seemingly according to an entirely different historical concept for which it is not certain that the concept of translation is appropriate).[69]

English, in fact, *is not* and will not be the "language of Europe."

It is already much *more* (the international globalized and globalizing language, the postmodern equivalent of the premodern role of Latin) and yet much *less* (one specific national language among others, occasionally in a minority situation itself, and threatened with breaking up into several relatively separate idioms).[70] My hypothesis, like that of Eco, is intentionally to the side of the legal problem: the "language of Europe" is not a code but a constantly transformed system of crossed usages; it is, in other words, *translation*. Better yet, it is the reality of social practices of translation at different levels, the *medium of communication* upon which all others depend (which poses the problem of access to communication between the codes). My goal is thereby to displace the question of identity, culture, and borders, to try to conceive of a practice that would be distinct from the globalized circulation of information and, in that sense, would be a means of cultural resistance and a countervailing power, but not on the traditionalist and communitarian bases of identitarian "national language-culture" cultivated for itself (and destined to decadence). If the "language of Europe" is translation (or, if you will, the concrete metalanguage made up of all the equivalences and all the attempts to overcome the "untranslatable" between idioms),[71] it is also an unevenly developed practice. For the moment, it is concentrated on the two "ends" of society: among intellectuals educated in the liberal arts and sciences, writers of uprooting and exile (inheritors of Heinrich Heine, Elias Canetti, James Joyce, or Joseph Conrad), and among anonymous migrants who generally occupy the lowest posts in the division of labor and employment (for the intermediary levels this virtually universal competence is prevented, blocked by the almost uniformly monolingual national education systems).[72] We must thus reduce—and not suppress—the gap and work to normalize it, which also means rediscovering on another level the spirit of the great "cultural revolutions" of learning: the generalization of literacy and schooling. The task is no less gigantic. It will be more than enough to occupy several generations of artists, teachers, and technicians and to reestablish the true aims of a "postnational" historical transformation.

The simultaneous opening of these worksites of democracy forms the concrete condition for turning public space back into a civic space: this is why the question of *European public opinion* (still practically nonexistent, and yet "insidious" in the similarity of questions and obstacles to democratization) is important, and so difficult, once it cannot be reduced in a unilateral way to the practices of communication between governments and the construction of European media networks (or the absorption of Europe into global networks of standardized information). In the absence of such a public opinion, it is out of the question to think of an "active citizenship" in the historical space we have now entered. But this is part of a more general question, namely that of the reversal of signs of value and priorities in action between the conquest of collective "powers" (as Spinoza would have put it), which are translated in inventions of ideas and institutions, and the formation of communal identities protected within more or less arbitrarily fixed borders. If Europe (that is, the real Europeans, the "residents" of Europe) manages to displace once again the motor of political action, it will not be the self-sufficient "everything" promised by Treaties and Summits, but—as the name of a people yet to come—it may become "something."

10

Democratic Citizenship or Popular Sovereignty? Reflections on Constitutional Debates in Europe

You know how titles work. You choose them before beginning work on writing out the talk, both in order to be able to print a poster and to give direction to your thinking, perhaps even to set a challenge for yourself. And then you have to try not to be too unfaithful to your initial intention. The exercise is particularly hazardous when you have to try to fill in the gap between two linguistic universes that, to a point, are also two distinct intellectual traditions, two different perspectives on history and society, and when you are trying to give a verbal formulation to working hypotheses rather than presenting the results of a completed research project.

What is called "European unification" is more the horizon than the object of my presentation this evening. As I have had the occasion to propose elsewhere, this construction, considered as the creation of an enduring political framework within which a new citizenship on the European continent—"European citizenship"—can emerge, and thus as the historical support for a transformation in the content of citizenship and the ways it is exercised (a signification contained in the expression "the Europe of citizens," *das Europa der Bürger*, which had been proposed from the beginning of the process), seems to me to be "impossible" to realize. But this impossibility, in the sense of an accumulation of historical obstacles whose combination can seem insurmountable, and partic-

Opening lecture of the 2001–2 academic year, Marc Bloch Center, Berlin, October 26, 2001.

ularly in the sense of obstacles to thought that are translated by the conjunction of apparently contradictory predicates in a single notion, seems nonetheless absolutely necessary. It is necessary because the steps that have already been covered leave no room, except in the form of a disaster, for turning backward or even halting at a status quo. It is further necessary because the invention of an original historical "solution" for the problem posed, however improbable it may seem, constitutes in my eyes (as, I believe, in the eyes of many among us), the only way to give a continuity to our common history, the only way to make our political culture take a step forward. From my viewpoint (and I do not think this is merely a matter of a pious wish, even if this sort of proposition does indeed contain an irreducible value judgment), this step forward can only be a democratic one, and it must even represent an innovation in the history of democracy, a "democratic invention" in the sense that Claude Lefort has given to this term.[1] This is why I believe that, at the least, we need to devote a renewed reflection to the paradoxes or even aporias that have characterized the invention, transformation, and development of democratic institutions throughout their history. These aporias are no doubt not proper to European unification but are rather characteristic of constituent processes in general. But precisely the fact that, rather than seeming to have been definitively left behind by European unification, they are once again coming to the fore in such an urgent and specific form at the current "moment" or "turning point," means that we are indeed dealing with a process of constitution, or that only this sort of process, whatever direction it may take (this is still entirely unpredictable), can represent a resolution of the paradox of impossible necessity from which I began.

My title gives an admittedly simplifying expression to these aporias, which are simultaneously old, permanent, and renewed by the current conjuncture. Furthermore, I encountered a difficulty that stems from semantic divergences between French and German. But such difficulties can also constitute a productive starting point for reflection. In moving from the French *Citoyenneté démocratique ou souveraineté du peuple?* to its German translation, *Demokratische Staatsbürgerschaft oder Volkssouveränität?*, a precision is added, making one of the dimensions of the problem more explicit, but at the risk of limiting the field of reflection in advance. The German language never naturalized *Citoyennität* in the way it did *Souveränität*, and *Bürgertum* has kept the double meaning that *bourgeoisie* gradually lost in French, which makes the extra precision in *Staatsbürgerschaft* necessary. The advantage of this is that it shows that the tension between "people" and "state" constitutes one of the unavoidable dimensions of our problem, and that citizenship is an institution that is inconceivable except in relation to the frame of a state, whatever its historical form may be. If the history of citizenship is not over, then the state too will have to undergo new developments. But the disadvantage is that it suggests, if not that the citizenship in question is by nature attached to the form of the nation-state within which, for the most part, it is currently realized, at least that the relationship between citizenship and the state is one of inclusion. It suggests that, by definition, citizenship is the quality or status that the state (and, in particular, the nation-state) confers on individuals, and which is inconceivable outside of this assignation (the term used in American political science is *ascriptive citizenship*).[2] This further suggests that citizenship cannot contribute to the formation of the state, or to giving it a particular form, on the basis of its own dynamic. This is nonetheless the hypothesis whose meaning and difficulties I would like to explore within the horizon of the "constituent problems" of Europe today, but at a more general philosophical level. This presentation will be organized in three moments. In a *first moment*, after having justified the way my title poses the question in the form of a dilemma, I will discuss a certain number of characteristics that modern political systems have attached to the conjunction of the ideas of democracy and sovereignty, in order to explain why "popular sovereignty" always returns from its officially announced decline to haunt political space. In a *second moment*, I will make a detour through the history of the *politeia*—the foundational Greek notion that, for reasons to be explained, I translate in a synthetic way as "constitution of citizenship"—so as to justify the thesis of a historical process that is both incomplete and incompletable. Citizenship is not only the foundation or the frame but the object of this process, a process that calls for new developments. Taking the opposite point of view—no longer that of the constitution as an objective form but that of the "subjectivity" that corresponds to it and supports it, and thus trying to bring together institutional and anthropological dimensions—I will show that the dichotomous choice posed between the ideas of democratic citizenship and popular sovereignty coincides with the problem opened by modernity of combining the conflicting values of liberty and equality and giving them an effective realization within a single public space. Finally, in a *third moment*, returning to the theme of the "worksites of democracy," which to me seems coextensive with that of the renewal of citizenship in the current context, and using the questions it poses to illuminate the old theme of the "marks of sovereignty" (in Jean Bodin's expression), I will try to formulate a few hypotheses with respect to the tasks of the political in the postmodern or postnational era.

I

I freely admit that the formulation in terms of a dilemma ("democratic citizenship *or* popular sovereignty") that I am using here is, to a large degree, suggested by my reading of Jürgen Habermas's theoretical developments and my desire to give a somewhat different response to the questions he poses.

In *Between Facts and Norms*, Habermas presents the construction of citizenship in the work of Rousseau and Kant as representing two successive and only partially satisfactory attempts to combine and reconcile two "principles" that are in an "unacknowledged *competition*," even though both of them "determined the normative self-understanding of constitutional democracies up to the present day." These two principles are the idea of the rights of man considered as the moral (or juridico-moral) foundation of the individual guarantees incorporated into every constitutional order, and the idea of popular sovereignty considered as the political foundation of the existence of a public sphere and its autonomy with respect to particular interests (that is, its generality).[3] It is not clear that the competition Habermas speaks of is quite so "unacknowledged" in that the history of the past two centuries is largely that of the privilege given to either one or the other of these ideas by different national political traditions, and their use against one another by antagonistic social forces and regimes. But it is clear that we are dealing with evidence of a fundamental duality.

The dominant tendency of current constitutionalism, and this is particularly true of debates relative to European unification, seems to express a marked preference for the notions of democratic principles, democratic guarantees of individual and collective rights, and democratic citizenship understood in the sense of belonging to a state governed by the rule of law and allowing participation in its institutions, over those of "popular sovereignty" or "sovereignty of the people" (except among theoreticians of what is called, at least in France, "sovereigntism," which essentially presents itself as a defense of the prerogatives of national sovereignty against any transfer of competencies to a supranational level insofar as the inevitable result would be the negation of popular sovereignty). There are two sorts of reasons for this, which, as sometimes happens, present a potentially contradictory combination of statement of fact and value judgment. The "people," the subject of sovereignty in the classical republican conception, is characterized as both unavailable and undesirable. It would be unavailable insofar as, even in a national and a fortiori in a transnational frame, the organic unity, both objective and subjective, that such a notion seems to demand has been exploded by the social and cultural diversification of political units. Unless one is willing to create the unity of a political community by force, the people can only be invoked in an ideal way. This also introduces the idea of an undesirable subject: the use of force to this end has been and is characteristic of totalitarian regimes (which frequently refer to popular sovereignty, only to transfer it in practice to "movements" or "leaders" that escape any democratic control on the part of citizens), with the consequence of extremely violent practices of internal exclusion and external antagonism.

But, on the other hand, it would seem that the disappearance of the reference to the sovereignty of the people leads the very idea of democratic citizenship to an unacceptable point of indeterminacy or even dissolution—not only on account of the fact that *dēmos* and "people" (*peuple, Volk*) are synonyms, and thus it is very difficult to conceive of a democracy without a *dēmos* or people, but also on account of the necessity for democratic procedures and forms of behavior to be defined not only as guarantees proposed or imposed by the state upon the individuals and groups who make up civil society but, more fundamentally, as the rules that these groups and individuals propose and impose *upon themselves and one another* within the framework of a "community of citizens," and which are thus the object of a self-determination. Democracy is never devoid of social content; it is never purely procedural, which amounts to saying that it is always measured by the reality of the rights effectively granted to those who, by heritage or social position, have no power other than the collective power or power of the community. This power cannot be constituted without a reference to the "people" as the *last instance of legitimacy and political decision making*, in the dual and conflictual (or, in any case, polemical) dimension that the notion of *dēmos* has contained since the beginning: the dimension of totality and the "popular" dimension, or if you prefer the principle of the *nonexclusion of its own "mass" or "multitude."*

This may be why, despite everything that, in both facts and values, seems to militate for eliminating the idea of popular sovereignty, with the decisionist and even mythical connotations it carries, from our definitions of citizenship, it never stops coming back to haunt it. Borrowing a favored term from Jacques Derrida, I would call this the "spectral" existence of sovereignty as popular sovereignty in the functioning of contemporary democracies and in projects to enlarge or transpose democracy beyond the limits of the nation-state. But it seems to me that the specter that haunts us here is in fact *the communal obsession*—the impossible requirement that the "community of citizens"[4] be both, and contradictorily, the *community of communities* before which every other principle of belonging and allegiance becomes relative so that universal rights and genuinely impartial guarantees can be put into effect, and also a *community without community*, or, if you prefer, a community without an "identitarian" substance of its own (in particular without ethnic, cultural, or ideological substance), so that it cannot be able to supplant those who compose it in a fearsome hypostasis of the collective. It must be *real* enough to exist in the face of the state whose legitimacy it founds and *unreal* enough not to absorb (or reject) rights-bearing individuals: such is the dilemma raised by the notion of popular sovereignty. The persistence of this truly insoluble dilemma constitutes the "life" of the constitutional problem of democratic citizenship, particularly in the form of an incessant dialectic between the notion of constituent power and that of the limitation or self-limitation of power.[5]

Before bringing this first point to a close, allow me to evoke, be it schematically, two more concrete aspects of this aporia of the political community, or community of citizens, which underlie the obsessive, spectral return of popular sovereignty in regimes of democratic citizenship. I connect them symbolically with the function and use of "we" as a self-designation of the sovereign people in proclamations of democratic rights (or rights of man and the citizen). It is well known that our republican constitutions begin explicitly or implicitly with such a self-reference: "We the People of the United States of America . . ."; "Nous, représentants du peuple français . . ."[6] This reference becomes particularly insistent in the insurrectional moments that open episodes of reconstitution, refoundation, or reaffirmation of democracy, or even constituent episodes. Remember the successive slogans of the demonstrators in Leipzig and Berlin in 1989: *Wir sind das Volk! Wir sind ein Volk!* Such performative utterances (the people exists insofar as it calls itself a people; it is what it says itself to be, that is, sovereign) bear within themselves complex, even contradictory characteristics. On the one hand a reciprocity of viewpoints (often considered as characteristic of the very idea of *Gemein-*

schaft) is established between individual singularity and the collective, since the people exists in each individual to the same degree, and each individual projects him or herself, as citizen, into the people (Rousseau called the citizen "an indivisible part" of the general will).[7] Hegel gave an admirable expression to this reciprocity in the chapter of the *Phenomenology of Mind* on "self-consciousness" (*Selbstbewußtsein*)—but in his eyes what he is formulating is a problem, not a solution or a factual reality—with the following formal equation, which he opposed to the sterile tautology of *Ich bin Ich* ("I am I"): *Ich, das Wir, und Wir, das Ich ist* ("'I,' that is 'We' and 'We' that is 'I'").[8] But, on the other hand, it seems that such performative utterances, communal proclamations, and claims to shared or collective sovereignty can have a concrete, institutional meaning only at the price of conflicts and exclusions. For the "us" denotes an identity that is affirmed, or whose constitutive properties (be they only the "common legacy" of a history, indissociable from some form of "normality") are affirmed, at the same time as other properties and their bearers, whether inside or outside its own "life space," are excluded.[9] And these conflicts and exclusions can only be inscribed in a process of democratic construction of the political sphere after passing through a painful dialectic (and even then not always successfully).

Consider the indivisibility of the community, or the equal, equivalent participation of all in the constitution of the state. This indivisibility, which represents the affirmation of a "We" in its absolute form, is particularly associated with what I would call the "insurrectional" moments of citizenship, taking the term insurrection in its broad historical sense, that of the "insurgents" of the classical bourgeois revolutions (which means, if we are willing to take the words literally, the revolutions of citizenship, both national and popular). At such moments we witness a real, if transitory, relativization of social differences and competing belongings in favor of a strong manifestation of democratic reciprocity. The definite rights inscribed in constitutional texts then appear as essentially "transindividual," that is, they overcome the opposition between the individual and the collective insofar as they are attributed to individuals and borne by them (whether it be the right to free expression, property, or existence) but are only conquered by a collective movement (in particular a movement that abolishes privileges and prohibitions). In other words, they are rights that individuals grant one another by conquering them together. In a sense, this is the very basis of the idea of popular sovereignty, which means that the people—contrary to Nietzsche's ironic phrase about the "new god": *Ich, der Staat, bin das Volk* ("I, the state, am the people")[10]—is not the pure and simple function or appearance of the state. There may be no democracy without a state, but nor is there any democracy if the "people" is merely an emanation of the state, the collective name that the state gives to its subjects.

But this first determination is at least partially contradicted by the equally democratic requirement of the *self-limitation of sovereignty*, as expressed in particular by the institution of *representation* and the "rules" by which it works (resulting from the parliamentary tradition). I am not thinking here of the idea (expressed by a certain legend of Rousseauism) according to which the insurrectional moment is inseparable from practices of direct democracy that exclude representation, for I am persuaded, to the contrary, that history has demonstrated the existence of an intimate link between the idea of an active citizenship, of an effective participation of citizens in the *res publica*, and an evolving variety of combinations of direct and representative democracy. Rather, I am thinking of the fact that representative democracy, without which popular sovereignty remains ineffective, introduces its own ferment of dissolution into the representation of the community. Representative democracy is the institution of a *distance* within the people, a distance "between the people and itself" or a distancing of the people from itself. In terms of real power (Spinoza's *potentia multitudinis*), its characteristic is contradictory. It represents both a *subtraction* from collective power—and this risk is quite real, as can be seen in the consequences of the delegation of power, which range from its monopolization by a political caste to its corruption—and yet also an *addition* or a supplement to it, in that it is the necessary condition of *openness* and thus of the *control* or rectification of legislative and governmental decisions. By instituting representation, and on the condition that it remains able to control it, the people in a sense gives itself the means to control itself. The idea of representative democracy operative here is a strong one, inspired not only by Tocqueville or Mill, but also by Spinoza, who thought that the greatest danger to a political community always comes from itself, from its own internal divisions, even as he rejected Hobbes's conclusion that the state is responsible for eliminating conflicts concerning the very nature of the community. In *democratic* representation, it is not only a question of guaranteeing and inspiring the *plurality* of opinions and parties, which is of course essential, but also of *representing social conflict*, bringing it out of the "repression" imposed on it by a given balance of power and into the light where it can be used in the service of a common good or common justice. This implies that conflict be neither denied nor made unavailable to argument and mediation ("communicative action"), even though the representation of conflict most often begins by violently exceeding the institutional framework established for the recognition of legitimate interests. But this brings an aporia into plain light: the community, at the very moment that it poses an autonomous "We," must always *continue to be represented in its multiplicity*, or *become once again a multiplicity* and be represented as such. Far from being able to be contained in the formula of a " 'We' that is 'I,' " or whose norm is self-identity, as Hegel (following Rousseau) had hoped, the community must on the contrary be instituted in a contradictory way, in the course of time, as a We that is (also) an Other, that alienates its identity.[11]

I would like to evoke more briefly a second difficulty, which concerns the inclusive or exclusive character of the community of citizens. Recent debates in both France and Germany—debates about republicanism, the universality or particularity of the nation-state, constitutional patriotism—have given rise to much discussion concerning the problem of the *inclusion* of immigrants in the political culture of democratic societies.[12] It seems to me most fruitful to approach this question from the perspective of the administration of justice. Once again it was Hegel who gave perhaps the most constrictive formulation of a fundamental democratic principle with his provocative proposition that *the criminal wills his own punishment.*[13] We must of course understand this proposition in a normative way, or upon a normative condition that bears precise implications. For punishment to have a legal meaning from the different perspectives of the criminal, the victim, and the collectivity, and thus for it to be inscribed in a process of construction or reconstruction of the community (rather than in an infinite spiral of vengeance that symbolically destroys the community), the criminal must be *a participant in the judgment of his own crime*, in other words, he must be able to consider himself (or, if you prefer, he must not be able to *refuse to consider himself*) to be represented in the tribunal that judges him. It is on this condition that we can say that *the criminal is still a citizen*, and correlatively that citizenship for all is guaranteed by the inclusion of the criminal.

This is an immediate and pressing problem in the context of multinational societies that have been led to treat as habitual offenders "foreigners" or "immigrants" who are manifestly excluded from any representation, even on a symbolic level, in the instances that render justice "in the name of the people." The fact that the principles of law applied by a tribunal are ultimately founded upon the universality of the rights of man, and consequently refer to a "human community" that encompasses all political communities or communities of citizens, is an insufficient guarantee. More precisely, this sort of reference to universality becomes violently contradictory if, at the same time, a particular community can be considered as *structurally excluded* from civic rights in a given space of citizenship and sovereignty. This was obviously the case in colonial societies, but it remains characteristic of the more or less rigorous situations of apartheid which, we are obliged to recognize, is what the condition of non-European populations in the current space of the European Union resembles. Sovereignty reverts to being an attribute of the state, a translation of its omnipotence or arbitrary power in the government of populations, even and above all if this state presents itself as the representative of one community in opposition to another, that is, as the representative of the limitation, incompleteness, and exclusive function of "We."[14]

Reflections on problems of this sort are what lead a theorist inspired by Hannah Arendt such as Herman van Gunsteren (mistakenly classified by Habermas as a "communitarian")[15] to make use of the notion of a "community of fate," that is, a community without community, or without a prior communal substance, without any *transcendence of sovereignty*. A "community of fate" results purely and simply from the recognition by individuals and groups that they have been "thrown together" by history, chance, or "fate" on the same territory or in the same "polity." No spontaneous harmony can arise between their interests and allegiances, but an institutionalization of the conflicts between them can allow them to survive together.[16] The groups that share such a community are neither simply "friends" nor "enemies," or perhaps are both at once. We must recognize that, more and more, this represents the condition of most of the "public spaces" in which we live. But we must also recognize the political paradox represented by the ultrademocratic *fiction* (or, better yet, the development of citizenship as an indefinite process of acquisition) that the practice of citizenship calls for in this situation, which tends to become its *material* condition of possibility, namely the at least symbolic *permanent recreation of the "community of citizens"* on the basis of their differences and conflicts (which cannot allow for any inherited "capital" or privilege of the "first occupant," any "nativism" [*autochtonie*]).

Whether described in terms of the reduction or preservation of the multitude, the representation of conflict (and not merely plurality) in the state, or the exclusion or inclusion of the other in the functioning of republican institutions that affect both the daily life and symbolic identity of the people, the spectral "return" of the question of popular sovereignty in the institution of citizenship does nothing more than manifest the irreducible character of the tensions or contradictions that affect that very notion of citizenship once it is no longer considered to be merely a status granted by a preexistent entity or authority, but has become once again a conquest or institution of autonomy. In order to try to understand better the different dimensions of this problem, we will now make a detour—unfortunately all too short—through the dual question of the constitution of citizenship and the subject of popular sovereignty.

II

In truth these two questions are bound together at a deep level, and it is not really possible to approach them separately. This is why I treat them as two facets of a single problem. This problem, that of the figures of *homo politicus* or the political institution of reciprocity, possesses both an "objective" and a "subjective" aspect, or an institutional dimension and an anthropological one. Both of them, as we shall see, are profoundly historical, but not in the sense of a simple progression or linear succession of figures, each of which would purely and simply replace its predecessor. There are thus both true "ruptures" as well as a political "memory" of humanity, which is one of the mainsprings of its inventiveness and its capacities for universalization. The notion of "constitution"—considered as both *Konstitution* and *Verfaßung*, and thus in a sense not exactly that of the jurists but one that I hope that at least some of them will find acceptable—is what represents in my view the point of contact between the objective and subjective aspects, between the institution and the human fact, and what therefore must be the first object of our reflection in order to elucidate the form of its historicity.

The thesis I would like to defend here lays claim to no originality, although it is by no means universally accepted. I ask merely that we take it seriously and examine all its consequences. It consists in the claim that the history of the political, of the *politeia*, is not over, but is unfinished and probably unfinishable, precisely on account of the ceaseless displacement of the historical conditions that frame the problem of the institution of citizenship and its relation to the "power of the people," formalized at a certain moment as popular *sovereignty*. The question remains, but the meaning of all the terms changes. Now, we should not neglect the fact that the contrary hypothesis, that of an essential completion of constitutional history, has defenders on different sides, among liberal theorists as well as sovereigntists. Both sides tend to regard as definitive the principles of political organization elaborated at the end of the eighteenth century and clarified, developed, and preserved through the nineteenth and twentieth centuries (in short, the principles of modernity). To paraphrase Marx, "there has been history, but there is no longer any."[17] We should be clear that this "no longer" is to be understood in a strong sense: there can and must be constitutional elaborations in new frameworks (nations gaining independence and democracy after a period of dictatorship, supranational groupings taking on all or part of a constitutional structure), not to speak of constant developments in the *content* of constitutions (including the definition and attribution of new democratic rights, of new "dimensions" of citizenship in T. H. Marshall's sense),[18] and extensions of the political community by the elimination of restrictions (as was the case for women, in particular, in Western democracies during the past century). But these elaborations and developments will not change anything about the *fundamental conception* of what a constitution is; to the contrary, they presuppose that the ideality and immutability of this conception be scrupulously respected. As a consequence they exclude the idea of new transformations in how we understand what a constitution is, that is, a new dialectic of institutional forms and figures of subjectivity, participation and political activity. It could be *politically* crucial to recognize that such transformations are historically "on the agenda," or perhaps simply that they are in fact occurring, and are thus in need of interpretation and orientation.

Habermas has clearly expressed this sort of position in recent years. In a lecture given in Paris in December 2000, for example, he stated, "we are not merely heirs to a long-established practice of constitution-making; in a sense, the constitutional question does not provide the key to the main problem we have to solve. For the challenge before us is not to *invent* anything but to *conserve* the great democratic achievements of the European nation-state, beyond its own limits."[19] What allows him to be so affirmative, as we know, is his conviction of having discovered, underlying the history of classical constitutional invention (which for him is the very invention of modernity) a *metaconstitutional* structure that is more operative, more constraining in moral and sociological terms, and less manipulable for antidemocratic ends: the *public sphere* in which citizenship is constituted as a set of rights and discursive practices. As a consequence, the question of a "European constitution" (of which

Habermas is a partisan, seeing it as an approximation of the Kantian cosmopolitan constitutional state) does not concern a *change* in the idea of a constitution, or in those of the people and sovereignty, but merely (and this is no small thing, of course) the emergence of a European public sphere.

The other position does exist, or at least it can be detected in the critical rereading some contemporary authors have proposed of the "definitions" of the constitution that have historically divided juridical and philosophical "schools." I am once again thinking of the work of Olivier Beaud, for example. Beaud is not content to account for the important historical transition between the "ancient" conception (revived during the Renaissance) of the constitution as a balance of powers (*archai*, often translated as "offices") within an organic totality that acts like an individual (whose model is the *polis*), and the modern conception resulting from the revolutions of the classical age, leading to the both universalist and positivist definition of a constitution as a "fundamental law" that incorporates the fundamental rights of citizens (derived from the rights of man) and makes possible both control over governmental action and measurement of the legitimacy of legislation in general. He carries this line of evolution further by suggesting that the appearance of a state defining itself as "social" represents the beginnings of a *third type* or *age* of constitutionalism, which he primarily presents as an alternative to a purely juridical conception (arousing the suspicions of many jurists). Indeed, it is less an issue of a codified formal relation between the extent of public powers and individual or collective freedoms (for example, the rights of minorities) than of the materiality of their *interventions* in the reproduction of the conditions of existence of individuals and in the conservation of the "social bond" itself.[20] A similar indication can also be found, I think, in the recent book by the Italian philosopher Giacomo Marramao, *Dopo il Leviatano*. Working on the basis of an opposition between "formal constitution" and "constitution in the material sense," Marramao argues that the movement of "deformalization of the state" has become irreversible as the notion of the state based on the rule of law (*État de droit*) has given way in part to that of the social state or state based on justice (*État de justice*). It can, of course, be objected that this movement is neither irresistible nor universal, but this does not negate the fact that a tendency has emerged and the question will not go away. In certain respects there is no way to limit demands for social rights and their constitutionalization other than to accentuate the corporate character of the state. This is why, whereas Beaud suggests that the question of the social state must sooner or later lead to a revalorization of the notion of "constituent power" (if not popular sovereignty) in such a way as to provide for a *political* reconceptualization of the collective "ends" of the state, Marramao in an apparently much more pessimistic way suggests that the ideas of popular sovereignty and the general will have lost all meaning and surrendered their functions to the set of "invisible" mechanisms of adjustment and power relations between "strategic groups" and the administration.[21]

I think that these indications are very valuable, but—with all the modesty required of a nonspecialist—I would want to reproach them for a dual limitation. On the one hand they essentially take into account *only one of the aspects* of the transformation of the sociological functions of the modern state, namely the "resistible" inscription into the structure and very definition of public power of the results of the class struggle during the nineteenth and twentieth centuries—that is, the transformation of the national "popular" state into a national "social" state and the trend to inscribe social rights (or at least some social rights, including the right to education, which in some sense works as a right of access to the abilities required to exercise citizenship) in the charter of "fundamental rights" guaranteed by the constitution and serving in return as its foundation. But they pay no attention to other aspects—in particular, the question of the repercussions of the progressive transnationalization of the economic, social, and intellectual conditions of life on the very idea of a constitution (heretofore always thought of as the constitution of a people, or a nation, or a state, perhaps of a federation). Does this not end up putting into question, *from both the top and the bottom of the social spectrum,* the exclusive relation between each individual and *a single community* of political belonging in which the status of citizens is recognized? What this implies is that the question (inscribed in the 1948 *Universal Declaration of Human Rights*) of the dual right of every person to *have a nationality* and to *change his or her nationality* (whose importance in this age of proliferation of refugees and stateless persons cannot be overestimated) is being displaced toward that of the right to combine or superimpose nationalities, pointing toward the emergence of a notion of "citizenship of residency" in competition with "citizenship of belonging."

Whence arises my second objection, which can be stated much more succinctly: these analyses of the limits or crisis of modern constitutionalism do not go so far as to consider the transformation and renewal of the idea of citizenship, without which it is impossible to historicize truly the meaning of the idea of a constitution. This sort of historicization presumes that we view the constitutional question from the perspective of changes in form and function of the state or transformations of the state-form, but also that we relate this perspective to its complement and dialectical antithesis, the transformation of the functions and practical modalities of the action of "citizens"—that is, the question (which in the end is an anthropological and not merely a juridical or sociological one) of *who the citizens are and what they do.*

This is why I suggest that we need to lengthen the detour and return, at least in a propaedeutic and pedagogical manner, to the way that questions of public power and citizenship were tied together in the ancient city-states from which we have inherited our notions of politics, civic consciousness, and civility, and further to the way that citizenship was refounded in the framework of the national state. This refoundation occurred in the form of a strong tension between participation in sovereignty and the exercise of individual freedoms, whose power explains, I think, at least to a large extent, why the link between citizenship and nationality, no matter how many ways it is "contradicted," is still impossible to abolish by a formal political decision: not, or not only, because individuals have an investment in nationality, but because they have an investment in citizenship (or at least that part of it they still possess).

As for the original connection between questions of the state and citizenship, we should first follow the hints contained within *words.* For some time now I have been astonished to see the single Greek word *politeia,* particularly in Aristotle's *Politics,* "translated" in some contexts as "citizenship" and in others as "constitution" or "form of government," whereas in reality it covers a single concept and pursues one development throughout.[22] This admittedly complex notion of a "constitution-of-citizenship" implies at once the delimitation of the community of citizens (the exclusion of dependents and their relegation to the private sphere of the *oikos,* the confinement of foreigners in a zone of lesser rights), the affirmation of the right of the mass of the people to deliberate upon public affairs, the foundation of offices and the exercise of power upon the notion of reciprocity (the governors are also governed or are at least answerable to the governed), and the distribution of these offices as a function of the abilities of each so as to avoid demagogy or the pure and simple identification of the general interest with the interests of the masses. At the heart of this initial presentation of the "constitution-of-citizenship" we thus find a powerful tension, clearly manifested by the tendency toward a conflict between the nonetheless inseparable notions of *politeia* and *isonomia* or *aequa libertas* (which we have translated as "equal liberty"). In a sense this means that the constitution (this is its perhaps inaccessible ideal of equilibrium) can be defined as the set of means used to resist the radical consequences of its own subversive principle.[23] This is why I do not hesitate to say that there is a certain constant of the constitutional problem, before and after the introduction of juridical universalism and the formalism proper to it, that allows us to understand why constitutionalists must periodically return to Aristotle, and that the democratic problem is posed from the origin of what, for us, is politics. In a sense the historicity of the idea of the constitution will never be anything but the necessity to reformulate periodically the terms in which the question of democracy is posed: not only its guarantees, but also its dangers, or rather, its constituent risks.

But as we move toward modernity we must envisage the question of citizenship and its history from what I called a subjective or anthropological angle. Here again I must go very quickly and state hypotheses schematically. I think that we can say that, at least ideally, the foundations of modern nation-states are to be found in insurrections, declarations of independence, or constitutions of "peoples," and that even states constituted "from above" (and it is well known that the idea of a *Revolution von oben* was invented in Germany with respect to Bismarck, if not by him)[24] end up having to be democratically refounded by a transfer of the "marks" of sovereignty to the people, or at least a pretense to have received those marks from the people. Now, the tendency in these nation-states has been for the figure of the citizen to be *doubled*. By this we do not mean that there are two sorts of citizens (in one sense there can only be one kind, and in another sense there are as many kinds as there are roles in the complex "civil societies" that are organized into nations), nor that there are two antithetical ways to institute juridical citizenship (even if it is true that the traditions that can be called "Atlantic" or Anglo-Saxon and "Continental" or European tend to choose to emphasize one of the two aspects). What this means is that the *rights of the citizen* refer to two forms of individuality that never purely and simply coincide and, in this sense, divide or distort the social *habitus* and self-consciousness of the "citizen." Both of them play an integral role in the inaugural revolutions that give them performative "definitions" in the great declarations of rights and inscribe their principles in constitutional texts (and thus in the norm if not, in an immediate and unconditional way, in practice).[25] Each of them represents a way of articulating the values or principles of liberty and equality, of instituting the citizen as the bearer of an affirmation of equal liberty that the state can limit or condition in all sorts of ways, but cannot purely and simply eliminate without provoking what Spinoza called *indignation,* which is to say, resistence or revolt, and thus without destroying itself (since this is the principle of its legitimacy).

There is thus an ongoing double genesis, a dual "production" of the citizen and his or her rights. In order to give some consistency to the discussion I will say that one genesis is closely tied to the history of the category of *sovereignty,* since it represents the paradoxical reversal of its hierarchical characteristics into egalitarian ones, the internalization of the subject's virtues of obedience (the "voluntary servitude" castigated by Étienne de la Boétie)[26] as capacities for autonomy (as can be clearly seen in both Rousseau and Kant), corresponding to what I elsewhere called the "perilous leap" from princely to popular sovereignty.[27] We must not dissimulate the fact that this figure is *uneasy*: it is difficult to conceptualize in a logical way, because it amounts to getting rid of what had constituted the essence of sovereignty—namely, the vertical distance between an instance of decision or authority (the German term *Obrigkeit* is quite "expressive" in this respect) and a subject who obeys that authority. At the same time it not only preserves both subject and obedience (to the government but above all to the law), but also identifies the collective subject with the sovereign and makes the community of citizens the sole sovereign. It is also difficult to conceptualize in a psychological way to the extent that it forces each individual, in order to be free, to "discipline" himself or herself, something that is impossible without a certain degree of cruelty, as Freud noted at some length. But despite this unease, or perhaps thanks to it, this figure of reversal and internalization represents the only way modernity knows to wrench the law away from transcendence, whether the transcendence be that of a divine, princely, or bureaucratic power (the last corresponding to the state's "expertise," which by definition is unverifiable so long as it is not subjected to a principle of "popular sovereignty," which in turn requires sovereign citizens, or citizen-subjects of sovereignty). The question posed is whether our postmodern (and perhaps postnational) societies have at their disposal any way to "reduce" the verticality inherent in political authority other than this paradoxical reversal of sovereignty, which is not purely and simply the same thing as a guarantee against the excesses of power. It seems to me that in order to find something substantially different we would have to renounce simultaneously the "principle" of popular sovereignty and the idea of the *law* and the generality proper to it.

But this genesis of the modern citizen has never been the only one, and cannot be the only one, among other reasons because liberty is not purely a question of autonomy in the Rousseauian and Kantian sense (being oneself the author of the law to which one conforms), but also of autonomy or independence in the Spinozist or Lockean sense: "self-ownership," ownership of the actions of one's body and the thoughts of one's mind. Equality, moreover, resides not only in the recognition of an equal status with respect to such fundamental public institutions as courts or elections, but also in the exercise of the equality of opportunity, at the very least an equal opportunity to develop one's capacities (and this explains why the school is always the site of particular conflict between the "public domain" and the "private domain"). Here again we are, of course, dealing with abstract ideas, but the important point is that they have acquired enough force that they cannot be openly denied, or that they can serve as a point of departure for democratic demands and protests. I am tempted to say that the horizontal dimension has primacy over the vertical dimension here—that is, that the constituent relation between equality and liberty is to be found in the element of contract and exchange or, better yet, in the element of reciprocity and reciprocal utility (what the classical age called "commerce"). Conceived in this way, the relation between liberty and equality is not given immediately in its totality but is a matter of degree; it is produced in a mediate way through conflict and the adjustment of productive capacities, the measure of the "values" that individuals bring to society.

It must be said that this process of adjustment of rights and values, of opportunities for access to social recognition, has been so profoundly destabilized by capitalism that we must wonder whether its contribution to the constitution-of-citizenship of modern societies has been merely a fiction, an original "Robinsonade." But the converse could be said as well: the development of capitalism and the social struggles that accompany it have maximized the dimension of conflict in the idea of access to citizenship, corrected the illusory appearance of a purely individualistic foundation of rights and of citizenship, and closely associated the viewpoint of individual equality with that of mass society (the obsession that haunts conservative theorists). In other words it has shown that the concrete processes by which individuals accede to the guarantee of fundamental rights and the exercise of the responsibilities of a citizen always pass through the treatment of entire social conditions: not the absorption of the individual into an undifferentiated mass, but the reciprocity of perspectives between the society of individuals and mass society, between contractualism and social struggles. Which means that this may be the best way to pose the question of the relation between "permissions" and "entitlements," or individual rights and social rights, which in reality *are the same*.[28]

III

It is entirely out of the question to claim either that the constitution-of-citizenship that is on the agenda for contemporary societies could be reduced to the ancient problematic of the distribution of offices or functions of command and obedience within the polity. Nor can we claim that this constitution-of-citizenship could be presented as the direct continuation of the "insurrectional" moment that founds (more or less) democratic societies on liberty and equality, that is on the problematic coexistence of the citizen as a "sovereign subject" (or a "subject member of the sovereign") and "self-owning individual" (that is, owner of the capacity to develop his or her capacities in reciprocal commerce with other individuals). This would contradict my hypothesis that the history of citizenship is *open* to new, *nonpredetermined* developments—even if it is the case that they "result" from contradictions or crises characteristic of the limit point reached by classical citizenship, and which European unification, in the end, only makes manifest. Still, we must try to carry forward in an entirely hypothetical way the trajectory I have just sketched, so as to continue to work with the hypothesis of a dynamics of *droit de cité*, or of a conquest of autonomy with a signification on both the individual and collective levels. This is what I would like to do, very schematically and in a necessarily partial way, in my concluding considerations.

The term I use to designate the sensitive questions, which probably complement one another but whose unity is not immediately apparent, and which are not experienced in the same way by different individuals, is that of "worksites of citizenship." I use this term in order to emphasize a *pragmatic* dimension: there is matter for trial and error, for apprenticeship on the basis of collective initiatives, some "global" and others "local," as well as on the basis of experiments in thought that necessarily depend upon the conjuncture. I am thus trying, in my own way, to put into practice the principle put forth by Herman van Gunsteren: politics today is universally condemned to an unstable balance of belonging and nonbelonging. We are obliged to engage in politics and to construct its conditions and rules within the framework of communities produced by history, but which must be conceived of as "communities of fate" rather than communities of descent. The rigorous correlate of this fact is that questions of citizenship can only be posed in terms of process and access.[29] We *are not* "citizens," but we can "become" citizens; we can *enter into* one or several processes of creation of citizenship. And we enter all the more deeply into them the more numerous and more different (I would almost say the more *divergent*) we are.

I began with a reflection on the aporetic relation between citizenship and sovereignty, on the reasons that the problematic of sovereignty continues in some sense to "haunt," like a ghost, democratic constructions that think they have been freed from this "metaphysical" or "totalitarian" reference. In the course of a discussion of the successive figures of the idea of the constitution and the "autonomous" political subject that, at least ideally, corresponds to these figures, I continued to maintain that a reference to popular sovereignty cannot be eliminated (unless we were to accept the integral technicization and bureaucratization of the "law"). Here again, I would then like to base my discussion on some of the components of the classical concept of sovereignty, be it at the cost of progressively deforming their meaning and submitting them to a differential treatment. The term I will use, *mark*, is at the heart of Bodin's inaugural definition of sovereignty (a term that, significantly, is systematically overlooked by Carl Schmitt in his extremely tendentious interpretation in terms of "decision on the state of exception," an idea that is totally inappropriate for Bodin).[30] Sovereignty presents itself as a set of "marks of sovereignty," that is, domains that cannot escape public power or be shared between its specific "monopoly" and competing powers. The entire question then becomes that of the extent to which the classical state in fact succeeds in exercising this monopoly, and to which the transition to a state of "popular sovereignty" represented either a more effective solution or the appearance of a definitive aporia—that is, the beginning of an era of constitutive incompleteness of sovereignty.

Here I will rapidly discuss three of these fundamental "marks" in terms of their current pertinence, in a slightly different way than I have done elsewhere. The first one concerns political control of economic processes and in particular the state's fiscal power, which in the twentieth century appeared as the condition of any "social policy," that is, any effective recognition of social rights and incorporation of them into the system of fundamental rights. It thus furnished, in a "dialectical" way, the necessary if not sufficient condition for individuals to be able to *use the state* in such a way as to assert effectively their fundamental rights (beginning with the *right to existence*) in the face of an occult "sovereignty" (that of capital and the pure logic of accumulation).

The issue here is not merely an imbalance, created by "globalization," between the economic power of multinational corporations and the economic power of even the richest states, but a certain relation between the *people* and the *territory*. Control of the territory on which economic activity occurred and, in particular, on which capital and labor power "met" was what allowed the state to intervene at a certain moment as a "mediator" between the two and, as a consequence, to assert a political sovereignty of a democratic (or democratizable) character. But this presupposes that economic processes are fundamentally "territorialized." But we all know that this is no longer the case, or at least that it is no longer so within the same borders, the same sort of borders. Economic processes are all the less "territorialized" insofar as they include, on a massive scale, not only processes of production and distribution of consumer goods, but processes of the economy of information and knowledge, processes of the economy of human life and its planetary conditions, even processes of the economy of violence. The question posed is thus whether a unity of democratic citizenship and popular sovereignty, through the intermediary of a "reterritorialization" of the economy, that is, a territorialization with different restrictions and within different borders, is conceivable and possible today, either in terms of taxation and universal redistribution (the "Tobin tax" or something similar, which would have as its corollary the embryo of transnational public finance), or in terms of negotiated limitations on the possibilities for exploiting terrestrial matter and human matter. But there is also another question, namely whether such a territorialization of the transnational economy is possible without a rethinking of the way in which communities and human groups are attached to their own "territory." To a large extent these two questions form a logical circle, since the same process that "deterritorializes" economic values multiplies controls over the displacements of people and the possibilities of combining citizenship by birth with citizenship by residence.

The second "mark" that I would like to associate with the idea of a "worksite of citizenship" concerns what is classically called the "theologico-political" problem, which can today be reformulated as the problem of the coexistence of cultures or civilizations ("religions" obviously occupying a large part, but not all, of this domain). From this point of view, it seems to me we see the following situation: popular sovereignty in democratic national states put into place a solution that preexisted it, even if it "democratized" this solution, that is, eliminated authoritarian procedures of control of beliefs by political authority. Still, it kept and even developed (as is particularly clear in the French case) the principle of the solution, which consists in relegating competing beliefs and cultures to the "private" sphere, while developing above them a sphere of *public neutrality* that in turn develops its own forms of "conviction" or "faith" (*Gesinnung* in Hegel's terms) around the recognition of the singular link that each individual maintains with the state (and I am by no means sure that the notion of "constitutional patriotism" is any exception in this respect: by definition it is still, ideally, a patriotism). But this solution is inapplicable in today's "world cities," and more generally it is inapplicable at the level of the "world people" that exists nowhere as a totality, but that is beginning to exist locally, often at the cost of quite violent conflicts that are experienced as absolute incompatibilities between different civilizations, or different "ages" of humanity, and thus between different eschatologies or visions of the world. This amounts to saying that there can be no new "Leviathan" that would regulate beliefs and officialize knowledge ("institute the truth," as the modern state has done through its schools and universities), and there is even less possibility for a new "civic religion" that would relativize "traditional" or "revealed" religions and relegate them to private choice.[31]

The world citizens that we are in the course of becoming—or that we are trying to become, or will have to become—are thus in some sense naked and alone before the constituent task par excellence, a "sovereign" task in the sense of the construction of a sphere of political communication on the basis of conflict, a task that consists in the need to "master" the action of our own religious or quasi-religious beliefs (many of us, perhaps all of us, "are still pious," as Nietzsche said in *The Gay Science*),[32] our own "ideological passions." This does not mean that we can expect nothing from the state, from existing states, or more precisely that we cannot demand anything from them. This is why, along with many others, I attach a fundamental importance to the need for citizens, and particularly European citizens, to organize and demand the establishment of a new program of Enlightenment, which would consist not in the denunciation of religious beliefs or the repression of cultural differences but, to the contrary, in their systematic study, in the removal of the prohibitions that (at least in some countries) prevent the comparative history of religions and moral and legal systems from becoming the object of *public* instruction, and in making available to all the elementary knowledge that will allow each of us to *think other people's thoughts* instead of ignoring them and fearing them (which does not mean thinking *as others do*).

Finally, but this would lead to such a difficult discussion that it would be better not to enter into it today, although we cannot fail to mention it, there is a third "mark of sovereignty" that, as we all know, has represented the core of classical sovereignty, the "monopoly of legitimate force." This is notorious for being the least democratic (or most resistant to democratization) aspect of sovereignty, even if the era of universal military service sustained some illusions about this in an entire sector of the liberal and social-democratic tradition. I do not need to justify at length—or I would have to devote such a long exposition to this point—the idea that this mark of sovereignty is inseparable from a fundamental anthropological characteristic, namely the *masculinity of power* or, more precisely, the phallic character of the representation of the community that has been associated, even in popular sovereignty, with citizenship as national citizenship. It is by no means evident that, from this point of view, transnational or postnational citizenship represents the slightest progress. But we can pose the problem in a different way by making it a worksite of citizenship situated at the limits of any relation with sovereignty. I hope that no one will have the hypocrisy to ask women to "end war" or even put a stop to the militarization of the public sphere, but neither can we avoid the question of what degree (and what forms) of "feminization" of politics would be necessary for the "community of citizens," wherever it may be, to abandon finally that particular "substance" or identity. Such a "feminization," going beyond all demands for parity or equality of opportunity between the sexes (or genders), could only be the common labor of men and women.

I am sure that you will have understood that my goal has not been to define the form and content of a new concept of the "constitution," whose necessity and approach I do nonetheless assert, or to fix in an a priori way the respective shares that law, politics, and culture should have in it. My goal has not even been to determine if the *droit de cité* for globalized societies that we are currently constructing in unease, in fear, and perhaps in suffering needs a new assignation of sovereignty. My aim has been to show that it is indeed in the collective rewriting of the "marks" of sovereignty that a new political order can emerge that might still call itself, rightly, democratic.

Europe: Vanishing Mediator?

Being invited by the Humboldt-Universität Berlin to give this year's first public George L. Mosse Lecture is one of the greatest honors that I have received. It is also for me a moving opportunity to return to Berlin and meet dear friends and excellent colleagues. Finally, it gives me the possibility to present before you some hypotheses on the function that European intellectuals can perform and the ideas that they should advocate in the current international situation, where the very project of a European community of nations and citizens is challenged. For all these generous gifts I want to thank you very sincerely.

I am especially pleased to speak under the auspices of George Mosse. I became aware of the importance of his work rather late in my life. Since reading *Nationalism and Sexuality* and his other books dealing with the relationships between nationalism, race, gender, and sexuality in the building of modern communities, I have always considered him a master of historical and political anthropology.[1] I have also realized the extent to which his life and career, marked by the consequences of the European catastrophe of the twentieth century, and shared among the universities of three continents, form an epitome of our cosmopolitan background and a key to the intelligence of our present. I draw a permanent inspiration from them.

Allow me to begin these considerations on the uncertainties of Europe's political identity at the beginning of the twenty-first century by

This chapter is a revised and expanded version of the first George L. Mosse Lecture at Humboldt-Universität Berlin for the academic year 2002, delivered on Thursday, November 21, 2002. The Mosse Lectures are sponsored by the Mosse-Zentrum Berlin, and the Hilde Mosse Foundation, New York.

referring to celebrated formulations from another European writer who, although belonging to a previous generation and writing along quite different lines, nevertheless shared some of the same experiences, namely exile and antifascist intellectual commitment: I am thinking of Thomas Mann. As we all know, Mann's attitude toward politics completely changed between the First World War and the period of the rise of Nazism leading to the Second World War. In 1918 he published *Betrachtungen eines Unpolitischen* (*Reflections of a Nonpolitical Man*), in which he rejected "democracy" along with "politics" in the name of the alleged opposition between the spiritual notion of "culture" developed in Germany and the intellectualized notion of "civilization" developed in France.[2] But already in 1935, in Nice, before the "Comité de cooperation intellectuelle" (European Committee for Intellectual Cooperation) he launched the famous call: "Achtung Europa!" (Europe Beware!), and in a 1939 essay, "Zwang zur Politik" (literally, "No Escape from Politics," translated into English during the war under the title "Culture and Politics"), he returned to the idea of the identity of "politics" and "democracy," but drew opposite conclusions. In this essay Mann criticized any concept of culture synonymous with "political passivity" (*politische Willenslosigkeit*), and called on intellectuals not to abandon the peoples and the cause of mankind at the hour of peril.[3] I find it especially remarkable that, in the case of Mann as of Mosse, it took the detour of exile to uncover the character of the European civil war, and draw therefrom universalist conclusions. Critical consciousness seems to be closely associated here with dislocation or decentering.

Should we say that, in the current situation, where it is again a question of waging wars between "cultures" and "civilizations," an "apolitical" temptation is on the agenda among intellectuals? This is not true without exceptions, to be sure, but it does seem present, particularly in the form of resignation, even despair, a feeling of powerlessness, which seem to have grown out of two main causes. One is the sensation that— in the age of globalization—the complexity of historical and social processes has escaped the grip of collectively debated strategies and resolution of conflicts (and this is one of the reasons why conflicts tend to become catastrophic). Another is the conviction—to which some great intellectual figures of the past century themselves paradoxically contributed—that the field of intellectual intervention is now mainly "expertise," that is, a specific and specialized one, which makes it difficult or impossible to address global or universal questions if one does not want to fall prey to the media type of sheer opinion.[4] There are remarkable exceptions to this nihilistic resignation, undoubtedly, in Germany, in France, and in many other parts of the world. Powerful voices of artists, writers, philosophers from Europe, America, Africa, Asia, and the Middle East, speak and win audiences. But there is an uncertainty as to how to recreate a civic function for intellectuals and intellectuality in general.

In this lecture I want to advocate the right and duty of intellectuals to address urgent political questions with their own instruments, calling on them to reject any "nonpolitical" temptation. But I want also to take into consideration some of the reasons that account for this temptation, one of them being the uneasiness with cultural identity, and the difficulty of giving a geographical, cultural, or institutional definition of the "place" or "position" where intellectuals are working, where they could "meet," where they write and talk from. This place has become, more than ever, *intermediary, transitory,* and *dialogic.* And it has to take into account the irreversible effects of the globalization of culture—very different from a simple uniformization, indeed. It cannot keep the traditional figure of a double but fixed location that Michel Foucault called the "empirico-transcendental doublet":[5] a particular location in the nation, the idiom, the academy, and a universal one in the ideal community of mankind. Nor can we believe that, by its sole virtue, the Internet will provide a technical solution for the problem of the constitution of the "global public sphere" by granting access for all to a single system of communications and data banks. Both our singularity and our universality must adopt more complicated patterns. Intellectuals must become "nomadic," traveling physically and mentally across borders. They must take risks to elaborate the discourses and patterns of their new transnational function.

When I speak of the right and duty of the intellectuals, I am specifically thinking of *European* intellectuals. In the world today, we are already perceived and addressed not only as "French" or "German," but as "European" intellectuals. In my opinion however, European intellectuals do not sufficiently exercise their capacity to cross political and cultural borders, translate discourses (other than specialized ones) within and beyond the official limits of the European Union, set the agenda of European politics before the *Öffentlichkeit,* the "public realm," and thus actively contribute to its emergence. They are not sufficiently acting as citizens of Europe, dare I say thinking European citizens. But I am also aware of the fact that such categories as "European citizenship," "European culture," and "European intelligentsia" are much too *narrow:* not only do they grant no automatic access to universality, but they are clearly *unilateral*—something that we will need to correct when we address the question of, precisely, "unilateralism." It is one of my claims that there exists nothing such as a "synoptic" or *singular-universal* point of view from which the "characters" of the present times, and the "justice" of any politics, could be decided: neither the point of view of the empire, nor those of some nation with a "manifest destiny," the multitude of its adversaries, or any specific continental region. This is not to say that we are forever enclosed within particular interests and beliefs. But the universality that we associate with the very idea of politics and the vocation of the intellectual has to be constructed practically and empirically; it has to be approached through confrontation and conflict. One of the ways to contribute to this process, for we European intellectuals, is to listen critically to objections and calls that we receive from other parts of the world: East, West, and South, including America.

Voices from America

Since September 11, many calls are directed toward Europeans. This is flattering for us, but also embarrassing. We understand that we really exist, but we fear some misunderstanding. I shall concentrate on the calls coming from the United States and, for the sake of simplicity, I will quickly review the *official* (or quasi-official) ones that express the view of the current administration, examining in more detail those coming from the *liberal* intellectuals of America.

Some such calls come from President Bush and his group of advisers, but also from speeches and writings of those who, at least temporarily, support his politics (this was notably the case of the group of well-known intellectuals who, in the wake of the war in Afghanistan, gathered around the "propositions" of the Institute for American Values—among them such different figures as David Blankenhorn, Jean Bethke Elshtain, Francis Fukuyama, Samuel Huntington, and Michael Walzer).[6] Their formulations vary from "Wake up, Europe! Fascism is back! " to "Join us in the just war," through the now famous "Whoever is not with us is against us" (which sounds more like a threat than an appeal, in fact). They refer either to American interests or common Western interests, much less often to the interest of international law and institutions. They insist on legitimacy or on efficiency (which in a sense meet on the diplomatic terrain, where in order to rally a broad international coalition efficiently, for example, you must also be legitimate). But they remain *unilateral* insofar as they embody a strong notion of *leadership*, based on material *hegemony* and, most often, on the idea of a global *mission* of the dominant power to keep peace, order, and civilization and to protect "democratic values." This leaves little room for self-criticism, for the discussion of goals and methods, not to speak of possible contradictions between the domestic interests of the hegemonic power and the universal or common interests that it claims to represent.

We should not, however, underestimate the extent to which a broad acceptance of this point of view, which by nature doesn't seem very attractive, has been helped, not only by the *overwhelming material hegemony* (economic and military as well as ideological, following the collapse of communism and Third World nationalism) of the American "hyperpower," but also by the traumatic effects of the September 11 attack on Manhattan: the "world city," the cosmopolitan city par excellence.[7] In a sense the United States "enjoys" a paradoxical combination of opposite statuses: dominant hyperpower *and* victim, a situation that produces powerful effects of identification.

Quite different, however, are the calls coming from the liberal intellectuals of America ("liberal" in the sense that, despite their obvious divergences, since they range politically from socialism to neorepublicanism, they advocate the same basic principles: the civil rights and legal protections of the individual are inalienable, governments are accountable before their constituencies, civil authorities must rule over the military, international law has primacy over national interests). This call is indeed self-critical; it is voiced by a "minority" that wants to distinguish itself from the "majority" in its own country, criticizing the choices that are imposed by the majority and their elected representatives. It is a call not only for *support* but also for *help* ("Help us, Europe!"), implying that the Europeans should *influence* American internal and external politics, for the sake of Europe itself, for the sake of America, and for the sake of all the others. The underlying idea ("multilateralist" in the broad sense) is that in a globalized world no power (not even the biggest) can "save" itself *alone* (not to speak of saving the others), but that it could very well "doom" itself and the others.

I shall recall some of the voices from America that could be heard in this sense in the last months, insisting at the same time on the importance of the idea that they contain and on some of the antinomies that I think they involve. I have selected four significant (and very diverse) voices: Bruce Ackerman, Immanuel Wallerstein, Timothy Garton Ash, and Edward Said.

To begin, Bruce Ackerman. In February 2002, the prominent jurist and political philosopher from Yale published an article in the *London Review of Books* with the title "Don't Panic!" Ackerman begins with the idea that "the attack of 11 September is the prototype of similar events that will litter the 21st century," and that "if American reaction is any guide, we urgently require new constitutional concepts to deal with the protection of civil liberties." Otherwise, he prophesies, "a downward cycle threatens. . . . Even if the next half-century sees only four or five attacks on the scale of 11 September, this destructive cycle will prove devastating to civil liberties by 2050." However, he does not see "an absolutist defense of traditional freedom" as the right response on the part of liberals (Ackerman defines himself as a *civil libertarian*). Not only would it not allow any democratic government to achieve popular support and would not help preventing future terrorist strikes, but it would leave totally unanswered the constitutional problems that emerge in situations of crisis. Declaring his concern to "prevent politicians from exploiting momentary panic to impose long-lasting limitations on liberty," Ackerman is especially critical of the notion of "war on terrorism" (a "war" already announcing itself as "without end"), which can and will be used both to cancel civil liberties (for Americans and non-Americans alike) and to destroy the democratic balance of powers between the administration, Congress, and the judiciary. What he advocates is a carefully controlled "state of emergency" with legal and temporal limits, where as many "normal" institutions as possible keep working under internal and external scrutiny of the "defenders of freedom." And he concludes:

> Europe is already influencing this political dynamic. The Spanish Government's refusal to hand over suspected terrorists has checked the Bush Administration's ardour for military tribunals. The French citizenship of the suspected "20th terrorist" helped persuade the Attorney General to try Zacarias Moussaoui in a civilian court. . . . In the future, it will not be enough to defeat proposals that threaten permanent damage to civil liberties. . . . A framework law emerging from any major European state would have worldwide influence. It would help us see the "war on terrorism" for what it is: an extravagant

metaphor blocking responsible thought about a serious problem.[8]

Even if you take into account that this was written for a European journal, it remains surprising and striking. The appeal seems to imply that certain traditions rooted in European politics form a legal pole of resistance against the tendencies toward the *militarization of politics*, inside and outside America, that threatens the very values in whose name the "war on terrorism" is declared and fought. It also suggests that Europe should and could act as a bulwark of *international law*, which is an essential safeguard against the corruption of constitutional principles (in particular, the balance of powers that lies at the core of American constitutionalism), that could result from a "war without an (ascribed) end," in other terms a permanent state of exception.

I want to take my second example from a very different author and context. In a public lecture delivered in December 2002, the Marxist historian and social scientist Immanuel Wallerstein, director of the Fernand Braudel Center at the State University of New York at Binghamton, explained how he saw the prospects of relationships between the United States and the world after the revelation of a completely new situation that the destruction of the twin towers had represented for Americans.[9] In the first part of his talk, he reminds us that the United States "had always defined itself by the yardstick of the world," which seemed to prove its continuous superiority.[10] In the second part ("Attack on America"), he quotes from Osama bin Laden's presentation of America as a "depraved" country, showing that bin Laden was the first person in history to become able to translate very widespread anti-American feelings into a physical attack initiated on American soil that left it momentarily helpless. As a consequence, a "war on terrorism" was declared, with "no reservations," that is, including measures against internal enemies. "It is clear at this point that, even if the events of September 11 will not alter the basic geopolitical realities of the contemporary world, they may have a lasting impact on American political structures."[11] In a certain sense, the powerful America discovers or fears to discover that it is vulnerable. In his third part ("America and World Power"), Wallerstein discusses the vulnerabilities of American hegemony, by comparing it with previous examples in history. Wallerstein's thesis is that the hegemony of the United States is no longer based on unchallenged economic superiority but only on military capacity. He describes the successive strategies that were implemented after World War II to eliminate forces and powers considered adversary to American interests in the world: containment, neutralization, interventions, subversion, and selective "antiproliferation" military policies:

> As a policy, non-proliferation seems doomed to failure. . . . But there is also a moral/political question here. . . . The U.S. trusts itself to use such [nuclear] weapons wisely, and in the defense of liberty (a concept seemingly identical with U.S. national interests). It assumes that anyone else might intend to use such weapons against liberty. . . . Personally, I do not trust any government to use such weapons wisely. I would be happy to see them all banned, but do not believe this is truly enforceable in the contemporary interstate system. So personally I abstain from moralizing on this issue.[12]

In his fourth part ("America: Ideals versus Privilege") Wallerstein distinguishes between the belief that "America and Americans are the cause of all the world's miseries and injustices," which he denies, and the belief that "they are their prime beneficiaries," which he endorses.[13] He expresses his fear that America, while trying to "rebuild" the power that the Twin Towers symbolized, might sacrifice the ideals of freedom and universality that went along with the traditional privileges. Finally, in his last part ("America: From Certainty to Uncertainty"), contrasting a rational view of the uncertainties of the world's future with the irrational attempt by President Bush to "offer the American people certainty about their future . . . the one thing totally beyond his power to offer," he addresses his fellow Americans with an eloquent plea for a contribution to the rebuilding of the world based on equality instead of privilege, universality instead of globalization. This is where a reference to Europe (among others) surfaces again:

> What the United States needs now to do is to learn how to live with the new reality—that it no longer has the power to decide unilaterally what is good for everyone. . . . It has to come to terms with the world. It is not Osama bin Laden with whom we must conduct a dialogue. We must start with our near friends and allies—with Canada and Mexico, with Europe, with Japan. And once we have trained ourselves to hear them and to believe that they too have ideals and interests, that they too have hopes and aspirations, then and only then perhaps shall

we be ready to dialogue with the rest of the world, that is, with the majority of the world.[14]

I understand Wallerstein's position as expressing a neo-universalist perspective. It takes the form of a defense of *multilateralism* against the attempt to recreate the conditions of a past economic hegemony through the implementation of a military superiority that remains unchallenged at its own level, but is entirely vulnerable to the new kind of threat that develops *within the limits* of the dominant system. It should be a permanent concern, therefore, to resist the polarization of the world into the mimetic figures of *Leviathan* (the world monopoly of "legitimate" violence) and *Behemoth* (the ubiquitous power of subversion based on "fundamentalist" religious creeds). Accordingly, it would be necessary to recreate a *multipolar equilibrium* of forces (be they national or postnational) that counteracts this polarization. In a more recent talk delivered at the World Social Forum in Porto Alegre, Wallerstein has publicly endorsed the necessity of backing the development of the European Union, precisely in order to counteract the American hegemony, even if Europe is also an "imperialist" power (there are "primary" and "secondary" contradictions—remember Mao!). A multipolar world offers more possibilities for democracy and social transformations than a world with a single superpower.[15]

I borrow my third example from the article published in the *New York Times* last April by the British historian and expert on Eastern European affairs, Timothy Garton Ash (who teaches in Oxford but also works at the Hoover Institution in Stanford University), with the unambiguous title: "The Peril of Too Much Power."[16] This is also a voice "from America." Professor Garton Ash begins by stating that "for most of the 20th century, the defining political question was: What do you think of Russia? At the beginning of the 21st century, it is: What do you think of America?" He deems the picture of America as "a dangerous selfish giant, blundering around the world" and "an anthology of what is wrong with capitalism" to be a caricature, especially if this serves to prove the moral superiority of Europe: "Of course America can't be reduced in this way. Apart from anything else, it is much too large, too diverse, too much a cornucopia of combinations and contradictions to allow any simple interpretation."

He goes on to recall how "America is part of everyone's imaginative life, through movies, music, television and the Web, whether you grow up in Bilbao, Beijing or Bombay. Everyone has a New York in their heads, even if they have never been there." In a sense it is not the existence of an American culture that is doubtful but rather that of a European one. But then comes the problem of the use of America's power and the effects of the enormous imbalance of power in the world. Not since Rome has a single power enjoyed such superiority, he explains, "but the Roman colossus only bestrode one part of the world. Stripped of its anti-American overtones, the French foreign minister Hubert Vedrine's term *hyperpower* is apt. . . . The fundamental problem is that America today has too much power for anyone's good, including its own." The example of U.S. policy in the Middle East clearly shows that there is a problem both when the Americans intervene and when they refuse to intervene. "When a nation has so much power, what it doesn't do is as fateful as what it does." Professor Garton Ash especially fears the consequences of a possible American (or American-led) war in Iraq, without any simultaneous initiative to negotiate a settlement of the Israeli-Palestinian conflict, which would unite the Islamic world against the West while dividing Europe from America, "with disastrous consequences for years to come." Finally he explains that, since "contrary to what many Europeans think, the problem with American power is not that it is *American*" but that it is *unchecked*. What applies to domestic politics (and is embodied in the American Constitution), namely the necessity for each power to be "checked by at least one other," also applies in world politics, hence the crucial question: "Who, then, should check and complement American power?" The internal democratic controls are no longer sufficient or working. "International agencies, starting with the United Nations, and transnational nongovernmental organizations are a place to start. But they alone are not enough. My answer is Europe—Europe as an economic equal to the United States and Europe as a close-knit group of states with a long diplomatic and military experience." A difficulty remains, however: "[T]he gulf between its military capacity and that of the U.S. grows ever wider." Europeans therefore face a "complicated double task": "to strengthen [their] capacity to act outside [their] own borders while disentangling the idea of a stronger Europe from its sticky anti-American integument." To make, in short, Europe a "partner" (with a capacity to resist), but not a "rival" of the United States. Timothy Garton Ash firmly believes that the United States itself has no real interest to remain in the position of "lonely" hyperpower.

Finally, I want to quote from a recent article by Edward Said (the Palestinian-American professor at Columbia University, author of *Orientalism* and *Culture and Imperialism* among other books): "Europe versus America."[17] Reporting from England, where he is currently teaching, Said emphasizes cultural differences between the United States and Europe, especially the disproportionate power of religious fundamentalism : "[R]eligion and ideology play a far greater role in the former than in the latter. . . . [T]he vast number of Christian fanatics in the US . . . form the core of George Bush's support and at 60 million strong represent the single most powerful voting block in US history." This American fundamentalism has merged with the conservative ideology of "American values" developed during the Cold War and has become "a menace to the world." It produces the "unilateralist" external policy, the belief that the United States as an "elect nation" has a divine mission to be fulfilled by all means. This leads to the only seemingly paradoxical combination of deep anti-Semitism ("these Christians . . . believe that all the Jews of the world must gather in Israel so that the Messiah can come again") and the global threat against the Arab-Islamic world confronting Israel. Said embarks then on a synthetic comparison of the ideologies and the political systems on both sides of the Atlantic: "There is no trace of this sort of thing in Europe that I can detect. Nor is there that lethal combination of money and power on a vast scale that controls elections and national policy at will." For Said, Europe remains more democratic in practice, the citizens have more effective control over the politicians and are less exposed to ideological blackmail when they dissent from the official policy (to be "un-American" is the cardinal sin), and have a less Manichaean view of the world. "No wonder then that America has never had an organized Left or real opposition party as has been the case in every European country."

But finally comes the concern, which is double: that Europe might lose its political identity, and that it might prove unable to act as a pole of resistance against American unilateralism: "Tony Blair's wholeheartedly pro-American position therefore seems even more puzzling to an outsider like myself. I am comforted that even to his own people he seems like a humourless aberration, a European who has decided in effect to obliterate his own identity. . . . I still have time to learn when it will be that Europe will come to its senses and assume the countervailing role to America that its size and history entitle it to play. Until then the war approaches inexorably."

Contradictions and Illusions

We certainly cannot ignore this call coming from the intellectuals of America (and also from other parts of the world, although not exactly in the same terms: each would deserve a special analysis). It really touches our common interests. We may observe that all these texts have a certain "family resemblance." But we suspect that they include deep contradictions, and we fear that they have substituted an imaginary Europe for the real one.

Obviously (and understandably), some American liberals share the view that America is the model democracy; they are especially concerned with the future of democracy in America, which they think should be an interest of the whole world, whereas others—from a more "global" or "systemic" point of view—believe that the democratic character of the United States will itself entirely depend on the way America behaves toward the rest of the world (any country that oppresses others cannot be itself a free country). Even more striking are the diverse ways in which these voices refer to the great divides of the world after the Cold War. Some of them ask us to be fully "Western," but others want us to be properly "European," that is, to destroy the false identity of the Western world (or bloc)—thus perhaps pushing America more effectively in the direction of its own "European" traditions. Others imagine that Europe may become the intermediary, at least one of the intermediaries in the great "negotiation" that should take place in the end : between the American "Empire" and its real "others," the peoples and cultures from East and South, the Mediterranean, the Third World. These considerable differences are indeed mirrored in our own reactions.

But what I find even more striking is the latent tension between two opposite ways of formulating the call to Europe: either as a demand for a *check and balance*, in order to countervail the American (super) power, or a demand for *mediation* within the "war of civilizations" that America is now apparently waging. If you choose the first formulation, you are in a "strategic" logic, where the relationships of forces ultimately resolve into military terms, quantitatively and qualitatively (how many troops and weapons, and how do you use them?). Why address Europe in this case rather than, say, Russia, Japan, or China? Perhaps because the authors of these texts more or less transfer onto Europe the ideal model of "force merged with right" (the rule of law, the constitution of liberty) that they fear America has now betrayed. If you choose the second formulation, you are in a logic of "moral" and "social" influences, which certainly does not ignore relationships of forces, but sees them as only one aspect of a more comprehensive process of cultural transformation. In that case, the apparently irreversible gap in military power between the United States and Europe is not necessarily a handicap for Europe. But the question of whether it really displays an *alternative* to American policy becomes more embarrassing. Clearly, "multilateralism" does not mean exactly the same thing from these two points of view. The first is compatible with a confrontation between rival "isolationisms" (more or less what has been reproached to Chancellor Gerhard Schröder during his last electoral campaign, when he "unilaterally" announced that Germany would not follow the United States in any war in Iraq),[18] whereas the second implies that political isolation today, among allies or even adversaries, has become obsolete and impossible to achieve. Rather than a "right of intervention," what we are confronted with would be a "fact of intervention," that is, interdependence: we cannot ignore it, only perhaps organize it and modify its consequences.

Certainly it would be interesting to examine how certain European voices, official or not, reacted to these demands. But let me refer instead to the way they have been quickly refuted in America. I am thinking in particular of the essay on "Power and Weakness" published by the former State Department expert and member of the Carnegie Endowment for International Peace, Robert Kagan, which has received considerable attention on both sides of the Atlantic.[19] "It is time to stop pretending that Europeans and Americans share a common view of the world, or even that they occupy the same world," writes Kagan, who is targeting the kind of "European opinion" on whose emergence and development American liberals place their hopes. "Europeans believe they are moving beyond power into a self-contained world of laws and rules and transnational negotiation and cooperation." But, while Europe would have entered "a post-historical paradise, the realization of Immanuel Kant's *perpetual peace*," the United States "remains mired in history, exercising power in the anarchic Hobbesian world where international rules are unreliable and where security and the promotion of a liberal order still depend on the possession and use of military might."[20]

One may wonder, then, whence the European rejection of the use of force as a means to solve international conflicts originates? This is not, according to Kagan, because Europeans possess a special character or nature: in past centuries, when they dominated the world, they never tired of using force to increase or keep their power, but they have become weaker, and quite simply they no longer have the capacities for power politics. Europe and America have "exchanged" their political cultures, as it were: it is now Europe that has adopted the Wilsonian discourse, dreaming of "civilizing the world" by putting an end to the wars and doing away with *Machtpolitik*, whose terrible effects Europeans have lived on their own soil. A nice project indeed but with one proviso: what makes European pacifism and moral consciousness materially possible is American military power itself! "The irony is that this trans-Atlantic disagreement is the fruit of successful trans-Atlantic policies. As Joschka Fischer and other Europeans admit, the United States made the new Europe possible by leading the democracies to victory in World War II and the Cold War and by providing the solution to the age-old 'German problem.' Even today, Europe's rejection of power politics ultimately depends on America's willingness to use force around the world against those who still do believe in power politics. Europe's Kantian order depends on the United States using power according to the old Hobbesian rules." Most Europeans do not realize that they can project themselves into "post-history" or "post-modern history" only because the United States did not follow this path. But as a result "this has put Europeans and Americans on a collision course."[21] Formally speaking, they remain allies, but the former see the latter as a "rogue colossus," and the latter see the former as a virtual obstacle, if not a potential traitor. Perhaps it would be better to acknowledge this contradiction, rather than desperately trying to fill the cultural gap.

I don't believe that I distort the meaning of Robert Kagan's analysis if I say in a nutshell: the "European" position, expressing something like a religion of law, is at the same time *powerless* ("Europe? how many divisions?" we might ask, echoing a famous question raised by Stalin), and *illegitimate* (since it disguises a historical regression as moral progress, misrepresenting its real weakness as an imaginary strength). Finally it is *self-destructive*: it undermines the defensive capacities of the Western democracies, everywhere under attack in the world, which remain its only safety. It is decidedly not America that has "too much power"; it is Europe that has too little.

A double question is at stake here. *There is a first question concerning the "power" of Europe.* In a sense, Europe as a sum is even *less* powerful (not *more*) than some of its constitutive nation-states, or its power is less effective, more difficult to implement (hence the project of many: to "reinforce" it, to achieve more "integration"). *There is also a second question concerning the "political capacity" of Europe* in today's world, in particular its capacity to help resolve conflicts (be they "old" or "new" in Mary Kaldor's terms),[22] and hence the concept of the political by which this capacity can be measured.

Here is the position that I want now to develop: undoubtedly, from a certain point of view, *Europe does not exist; it is not a political* "*subject*" (the subject of a political power). And in this sense to ask Europe to disturb the ongoing processes and plans, to "check and balance" other powers, is a pure illusion. But on the other hand you cannot (or you can less and less) reduce the idea of "mediation" to *the alternative of power politics (ultimately relying upon military force) and "moral" powerlessness,* even if you admit that a diplomatic and institutional expression has to be found for such a mediation at some moment. The question then becomes: how to imagine *a change in the relationship between "politics" and "power" or, perhaps better, in the very notion of "power."*

I agree that European political capacity, which is a necessary condition of its autonomy, in a sense simply does not exist. "Economic weight" is a weak argument, especially in a globalized economy. Even if you crown it with a (partially) common currency, it represents only a variable statistical aggregate, precisely so long as no corresponding "strategy" or "economic (therefore also social) policy" exists. If you reflect further on the recent confrontation at the United Nations Security Council about the right of the United States to launch what it called a "preventive war" against Iraq, which (provisionally) ended with a compromise (the United States accepting an international procedure that, at least in theory, leaves Iraq the possibility to prove its "innocence"),[23] you see clearly that it is not "Europe" that, to some extent, has checked American power. It is a conjunctural (and highly fragile) convergence of middle-range powers (France, Germany, Russia, China, Mexico) that refused to become completely "marginalized" in international relations. They are not all of Europe, and not all of them are European. In addition, they would not have achieved anything without certain internal divisions within American strategy itself.

Above all, there is a strong case to be made for Europe's incapacity to *solve its own problems without American "help."* When I say its "own" problems, I am also thinking of neighboring problems where Europe is necessarily involved. This is exactly the opposite of the liberal dream, but there are numerous dramatic and recent examples, of which we can list but a few. Europe remains unable to solve the Irish problem, where two of its old nations are involved, each with its own "diaspora." It proved unable to prevent the civil war in (former) Yugoslavia, which produced the worst crimes against humanity since Nazism, whether by offering a framework for development and coexistence to the various Balkan communities (which belong since time immemorial to the European ensemble) or by launching a military intervention to neutralize the agressors and protect the populations with some chance of success (when this was finally undertaken by NATO under American leadership, it was with questionable results). The United States then has good reasons to explain that, beginning with the two world wars, it has been American intervention that has stopped bloodshed and opposed savagery on European soil (although Americans tend to "forget" that the Soviet "patriotic war" against Nazism played an equally important role, which the contemporaries still remember, associating Omaha Beach with Stalingrad in their memories of World War II). What seems to be a characteristic of the twentieth century, and could characterize the twenty-first as well, is not a "European mediation" in conflicts involving America, but rather an "American mediation" in conflicts that rend Europe and prove that it is unable to provide an effective political expression for the historical and moral identity it claims to represent.

This is equally true concerning the way Europe deals with violent situations that have developed at its "borders" (and, in fact, where it is so intimately mixed, and affected, that the distinction with the previous "internal" cases sometimes seems quite artificial). Algeria, Palestine-Israel, Chechnya: these are the names of a long series of shameful collective resignations of Europe. Each time in different ways, tracing back to colonial history, to its own ethnic and religious divisions, its wars and genocides, Europe was involved as a cause or a mirror of these "impossible to solve" conflicts, whose continuous degradation threatens its own civility and moral identity. History seems to show that any political entity (call it a "state" in the broad sense), in order to exist, needs an "idea" or a universal project to unify its human and material forces. But Europe's project can no longer be to subjugate the world, as in the colonial era. Nor can it be a messianic project of announcing (after the Christian or the communist model) the birth of the "new man." Europe can indeed try to exercise a "civilizing" influence in the world, as well as to build the moral conditions of its own construction, but in order to do so it has to be more active. By abandoning the Chechens to the total war waged against them by post-Soviet Russia, Europe keeps in the traditional line of blindness before genocidal processes, and it practically denies the "European" character of Russia, destroying the possibilities of finally lifting the "iron curtain" (or its latest replica). The Russians can do what they like, they are not "applying" to the European Union. By practically endorsing the plans of the U.S.-Israel alliance in the Middle East (with some limited counterweights: periodical statements that the United Nations resolutions should be enforced, humanitarian projects that neither protect the Palestinians from colonization and state terrorism nor completely convince them to reject terrorism), the Europeans help the development of a new "generalized" anti-Semitism in the world, where judeophobia and arabophobia paradoxically merge. By keeping silent on the crimes of the Algerian army (which seem to match the crimes of the Islamic terrorist groups) and backing the repression of democratic movements by other authoritarian regimes in North Africa, while at the same time racially and culturally discriminating against their own "immigrant" populations from the Maghreb, they provoke a disastrous collapse of the "Euro-Mediterranean" project (a theme to which I return).

But, we may ask, is this the only way to analyze the situation? I would suggest that the new "global" conjuncture offers other alternatives. Undoubtedly the cultural divisions and conflicting interests of the world also affect us in Europe and could become acute. There is to date no strong symbol of a common identity that could help neutralize or suppress them. Undoubtedly Europe and America are not separated spaces, any more than Europe and Eurasia, or Europe and the Middle East. In this respect some countries owe to their history or their geography or their demographic composition the virtual capacity to "open gates" and "build bridges." Whether you think of Britain, the Ukraine, Turkey, or the Balkans, it would be absurd to forcefully locate them on a single side of an external "European border." Undoubtedly Europe does not have the capacity to build a *Grossraum* on the continent, to impose a kind of European "Monroe Doctrine" (a geostrategic idea that was invented in the 1930s by Carl Schmitt to justify German imperialism and that is now retrieved by some in a democratic context).[24] But you can read all this in the opposite sense. No European "identity" can be *opposed* to others in the world because there exist no absolute *border lines* between the historical and cultural territory of Europe and the surrounding spaces. There exist no absolute border lines *because Europe as such is a "border line"* (or "a Borderland," to borrow Scott Malcomson's beautiful title for a beautiful book on the Bosphorus and its region).[25] More precisely it is a superposition of border lines, hence a superposition of heterogeneous relations to the other histories and cultures of the world (at least many of them), which are reproduced within its own history and culture.

We must therefore concentrate our attention on a very singular pattern of dialectical interactions between the "interior" and the "exterior." This was precisely the theme of a recent essay by the director of the Institut français des Relations Internationales, Thierry de Montbrial, acting chair of the French Académie des Sciences morales et politiques, "Europe: La Dialectique intérieur-extérieur."[26] After many others, Montbrial draws lessons from the recent international events. He too agrees that there is an amazing disproportion between Europe's limited influence in international negotiations and its economic prosperity, a military gap that automatically confers upon the United States the responsibility of decision making in security matters, and he pictures a sharp contrast between Europe's incapacity to define a common foreign policy and the "strong demand upon Europe" that he perceives in the world, from the former Soviet Empire to Latin America. He quotes from a "Brazilian authority" who would explain this "insufficient offer" as a consequence of Europe's remaining "ashamed of the way it destroyed itself in the first half of the 20th century." His own explanation is different, however, taking the form of a dialectical reversal. In the history of the building of nation-states, it was the strong preexisting national unity, the feelings of belonging and identity, that made it possible for the state to mobilize all the human and material resources needed to achieve international goals. But now, in the case of the European unification, however impressive the achievements since 1957 may appear, the reverse is true: a "European Europe" can emerge only if foreign policy shapes domestic policy. A truly unified foreign policy and defense policy are impossible in the immediate situation, but a "combined intervention" of European nations in the "high politics" of world affairs (decisions concerning war and peace, as in the case of Iraq, for example) can result from a permanent alliance between the three major European powers (Great Britain, France, and Germany) if they agree to consult each other following certain established rules.

This idea of a "dialectical relationship" between interior and exterior is well meant, but I fear there is something like a *petitio principii* in the (very conventional) way it is used here. Why should it be easier for a "common political will" to emerge at the level of the three European "great powers" (in reality, medium powers), rather than at the level of all members of the European Union, or rather than developing a majoritarian opinion on the European scale, especially when it comes to discussing "world affairs"? The reverse could very well be the case. But above all I think that the change of method as it is advocated here should be much more radical, if we are to cope with the new situation we have entered. I myself would suggest that we must draw all the consequences from the fact that *Europe is a borderland* rather than an entity that "has" *borders* (or "will have" them in the future). This quite naturally leads us to completely reexamine the relationships between "strategy," "power," "agency," and "subjectivity" (or "identity"). In order to overcome the dilemma of a strategy that presupposes the autonomy of the subject that conceives and implements it, *agency* must have a privilege over *identity*. What is at stake is indeed a complete change in the way *relations of power* are calculated, imputed, and recognized on the world scale.

Toward a European "Antistrategic" Policy?

I am convinced that only a transformation in the way we understand the concept of politics in relation with the idea of "power" will allow us to begin to escape the aporias affecting the notion of a "European policy" and to give a realistic content to the notion of a "European mediation," which combines such opposite demands as increasing Europe's specific role in world affairs and deconstructing the myths of European closure and exclusive identity ("Fortress Europe," to quote its most aggressive formulation). How then both to *individualize and desubstantialize Europe?* Is that really possible?

It will become possible only if, reacting to the calls addressed to us and drawing lessons from historical experience, we criticize to the roots the proposition presupposed by most of the arguments concerning politics and power: that an efficient action can take place only when the agent has an exclusive control over some resources and is able to use them as a unified "sovereign subject," at the very least enjoying a stable and recognized identity. This was typically the objective of the classical nation-states, and the European Union seems to be in permanent search of similar constitutional and administrative tools to achieve the same result. What I suggest is that we need to explore a completely different path, where *power does not predate action but is rather its result*, in a sense that depends upon the goals that one wants to achieve. It is action, or agency, that produces the degree and distribution of power, not the reverse. As Michel Foucault used to explain, agency is "power acting upon power"; therefore it is the (efficient) use of *the other's power*, also resulting from its own orientation.[27] For the same reason, a "collective identity" is not a given, a metaphysical prerequisite of agency, and it is certainly not a mythical image that could be forcefully imposed upon reality by inventing this or that historical criterion (for example, "Christian Europe").[28] It is a *quality* of collective agency, which changes form and content in time, as new agents come into play and new solidarities are built among those who, not long ago, were ignoring or fighting each other.

It will be useful to remind ourselves, in a schematic manner, of historical experiences that contributed to shaping contemporary Europe, especially in the past century. The lessons that we can draw from them are clearly not beyond dispute; they can be interpreted diversely in different places on the continent and according to the social and political affiliations of each of us. But they have become to a large extent part of our collective memory, which is active in our intellectual elaborations and the institutional realities of Europe.

A first lesson—let us call it *the lesson of tragedy*, because it concerns the "civil wars" that devastated the European community of peoples—seems initially to be purely negative. However, it gives its deep roots to what I would call, following Monique Chemillier-Gendreau, a "transnational public order" (not reducible to a form of moral "pacifism") that contradicts the "Clausewitzian" equivalence of the "means" of war and the "means" of politics.[29] Retrospectively, the interstate national wars that periodically broke into the history of the "peoples" and modified their respective powers, leading in the end to the mass exterminations during the world wars and even after (as I recalled), are only one aspect of a more general system of violent conflicts, which includes also "wars" between classes, religious communities, ideologies. Always distinguishing clearly what mainly depends on ethnic or religious as opposed to social and ideological determinations is far from easy. If a lesson can be drawn from the long twentieth-century "European civil war,"[30] it should be that no "absolute victory" is possible, no final suppression or neutralization of the "enemy." Whenever you believe to be able to reach this "final" solution, you create the conditions for more destruction and self-destruction. Mutual extermination as such does not have an "end"— or, better said, it can reach an end only when it is radically deprived of its legitimacy, and if collective institutionalized counterpowers emerge.

But this is an incomplete lesson and, in some sense, a blind one. It takes the problem of violence *within a "metropolitan" framework* that cannot really be isolated. Only recently, and with considerable difficulties, have we become conscious of the fact that "barbarity" indeed circulated for centuries between the dominant center and the dominated periphery. The critical labor of memory concerning the violence of European conquest and rule did not immediately start with decolonization but long after the event, as in the case of the French War in Algeria. It was clearly encouraged by the massive presence, increasingly legitimate in spite of all the remaining discriminations, of "postcolonial" populations within the European nations. Much remains to be uncovered and acknowledged, but this growing consciousness of the realities of colonial history, a history that has made Europe what it is, has now profoundly disturbed Eurocentric visions that used to contrast "our" civilization with "their" barbarity: the greatest barbarity certainly was not on the side that we imagined, although it is not an "imperialist" privilege either (witness the tragic development of postcolonial ethnic conflicts in Africa and elsewhere). The *positive* counterpart of all this is a powerful, irreversible phenomenon of hybridization and multiculturalism now transforming Europe in a way that considerably differs from the American "melting pot," even if you consider such "cosmopolitan" cities as New York and Los Angeles. It started with specific, reciprocal ties between former metropolises and their former empires (France and northern and western Africa, Britain and India, Pakistan, and the West Indies, the Netherlands and Indonesia), but is now quite generalized as a pattern of interaction between Europe as such and its "exterior." If the first lesson to be drawn from recent European history could be called a tragic lesson of public order, we might call this other one a lesson of *otherness*. It leads Europe to recognize, albeit with considerable hesitations and drawbacks, that the Other is a necessary component of its "identity," therefore its future vitality, its "power."

I would like to add a third lesson. It cannot be isolated from the other aspects of European history but has its own specific implications. It concerns the possibility of a gradual transformation of the violence of social antagonisms into collective political capacities by combining the different resources of *institutionalizing conflicts* (providing antagonistic interests with a formal "representation" within the state, instead of suppressing and criminalizing them), setting up *public and private* instances of social regulation (or distributing in a more or less stable manner the regulating functions between "law" and "contract"), and progressively introducing *new basic rights*, which add new positive "liberties" or, as Amartya Sen calls them, "capabilities,"[31] to the existing rights of the individual, thus becoming an essential component of citizenship. We might call this lesson "Machiavelli's Theorem," referring to the political model that can be found in famous pages in his *Discorsi sopra la prima deca di Tito Livio*.[32]

I would admit that globalization has weakened this lesson, or confronts it with a dilemma, because it places nation-states in a defensive position, restricting their possibilities to mediate social conflicts and leaving without solution the urgent problem of the constitution of a new "citizenship" in Europe. But the fact remains that Europe, in this respect, has a singular, if not privileged, position in the world. Europe certainly has no monopoly of pluralist representative democracy. But its own history of social movements (acute class struggles, if we want to be explicit) has produced a level of institutional recognition of basic social rights that is still unrivaled in today's world. It has no monopoly of either religious tolerance or intolerance. But its own history of confessional divisions, heresies, and wars of religions has produced a form of "secularization" of politics and society that goes far beyond the classical idea of "tolerance," allowing a recognition that religious memberships are an important aspect of the constitution of the "civil society" but without either creating state religions or, conversely, accepting a "free" development of religious sects in the form of what Max Weber called the "market of salvation goods."[33]

It would seem that this last lesson has to do with an original elaboration of *conflictual democracy*, where different heterogeneous constitutional principles are combined (therefore contributing to a revival of the old notion of the "mixed constitution," but again in a way that significantly differs from the American experience). This combination includes a development of *legal or formal democracy*, making sure that the individuals who vindicate them are recognized, ultimately, as the true bearers of rights. It also includes a development of *social* or *substantial democracy*, making sure that inequalities are addressed and conflictual interests taken into account, so that individual freedom is not pure and simply equivalent with competition, and competition with an elimination of the weakest within the "city." Finally, it refers to an idea of *expansive democracy* (in the language of Antonio Gramsci) or *democratic invention* (in the language of Claude Lefort), which means that politics remains open to the integration of new elements into the "common part" of mankind, and there can be no "end of history."[34]

I would not be misunderstood: none of these "lessons" seems to me irreversible, valid forever, or unquestionable. All of them remain clearly fragile and ambiguous. After experiencing extermination processes on its own soil, Europe believed that it had become the natural champion of international law, which in many cases it does not obey itself. It has become conscious of the positive value of the other as such, but it keeps excluding people by systematically combining criteria of culture (practically equivalent to race) and economic discrimination. To be poor and colored in Europe is not a good situation; it means overexploitation and insecurity, a condition of pariah. Europe has invented a secular state and society but in an environment where Christian denominations were completely dominant. Many European historians and theologians even believe that it is Christianity that has separated the sacred and the secular realms in general. As a consequence secularism can be brandished as a shield against other forms of religious universalism (above all Islam), antagonistic with Christianity, and becomes an instrument to protect "domestic" cults (the attitude toward Judaism in this respect being highly ambivalent, combining age-old anti-Semitism with the recognition generated by the Holocaust). The dominant form of European "secularism" (this is particularly the case with French *laïcité*) is also a form of resistance to real multiculturalism, since many cultures are deemed to be too "religious" to become acceptable in the picture. This is not far from transforming Western culture into a secular form of religion indeed. Finally the "European" conception of conflictual democracy that I have described is more a past ideal than a living reality today: it has a tendency to return to purely corporatist forms, since economic deregulation and globalization deprive it of its material possibilities to protect citizens from the brutal variations in the labor market and the continuous decrease in the level of welfare.

These deep contradictions, however, are part of a dynamic whose consequences should and could be to continue and broaden the European experience of politics by mobilizing all our forces, be they economic, cultural, intellectual, social, or legal, but also "external" forces, to transform international relations. Such a project is not an exercise of power politics; it does not aim at constituting a new (great) power, but rather at constituting a *new type of power*, one that nobody can appropriate (not even the forces that could more effectively push in that direction). This type of power is essentially a new *correlation among the existing forces*; it becomes effective inasmuch as structures and relations of forces are evolving, and resistances and alternatives to the dominant tendencies become more consistent. This explains why I preferred the expression "antistrategic politics." But it is not to say that we can do without initiatives, orientations, and even mottoes. I have no intention to define a "program," but I will try to list some priorities, being aware that they concern long term evolutions, where obstacles and setbacks and rectifications will inevitably take place.

Collective Security: For Protection, against Fortifications

In order to transform international relations, we need a *model of collective security* that can open the possibility of escaping the confrontation between "terrorist" and "counterterrorist" forces. But the notion of "collective security," which is constitutive of the texts on which international institutions are based (in particular the Charter of the United Nations),[35] can not remain purely formal. It cannot simply demand that the use of military force be subjected to the (admittedly very restrictive) conditions registered in international law. It must become (again) a *political goal* and therefore involve *decisions* on certain crucial issues. In my view the demarcation line clearly passes between a *necessity* and an *impossibility*. It is necessary to take into account the real complexity and deep social roots of the *causes* that feed violence and encourage the recourse to terrorist practices and ideologies everywhere in the world: not only in the "peripheries" ridden with poverty, humiliation, and corruption, but also in the "centers" where inequalities and discriminations are growing, with probably no less corruption. But it is impossible to accept blindly violence and terrorism as real answers to exploitation and domination. This answer is neither legitimate nor effective; it destroys the very cause in the name of which it is exercised. Collective security (which we should not identify with the "unilateral" defense of the *established order*, especially if this "order" more and more resembles a violent disorder) therefore requires us to reject the projective illusion of transforming the main victims of insecurity into its ultimate authors, but also to leave aside prophetic discourses picturing "the capitalist system" as the hidden cause of every violence and all conflicts, including those which are obstacles to its own development.

What are then the complementary requisites of a viable model of collective security? It must allow the possibility for both actively fighting against injustice *and* having intelligence and police services combine their actions under legal control against terrorist networks, if their existence is proved (which seems to be the case of Al Qaeda, although the various powers involved—beginning with the United States—clearly don't want all its dimensions to be clarified). If we agree that, for various reasons, there currently is a special threat of "Islamic terrorism" (or terrorism fueled by a fundamentalist Islamic ideology), there is no doubt in my mind that the ultimate condition for an effective "counterterrorist" policy is an active commitment to promoting the emergence of democratic regimes within the Islamic world. Only the ensemble of societies and states where Islam is the essential cultural reference, with the assistance of the international community, will prove able to "uproot" Islamic fundamentalism and terrorism. A model of collective security therefore rules out the substitution for joint operations that prove either too difficult or too embarrassing for the hegemonic power and its clients, of potentially exterminist and imperialist wars that serve mainly objectives of regional domination and prestige. The same could be said, indeed, concerning plans to develop the "antimissile shield" (or star wars) program. Above all, a policy of collective security must systematically eliminate all the factors that lead to a merging of violence "from above" and "from below," creating a symmetrical alignment of fundamentalist ideologies and economic interests in the world.

General Disarmament: Who Is in Charge?

It is meaningless to talk about collective security if the global level of armaments is not reduced. International institutions are not only in charge of negotiating and settling conflicts; they have been created with a goal of generalizing and controlling the process of disarmament. This is the true basis of the idea of "multilateralism," and it cannot be left aside from the moment when it becomes officially a question of obtaining (if necessary, compelling) the "disarmament" of one or several states whose weapons, quantitatively and qualitatively, are dangerous "for the whole of mankind" (many of them, be it said in passing, former allies and clients of this or that superpower who changed sides). By definition no state ("rogue" or not) can be excepted from this rule, since precisely the populations of the whole world are likely to become victims of aggressions or, conversely, of retaliations and preventive wars against particular aggressors. It has been repeatedly proven that the origin of the proliferation of weapons of mass destruction and more generally the constant elevation of the level of military equipment in the world has to be traced back to the great powers themselves, which produce them or develop most of the corresponding research programs (Iraq bought its lethal germs in the United States). More generally, it is meaningless to speak of a multilateralism of warfare, which in practice means an arms race, whereas a multilateralism of disarmament is surrounded with obstacles, but thinkable.

The practical consequence is that Europe should not accept the comparison currently drawn (including by honest commentators) between the "war on terrorism" and the war against Nazism, raising once again the specter of "Munich" when the idea of disarmament is suggested. It should refuse NATO plans to start a new cycle of development of its military capacities (including the capacities to "project" forces outside Europe, to join or replace the special forces of the U.S. Army in some of its operations).[36] On the contrary, it should immediately raise the question of a long-term reduction in the level of armaments in the world, concerning both the "new" and the "old" concentrations of nuclear, biological, and chemical weapons, which include the European concentrations and exportations, under international control and inspections.

There are obvious difficulties with such a perspective, which are only too likely to lead to its abandonment. It contradicts powerful private and public interests in the production and consumption of arms, which continuously increase the level of insecurity throughout the world, producing a general phenomenon of militarization of social life, and transforming large regions of the world into zones of endemic violence and death. To speak of disarmament, one might say, is to beg the question, to suppose that the lack of trust between mutually hostile societies that did not share the same historical experiences and have opposite conceptions of law and politics, which can be either very rich or very poor, has already been overcome. This is true enough; it proves that any serious program of disarmament involves a number of material conditions, including social and political changes all over the world. This is also the reason why we should not simply identify disarmament with pacifism. Controlled disarmament should be compatible with modernized national or supranational defense policies, provided only that negotiations take place to replace offensive programs by defensive ones. Consequently and above all, it means that "the world" agrees to offer *guarantees and means of security to the American people* that, in the long run, would appear better than the prospects of isolation, fortification, and counterterror on a world scale. This may indeed require the experience of tragic events, such as the attacks on September 11 (or worse, which is thinkable).

Local and Global Processes: Who Is Accountable, Who Can Mediate?

I am not trying to introduce a new brand of pacifism. I speak of collective security and advocate, against the current, a new cycle of general disarmament, but I don't speak against "interventions"—at least against *any intervention*—in the violent conflicts and civil wars that tend to shape world politics today. I have recalled the recent examples, both inside Europe and close to it, of Ireland, Yugoslavia, Chechnya, and Palestine, that show the necessity of interventions: not only *humanitarian* interventions, but *coercive* interventions, making use of the means that derive from the contemporary intersections of economic, technological, and cultural processes. Not even military "forces of interposition" should be excluded as a matter of principle, if the conditions exist for their introduction. However, Europe might draw another lesson from its own experience: military conflicts where ethnic, religious, and cultural communities confront each other, which are at the same time extremely unequal and mixed with one another (a general characteristic of what Mary Kaldor calls the "new wars,"[37] expressing "organized violence in the era of globalization"), can be resolved only *locally*. Better said, *the local and global determinations should invert their roles*. The Israeli-Palestinian conflict is exemplary here. Everybody understands now that the roots of further hostilities were present in the very terms of the Oslo Accords and the "peace process" based on them,[38] because they masked objective contradictions under carefully imprecise formulations and could be immediately manipulated, not only by the Israeli government but also by the Palestinian Authority. But the Oslo Accords had one important positive aspect: they implied that, with the help of external mediating forces, the solution should be found *by the conflicting groups themselves*. You frequently hear just the opposite nowadays, both in America and in Europe: that "the Israelis and Palestinians have proved incapable of discussion." The result is a merging of the causes of the conflict into elements of a global conflict (including the identification of local adversaries with the macroforces of "terrorism" and "counterterrorism"), producing destructions and hatreds that become more irreversible every day.

What I tentatively call an "antistrategy" therefore also implies giving a systematic primacy to local determinations over the "global" ones, because they refer to the specific historical and geographical roots of the conflict, which are also dialectically the premises of its solution, and because they allow us to assign responsibilities and make concrete forces accountable for their actions, whereas the primacy of the global nourishes passivity by suggesting that everything is determined at the "global" level, that is, nowhere. But to emphasize the importance of the local level is not to isolate it: we should neither deny globalization nor fetishize it as a "destiny," but rather explore all the possibilities that it provides in order to set up "multilateral" interventions that provide the conflicting subjects with observers, mediators, and witnesses who are *themselves accountable*, in order to build a space for coexistence. On the stage of globalized violence, there are today many actors more or less powerful and dangerous, but apparently only one "judge," who is or seems to be as powerful (and therefore also as dangerous) as all the others combined. But seen from another angle, this stage also offers many potential "mediators": Europe is one of them, albeit not the only one. It is perhaps not by chance that many of them, like Europe itself, are transnational orders, which can be found or will emerge in a near future in East Asia, in the *Cono Sur* of Latin America, in southern Africa, perhaps even in the Middle East, where a renovated "Arab League," both democratized and liberated from the dream of the "Arab Nation" (or transferring it onto more rational prospects) could play a decisive role. Maybe we could say that these potential "mediators" are the true "antisystemic forces" of today and tomorrow, to borrow one of Immanuel Wallerstein's favorite categories.[39]

The "Fault Line" Reduced, or the Euro-Mediterranean Ensemble

In order to be more precise, I will now make a critical use of the great debate raised by the publication of Samuel Huntington's book *The Clash of Civilizations*, with its strategic proposal of a new "world order" based on the simultaneous acceptance of a "multicultural world" and rejection of "multiculturalism" within the West, more specifically within America (the idea that America and Europe belong to a single "Western civilization" being one of the unquestioned assumptions of Huntington's book).[40] My "antistrategic" idea that we ought to push in the direction of the primacy of local determinations over global determinations within the relation constitutive of both, in order to promote the "mediated" resolution of conflicts, will remain meaningless unless it proves possible to define an *open, nonexclusive* framework that would nevertheless be *sufficiently binding* in geographical and historical (and therefore "cultural") terms. In such a framework conflicts would ultimately appear as "civil wars," that is, as wars whose very violence and "irreconcilable" character force the community to assert itself, offering simultaneous recognition to the conflicting camps, and thus paving the way for mutual recognition or the building of "civil peace." There seems to be an enigma, if not a logical flaw in such a formulation: *which community* is able to play such a role? To answer the question, we must fully admit the circle that is involved in the idea of creating a community in order to promote a solution for the problems that are its obstacles. No *preexisting community*, based on traditional membership and "roots," can play this historic role, but only a community of alliances that is instituted *with a view toward favoring this kind of recognition*. Let us note in passing that, to a large extent, this was precisely the way in which modern nation-states were "invented," as a *nonexisting* solution for the problem of religious, feudal, and regional conflicts, but at a different scale and following procedures that are now obsolete.[41]

I believe that the "Euro-Mediterranean ensemble," whose development is both advocated and constantly hindered by multiple obstacles, including phobias profoundly buried in the collective unconscious that trace back to centuries of religious and colonial conflicts, is nevertheless exactly such a framework.[42] Its progressive construction, through negotiations, common projects, and simultaneous mediations in the common interest, is itself a way to affirm the originality of Europe's position in international relations, where the assertion of a specific identity goes hand in hand with its (seeming) opposite: the inclusion of the Other within itself. This is where Huntington's conceptualization can give us a precious *inverted* indication (a *counterfactual,* as logicians would say), since the central notion in his book is not only the concept of "border line" separating heterogeneous populations and territories, but more precisely the concept of a *global border line* (now replacing the geopolitical one that used to separate the "blocs" in the Cold War), which appears as a real "fault line." Along such "fault lines" the new (coming) type of wars would develop (for example, wars between the West and the Islamic world, or the West and the rising "Asian" ensemble around China). According to Huntington, *it is impossible to reduce fault lines:* you can only "freeze" the violence they tend to unleash and organize the world order around the fragile equilibrium of competing, ultimately incompatible civilizations, which are essentially external to one another. This idea clearly derives from the geopolitical notions that were theorized around World War II by the German (pro-Nazi) jurist and philosopher Carl Schmitt, who explained that every political institution was based on the absolute primacy of the "friend versus foe" divide and sought to transfer this notion to the new "spatial distribution of power" (Nomos *of the Earth*) emerging after the Second World War.[43] Clearly, the idea of a "Euro-Mediterranean" ensemble (or alliance) expresses the exactly opposite axiom: it does not say that there are no "fault lines," no vested hostilities around them, but it does say that political institutions (the "polity" and the "civility") precisely arise when hostility becomes a focal point for the elaboration of common interests and historic compromises. Such common interests express the "complementarity of the enemies," to borrow an expression from the French anthropologist Germaine Tillion that I have commented on elsewhere, and this is what makes them politically significant.[44]

Recent debates—sometimes quite virulent—about the possible admission of Turkey into the European Union, which followed the electoral victory of the Party for Justice and Development (AKP) (a party that defines itself as "conservative" and is pictured by political scientists as "moderate Islamic") and were prompted by the declarations of Valéry Giscard d'Estaing, former French president and now chair of the European Constitutional Convention, to the effect that Turkey was "non-European" and its admission would ruin the European construction,[45] have had at least one good effect: they have manifested a reality that does not belong to utopia or a distant future but is approaching fast. Whatever the (probably very great) diversity of institutional solutions, ranging from formal inclusion to close association, Turkey will not remain an isolated case. The whole of the southern shore of the Mediterranean will become progressively involved in the construction of a common space of interdependence, a laboratory for new relationships between "developed" and "developing" countries, and between cultures that have their religious roots in antithetical versions of the same monotheistic theology—provided, of course, that the political conditions are consciously and tenaciously forged.

If such an ensemble were to gain consistency, it would become at the same time an instrument to correct inequalities in the rates of development, an intermediary structure making it easier for Europeans to influence world affairs effectively, and a powerful force for democratizing Arab-Islamic regimes in the Middle East. This is the real way to overcome the old patterns of opposition between "Occidental" and "Oriental" cultures (which are only one figure among many for understanding the history of mankind, but still project a substantial shadow on contemporary thought and politics). It seems to me obvious that, in conjunction with other, similar processes, it could play a very effective role in promoting collective security and activating the working of international institutions. The alternative is quite gloomy: that the "global" logic keeps igniting "fault lines" for decades.

I have been following the guiding thread provided by the obligation to "answer" (at least answer *something*) to the call of American liberals (among whom I include those who, like George Mosse in the past, or Edward Said nowadays, were driven to America by exile, and became essential contributors to its intellectual life), and it took us some distance further away. Allow me to summarize this path, leaving aside some inevitable detours: starting with the critique of the equivocalities of any demand addressed to Europe to act as a counterweight or a mediator, I advocated in the end an "antistrategic" metamorphosis in our conception of the relation between power and political capacity. Meanwhile, I made some concrete suggestions concerning the way European nations, European states, European institutions, and European social forces and public opinion could favor a new system of international relations. It will be said that any "antistrategy" remains a strategy.[46] This is, of course, true; if it was not the case, there would be no point in offering this idea to determinate actors, in a situation that is critical, both urgent and antagonistic. What was important in this choice of terms was to make clear how deeply we must locate the inversion of perspectives necessary to *answer the call* that we receive: we must displace the call, we must call in return upon the Americans to think in different terms, we must question the very presuppositions of the demands. We must *start changing the concept of the political*. As a way of concluding, I would like to explain why I chose this title ("Europe, Vanishing Mediator?"), and I will return to the function of the intellectuals.

As a matter of fact, while I was sketching the elements of this presentation,[47] I happened to read (with considerable delay: almost thirty years!) Fredric Jameson's brilliant essay "The Vanishing Mediator; or, Max Weber as Storyteller."[48] Jameson attempts to show that, at the core of Weber's interpretation of the process of modernization or rationalization (which is basically a European or Eurocentric process), but also of certain Marxian descriptions of revolutionary processes in the past, there lies a dialectical figure that can be called the figure of the vanishing mediator. This is the figure (admittedly presented in speculative terms) of a *transitory* institution (or force, community, or spiritual formation) that creates the conditions for a new society and a new civilizational pattern, albeit in the horizon and the vocabulary of the past, and by rearranging the elements inherited from the very institution that has to be overcome. This is notoriously the case of the "Protestant ethic," centered around the paradoxical notion of a "worldly asceticism," or an immanent spiritual calling, where a twist in the meaning of religious beliefs in fact prepares the subjective conditions for a secularized behavior of individuals and the whole society, the emergence of "rational" economic subjects. It creates therefore the conditions for its own suppression and withering away. But without this "vanishing" mediation no transition from the old to the new fabric of society would have been possible.

It seemed to me that I could in fact play on the double meaning of this remarkable dialectical expression to discuss the paradoxical situation in which Europe and European intellectuals find themselves today. On the one hand, I should critically assess the limits of Europe's capability to influence and mediate conflicts and historical processes that are changing the structure of the world under our eyes. On the other hand, I should explore the possibilities for Europe to use its own fragilities and indeterminacies, its own "transitory" character in a sense, as an effective mediation in a process that might bring about a new political culture, a new pattern of the political institution as such, in our context of acute national and international crisis. Or perhaps, even more paradoxically, I should explore the possibilities for Europe to offer itself as an instrument that other forces in the world, aiming at a transformation of politics, could use and shape to cope with the crisis.

The idea of the vanishing mediator is probably not so different from the idea of the *translator*, the *intermediary*, or the *traveler* that I have associated with the essential function of the intellectual. In "our" case—we the people of Europe—the similitude becomes almost a fusion. As Umberto Eco has proposed, the only genuine "idiom of Europe" (and we know that any political entity needs an idiom or a linguistic institution) *is the practice of translation.*[49] This might well be the "exceptional" character of Europe, due to its specific history, in particular its global expansion and the past competition between its imperialist powers, followed by the "striking back" of the empires. Europe is not the only region in the world where translations are made, where technologies, professional instructions, literary works, and sacred texts continuously pass from one idiom to another. But nowhere—not even in India or in China—was it necessary to organize to the same degree the political and pedagogical conditions of linguistic exchanges. It seems actually possible to imagine how this age-old institutional practice of translation, which is both typically "European" and impossible to enclose in the "borders of Europe" (since almost none of the great European idioms has remained a national "property"), could be expanded, in two directions. It could be expanded by including new elements in the group of languages taught and practiced for the sake of labor and culture, thus broadening the circle of legitimate translations (starting with Arabic, Turkic, Urdu, and others that are already widely practiced on European soil). It could be expanded also by stretching the idea of "translation" from the merely linguistic to the broader *cultural* level. This is a decisive but still enigmatic task, one that involves acknowledging certain impossibilities ("nontranslatable" ideas and forms) *and* looking for equivalences: scientific, literary, legal and religious "universals."

We are thus led to an additional meaning of the idea of the "vanishing mediator"—perhaps our utopia or our myth: Europe as the *interpreter of the world*, translating languages and cultures in all directions. This is an attempt to restore the political function of intellectuals: notwithstanding other activities and commitments, intellectuals would continuously broaden the horizon of their translating capacities. It also points at a *broad*, "organic," function of the intellectuals. Intellectuals would "disappear into [their] own intervention," as Louis Althusser used to say.[50] They would be necessary, but without monopoly. They would be border lines themselves.

NOTES

Preface

1. Étienne Balibar, *Nous, citoyens d'Europe? Les Frontières, l'État, le peuple* (Paris: La Découverte, 2001).

2. In reality, the American volume having been planned first, it was the true "original," but for technical reasons, above all the necessity to translate most of the texts, the French appeared first, leaving the possibility to make changes in the initial plans.

3. Essays omitted from this translation include "Identité/Normalité"; "Vers la citoyenneté imparfaite"; "*Es gibt keinen Staat in Europa*," available in English as "'*Es gibt keinen Staat in Europa*': Racism and Politics in Europe Today," *New Left Review* 186 (March–April 1991): 5–19; "Une citoyenneté européenne est-elle possible?" an expanded version of which is now available as "Is a European Citizenship Possible?" in Étienne Balibar, *Politics and the Other Scene* (London: Verso, 2002), pp. 104–28.

Chapter I

1. See Étienne Balibar, "'*Es gibt keinen Staat in Europa*': Racism and Politics in Europe Today," *New Left Review* 186 (March–April 1991): 5–19.

2. Ismail Kadaré, "Il faut européaniser les Balkans," *Le Monde*, April 10, 1999, pp. 1, 16.

3. Jean Chesneaux, "Quelle paix au Kosovo?" *Le Monde*, June 3, 1999, p. 17.

4. Carl Schmitt, *The Nomos of the Earth in the International Law of the Jus Publicum Europaeum*, trans. G. L. Ulmen (New York: Telos Press, 2003).

5. See Étienne Balibar, "The Borders of Europe," in *Politics and the Other Scene*, trans. Christine Jones, James Swenson, and Chris Turner (London: Verso, 2002), pp. 87–103.

6. Federico Chabod, *Idea di Europa e politica dell equilibrio*, ed. Luisa Azzolini (Bologna: Il Mulino, 1995).

7. H. D. Schmidt, "The Establishment of 'Europe' as a Political Expression," *Historical Journal* 9 (1966): 172–78.

8. Étienne Balibar and Immanuel Wallerstein, *Race, Nation, Class: Ambiguous Identities*, trans. Chris Turner (London: Verso, 1991).

9. This difficulty is not a purely speculative question. It continually interferes with concrete legal and political problems. An example of this occurred when the French Constitutional Council challenged the "symbolic" phrase proposed by the government as a resolution of the Corsican issue ("the Corsican people are a component of the French people") because of its apparent incompatibility with the idea of the nation as "one and indivisible" written in successive republican constitutions (decision of May 9, 1991).

Chapter 2

1. Aleida Assmann,"Die Gleichzeitigkeit des Ungleichzeitigen: Nationale Diskurse zwischen Ethnisierung und Universalisierung," in *Bilder der Nation: Kulturelle und politische Konstruktionen des Nationalen am Beginn der europäischen Moderne,* ed. Ulrich Bielefeld and Gisela Engel (Hamburg: Hamburger Edition, 1998), pp. 379–400. See also Assmann, *Arbeit am nationalen Gedächtnis: Eine kurze Geschichte der deutschen Bildungsidee* (Frankfurt: Campus Verlag, 1993).

2. In today's world "national" tends to become a privileged status in itself: certain individuals are *nationals,* that is, they *have* a nationality with an effective signification, whereas for others nationality has only a fictive signification that gains them no recognition, not to speak of refugees and stateless persons (such as the Palestinians). It should be recalled that the Universal Declaration of Human Rights, adopted by the General Assembly of the United Nations in 1948, inscribed among fundamental rights the "right to a nationality" (and also the right "to change [one's] nationality") (article 15).

3. This is the fundamental position advanced by E. J. Hobsbawm, *Nations and Nationalism since 1789: Programme, Myth, Reality* (Cambridge: Cambridge University Press, 1990). We should salute the fact that, in the second paperback edition (1992), which appeared after the civil war in Yugoslavia broke out, Hobsbawm took recent events into account while maintaining his point of view.

4. See the brilliant essay by Tom Nairn, *The Break-up of Britain: Crisis and Neo-Nationalism* (London: New Left Books, 1977).

5. See Gian Enrico Rusconi, *Se cessiamo di essere una nazione: Tra etnodemocrazie regionali e cittadinanza europea* (Bologna: Il Mulino, 1993).

6. We should recognize that Hélène Carrère d'Encausse predicted the breakup of the USSR (see *Decline of an Empire: The Soviet Socialist Republics in Revolt,* trans. Martin Sokolinsky and Henry A. La Farge [New York: Newsweek Books, 1979]), but on the foundation of the idea of a *multicultural empire,* prefiguring the thesis of Samuel P. Huntington, *The Clash of Civilizations and the Remaking of World Order* (New York: Simon and Schuster, 1996), about confrontation between "Christian" Russia and the "Muslim" East.

7. See Samir Amin, *Delinking: Towards a Polycentric World,* trans. Michael Wolfers (London: Zed Books, 1990).

8. It is not necessary to insist at length on the murderous way in which this sort of "double bind" works in Africa, in the areas of "civil war" that cover almost

the entire continent. At the same time, the formation of "strong," "civilized" *nation-states* continues to be demanded, even as the conditions for such a development, namely those of a "self-centered" economic, political, and cultural sovereignty, and of regional Pan-African solidarity and security, are forbidden.

9. Paul Valéry, "The Crisis of the Mind," in *The Collected Works of Paul Valéry*, ed. Jackson Matthews, 15 vols. (Princeton: Princeton University Press, and New York: Pantheon, 1956–75), 10:23.

10. For the comparison between France and Germany, see particularly Louis Dumont, *German Ideology: From France to Germany and Back* (Chicago: University of Chicago Press, 1994).

11. Jean-Jacques Rousseau, *Of the Social Contract*, book 1, chap. 6, in *The Social Contract and Other Later Political Writings*, ed. and trans. Victor Gourevitch (Cambridge: Cambridge University Press, 1997), p. 50.

12. Ernest Renan, *Qu'est-ce qu'une nation?/What Is a Nation?* trans. Wanda Romer Taylor (Toronto: Tapir Press, 1996), pp. 48–49.

13. See, for example, Niklas Luhmann, *The Differentiation of Society*, trans. Stephen Holmes and Charles Larmore (New York: Columbia University Press, 1982), pp. 92–93.

14. Immanuel Wallerstein, *The Politics of the World-Economy: The States, the Movements, and the Civilizations* (Cambridge: Cambridge University Press, and Paris: Éditions de la Maison des sciences de l'homme, 1984).

15. In other circumstances, I called this "Machiavelli's theorem" because of the way Machiavelli bases his account of the power and stability of the Roman Republic in the *Discourses on Livy* on the institutional solution found for the conflict between the plebs and the patricians (the "tribunate of the plebs," which gives it a representation within the state and institutionalizes class conflict). See Étienne Balibar, "Is a European Citizenship Possible?" in *Politics and the Other Scene*, trans. Christine Jones, James Swenson, and Chris Turner (London: Verso, 2002), p. 123.

16. I developed this idea, derived from Louis Althusser's notion of the "absent cause," in the series of essays in part 2 of Étienne Balibar, *Masses, Classes, Ideas: Studies on Politics and Philosophy before and after Marx*, trans. James Swenson (New York: Routledge, 1994).

17. This is why, despite its interest, I keep a distance from the still functionalist analysis of Immanuel Wallerstein, "Culture as the Ideological Battleground of the Modern World-System," in *Geopolitics and Geoculture: Essays on the Changing World-System* (Cambridge: Cambridge University Press, and Paris: Éditions de la Maison des sciences de l'homme, 1991), pp. 158–83.

18. Étienne Balibar and Immanuel Wallerstein, *Race, Nation, Class: Ambiguous Identities*, trans. Chris Turner (London: Verso, 1991).

19. On the background of a contested or claimed reference to Freudian "group psychology" (*Massenpsychologie*: see Sigmund Freud, *Group Psychology and the Analysis of the Ego* [1921], in *The Standard Edition of the Complete Psychological Works of Sigmund Freud*, ed. James Strachey [London: Hogarth Press, 1953], vol.

18), one can refer here in a "contradictory" way to the work of Michel Foucault (in particular the collective volume *I, Pierre Rivière, Having Slaughtered My Mother, My Sister and My Brother . . .* , ed. Michel Foucault, trans. Frank Jellinek [Lincoln: University of Nebraska Press, 1982]) and Pierre Legendre (in particular *Leçons VIII: Le Crime du caporal Lortie: Traité sur le Père* [Paris: Fayard, 1989]). Hans Kelsen had already tried to put Freudian theory at the service of political and juridical science; see Kelsen, "God and the State" (1922–23), in *Essays in Legal and Moral Philosophy*, ed. Ota Weinberger, trans. Peter Heath (Dordrecht: D. Reidel, 1973), pp. 61–82; and Kelsen, "Der Staatsbegriff und die Psychoanalyse" (1927), reprinted in Hans Kelsen, Adolf Merkl, and Alfred Verdross, *Die Weiner rechtstheoretische Schule*, 2 vols. (Vienna: Europa Verlag, 1968), 1: 209–14. The intersection between the paternal reference and the theological reference, which is also at the heart of Weber's conception of "charismatic power," deserves an extended discussion.

20. Cf. Jean-Claude Milner, *For the Love of Language*, trans. Ann Banfield (London: Macmillan, 1990); Milner, *Les Noms indistincts* (Paris: Seuil, 1983); Françoise Gadet and Michel Pêcheux, *La Langue introuvable* (Paris: Maspero, 1981).

21. I call "anthropological difference" not any codified social or cultural difference but a difference that fulfills two conditions: first, that humanity cannot be conceived of *without it* (or, its negation represents a denial of humanity); and, second, that its "dividing line" can never be drawn in a stable, objective fashion (so that individuals could be split up, once and for all, without intersections or remainders, *on one side or the other*). This is obviously true in the case of sexual difference, whose social institution engenders genealogical structures, and of intellectual difference, whose academic and professional institution produces a division between "manuals" and "intellectuals," or the ignorant and the educated (see Jacques Rancière, *The Ignorant Schoolmaster: Five Lessons in Intellectual Emancipation*, trans. Kristin Ross [Stanford: Stanford University Press, 1991]). Doubtless we should also mention the difference between *sickness* and *health* ("mental" as well as "physical"), which would lead us directly to the necessity of integrating into the preceding sketch the Foucauldian notion of "biopower" and the study of the relations between the *nationalization* and the *medicalization* of modern societies, outside of which the tight link between nationalism and eugenics or medical prophylaxis (even when it stays short of programs of elimination) would remain incomprehensible.

22. Cf. Ernst Kantorowicz, "*Pro Patria Mori* in Medieval Political Thought," in *Selected Studies* (Locust Valley, N.Y.: J. J. Augustin, 1965), pp. 308–24.

23. Ernest Gellner, "Tractatus Sociologico-Philosophicus," in *Culture, Identity, and Politics* (Cambridge: Cambridge University Press, 1987), pp. 166–84. This is precisely what a certain "postmodernity" seems to destroy irreversibly; see Zygmunt Bauman, *Life in Fragments: Essays in Postmodern Morality* (Oxford: Blackwell, 1995), particularly pp. 235–40 on "The Social Dislocation of Intellectuals."

24. Charles de Gaulle, *War Memoirs*, trans. J. Griffith and Richard Howard, 3 vols. (New York: Viking, 1955–59), 3: 284.

25. See Benedict Anderson, *Imagined Communities: Reflections on the Origins*

and Spread of Nationalism (London: Verso, 1983); Anderson, *The Spectre of Comparisons: Nationalism, Southeast Asia and the World* (London: Verso, 1998).

26. See Friedrich Balke, Rebekka Habermas, Patrizia Nanz, and Peter Sillem, eds., *Schwierige Fremdheit: Über Integration und Ausgrenzung in Einwanderungsländern* (Frankfurt: Fischer Taschenbuch Verlag, 1993); Uli Bielefeld, ed., *Das Eigene und das Fremde: Neuer Raßismus in der Alten Welt?* (Hamburg: Junius, 1991).

27. On the problem of political programs of struggle against discrimination, see Véronique de Rudder, Christian Poiret, and François Vourc'h, *L'Inégalité raciste: L'Universalité républicaine à l'épreuve* (Paris: Presses universitaires de France, 2000).

28. Assmann,"Die Gleichzeitigkeit des Ungleichzeitigen."

29. Gramsci's principal texts on the notion of hegemony are to be found in notebooks 12 to 16 of the *Prison Notebooks*. See Antonio Gramsci, *Quaderni del carcere*, Edizione critica dell'Istituto Gramsci, ed. Valentino Gerratana, 4 vols. (Turin: Einaudi, 1975). The complete translation currently in process (*Prison Notebooks*, trans. Joseph A. Buttegieg [New York: Columbia University Press, 1991–], 2 vols. to date) so far includes only notebooks 1–5. The older translations (*Selections from the Prison Notebooks*, trans. Quintin Hoare and Geoffrey Nowell-Smith [New York: International Publishers, 1971], and *Further Selections from the Prison Notebooks*, trans. Derek Boothman [Minneapolis: University of Minnesota Press, 1995]) are eclectic in organization. See also Giorgio Baratta, *Le rose e i quaderni: Saggio sul pensiero di Antonio Gramsci* (Rome: Gamberetti Editrice, 2000).

30. A very interesting use of the distinction between "primary" and "secondary" identities can be found in Élise Marienstras, *Nous le peuple: Les Origines du nationalisme américain* (Paris: Gallimard, 1988).

31. Freud, *Group Psychology and the Analysis of the Ego*; George Devereux, "Ethnic Identity: Its Logical Foundations and Its Dysfunctions," in *Ethnopsychoanalysis: Psychoanalysis and Anthropology as Complementary Frames of Reference* (Berkeley: University of California Press, 1978), pp. 136–76; Michel Kail and Geneviève Vermès, eds., *La Psychologie des peuples et ses dérives* (Paris: Centre national de documentation pédagogique, 1999).

32. Before Freud, this complexity-conflictuality was seen with admirable clarity by Nietzsche, who related it to the *reversibility* of questions posed by the individual "I" and by the "community" and political "sovereignty." See Friedrich Nietzsche, *Beyond Good and Evil: Prelude to a Philosophy of the Future*, trans. Judith Norman (Cambridge: Cambridge University Press, 2002), §19, pp. 18–20. It is no doubt not an accident if the question of "multiple personalities" arises as a theoretical problem at the moment when classical right and the classical national state are constituted, at the cost of a primary and fundamental rupture with the theological conception of the subject and of obedience. See, for example, John Locke, *An Essay concerning Human Understanding*, ed. Peter H. Nidditch (Oxford: Clarendon Press, 1975), book 2, chap. 27, "Of Identity and Diversity," pp. 328–48, and my commentary in John Locke, *Identité et différence: L'Invention européenne de la conscience*, ed. and trans. Étienne Balibar (Paris: Seuil, 1998). It will then go on to lead a subterranean

life, to reemerge in the philosophical, literary, and psychological discourse contemporary with the "age of mass society," that is, of social normalization in democratic nations (William James, Pierre Janet), to which Freud was to respond.

33. It is striking that Nazism and "totalitarian" regimes in general (all of which are ultranationalist, including in the form of "national communism" or state communism) constantly alternated between these two types of forced reduction to the univocality of identities: whence a characteristic uncertainty—which is, in fact, valorized in the name of (the) "movement"—in the separation between private and public sphere, but also a "forcing" in the distribution of sexual roles assigning women to the private and men to the public sphere (particularly in the case of Nazism and fascism). These problems are at the heart of Hannah Arendt's reflections in *The Origins of Totalitarianism* (San Diego: Harcourt, 1968) and beyond. They have been studied from a historical and anthropological point of view by George L. Mosse (*Nationalism and Sexuality: Middle-Class Morality and Sexual Norms in Modern Europe* [Madison: University of Wisconsin Press, 1985]) and Klaus Theweleit (*Male Fantasies*, vol. 1: *Women, Floods, Bodies, History*, trans. Stephen Conway [Minneapolis: University of Minnesota Press, 1987]). In a forthcoming book entitled *Le Sexe de la nation*, Rada Ivecovic suggests that every collective formation of national identities is specifically associated with a "communitarian" distribution of sexual roles that is projected back onto the sexualized images of the "nation" and its "body." See also Ivekovic, "The Bosnian Paradigm," *Dialogue* (Sarajevo) 9–10 (1998): 61–85, and Nira Yuval-Davis, *Gender and Nation* (Thousand Oaks, Calif.: Sage Publications, 1997).

34. It is important here not to conflate all discourses abusively. In particular, it would be appropriate to devote detailed readings to the analyses of "becoming a minority" in Deleuze (see Gilles Deleuze and Félix Guattari, *A Thousand Plateaus: Capitalism and Schizophrenia*, trans. Brian Massumi [Minneapolis: University of Minnesota Press, 1987], pp. 291–93) or of the "performative subversion of sexual roles" in Judith Butler's *Gender Trouble: Feminism and the Subversion of Identity* (New York: Routledge, 1990), which constitute esthetico-philosophical inversions of this tendency. The problematization of these questions is also at the center of the important work of Zygmunt Bauman, which is just beginning to be known in France.

35. The accelerated professionalization of the former armies of conscription is a characteristic sign of the crisis of the "nation-form," which has not escaped the attention of the spokesmen of French "national republicanism." A social, cultural, and psychosocial history of the military in modern nations remains, to the best of my knowledge, entirely unwritten. The comparison of its different variants, in relation to different models of imperialism, demands particular attention.

36. So destructive that some (sometimes many, in mass), in order to escape this risk, are ready to accept the most extreme forms of individual subjection and to reverse the injunctions of morality and humanity generally associated with *Sitt-*

lichkeit into injunctions of barbarism and self-destruction. See Étienne Balibar, "De la 'préférence nationale' à l'invention de la politique," in *Droit de cité: Culture et politique en démocratie* (Paris: Éditions de l'Aube, 1998), pp. 89–132.

37. See Robert Castel, *From Manual Workers to Wage Laborers: Transformation of the Social Question*, trans. Richard Boyd (New Brunswick, N.J.: Transaction Publishers, 2003).

Chapter 3

1. The expression *droit de cité*, generally left untranslated here, designates the right of entry and residence in the classical or medieval city-state. In contemporary French, it is most often used in a metaphorical sense to indicate the acceptability of an idea or an expression within a particular discipline or discourse.

2. See Jacques Rancière, *Disagreement: Politics and Philosophy*, trans. Julie Rose (Minneapolis: University of Minnesota Press, 1999); Rancière, *On the Shores of Politics*, trans. Liz Heron (London: Verso, 1995).

3. See the presentations of these debates by Jean Leca, "Questions on Citzenship," trans. Anna Marie Smith, in *Dimensions of Radical Democracy: Pluralism, Citizenship, Community*, ed. Chantal Mouffe (London: Verso, 1992), pp. 17–32; Jacqueline Costa-Lascoux, *De l'immigré au citoyen* (Paris: La Documentation française, 1989); Dominique Schnapper, *La France de l'intégration: Sociologie de la nation en 1990* (Paris: Gallimard, 1991); and Étienne Balibar, *Les Frontières de la démocratie* (Paris: La Découverte, 1992).

4. These are the formulations proposed respectively by the Declarations of the Rights of Man and the Citizen of 1795, 1793, and 1789 to designate the instance that bears the democratic "general will."

5. Roger Establet, *Comment peut-on être français? 90 ouvriers turcs racontent* (Paris: Fayard, 1997), presents a remarkable investigation of the way a "community" often accused of isolationism perceives the opportunities and risks of integration into French society and particularly the egalitarian and civilizing dimension of social rights.

6. Albert O. Hirschmann, *The Rhetoric of Reaction: Perversity, Futility, Jeopardy* (Cambridge, Mass: Belknap Press, 1991), studies the great models, taken up over and over since the French Revolution, that serve to disqualify democratic projects by prognosticating their failure or the danger that they represent for civic liberties.

7. The expression has also been employed, in a similar sense, by Michel Wieviorka, "Racisme, antiracisme et mutation sociale: L'Expérience française," in *Immigration et racisme en Europe*, ed. Andrea Rea (Brussels: Éditions complexe, 1998), p. 43. One can find an analysis of national-republican language in Pierre Tévanian and Sylvie Tissot, *Mots à maux: Dictionnaire de la lepénisation des esprits* (Paris: Éditions Dagorno, 1998).

8. On the "hardening of attitudes" in similar affairs whose flames are peri-

odically fanned by secularist activists, see Madeleine Rebérioux, "A propos du foulard: Lettre aux enseignants," *Homme et libertés: Revue de la Ligue des droits de l'homme* 103 (February–March 1999): 9.

9. This practice has occasioned repeated appeals to the European Court of Human Rights; see Andrea Rea, "Le Racisme européen ou la fabrication du 'sous-blanc,'" in Rea, *Immigration et racisme en Europe*, p. 183.

10. See the justification of double jeopardy as the equivalent of a "suppression of civic rights" affecting a French citizen by Sami Naïr, "À propos de l'immigration," *Lignes* 35 (October 1998): 162: "*It does not violate the principle of republican equality but to the contrary establishes it,* taking into account the fact that foreigners and Frenchmen do not possess the same political rights."

11. Nothing has fundamentally changed in this domain since the same Sami Naïr wrote, "The affair of the *'sans-papers'* . . . shows how much the violation of legality by the police is a current practice in this domain" (*Contre les lois Pasqua,* 2nd ed. [Paris: Arlea, 1997], p. 113). See also Association nationale d'assistance aux frontières pour les étrangers, *Zones d'attente des ports, des aéroports et des gares ferroviaires: Visite des associations habilitées* (Paris: ANAFE, 1998).

12. Étienne Balibar, *Droit de cité: Culture et politique en démocratie* (Paris: Éditions de l'Aube, 1998), pp. 109–13. It is striking that the National Front, apart from a few "excesses" (skinheads, etc.), concentrates its efforts on the development of an institutional violence exercised by the agents of authority, which gives it the opportunity to affirm, not without foundation, that its influence has grown.

13. Let us recall that this notion, originally theorized by the Club de l'Horloge (Jean-Yves Le Gallou and le Club de l'Horloge, *La Préférence nationale: Réponse à l'immigration* [Paris: Albin Michel, 1985]), is the keystone of the proposals for a "final solution to the immigration problem" whose effectuation is demanded by the National Front. But it has not remained without influence on the ideology and practice of other political formations, in particular on the municipal level.

14. On all these points, see the fundamental work of Gérard Noiriel, in particular *The French Melting Pot: Immigration, Citizenship, and National Identity,* trans. Geoffroy de Laforcade (Minneapolis: University of Minnesota Press, 1996); as well as Rogers Brubaker, *Citizenship and Nationhood in France and Germany* (Cambridge, Mass.: Harvard University Press, 1992).

15. Pierre Legendre, *Trésor historique de l'État en France: L'Administration classique,* rev. ed. (Paris: Fayard, 1992), speaks of "colonial projection" in order to characterize the constitution of the administrative bodies of the French Empire. See also in the important book by Paul Rabinow, *French Modern: Norms and Forms of the Social Environment* (Cambridge, Mass.: MIT Press, 1989), the description of the "laboratory of experimentation for new arts of government" (p. 289) constituted by Morocco during the French Protectorate before World War II.

16. See Claude-Valentin Marie, "L'Europe: De l'empire aux colonies intérieures," in *Face au racisme,* ed. Pierre-André Taguieff, 2 vols. (Paris: La Découverte, 1992), 2: 296–310. The DOM-TOM are former colonies now integrated into France

as Départements d'Outre-Mer and Territoires d'Outre-Mer (Overseas Departments and Territories).

17. See Gérard Noiriel, *Population, immigration et identité nationale en France, XIXe–XXe siècle* (Paris: Hachette, 1992), chap. 2.

18. Robert Castel, *From Manual Workers to Wage Laborers: Transformation of the Social Question*, trans. Richard Boyd (New Brunswick, N.J.: Transaction Publishers, 2003).

19. An interesting comparison could be drawn on this point between the analyses of Suzanne de Brunhoff, *L'Heure du marché* (Paris: Presses universitaires de France, 1985), and Immanuel Wallerstein, *After Liberalism* (New York: New Press, 1995).

20. Immanuel Wallerstein, "The Construction of Peoplehood: Racism, Nationalism, Ethnicity," in Étienne Balibar and Immanuel Wallerstein, *Race, Nation, Class: Ambiguous Identities*, trans. Chris Turner (London: Verso, 1991), pp. 71–85.

21. Emmanuel Terray, "Le Travail des étrangers en situation irrégulière ou la délocalization en place," in Balibar et al., *Sans-papiers: L'Archaïsme fatal*, pp. 9–34.

22. An expression proposed by Pierre-Noël Giraud, *L'Inégalité du monde: Économie du monde contemporain* (Paris: Gallimard, 1996).

23. See Olivier Le Cour Grandmaison, "Immigration, politique et citoyenneté: Sur quelques arguments," in *Les Étrangers dans la cité: Expériences européennes*, ed. Olivier Le Cour Grandmaison and Catherine Wihtol de Wenden (Paris: La Découverte, 1993), pp. 81–103.

24. The expression is taken from the Dutch political theorist Herman R. van Gunsteren, *A Theory of Citizenship: Organizing Plurality in Contemporary Democracies* (Boulder, Colo.: Westview Press, 1998).

25. Catherine Wihtol de Wenden, *La Citoyenneté européenne* (Paris: Presses de la Fondation nationale des Sciences politiques, 1997), p. 99.

26. Rea, "Le Racisme européen," pp. 194–95.

27. See Monique Chemillier-Gendreau, *L'Injustifiable: Les Politiques françaises de l'immigration* (Paris: Bayard Éditions, 1998), pp. 151–70.

28. Reports by Patrick Weil on the right of nationality and on immigration submitted to the prime minister on July 31, 1997, published as *Mission d'étude des législations de la nationalité et de l'immigration: Des conditions d'application du principe du droit de sol pour l'attribution de la nationalité française; Pour une politique de l'immigration juste et efficace* (Paris: La Documentation française, 1997).

29. See Castel, *From Manual Workers to Wage Laborers.*

30. Radio interview, Club de Presse d'Europe 1, July 5, 1998, available at <http://www.archives.premier-ministre.gouv.fr/jospin__version2/PM/D050798.HTM>.

31. We are thinking here not only of the support of certain labor-union officials and municipal politicians, among whom are the "reformist" communist mayors of some large suburban towns, but also of the striking evolution of the Immigration Commission of the French Communist Party directed by Serge Guichard and of the initiative of a collective of socialist elected officials in favor of regulariza-

tion. See the article by the Parisian Deputy Serge Blisko, "Sans-papiers: Jospin, encore un effort," *Libération*, March 22, 1999, p. 7.

32. See Marie-Claire Caloz-Tschopp, Axel Clément, and Maria-Pia Tschopp, eds., *Asile, Violence, Exclusion en Europe: Histoire, analyse, prospective* (Geneva: Groupe de Genève "Violence et droit d'Asile en Europe" and Cahiers de la section des sciences de l'éducation de l'Université de Genève, 1994).

33. Rancière, *Disagreement*.

34. Dominique Schnapper, *Community of Citizens: On the Modern Idea of Nationality*, trans. Séverine Rosée (New Brunswick, N.J.: Transaction Publishers, 1998), p. 85.

Chapter 4

1. See Étienne Balibar, "Sur la désobéissance civique," in *Droit de cité: Culture et politique en démocratie* (Paris: Éditions de l'Aube, 1998), pp. 17–22.

2. Dominique Schnapper, *Community of Citizens: On the Modern Idea of Nationality*, trans. Séverine Rosée (New Brunswick, N.J.: Transaction Publishers, 1998).

3. These notions or labels are of course subject to significant variations, both within and outside of France. In particular, in the case of Italy, see the series of recent publications by Gian Enrico Rusconi: *Se cessiamo di essere una nazione* (Bologna: Il Mulino, 1993); *Patria e repubblica* (Bologna: Il Mulino, 1997); and *Possiamo fare a meno di una religione civile?* (Bari: Laterza, 1999).

4. Frequently cited in this context is Ernest Renan's lecture, *Qu'est-ce qu'une nation?/What Is a Nation?* trans. Wanda Romer Taylor (Toronto: Tapir Press, 1996), in which is found the famous formula defining the nation as a "daily plebiscite" (pp. 48–49). We cannot discuss the difficult questions this formula raises here.

5. Schnapper, "The Logic of the Civic Nation," in *Community of Citizens*, pp. 76–91.

6. Ibid., p. 169: "In historicizing all concepts and relativizing all institutions, modern thought—aided by the horrors perpetrated in the twentieth century in the name of political values—had the effect of disenchanting [*désacraliser*] the political, after having already disenchanted the religious. But all power emanates from the sacred."

7. See Régis Debray, Max Gallo, Jacques Julliard, Blandine Kriegel, Olivier Mongin, Mona Ozouf, Anicet Le Pors, and Paul Thibaud, "Républicains, n'ayons plus peur!" *Le Monde*, September 4, 1998, p. 13.

8. Schnapper, *Community of Citizens*, p. 169: "It is by no means certain, then, that the democratic nation can continue to control the inevitable conflicts provoked by the sharing of resources by means of the rational ambition of citizenship. In a commercial democracy, material aspirations by definition know no limits. It is by no means certain that the democratic nation may continue to control the behaviors inspired by feelings of belonging or identification with ethnic communities. There is no guarantee whatsoever that the democratic nation will be able to preserve the social bond. Europeans witnessed the weakening of the monarchical

system in the eighteenth century, which was poorly prepared to respond to the new aspirations of peoples; it may be the case today that the national political form has been similarly exhausted." One of the essential inspirations for Dominique Schnapper's recent work was her participation in the Commission on Nationality created in 1987. Contrary to what many had expected, the commission, established following a first set of polemics about the evolution of the French population toward a "multicultural" composition and on the "right to difference," did not reintroduce the idea of *jus sanguinis*, still dominant at the time in some European nations (particularly Germany), but confirmed the tradition of *jus soli* as the route of access to citizenship and nationality. But it did not, in the other direction, evoke the possibility of founding citizenship on a *right of residency*. See Marceau Lang, Olivier Fouquet, Jean-Claude Maillet, and Jean Merline, *Être français aujourd'hui et demain: Rapport de la commission de la nationalité*, 2 vols. (Paris: Union générale d'édition, 10/18, 1988); and Dominique Schnapper, *La France de l'intégration: Sociologie de la nation en 1990* (Paris: Gallimard, 1991).

9. Schnapper, *Community of Citizens*, p. 85.

10. Pierre Hassner, "Construction européennes et mutations à l'Est," in *L'Europe au soir du siècle: Identité et démocratie*, ed. Jacques Lenoble and Nicole Dewandre (Paris: Éditions Esprit, 1992), p. 279.

11. Jürgen Habermas, *The Postnational Constellation: Political Essays*, trans. Max Pensky (Cambridge, Mass.: MIT Press, 2001), p. 107. The sentence continues: "The self-referential concept of collective self-determination demarcates a logical space for democratically united citizens who are members of a particular political community."

12. Ibid.

13. Ibid., pp. 109–12.

14. Carl Schmitt, *Theorie des Partisanen: Zwischenbemerkung zum Begriff des Politischen* (Berlin: Duncker und Humblot, 1963).

15. Habermas, *The Postnational Constellation*, p. 108.

16. Schnapper herself undertakes a number of transhistorical comparisons between "political organizations," in particular between the modern nation and the ancient city-state (whence the name *citizen*, possessor of a *droit de cité*). She notes that the Greeks "formulated the values of liberty and equality, which formed the basis for modern democratic thought. . . . However, the Greek *polis* remained limited by a conception that we would characterize in modern language as ethnic. Citizens were defined by their birth and their belonging." She describes Rome and the Romans as the inventors of "the conception of citzenship . . . defined in terms of juridical status, [which implies that] the principle of openness to foreigners was inscribed in the definition of political society" (Schnapper, *Community of Citizens*, pp. 67–69), but she does not discuss the possibility of thinking of Rome as a "protonational" type of state (in contrast, for example, to Claude Nicolet, *The World of the Citizen in Republican Rome*, trans. P. S. Falla [London: Batsford Academic and Educational, 1980]).

17. See the remarkable book by Nestor Capdevila, *Las Casas, une politique de l'humanité: L'Homme et l'empire de la foi* (Paris: Éditions du Cerf, 1998).

18. Carl Schmitt, *The* Nomos *of the Earth in the International Law of the* Jus Publicum Europaeum, trans. G. L. Ulmen (New York: Telos Press, 2003).

19. Étienne Balibar, "The Nation Form," in Étienne Balibar and Immanuel Wallerstein, *Race, Nation, Class: Ambiguous Identities*, trans. Chris Turner (London: Verso, 1991), pp. 86–106.

20. Of course, extensive universalism in this sense has known other historical realizations, always connected to both the form of an empire and the idea of a civilizing mission, whether with or without a theological foundation; examples include Alexandrian Hellenism, Confucian China, republican and imperial Rome, Islam.

21. Dominique Colas's presentation in "La Citoyenneté au risque de la nationalité," in *La Démocratie en France*, ed. Marc Sadouan, 2 vols. (Paris: Gallimard, 2000), 2: 116–223, is perhaps overly vehement but strikes the mark on this point.

22. How this idea, inherent in the idea of "fraternity" between men (each of whom is the other's "neighbor" who must be loved as oneself) as well as in that of "natural right" (founded on liberty and equality), passed from religious to political discourse is a fundamental question. Before engaging in a general discussion, a particularly luminous starting point can be found in Tocqueville's reflections in book 1, chap. 3 of *The Old Regime and the Revolution* on "How the French Revolution Was a Political Revolution Which Acted Like a Religious Revolution, and Why" (Alexis de Tocqueville, *The Old Regime and the Revolution*, ed. François Furet and Françoise Mélonio, trans. Alan S. Kahan, 2 vols. [Chicago: University of Chicago Press, 1998–2001], 1: 99–101).

23. Or *equaliberty*, as it can be written to emphasize the fusion of the two notions, each of which functions as the presupposition of the other. See Étienne Balibar, "'Rights of Man' and 'Rights of the Citizen,'" in *Masses, Classes, Ideas: Studies on Politics and Philosophy before and after Marx*, trans. James Swenson (New York: Routledge, 1994), pp. 39–59.

24. See Alain Badiou, *Saint Paul: The Foundation of Universalism*, trans. Ray Brassier (Stanford: Stanford University Press, 2003).

25. The "case" of "abnormal" or "handicapped" individuals, apparently "halfway" between the two preceding cases, has long posed particularly difficult problems and has once again taken on a crucial importance today.

26. One of the consequences of the modern definition of the "nation" pointed out by Hannah Arendt, *The Origins of Totalitarianism* (San Diego: Harcourt, 1968), book 2, "Imperialism."

27. As the following examples show, I call "anthropological differences," absolutely speaking, those without which the constitution of humanity cannot be represented, since it resides precisely in their complementarity, even though it is impossible to *establish the dividing line* in a clear and unequivocal way. Thus the human cannot be represented without the possibility of illness, but one cannot say in an exact ("objective") way *who is "healthy" and who is "sick."*

28. Schnapper, *Community of Citizens*, p. 159.

29. "Permissions" (*droits libertés*) and "entitlements" (*droits créances*) in the terminology proposed by Raymond Aron; see Luc Ferry and Alain Renaut, *Political Philosophy*, vol. 3: *From the Rights of Man to the Republican Idea*, trans. Franklin Philip (Chicago: University of Chicago Press, 1992).

30. See Robert Castel, *From Manual Workers to Wage Laborers: Transformation of the Social Question*, trans. Richard Boyd (New Brunswick, N.J.: Transaction Publishers, 2003).

31. Schnapper, *Community of Citizens*, p. 159.

32. Regardless of what may be said, this makes it impossible for any logic of "depreciation" or "devaluation" of labor as a social activity to be taken to its conclusion without putting "national cohesion" itself into danger. For a good representation of this naive belief, see Dominique Méda, *Le Travail, une valeur en voie de disparition* (Paris: Aubier, 1995).

33. Balibar, *Droit de cité*, pp. 109–13.

34. See Gilles Deleuze and Félix Guattari, *A Thousand Plateaus: Capitalism and Schizophrenia*, trans. Brian Massumi (Minneapolis: University of Minnesota Press, 1987), pp. 214–15.

35. The granting of the right to vote in local elections to foreign residents of all nationalities continues to be periodically held out as a promise, bait, or bogeyman by a large part of the political class, without the slightest serious effort actually to introduce it, despite the confirmed evolution of public opinion on this point.

36. We should be clear about this "invisibility": it is a matter of the public sphere and thus of the reality or transgression of rights, but individuals and practices themselves have by no means become invisible. It is enough to go out to the "territories" where stigmatized populations encounter (or often are confronted by) the repressive apparatus—suburban ghettos, public transit systems, social agencies, etc.—to see nonright displayed openly. One could even hold the position that the function of a good part of racist practices is to make discriminatory stigmata *visible*, provoking a reflex of rejection and fear in the "national" population. Still, this contradiction is what makes the body of citizens *blind* to the degeneration of the *res publica*, and all the more so as it is obstinately and loudly denied in "republican" discourse.

37. One could argue that, in the French case as well as others, this discriminatory logic stems from the persistence of a colonial image and definition of the "territory" within the world; see on this point the analyses proposed by Colas, "La Citoyenneté au risque de la nationalité." But is it not, at a more profound level, the logic of *sovereign* territory that implies considering the population as something that "belongs" to it? Still, one would have to examine in detail the question of whether, *historically*, "European" sovereign territory and the colonial division of the world are in fact independent phenomena.

38. The symbolic point of departure can be dated from the appearance, during the controversy over Muslim girls wearing veils to school (*l'affaire des foulards*)

in 1989, of a group of intellectuals seeking to recompose the ideological landscape by substituting a split between democrats and republicans (articulated in terms of an opposition between the liquidation and the defense of national sovereignty) for the split between left and right. See Françoise Gaspard and Farhad Khosrokhavar, *Le Foulard et la République* (Paris: La Découverte, 1995).

39. Or, as Alain Badiou puts it, the "counts-as-one" of a multiplicity of individuals. See Alain Badiou, *L'Être et l'événement* (Paris: Seuil, 1988), pp. 104–7.

40. *Aoristos archē*: the expression used by Aristotle in his first definition of *politeia* or citizenship in the third book of the *Politics* (1275a32), in relation with the idea that in every city there is as much "citizenship" as there is "democracy" or popular force (in the standard English translation by Benjamin Jowett, in *The Politics and The Constitution of Athens*, ed. Stephen Everson [Cambridge: Cambridge University Press, 1996], p. 62, this is rendered as "indefinite office").

41. Just as, in another dimension, one often hears that Europe cannot take charge of dealing with the historical consequences of communism, which essentially means that the former USSR and its various "national" components must be kept in an *exterior*, non-European space.

42. See Étienne Balibar, "Exclusion ou lutte des classes," in *Les Frontières de la démocratie* (Paris: La Découverte, 1992), pp. 191–205.

43. Jean-Luc Nancy, *The Inoperative Community*, trans. Peter Connor, Lisa Garbus, Michael Holland, and Simon Sawhey (Minneapolis: University of Minnesota Press, 1991).

44. In particular, Jean-Luc Nancy, *The Experience of Freedom*, trans. Bridget McDonald (Stanford: Stanford University Press, 1993); and *Being Singular Plural*, trans. Robert D. Richardson and Anne E. O'Byrne (Stanford: Stanford University Press, 2000).

45. Nancy, *The Inoperative Community*, pp. 28–30.

46. Ibid., pp. 72, 74–75.

47. Ibid., pp. 76–77.

48. This conception of the "exposition of the community" is particular to Nancy but does have a relation with the way in which Hannah Arendt defines the public sphere or sphere of *action* as a sphere of co-presence of reciprocal "visibility," which is what makes possible self-presence. See Adi Ophir, "Between Eichmann and Kant: Thinking on Evil after Arendt," *History and Memory* 8, no. 2 (1996): 89–136.

49. Roberto Esposito, *Communitas: Origine e destino della communità* (Turin: Einaudi, 1998).

50. Jacques Rancière, *Disagreement: Politics and Philosophy*, trans. Julie Rose (Minneapolis: University of Minnesota Press, 1999), pp. 8–9, 11–12. Such formulations naturally have a background that Rancière himself indicates in the place of *isonomia* in Greek thought. But, closer to us, they could have been influenced by the pages that Maurice Merleau-Ponty devoted to the relation between Machiavelli and Marx: "The problem of a real humanism that Machiavelli set was taken up

again by Marx a hundred years ago. Can we say the problem is solved? What Marx intended to do to create a human community [*pour faire une humanité*] was precisely to find a different base than the always equivocal one of principles. . . . But it became apparent that the whole problem was to constitute a power of the powerless" (Maurice Merleau-Ponty, "A Note on Machiavelli," in *Signs*, trans. Richard C. McCleary [Evanston, Ill.: Northwestern University Press, 1964], p. 222). One might say that in a sense Rancière proposes as a solution to be forever reconstructed what Merleau-Ponty saw as an always inaccessible task.

51. Rancière, *Disagreement*, pp. 35–37.

52. Ibid., pp. 120–21.

53. We should emphasize that when the history in question has been acquired through a long colonial past, as is the case in France and more generally in Europe, such a putting into question must begin with a real *knowledge* of the past from which it results.

54. Jean-Claude Milner, *Les Noms indistincts* (Paris: Seuil, 1983), pp. 116–23. Each of the cases evoked obviously raises particular difficulties, often considerable ones. But it is striking that all, in one way or another, have been "put on the agenda" by the transnational experience that contemporary societies have of the exclusions from and limits to citizenship that characterize them, correlative to a delegitimation of politics. Whence the insistences of notions or programmatic watchwords such as "parity" (or effective participation of both sexes in political functions), "citizenship of residence," "citizenship of the sick" (responsibility for oneself, equality of access to treatment, etc.), even of "citizenship of the incarcerated," marking the fact that a criminal is still—more than ever, in a sense—a citizen, as Hegel already showed. See G.W.F. Hegel, *Elements of the Philosophy of Right*, ed. Allen W. Wood, trans. H. B. Nisbet (Cambridge: Cambridge University Press, 1991), §100, p. 126.

55. Close in this respect to the idea developed by Colas ("La Citoyenneté au risque de la nationalité") when he places the general notion of *civitas* at the point of divergence between the two models of the "club" or statutory monopoly and democratic "concitizenship."

56. We must here refer to what Herman R. van Gunsteren, *A Theory of Citizenship: Organizing Plurality in Contemporary Democracies* (Boulder, Colo.: Westview Press, 1998), calls a "community of fate."

57. Balibar, "'Rights of Man' and 'Rights of the Citizen.'"

Chapter 5

1. See Georges Labica, "Le communisme enfin possible," *M (Mensuel, marxisme, mouvement)* 36 (March–April 1990).

2. François Furet, "Les Russes finissent la Révolution française," *Libération*, August 27, 1991, p. 13.

3. It would, of course, be appropriate to ask whether this description is universally valid, or whether it only applies to Europe. I am thinking here not so much

of Cuba, whose fate will be played out shortly in the relations of forces in America's "backyard," but of China (if not of other "Marxist" states in Asia). One factor at least will be very different: the attitude of the external world, which as we have seen since Tiananmen, has a much greater investment in the stability of power in Beijing than in its reversal. Moreover, the relation between the revolutionary tradition and nationalism there is fairly different from what can be observed in Europe. It seems probable to me that China will go completely "out of communism" but doubtful that this departure will take the form of a dismantling of the state.

4. Antonio Gramsci, *Selections from the Prison Notebooks*, trans. Quintin Hoare and Geoffrey Nowell Smith (New York: International Publishers, 1971), pp. 235–39.

5. Jean-Denis Bredin, "Est-il permis?" *Le Monde*, August 31, 1991, p. 7.

6. [Editorial board], "La Gauche orpheline," *Esprit* 175 (October 1991): 4.

7. See Lucien Sève, *Communisme: Quel second souffle?* (Paris: Messidor/Éditions sociales, 1990); see also, on opposite premises, Alain Badiou, *D'un désastre obscur: Droit, État, Politique* (La Tour d'Aigues: Éditions de l'Aube, 1991).

8. See Louis Althusser, "The Crisis of Marxism," in *Il Manifesto: Power and Opposition in Post-Revolutionary Societies* (London: Ink Links, 1979), pp. 225–37; Althusser, "Entretien," *Dialectiques* 23 (Spring 1978): 5–12.

9. It is important here to make an exception for the Italian Communist Party, going back at least as far as Palmiro Togliatti's famous interview of 1956 in *Nuovi Argomenti*, whose "polycentric" thesis represented both a demand for autonomy and an embryonic analysis of the real articulation of the communist movement. See Palmiro Togliatti, "Interview with *Nuovi Argomenti*," in *On Gramsci and Other Writings*, ed. Donald Sassoon (London: Lawrence and Wishart, 1979), pp. 115–42.

10. An extremely revelatory episode in this respect is that of 1956, which saw different communist parties of the "West," beginning with the French Communist Party under the direction of Maurice Thorez, intervene in the internal struggles of the Soviet Communist Party to counteract the reformist orientation of Khrushchev.

11. Jean-Paul Sartre, "Les Communistes ont peur de la révolution," in *Situations VIII* (Paris: Gallimard, 1972), pp. 208–25.

12. The other side of the picture I have evoked is this: the parties of "external" communism (at least some of them) have most closely approached "totalitarianism" in the strict sense, the uniformization of collective thought cemented by the identification of politics and truth. The consequences of this have been less tragic (except on certain individual lives) than those of "democratic centralism" in the USSR (where for a long time it has no longer been a matter of belief but of functionalism and privileges: Andrzej Wajda's 1977 film *Man of Marble* remains a great expression of this particular form of "routinization of charisma"). But it is probable that the proximity of Western state parties has greatly contributed to increase the projection of the category of "totalitarian" onto the party-states of the East.

13. See Étienne Balibar, "'*Es gibt keinen Staat in Europa*': Racism and Politics in Europe Today," *New Left Review* 186 (March–April 1991): 5–19.

14. It might be suggested that the last trace of a *historical* problematic, in the strong sense, for the political scientists disappeared with the discussion of a dozen years ago on the "convergence of systems" and the development of a "technostructure" in both East and West.

15. If I thus agree, at least in a first approximation, with their notion of insurrection (which integrates and surpasses that of resistance), I cannot agree with that of *communist invariants* as recently advanced by Alain Badiou and François Balmès, *De l'idéologie* (Paris: Maspero, 1976), pp. 67–75. The word "communist" was first used in Latin and in Polish in the sixteenth century to refer to Czech Anabaptists (also known as the Moravian brothers); "communism" was invented in 1797 by Restif de la Bretonne. See the thesis by Jacques Grandjonc, *Communisme/ Kommunismus/Communism: Origine et développement international de la terminologie communautaire prémarxiste des utopistes aux néo-babouvistes, 1785–1842* (Trier: Schriften aus dem Karl-Marx-Haus, 1989).

16. See Jacques Rancière, "The Community of Equals," in *On the Shores of Politics*, trans. Liz Heron (London: Verso, 1995), pp. 63–92.

17. See the extraordinary essay on medieval debates on property by Janet Coleman, "Property and Poverty," in *The Cambridge History of Medieval Political Thought*, ed. J. H. Burns (Cambridge: Cambridge University Press, 1988), pp. 607–48.

18. On Winstanley, see the works of Christopher Hill, in particular *The World Turned Upside Down: Radical Ideas during the English Revolution* (Harmondsworth: Penguin Books, 1975); for Babeuf, see Gracchus Babeuf, *Écrits*, ed. Claude Mazauric (Paris: Messidor/Éditions sociales, 1988).

19. On the vicissitudes of communist internationalism, see Jean Robelin, "L'Internationale sans le genre humain," in *La Rationalité du politique* (Paris: Les Belles Lettres, Annales littéraires de l'Université de Besançon, 1995), pp. 187–219.

20. See Michel Foucher, *Fronts et frontières: Un Tour du monde géopolitique* (Paris: Fayard, 1988), pp. 391–406, for a striking description of the tangle of internal and external boundaries of the "socialist bloc."

21. Recall, however, that the United States is also extraordinarily marked in its history and culture by a "siege mentality" and obsession with the permeability of boundaries.

22. See the evocation of the "spirit of fortification" proper to Soviet imperialism in Alain Joxe, *Voyage aux sources de la guerre* (Paris: Presses universitaires de France, 1991), pp. 418–19.

23. German history is an extraordinary precipitate of this whole scenario. We could rewrite each sentence, substituting for the indication of the body in pieces of Europe that of Germany. This is also why Germany today is more than ever the "European" nation par excellence.

24. If I were asked for a "definition" of "European peoples" that would be historical rather than mythical, I would propose the following, no more or less arbitrary than any other: Europeans are the peoples who participated in World War I. This is why the Americans (of the United States) and the Senegalese cannot be totally excluded from it, whereas the place of the Swiss is problematic.

25. It is hardly a chance occurrence if the most original among the Marxist theoreticians of the 1930s and 1940s—Brecht, Walter Benjamin, Gramsci, Wilhelm Reich—are precisely those who anticipated or designated the "blind spot" of Marxism as such. See Étienne Balibar, "Fascism, Psychoanalysis, Freudo-Marxism," in *Masses, Classes, Ideas: Studies on Politics and Philosophy before and after Marx*, trans. James Swenson (New York: Routledge, 1994), pp. 177–89. On the combination of social and national dimensions of interwar antifascism, see the somewhat different analysis by E. J. Hobsbawm, *Nations and Nationalism since 1789: Programme, Myth, Reality* (Cambridge: Cambridge University Press, 1990), pp. 145–50.

26. Karl Marx and Frederick Engels, *Manifesto of the Communist Party, Political Writings*, vol. 1: *The Revolutions of 1848*, ed. David Fernbach (New York: Vintage, 1974), p. 79.

27. A characterization systematized in the excellent study by Jean Rony, "Préliminaires à une 'troisième voie': Le Parti communiste italien et l'URSS," in *L'URSS vue de gauche*, ed. Lilly Marcou (Paris: Presses universitaires de France, 1982), pp. 211–29. See also Alexandre Adler and Jean Rony, *L'Internationale et le genre humain* (Paris: Mazarine, 1980).

28. Here I am following the suggestions of Giovanni Arrighi, Terence K. Hopkins, and Immanuel Wallerstein, "1989, the Continuation of 1968?" *Review* (Fernand Braudel Center for the Study of Economies, Historical Systems, and Civilizations) 15 (1992): 221–42.

29. The most significant theoretical product, perhaps, of this vision of things, is the book by Rudolf Bahro, *The Alternative in Eastern Europe*, trans. David Fernbach (London: New Left Books, 1978).

30. In France, this utopia has been particularly active in the CFDT (French Democratic Confederation of Labor); moreover, it has corresponded to the highest point of the CFDT's power of intellectual attraction and attempt to replace communism as the center of initiative on the left.

31. This fatalism is supported by the general impression that the process of the exacerbation of nationalisms *continues to surpass* the limits set by reason or history. Hence, Alexandre Adler ("Après le marxisme, le problème des nationalités?" *Libération*, March 27, 1990, p. 4) dissociates democratic nationalism, "that generosity of the great nations of the East," from "true nationalisms, those that do not compromise." At the time, Adler thought it possible to assure that "in the same way we must exclude the possibility of a separation of the Ukraine."

32. See Ronald Suny, "The Revenge of the Past: Socialism and Ethnic Conflict in Transcaucasia," *New Left Review* 184 (November–December 1990): 5–34.

33. See Pierre Hassner, "L'Europe et le spectre des nationalismes," *Esprit* 175

(October 1991): 6: "The renewal of nationalism in Eastern Europe is less the cause of the current situation than its consequence"; E. J. Hobsbawm, "The Perils of the New Nationalism," *Nation*, November 4, 1991, p. 556: "Baltic and Caucasian separatism, and conflicts between Serbs and Croats, and Czechs and Slovaks, were not serious problems in 1917, or could not have existed before the establishment of Yugoslavia and Czechoslovakia. What has made those problems so acute is not the strength of national feeling, which was no greater than in countries like Britain and Spain, but the disintegration of central power, for this has forced even Soviet or Yugoslav Republics that did not dream of separation . . . to assert independence as a means of self-preservation."

34. Its only equal is the rapidity with which the best-placed representatives of the nomenklatura reappeared in private enterprise (a reclassification that was long prepared by a whole "mafia"-style operation).

35. See Immanuel Wallerstein, "Semiperipheral Countries and the Contemporary World Crisis," in *The Capitalist World Economy* (Cambridge: Cambridge University Press, and Paris: Éditions de la maison des sciences de l'homme, 1979), pp. 95–118; Giovanni Arrighi, Terence K. Hopkins, and Immanuel Wallerstein, *Antisystemic Movements* (London: Verso, 1989).

36. Samir Amin, *Delinking: Towards a Polycentric World*, trans. Michael Wolfers (London: Zed Books, 1990).

37. Joxe, *Voyage aux sources de la guerre*, pp. 418–22.

38. See Hassner, "L'Europe et le spectre des nationalismes," pp. 20–21: "The cold war brought about the primacy of East-West problems. With its end, they lost at once their priority and their specificity in favor of North-South relations. The situation is most dramatic in the third world, particularly in Africa. The greatest number of victims of racism, candidates for emigration, and refugees wandering across the seas and the continents are to be found among Asians and Africans. But above all, East-West relations themselves more and more resemble North-South relations. Of course, neither poverty nor cultural distance from the West is the same in Central Europe or even the Soviet Union as it is in Africa. But the primacy of socioeconomic divisions and conflicts in relation to ideological and military oppositions has reached an equal degree in Europe. The problem of relations with Poland, as with a large part of the nations of the third world, is centered on debt and immigration. What Mexico is to the United States and the Maghreb is to France, the South and East of Europe (Turks, Yugoslavians, and now East Germans, *Aussiedler* from Russia, and Poles) is to Germany and Austria."

39. See Robert Dahl, "Social Reality and 'Free Markets,'" and James Tobin, "One or Two Cheers for the 'Invisible Hand,'" *Dissent* (Spring 1990): 224–36; see also the opinion of Alexander Iakovlev, cited by Lilly Marcou, "Le 'Socialisme réel,' un avenir disparu," *Les Temps modernes* 543 (October 1991): 55.

40. Marcou, "Le 'Socialisme réel,' un avenir disparu," p. 56.

41. See Christoph Dieckmann, "Wenn das Wunder zum Alltag wird: Zwei Jahre nach dem Fall der Mauer: Die DDR Geschichte wirkt weit," *Die Zeit*, Novem-

ber 8, 1991, p. 1: "[T]oday the East Germans live anew under the pressure of a compulsory loyalty to the state that they cannot even recognize as such. The history of the GDR is presented [*diktiert*] to them as a time that was lost, like a guilty history [*Schuldgeschichte*], but with which, perhaps to 'better teach them,' they must no longer have anything to do."

42. The sorcerer's apprentices thus "discover" with terror that they have not had the time to eliminate nuclear arms (which is difficult, without a concession in return), and that they will be "disseminated." Beside the great nuclear power, there will now be one medium power (Russia) and a number of small powers (France, Germany, the Ukraine, China, Iran, Pakistan, etc.).

Chapter 6

1. Georg Vobruba, "The Limits of Borders," in *Social Policy beyond Borders: The Social Question in Transnational Perspective*, ed. Abram de Swaan (Amsterdam: Amsterdam University Press, 1994), pp. 7–13.

2. A detailed exposition of this extreme hypothesis can be found in Masao Miyoshi, "A Borderless World? From Colonialism to Transnationalism and the Decline of the Nation-State," *Critical Inquiry* 19 (1993): 726–51.

3. For a review of the history and development of uses of the term "globalization," see Robert Boyer, "La Globalisation: Mythes et réalités," *Actes du GERPISA Réseau International* 18 (Université d'Évry-Val d'Essonnes, November 1996), available at <http://www.univ-evry.fr/labos/gerpisa/actes/18/article2.html>.

4. We can recall the declaration by the president of Volkswagen suggesting that politics is now a field of maneuver limited by the economy and that the economy is more and more constrained by the stock market.

5. Immanuel Wallerstein, *The Modern World-System*, 3 vols. (New York: Academic Press, 1974–89); Giovanni Arrighi, Terence K. Hopkins, and Immanuel Wallerstein, *Antisystemic Movements* (London: Verso, 1989).

6. See Pierre-Noël Giraud, *L'Inégalité du monde: Économie du monde contemporain* (Paris: Gallimard, 1996), which shows that "competition between territories" and "competition between capitals" are equally important for the orientation of the still uncertain evolution of the world-economy. In the absence of a state authority on the global scale, "global Keynesian regulation" remains a utopia.

7. Pierre-Noël Giraud, *Le Commerce des promesses: Petit traité de la finance moderne* (Paris: Seuil, 2001).

8. See E. J. Hobsbawm, *The Age of Extremes: A History of the World, 1914– 1991* (New York: Vintage Books, 1996).

9. Samuel P. Huntington, *The Clash of Civilizations and the Remaking of World Order* (New York: Simon and Schuster, 1996).

10. Which, let us not forget, is also a system of surveillance, as has recently been recalled by the discovery by a commission of the European parliament of the spy system "Echelon," established in Great Britain by the United States in order to

"listen" to European telephone conversations (see "Comment les États-unis vous es-pionnent," *Le Monde*, February 23, 2000, pp. 1–3, and Jacques Isnard, "La Sainte alliance de l'espionnage," *Le Monde*, March 30, 2000, p. 16).

11. It is likely that the image proposed here of the "sources" of the idea of globalization is profoundly marked by a "Northern" point of view, even as global-ization wants to be seen as a questioning and a complication of the idea of a split between North and South. But it is also possible that *the very idea of globalization is a "Northern" idea.* In the South it is not yet a dominant discourse (in comparison, for example, with the ideas of imperialism or of a new stage in the history of impe-rialism). This dispute is not a merely verbal one, and it is far from decided.

12. See Perry Anderson, "The Ends of History," in *A Zone of Engagement* (London: Verso, 1992), particularly pp. 294–308.

13. See Karl Marx, *The Poverty of Philosophy*, ed. C. P. Dutt and V. Chat-topadhyaya (New York: International Publishers, [n.d.]), pp. 146–47; Karl Marx and Frederick Engels, *Manifesto of the Communist Party, Political Writings*, vol. 1: *The Revolutions of 1848*, ed. David Fernbach (New York: Vintage, 1974), p. 87.

14. Étienne Balibar, "Exclusion ou lutte des classes," in *Les Frontières de la démocratie* (Paris: La Découverte, 1992), pp. 191–205.

15. In some respects, the Deleuzian idea of a "control society" leads in the same direction. See Gilles Deleuze, *Negotiations, 1972–1990*, trans. Martin Joughin (New York: Columbia University Press, 1995), pp. 177–82.

16. Francis Fukuyama, *The End of History and the Last Man* (New York: Free Press, 1992).

17. See the text by the Forum mondial des Alternatives, *Manifeste: Il est temps de renverser le cours de l'histoire* (available on line at <http://www.forumalternatives. net/fr/manifesto.lasso>), and the manifesto-like text published by subcommandant Marcos himself, "Pourquoi nous combattons: La 4e guerre mondiale a commencé," *Le Monde diplomatique* 521 (August 1997): 1, 4–5 (available in English, "Why We Are Fighting: The Fourth World War Has Begun," trans. Ed Emery, at <http:// mondediplo.com/1997/09/marcos>).

18. Jacques Derrida, *Specters of Marx: The State of the Debt, the Work of Mourning, and the New International*, trans. Peggy Kamuf (New York: Routledge, 1994), chap. 3, "Wars and Tears (Tableau of an Ageless World)," pp. 77–94. This text can be contrasted with the beautiful lecture delivered at the Premier Congrès des Villes-Refuges in Strasbourg, published in *On Cosmopolitanism and Forgiveness*, trans. Mark Dooley and Michael Hughes (London: Routledge, 2001), pp. 1–24.

19. A schema of this sort is incontestably present in Wallerstein's most recent work, counterbalancing an apparently more "positive" description of the evolution of the world-system that tends to give an approximation of a "zone of instability" in which the "bifurcation of the system" is becoming more likely. It is essential to Wallerstein's argument (which takes up here the apocalyptic language of *kairos*) that this event be presented as both sociological and moral, where necessity and freedom

come together. See, for example, Immanuel Wallerstein, "The Inventions of Time-Space Realities: Towards an Understanding of our Historical Systems," in *Unthinking Social Science: The Limits of Nineteenth-Century Paradigms* (Philadelphia: Temple University Press, 2001), pp. 135–48; and more recently, *Utopistics, or Historical Choices of the Twenty-First Century* (New York: New Press, 1998).

20. Étienne Balibar, "What Is a Border?" and "The Borders of Europe," in *Politics and the Other Scene*, trans. Christine Jones, James Swenson, and Chris Turner (London: Verso, 2002), pp. 75–103. Lucien Febvre's classic study, "*Frontière*: The Word and the Concept" (1928), in *A New Kind of History: From the Writings of Febvre*, ed. Peter Burke, trans. K. Folca (New York: Harper and Row, 1973), pp. 208–18, remains indispensable. See also Febvre, *Le Rhin: Histoire, mythes et réalités*, ed. Peter Schöttler (Paris: Librairie académique Perrin, 1997).

21. See in particular the work of the Centre for New Ethnicities Research at the University of East London (Dagenham), directed by Phil Cohen, especially the December 1996 conference on Frontlines, Backyards.

22. See James Holston, ed., *Cities and Citizenship* (Durham, N.C.: Duke University Press, 1999).

23. See Marie-Claire Caloz-Tschopp, ed., *Frontières du droit, frontières des droits: L'Introuvable statut de la "zone internationale"* (Paris: L'Harmattan/ANAFE, 1993).

24. Stuart Hall, "New Ethnicities," in *Stuart Hall: Critical Dialogues in Cultural Studies*, ed. David Morley and Kuan-Hsing Chen (London: Routledge, 1996), pp. 441–48.

25. Abdelwahab Meddeb, "L'Interruption généalogique," *Esprit* 208 (January 1995): 74–81; cf. Étienne Balibar, "Algeria, France: One Nation or Two?" trans. Adele Porter, in *Giving Ground: The Politics of Propinquity*, ed. Joan Copjec and Michael Sorkin (London: Verso, 1999), pp. 162–72.

26. On Turks in France, see the recent study by Roger Establet, *Comment peut-on être français? 90 ouvriers turcs racontent* (Paris: Fayard, 1997).

27. Roland Hureaux, "Les Trois Fractures sociales," *Libération*, August 7, 1997, p. 4; Lester C. Thurow, *The Future of Capitalism: How Today's Economic Forces Shape Tomorrow's World* (New York: Morrow, 1996). Michel Aglietta presented a similar idea at the Hamburg conference where this paper was first read.

28. Nigel Thrift, "A Phantom State? International Money, Electronic Networks and Global Cities," in *Spatial Formations* (Thousand Oaks, Calif.: Sage, 1996), pp. 213–55.

29. We should not forget that they were both invented as mechanisms of *interior* police for the regulation of the "dangerous classes," that is, the poor and the workers. See Gérard Noiriel, *La Tyrannie du national: Le Droit d'asile en Europe (1793–1993)* (Paris: Calmann-Lévy, 1991).

30. Étienne Balibar, "Is European Citizenship Possible?" in *Politics and the Other Scene*, pp. 104–28.

Chapter 7

1. See Étienne Balibar, "Three Concepts of Politics: Emancipation, Transformation, Civility," in *Politics and the Other Scene*, trans. Christine Jones, James Swenson, and Chris Turner (London: Verso, 2002), pp. 1–39.

2. Hannah Arendt, *The Origins of Totalitarianism* (San Diego: Harcourt, 1968), book 2, "Imperialism," ch. 9.

3. Jacques Rancière, *Disagreement: Politics and Philosophy*, trans. Julie Rose (Minneapolis: University of Minnesota Press, 1999).

4. "Lettre ouverte en mémoire de 19 paysans sans-terre massacrés à El Dorado dos Carajas le 17 avril 1996," *Réseau contre l'impunité au Brésil: Justice pour les sans-droits*.

5. See chapter 3 and the collection in which it was originally published: Étienne Balibar, Jacqueline Costa-Lascoux, Monique Chemillier-Gendreau, and Emmanuel Terray, *Sans-papiers: L'Archaïsme fatal* (Paris: La Découverte, 1999).

6. Catherine Wihtol de Wenden, *La Citoyenneté européenne* (Paris: Presses de la Fondation nationale des Sciences politiques, 1997), p. 99.

7. See Center for Contemporary Cultural Studies, *The Empire Strikes Back: Race and Racism in 70s Britain* (London: Hutchinson in association with the Centre for Contemporary Cultural Studies, University of Birmingham, 1982).

8. See Rogers M. Smith, *Civic Ideals: Conflicting Visions of Citizenship in U.S. History* (New Haven: Yale University Press, 1997).

9. Pierre de Senarclens, *L'Humanitaire en catastrophe* (Paris: Presses de la Fondation nationale des Sciences politiques, 1999), p. 65.

10. Ibid., p. 70.

11. See Mary Kaldor, *New and Old Wars: Organized Violence in a Global Era* (Stanford: Stanford University Press, 1999).

12. Samuel P. Huntington, *The Clash of Civilizations and the Remaking of World Order* (New York: Simon and Schuster, 1996).

13. Edward P. Thompson, et al., *Exterminism and Cold War* (London: Verso, 1982).

14. See Carl Schmitt, *The Nomos of the Earth in the International Law of the Jus Publicum Europaeum*, trans. G. L. Ulmen (New York: Telos Press, 2003).

15. Loïc Wacquant, *Les Prisons de la misère* (Paris: Raisons d'agir/Darantière, 1999).

16. Giorgio Agamben, *Homo Sacer: Sovereign Power and Bare Life*, trans. Daniel Heller-Roazen (Stanford: Stanford University Press, 1998).

17. Michel Foucault, *"Society Must Be Defended": Lectures at the Collège de France, 1975–1976*, ed. Mauro Bertani and Alessandro Fontana, trans. David Macey (New York: Picador, 2003), pp. 240–41.

18. See Bertrand Ogilvie, "Violence et représentation: La Production de l'homme jetable," *Lignes* 26 (October 1995): 113–42.

19. See Daniel Pécaut, "En Colombie, une guerre contre la société," *Le Monde*, October 22, 1999, p. 15.

20. Benedict Anderson, *Imagined Communities: Reflections on the Origins and Spread of Nationalism* (London: Verso, 1983).

21. Among many other publications, see Jürgen Habermas, *Between Facts and Norms: Contributions to a Discourse Theory of Law and Democracy*, trans. William Rehg (Cambridge, Mass.: MIT Press, 1996).

22. Michael Hardt and Antonio Negri, *Empire* (Cambridge, Mass.: Harvard University Press, 2000).

23. E. J. Hobsbawm, *The Age of Extremes: A History of the World, 1914–1991* (New York: Vintage Books, 1996).

24. Herman R. van Gunsteren, *A Theory of Citizenship: Organizing Plurality in Contemporary Democracies* (Boulder, Colo.: Westview Press, 1998).

25. Gayatri Chakravorty Spivak, *Imperative zur Neuerfindung des Planeten/Imperatives to Re-Imagine the Planet* (Frankfurt am Main: Passagen Verlag, 1999).

26. Immanuel Kant, "Toward Perpetual Peace," in *Practical Philsophy*, trans. and ed. Mary J. Gregor, in *The Cambridge Edition of the Works of Immanuel Kant*, ed. Paul Guyer and Allen W. Wood (Cambridge: Cambridge University Press, 1996), p. 329 (Third Definitive Article).

Chapter 8

1. Chantal Millon-Delsol, *L'État susidiaire: Ingérence et non-ingérence de l'État: Le Principe de susidiarité aux fondements de l'histoire européenne* (Paris: Presses universitaires de France, 1992).

2. Olivier Beaud, "La Fédération entre l'État et l'empire," in *L'État, la finance et le social: Souveraineté nationale et construction européenne*, ed. Bruno Théret (Paris: La Découverte, 1995), pp. 282–305; see also Gérard Mairet, *Discours d'Europe, ou, souveraineté, citoyenneté et démocratie* (Paris: La Découverte, 1994).

3. Michael Hardt and Antonio Negri, *Empire* (Cambridge, Mass.: Harvard University Press, 2000). For Hardt and Negri, empire is both a mutation of sovereignty and the realization of one of its original tendencies.

4. Friedrich Nietzsche, "On the New Idol," in *Thus Spoke Zarathustra: A Book for All and None*, trans. Walter Kauffman (New York: Viking, 1966), p. 48.

5. Jürgen Habermas, *The Postnational Constellation: Political Essays*, trans. Max Pensky (Cambridge, Mass.: MIT Press, 2001).

6. Étienne Balibar, "'Es gibt keinen Staat in Europa': Racism and Politics in Europe Today," *New Left Review* 186 (March–April 1991): 5–19.

7. As in French, Schmitt's work has only begun appearing in English fairly recently, and much of it remains untranslated. See the bibliographies contained in Chantal Mouffe, ed., *The Challenge of Carl Schmitt* (London: Verso, 1999), and Gopal Balakrishnan, *The Enemy: An Intellectual Portrait of Carl Schmitt* (London: Verso, 2000).

8. Olivier Beaud, *La Puissance de l'État* (Paris: Presses universitaires de France, 1994).

9. Jacques Derrida, "Force of Law: The 'Mystical Foundation of Authority,'"

trans. Mary Quaintance, in *Deconstruction and the Possibility of Justice*, ed. Drucilla Cornell, Michel Rosenfeld, and David Gray Carlson (New York: Routledge, 1992), pp. 3–67; Derrida, *Politics of Friendship*, trans. George Collins (London: Verso, 1997).

10. Antonio Negri, *Insurgencies: Constituent Power and the Modern State*, trans. Maurizia Boscagli (Minneapolis: University of Minnesota Press, 1999).

11. Jürgen Habermas, "Kant's Idea of Perpetual Peace: At Two Hundred Years' Historical Remove," in *The Inclusion of the Other: Studies in Political Theory*, trans. Ciaran Cronin and Pablo De Greif (Cambridge, Mass.: MIT Press, 1998), pp. 165–201.

12. Carl Schmitt, *The Nomos of the Earth in the International Law of the* Jus Publicum Europaeum, trans. G. L. Ulmen (New York: Telos Press, 2003).

13. Carl Schmitt, *Political Theology: Four Chapters on the Concept of Sovereignty*, trans. George Schwab (Cambridge, Mass.: MIT Press, 1985), p. 5.

14. Ibid., p. 12.

15. Writing in German, Schmitt is not explicitly concerned with the paradox inherent in the idea of a "sovereign subject" or "subject of sovereignty" grounded in the Latin etymology of "subject" as meaning "dependent" or "subjected" (*subjectus/subjectum*). It was Georges Bataille who, at about the same time, began to pose this problem, sketching out an inner reversal of the idea of sovereignty. See Roberto Esposito, "Sovranità," in *Nove pensieri sulla politica* (Bologna: Il Mulino, 1993), pp. 87–111.

16. An index can be seen in the fact that, when Schmitt republishes his fundamental works (*Political Theology*; *The Concept of the Political*, trans. George Schwab [New Brunswick, N.J.: Rutgers University Press, 1976]) after 1950, he systematically accompanies them with notes and complements that resume the arguments of the *Nomos of the Earth* on the "constituent" territorial order. *The Nomos of the Earth* is in many respects an astonishing book. Written between 1940 and 1950, it contains no allusions to either Nazism or the Second World War, but pursues a polemic against the Treaty of Versailles and attributes what it calls the "collapse" of the international juridical order to the consequences of the First World War and the "criminalization" of certain states that followed it.

17. Carl Schmitt, *The Leviathan in the State Theory of Thomas Hobbes: Meaning and Failure of a Political Symbol*, trans. George Schwab and Erna Hilfstein (Westport, Conn.: Greenwood Press, 1996).

18. On these classic medieval formulas, see K. Pennington and J. P. Canning, "Law," in *The Cambridge History of Medieval Political Thought*, ed. J. H. Burns (Cambridge: Cambridge University Press, 1988), pp. 424–76.

19. Thomas Hobbes, *Leviathan, or the Matter, Forme, and Power of a Commonwealth, Ecclesiaticall and Civill*, ed. Richard Tuck (Cambridge: Cambridge University Press, 1996), book 2, chap. 18, p. 127.

20. To the contrary, jurists such as Raymond Carré de Malberg see in it a disastrous "confusion" between the concept of sovereignty and that of public power:

see Raymond Carré de Malberg, *Contribution à la théorie générale de l'État*, 2 vols. (1920; reprint, Paris: CNRS, 1962), 1: 76–77. For an important recent discussion, see Beaud, *La Puissance de l'État*.

21. Carl Schmitt, *Die Diktatur: Von den Anfängen des modernen Souveränitätsgedanken bis zum proletarischen Klassenkampf* (1921; reprint, Berlin: Duncker und Humblot, 1994).

22. Jean Bodin, *On Sovereignty*, ed. and trans. Julian H. Franklin (Cambridge: Cambridge University Press, 1992), p. 21 (book 1, chap. 8 of *Six Livres de la République*).

23. Ibid., p. 1. Franklin generally translates *république* as "commonwealth"; "republic" has been restored here.

24. Schmitt, *Political Theology*, p. 8.

25. Jean Bodin, *Les Six Livres de la République*, 6 vols. (Paris: Fayard, 1986), 1: 112.

26. Without considering Bodin's thesis reserving the validity of divine law above that of human law, we can admit that it expresses essentially the same requirement for rationality and justice already immanent in "well-ordered" politics.

27. Bodin, *On Sovereignty*, p. 56.

28. Ibid., p. 59.

29. Ibid., p. 64.

30. Ibid., p. 67.

31. Ibid., p. 73.

32. On the classical doctrine of the "parts of sovereignty" and the debates it involves, see Robert Derathé, *Jean-Jacques Rousseau et la science politique de son temps*, 2nd ed. (Paris: Vrin, 1988), pp. 280–94.

33. Norberto Bobbio calls the distinction between the public and private a "grande dichotomia," foundational, in his view, of the very idea of a juridical order. The question posed here is to what extent, being implied in the constitution of sovereignty, it is, in turn, inseparable from it. The question is capital as soon as the problem is posed of what a public sphere, public interests, even public service could be beyond the national framework. See Norberto Bobbio, *Dalla struttura alla funzione: Nuovi studi di teoria del diritto* (Milan: Comunità, 1977).

34. Lefort calls the effect of the democratic revolution a "disincorporation" of individuals in that it violently dissolves the "great imaginary body" to which they were attached during the Old Regime, whose symbolic model is provided by the "King's two bodies" as described by Ernst Kantorowicz (*The King's Two Bodies: A Study in Medieval Political Theology* [Princeton: Princeton University Press, 1957]). See Claude Lefort, "The Image of the Body and Totalitarianism," in *The Political Forms of Modern Society: Bureaucracy, Democracy, Totalitarianism*, trans. John B. Thompson (Cambridge, Mass.: MIT Press, 1986), pp. 292–306.

35. See Louis Althusser, "Ideology and Ideological State Apparatuses (Notes toward an Investigation)," in *Lenin and Philosophy and Other Essays*, trans. Ben Brewster (London: New Left Books, 1971), p. 160.

36. On medieval and modern "corporatism," see, in the heritage of Otto

Gierke, Antony Black, *Guilds and Civil Society in European Political Thought from the Twelfth Century to the Present* (Ithaca, N.Y.: Cornell University Press, 1984).

37. Michel Foucault, "*Omnes et singulatim*: Toward a Critique of Political Reason," in *Essential Works of Foucault*, ed. Paul Rabinow and James D. Faubion, 3 vols. (New York: New Press, 1997–99), 3: 298–325. I cannot here enter the question, which was the object of Foucault's research and more recently that of Michel Senellart, of the relations between sovereignty and "police."

38. Confronting Bodin's formulations with those of Hobbes would lead not to rejecting but to complicating this analysis. At first sight, Hobbes is much less concerned with territoriality in his definition of the "Leviathan," and he grants intermediary bodies ("systemes subjects" [see *Leviathan*, book 2, chap. 22]) a much greater importance. In reality Hobbes's demonstration, conducted on the basis of the theory of "representation" in the very particular meaning he gives to the term, consists in showing that all "political" bodies, that is, associations generally that have a public status (notably commercial and colonial societies) must admit the authority of the sovereign within themselves: they cannot be judges of conflicts opposing them to their own members or employees. As for "private" bodies, either they are legal (families), in which case they too admit the primacy of the law over their internal authority (the "real father" is never the "symbolic father"), or they are illegal and the *de facto limitation of sovereignty is reached*, constituting the institution's permanent horizon of violence, that is, the menace to the institution represented by the uncontrollable "mass" (here evoked by enumeration: beggars, gypsies and other vagrants, foreign agents, factions or politico-religious parties, assemblies too large to be controlled by the state). Within the limits of its power to discipline the mass, the sovereign *commonwealth* is thus conceived as a "body of bodies" before being a coupling of population and territory. But in the last instance it is indeed individuals who are subjected and not the bodies to which they belong. The two points of view will be ever more fused in Rousseau. The difference between them is no doubt to be explained, as Schmitt suggests, by the fact that Hobbes theorizes the absoluteness of sovereignty in a "nation" that is also "universal," or that exercises the function of guardian of the political order for the entire earth, beyond boundaries.

39. Julian H. Franklin, *Jean Bodin and the Rise of Absolutist Theory* (Cambridge: Cambridge University Press, 1973).

40. On Bodin's positions concerning sovereignty and fiscality (and more generally on the origins of the "fiscal state"), see Richard Bonney, "Early Modern Theories of Public Finance," in *Economic Systems and State Finance*, ed. Richard Bonney (Oxford: Clarendon Press, 1995), pp. 163–229.

41. Étienne Balibar, "The Nation Form: History and Ideology," in Étienne Balibar and Immanuel Wallerstein, *Race, Nation, Class: Ambiguous Identities*, trans. Chris Turner (London: Verso, 1991), pp. 86–106.

42. Étienne Balibar, "De la préférence nationale à l'invention de la politique," in *Droit de cité: Culture et politique en démocratie* (Paris: Éditions de l'Aube, 1998), pp. 109–13.

43. Karl Marx, "Critique of Hegel's Doctrine of the State," in *Early Writings*,

trans. Rodney Livingston and Gregor Benton (London: Penguin, 1992), pp. 57–198. See the commentary by Miguel Abensour, *La Démocratie contre l'État: Marx et le moment machiavélien* (Paris: Presses universitaires de France, 1997).

44. The study of John Maynard Keynes's trajectory from *The Economic Consequences of the Peace* (New York: Harcourt, Brace and Howe, 1920) to the interventions that inspired the international monetary system and the institution of social policy in a national framework, astonishingly parallel to that of Schmitt but leading to the adoption of totally opposite positions, remains to my knowledge entirely undone. A few interesting indications can be found in Suzanne de Brunhoff, *L'Heure du marché* (Paris: Presses universitaires de France, 1985), and Michel Aglietta, *A Theory of Capitalist Regulation: The US Experience* (London: New Left Books, 1979).

45. Jean-Jacques Rousseau, *Of the Social Contract*, book 1, chap. 7, in *The Social Contract and Other Later Political Writings*, ed. and trans. Victor Gourevitch (Cambridge: Cambridge University Press, 1997), p. 52.

46. But the *Declaration* also includes other statements—of Lockean rather than Rousseauist inspiration—that insist, to the contrary, on the guarantee of natural rights preexisting the institution of politics. See Florence Gauthier, *Triomphe et mort du droit naturel en Révolution, 1789–1795–1802* (Paris: Presses universitaires de France, 1992).

47. "This doctrine contains two contradictory terms: subjection and power of domination are two things that exclude one another, even when an attempt is made to make them function in alternation. If the nation is subject, it cannot be sovereign. And on the other hand a power of domination over oneself is complete nonsense from a juridical point of view" (Carré de Malberg, *Contribution à la théorie générale de l'État*, 1: 244).

48. Ibid., pp. 250–51.

49. Ibid., pp. 83–88.

50. Rousseau, *Social Contract*, book 1, chap. 7, p. 53.

51. Carré de Malberg, *Contribution à la théorie générale de l'État*, 1: 250, 254, 246 and note.

52. Rousseau, *Social Contract*, book 1, chap. 7, p. 51.

53. Sieyes does not use the word sovereignty but gives a particularly restrictive definition of it by substituting *nation* for *people* where Rousseau used the latter term. See Emmanuel-Joseph Sieyes, *What Is the Third Estate?* trans. M. Blondel (New York: Praeger, 1963), p. 126: "Not only is the nation not subject to a constitution, but it *cannot* be and *must not* be, which is tantamount to saying that it is not."

54. Marx, "Critique of Hegel's Doctrine of the State," pp. 119–20. Negri's *Insurgencies* constitutes an astonishing attempt to combine the viewpoints of Sieyes and Marx.

55. Karl Marx and Frederick Engels, *Manifesto of the Communist Party, Political Writings*, vol. 1: *The Revolutions of 1848*, ed. David Fernbach (New York: Vintage, 1974), pp. 67–68.

56. Balibar, "De la préférence nationale," pp. 102–9.

57. Pierre Rosanvallon's works, *Le Sacre du citoyen: Histoire du suffrage universel en France* (Paris: Gallimard, 1992) and *Le Peuple introuvable: Histoire de la représentation démocratique en France* (Paris: Gallimard, 1998), are indispensable here. They show how the representation of the people is constantly rubbing up against corporatism but can only fulfill its function of political legitimation on the condition of distinguishing itself from it. At most I would wish to add that it is precisely the effectiveness of class struggles, in their various forms of representation or "consciousness," that periodically assures this regeneration of the political (or that has assured it in the historical period from which we are now emerging).

58. The expression "organic sovereignty" is at the heart of Hegel's *Elements of the Philosophy of Right*, ed. Allen W. Wood, trans. H. B. Nisbet (Cambridge: Cambridge University Press, 1991). It designates a "functional" conception of sovereignty in which the division of powers is put in the service of the state's supervision of civil society. This conception is particularly elaborated as far as the primacy of the political in the "theological" field is concerned, through the definitions of private religion, political disposition (*politische Gesinnung*), social morality (*Sittlichkeit*), and public opinion under the control of civil servants. It is more equivocal on the "economic" side, where Hegel oscillates between corporatism and the recognition of economic exclusions, leading him into the immediate neighborhood of a "social" version of Schmitt's state of exception. See Jean-François Kervégan, *Hegel, Carl Schmitt: Le Politique entre spéculation et positivité* (Paris: Presses universitaires de France, 1992).

59. For an analysis of the substitution of the "network" for the "territory" as the dominant form of organization of markets, which implies a separation of economic space from political space and obliges states to abandon the "Keynesian" model of sovereignty and appear on the global market as "enterprises" among others, see Marco Revelli, "Economia e modello nel passaggio tra fordismo e toyotismo," in *Appuntamenti di fine secolo*, ed. Pietro Ingrao and Rossana Rossanda (Rome: Manifestolibri, 1995), pp. 202–26. See also Pierre-Noël Giraud, *L'Inégalité du monde: Économie du monde contemporain* (Paris: Gallimard, 1996), on the competition between "national territories" for foreign investment, whose principle instrument is the abolition of taxes on capital movement and thus the dismantling of fiscal sovereignty.

Chapter 9

1. Aristotle, *Nicomachean Ethics*, trans. Roger Crisp (Cambridge: Cambridge University Press, 2000), 1094a28, p. 4 (Crisp translates *architektonikēs* as "master science").

2. G.W.F. Hegel, "The Constitution of Germany," in *Political Writings*, ed. Laurence Dickey and H. B. Nisbet (Cambridge: Cambridge University Press, 1999), p. 6.

3. Étienne Balibar, "'*Es gibt keinen Staat in Europa*': Racism and Politics in Europe Today," *New Left Review* 186 (March–April 1991): 5–19.

4. M. Rainer Lepsius, "Ethnos und Demos," in *Interessen, Ideen und Institutionen* (Opladen: Westdeutscher Verlag, 1990), pp. 247–55.

5. Carl Schmitt, *The* Nomos *of the Earth in the International Law of the* Jus Publicum Europaeum, trans. G. L. Ulmen (New York: Telos Press, 2003).

6. Jean Bodin, *Les Six Livres de la République,* 6 vols. (Paris: Fayard, 1986), 1: 112.

7. Jean-Jacques Rousseau, *Of the Social Contract,* book 1, chap. 7, in *The Social Contract and Other Later Political Writings,* ed. and trans. Victor Gourevitch (Cambridge: Cambridge University Press, 1997), p. 51.

8. See Baruch Spinoza, *Theological-Political Treatise,* trans. Samuel Shirley (Indianapolis: Hackett, 1998), particularly the preface and chap. 20 (pp. 1–8, 220–30). There is no way to know whether Spinoza was familiar with Étienne de la Boétie's *Traité de la servitude volontaire* (*Slaves by Choice,* trans. Malcolm Smith [Egham, Surrey, England: Runnymede, 1988]).

9. On the history and uses of the central notion of *Bildung* in Germany, see Aleida Assmann, *Arbeit am nationalen Gedächtnis: Eine kurze Geschichte der deutschen Bildungsidee* (Frankfurt: Campus Verlag, 1993); on the perennial ideal of civil religion among contemporary republicans, see Gian Enrico Rusconi, *Possiamo fare a meno di una religione civile?* (Bari: Laterza, 1999).

10. Which allows us to understand how this *particular* schema, under very restrictive conditions, also worked as a *universal* model of state formation.

11. Here it is important to see the contrast with the way that the International Monetary Fund "sets" (that is, puts into tutelage) budgets and exchange policies for "underdeveloped" countries, showing an essential default in their sovereignty.

12. See, for example, the headline in *Le Monde,* February 10, 2000: "The German Social-Democrats Launch Fiscal Competition in Europe" (i.e., by lowering taxes). See Pierre-Noël Giraud, *L'Inégalité du monde: Économie du monde contemporain* (Paris: Gallimard, 1996); but also, some time ago, James O'Connor, *The Fiscal Crisis of the State* (New York: St. Martin's Press, 1973).

13. Emmanuel-Joseph Sieyes, *What Is the Third Estate?* trans. M. Blondel (New York: Praeger, 1963); Carl Schmitt, *Verfassungslehre* (1928; reprint, Berlin: Duncker und Humblot, 1957); Antonio Negri, *Insurgencies: Constituent Power and the Modern State,* trans. Maurizia Boscagli (Minneapolis: University of Minnesota Press, 1999).

14. Whereas they frequently refer to the judicial decisions of European courts.

15. Unless we presume, as Antonio Negri and Michael Hardt do in *Empire* (Cambridge, Mass.: Harvard University Press, 2000), that we are currently seeing the emergence of a qualitatively new concept of "global sovereignty" that coincides with its own "crisis" and its own "corruption" insofar as, having no outside, it must exercise its power upon itself.

16. Which of course does not prevent a genuine inflation in the use of the

words "citizen" and "citizenship" ("citizen initiatives," etc.) that devalues and dilutes their sense.

17. I argue that this is how we should translate the unitary notion of *politeia* used by the Greeks and Aristotle in particular, making it the founding notion of political "theory." Existing translations, depending on the context, alternate between "constitution" (or "regime," "form of state," etc.) and "citizenship" (in the dual sense of institution and exercise of the rights of a citizen), whereas there is a single debate being pursued in all the uses. *Droit de cité* would be an interesting equivalent.

18. See Jürgen Habermas, *The Inclusion of the Other: Studies in Political Theory*, trans. Ciaran Cronin and Pablo De Greif (Cambridge, Mass.: MIT Press, 1998). The Austrian affair provoked an outburst of interventions on this theme, particularly as a way of removing the "constitutional obstacles" raised by a collective, majoritarian intervention in the electoral and governmental process of a member country in the name of what French President Jacques Chirac called a "European contract." The distant model is clearly the debate in America before the Civil War on whether certain states could continue to justify (and practice) slavery.

19. Olivier Beaud gives an admirable analysis of this vicious circle in the general conclusion to his *La Puissance de l'État* (Paris: Presses universitaires de France, 1994). Beaud's argument goes against the grain of all those who see a "dissolution of sovereignty" in the European framework on account of the constitutional ambiguity that refers, on one hand, to the autonomization of a "supranational sovereignty" inherent in the European treaties and, on the other, to the inalienable "reservation of sovereignty" they recognize in national states. See M. Rainer Lepsius, "Nationalstaat oder Nationalitätenstaat als Modell für die Weiterentwicklung der Europäischen Gemeinschaft," in *Demokratie in Deutschland: Soziologisch-historische Konstellationsanalysen: Ausgewählte Aufsätze* (Göttingen: Vandenhoeck und Ruprecht, 1993), pp. 265–85.

20. On the idea of a "constitution in the material sense" (theorized in particular by the Italian jurist Costantino Mortati) and on the light the antithesis between the two senses of the word "constitution" can throw on the processes of "deformalization" of the state to which the development of the social state gives rise, see Giacomo Marramao, *Dopo il Leviatano: Individuo e comunità nella filosofia politica* (Turin: Giappichelli editore, 1995), pp. 356–59.

21. See the references in Bino Olivi, *L'Europe difficile: Histoire politique de la communauté européenne* (Paris: Gallimard, 1998); Chistina Giannoulis, "Die Idee des 'Europa der Bürger' und ihre Bedeutung für den Grundrechtsschutz," Ph.D. dissertation, Universität des Saarlandes, Europa-Institut, Sektion Rechtswissenschaft, 1992; and Catherine Wihtol de Wenden, *La Citoyenneté européenne* (Paris: Presses de la Fondation nationale des Sciences politiques, 1997).

22. As is well known, one of Jacques Delors's favorite themes for some years now has been that there is an insoluble contradiction between the two goals that

European Union as presently composed has officially set for itself, namely the (limited) opening to a certain number of "candidate" countries to the East, and the reinforcement of the cohesion and powers of the European Commission and European Parliament. If there is a contradiction between the goals of enlargement and integration, and a fortiori the goal of developing "social Europe," what would be said of the contradiction that would arise if we were to put into question the boundaries and procedures of exclusion that have been incorporated into the very definition of European identity.

23. Edgar Morin, *Penser l'Europe* (Paris: Gallimard, 1987).

24. Antonio Gramsci, *Selections from the Prison Notebooks*, trans. Quintin Hoare and Geoffrey Nowell Smith (New York: International Publishers, 1971), pp. 5–23.

25. The "constitutionalization" of social rights is more or less explicit depending on the state. The most striking example is that of Italy, whose 1948 constitution stipulates that "Italy is a democratic Republic founded on labor" (*L'Italia è una Repubblica democratica fondata sul lavoro*). The French constitution of 1958, under the heading of "Sovereignty" (article 2), stipulates that "France is an indivisible, secular, democratic and social Republic" (*La France est une République indivisible, laïque, démocratique et sociale*). The 1949 *Grundgesetz* of the Federal Republic of Germany (today applicable to the whole country) stipulates in article 20.1 that "The Federal Republic of Germany is a democratic and social federal state" (*Die Bundesrepublik Deutschland ist ein demokratischer und sozialer Bundesstaat*), which is further specified by article 28.1: "Regulations having constitutional value in individual states must correspond to the fundamental principles of a republican, democratic, and social state in the sense defined by this Fundamental Law" (*Die verfassungsmässige Ordnung in den Ländern muss den Grundsätzen des republikanischen, demokratischen und sozialen Rechtsstaates im Sinne dieses Grundgesetzes entsprechen*).

26. Most often an opposition is drawn between a "Beveridgian model" and a "Bismarckian model," with the French case being located halfway in between. On the methodological problems posed by the definition of a "European social model," see Daniel Lenoir, *L'Europe sociale* (Paris: La Découverte, 1994).

27. T. H. Marshall, "Citizenship and Social Class," in *Class, Citizenship, and Social Development: Essays by T. H. Marshall* (Garden City, N.Y.: Anchor Books, 1965), pp. 65–122.

28. Robert Castel, *From Manual Workers to Wage Laborers: Transformation of the Social Question*, trans. Richard Boyd (New Brunswick, N.J.: Transaction Publishers, 2003).

29. See Donald Sassoon's account of the "Beveridgian" orientation of universalizing social rights as rights of the citizen in *One Hundred Years of Socialism: The West European Left in the Twentieth Century* (New York: New Press, 1996), particularly chap. 6, "Building Social Capitalism 1945–50."

30. See the opposition between "permissions" and "entitlements," formulated by Raymond Aron and taken up by many authors, in particular Luc Ferry and

Alain Renaut, *Political Philosophy*, vol. 3: *From the Rights of Man to the Republican Idea*, trans. Franklin Philip (Chicago: University of Chicago Press, 1992). It is remarkable that an author such as Amartya Sen, coming from the utilitarian tradition, has been led by the study of problems of development in the Third World and of inequalities connected with globalization to give a vigorous reaffirmation of the principle of equality of opportunity. See Amartya Sen, *Inequality Reexamined* (Cambridge, Mass.: Harvard University Press, 1992), and the special issue of the journal *Cités* 1 (2000) devoted to his work.

31. See Karl Polanyi, *The Great Transformation* (Boston: Beacon Press, 1971).

32. See chapter 5.

33. See, most recently, Olivi, *L'Europe difficile.*

34. Political leaders in Hungary, Poland, and the Czech Republic, which are candidates together for admission to the European Union, often insist on the "non-European" character of Russia, on the Russian people's lack of "democratic traditions," and so forth.

35. An expression popularized by the political scientist and former European commissioner Lord Ralf Dahrendorf, *Reflections on the Revolution in Europe* (New York: Times Books, 1990).

36. This would be the time to read the prophetic pages in John Maynard Keynes, *The Economic Consequences of the Peace* (New York: Harcourt, Brace and Howe, 1920), which also presents the advantage of illustrating in a striking way the relativity of representations of European identity and of the "borders" of Europe with respect to determinate conjunctures and political objectives. Sometimes what is "problematic" is Great Britain's membership in the "system" of European nations, at other times it is the Slavic or more precisely Russian space, and at others still it is the Mediterranean region, which is capable of overflowing both shores (as can be seen today from Turkey to the Maghreb). Nothing durable nor (a fortiori) natural is to be found in these exclusions.

37. A point of agreement between the work of two historians who are diametrically opposed about everything else: Ernst Nolte, *Der Europäische Bürgerkrieg, 1917–1945: Nationalsozialismus und Bolschewismus*, 5th ed. (Munich: F. A. Herbig Verlag, 1997); and E. J. Hobsbawm, *The Age of Extremes: A History of the World, 1914–1991* (New York: Vintage Books, 1996).

38. On the "new wars" in Europe and the relations that they entertain with traits of "globalization" after the end of the "Cold War," see Mary Kaldor, *New and Old Wars: Organized Violence in a Global Era* (Stanford: Stanford University Press, 1999).

39. An expression invented by Jacques Rupnik, *The Other Europe* (New York: Schocken Books, 1989).

40. See Imre Marton, "Transition démocratique ou démocratisation transitoire dans les pays de l'Europe de l'Est," *M* 45 (April 1991); see also the special issue of *Mouvements* 6 (November–December 1999) on "Est 89–99: Que sont les espoirs devenus?"

41. This text was written before the withdrawal or overthrow of Slobodan Milošević and his replacement by Vojislav Kostunica, a process whose goals and means remain obscure. What is clear is that the disastrous consequences of the 1999 bombing campaign led the allies to favor this solution without posing any conditions.

42. "A procedural and pluralist identity with moving borders," in the formula of Pierre Hassner, "Construction européenne et mutations à l'Est," in *L'Europe au soir du siècle: Identité et démocratie*, ed. Jacques Lenoble and Nicole Dewandre (Paris: Éditions Esprit, 1992), p. 273. The effectiveness of this "procedure" between 1950 and 1997 is one of the major themes of Olivi, *L'Europe difficile*.

43. Quite recently taken up by Alexandre Adler, "La Grande Europe," *Philosophie politique* 1 (1991): 151–61.

44. See Ismail Kadaré, "Il faut européaniser les Balkans," *Le Monde*, April 10, 1999, pp. 1, 16.

45. Timothy Garton Ash, "L'Europe a raté une extraordinaire opportunité" (interview), *Libération*, November 9, 1999, p. 4.

46. See, in particular, Étienne Balibar, "Is European Citizenship Possible?" in *Politics and the Other Scene*, trans. Christine Jones, James Swenson, and Chris Turner (London: Verso, 2002), pp. 104–28.

47. The Maastricht Treaty defines European citizenship as belonging to those who hold citizenship in one of the member countries of the Union.

48. I by no means regret this provocation today when we consider the developments of the Austrian affair: the hypocrisy of the reactions by other European countries (with France at their head), since everywhere Jörg Haider's explicit goal— legislation creating an "internal exclusion" of "extracommunal" immigrants as a precarious labor force—is already, to one degree or another, in place.

49. See Wihtol de Wenden, *La Citoyenneté européenne*, p. 99. Another significant use of the comparison with apartheid can be found in the way some intellectuals currently characterize relations of neocolonial domination within the combined Israeli-Palestinian space. See, for example, Ariella Azoulay and Adi Ophir, "100 Years of Zionism, 50 Years of a Jewish State," *Tikkun* 13, no. 2 (March–April 1998): 68–71.

50. See Andrea Rea, ed., *Immigration et racisme en Europe* (Brussels: Éditions complexe, 1998).

51. See chapter 7.

52. Gramsci, *Selections from the Prison Notebooks*, pp. 229–43.

53. Jean-Marc Ferry, *La Question de l'État européen* (Paris: Gallimard, 2000).

54. Yves Sintomer, *La Démocratie impossible? Politique et modernité chez Weber et Habermas* (Paris: La Découverte, 1999), p. 369.

55. See Giorgio Baratta, *Le rose e i quaderni: Saggio sul pensiero di Antonio Gramsci* (Rome: Gamberetti Editrice, 2000).

56. Herman R. van Gunsteren, *A Theory of Citizenship: Organizing Plurality in Contemporary Democracies* (Boulder, Colo.: Westview Press, 1998).

57. Aristotle, *The Politics and The Constitution of Athens*, ed. Stephen Everson, trans. Benjamin Jowett (Cambridge: Cambridge University Press, 1996), book 3, particularly 1275a19–34, p. 62.

58. G.W.F. Hegel, *Elements of the Philosophy of Right*, ed. Allen W. Wood, trans. H. B. Nisbet (Cambridge: Cambridge University Press, 1991), §100, p. 126.

59. See Blandine Kriegel, *Philosophie de la République* (Paris: Plon, 1998), pp. 306–7: "As for us, we must accept that our administrative law and our centralization, which, as Tocqueville pointed out is more admininstrative than political, have had their time and that, if we want to preserve political centralization, we will have to sacrifice administrative centralization. We will have to accept, if we do not want to see a pendulum swing between the dictatorship of corrupt Parliaments and that of avenging judges, the installation of a true European judicial power that is every bit as structured and autonomous and that founds its justifications on a more active and up-to-date jurisprudence than ours. . . . Scattered elements exist that would allow us to constitute the beginnings of the rule of law . . . from the set of European Courts, which constitute a genuine balance to the administrative power of the Commission. . . . What we do not have is a common European citizenship."

60. See Lepsius, "Nationalstaat oder Nationalitätenstaat."

61. The question does not only concern private litigation, criminal and civil matters, but also matters of humanitarian law, now that the question of a true "cosmopolitan penal law" is being posed. The episode of the Pinochet affair, set in motion by Spanish judges, shows that there is a competition between two sorts of proceedings: those of special penal tribunals and that of "universal jurisdiction," which would seem to be much more democratic but which for that very reason is dependent on the way in which public opinion in each country progressively takes into account issues of justice concerning all of humanity. We can hope that a "European doctrine" will be formed on this point that will not merely be the reflection of conjunctural relations of power on the world scale.

62. See Pierre Bourdieu, *Acts of Resistance: Against the Tyranny of the Market*, trans. Richard Nice (New York: New Press, 1998); Bourdieu, *Backfire: Against the Tyranny of the Market*, trans. Chris Turner (New York: New Press, 2002).

63. Negri and Hardt, *Empire*, pp. 22–41.

64. A particularly disturbing prefiguration of this trend is the trade in children offered for adoption (which, thanks to the Internet, is now becoming completely internationalized).

65. We can only hope that the information center created in Sweden by Nicholas Bush is able to resume its activities with more appropriate means at its disposal: *Fortress Europe*, Blomstervägen 7, S-791 33 Falun, Sweden.

66. See Umberto Eco, *The Search for the Perfect Language* (*The Making of Europe*) (Oxford: Blackwell, 1995), pp. 350–51: "These are possibilities for more than just the practice of translation; they are the possibilities for co-existence on a continent with a multilingual vocation. Generalized polyglottism is certainly not the solution to Europe's cultural problems. . . . The solution for the future is more likely

to be in a community of peoples with an increased ability to receive the spirit, to taste or savor the aroma of different dialects. Polyglot Europe will not be a continent where individuals converse freely in all the other languages; in the best of cases, it could be a continent where differences of language are no longer barriers to communication, where people can meet each other and speak together, each in his or her own tongue, understanding, as best they can, the speech of others. In this way, even those who never learn to speak another language fluently could still participate in its particular genius, catching a glimpse of the particular cultural universe that every individual expresses each time he or she speaks the language of his or her ancestors and his or her own tradition." To which it would be appropriate to add that the "community of translation" is also not that in which everyone speaks or understands everyone else's language but, on the contrary, that in which the role of "interpreter," depending on the situations and configurations of exchange, is capable of falling on anyone in turn, passing from the "majority" to the "minority" position.

67. The "Humboldtian" tradition, founded on the idea of a homology between language and culture considered as "totalities," does not in fact correspond to Humboldt's own practice. See Antoine Berman, *The Experience of the Foreign: Culture and Translation in Romantic Germany*, trans. S. Heyvaert (Albany: State University of New York Press, 1992).

68. The charter, unequally accepted by member states (who have the latitude to apply it in whole or in part), has the advantage of including in a single document "territorial" languages such as Corsican or Basque and languages "of immigration" such as Arabic or Turkish, but it does not unite them in a single concept, which means that it does not manage to conceptualized the equality between the different communities that contribute to the formation of the "European people."

69. There is obviously a relation between the fact that the European continent has preserved a multiplicity of idioms for a relatively limited population, and the fact that each of these languages has been associated with projects of colonial universalization that have globalized them to some extent: compare this with the American continent or China.

70. We should not be too quick to think that "minority" status is the seed of a language's decline as a means of access to cultural universality, particularly if it can be transformed into an aesthetic problem. See the beautiful pages Pierre-Yves Pétillon devotes to the English of Irish writers in *L'Europe aux anciens parapets* (Paris: Seuil, 1986).

71. Barbara Cassin has set the concept of "untranslatable" as a means of translation itself at the center of the collective project she organized for a *Vocabulaire européen des philosophies* (forthcoming).

72. But with considerable differences; the "small countries" (Netherlands, Scandinavia, Greece, and Portugal) show a considerable advance in this respect (and demonstrate that mass plurilinguism is perfectly possible).

Chapter 10

1. See Claude Lefort, *The Political Forms of Modern Society: Bureaucracy, Democracy, Totalitarianism*, trans. John B. Thompson (Cambridge, Mass.: MIT Press, 1986) (many of the essays in this collection were collected in French under the title *L'Invention démocratique: Les Limites de la domination totalitaire* [Paris: Fayard, 1981]).

2. See Rogers M. Smith, *Civic Ideals: Conflicting Visions of Citizenship in U.S. History* (New Haven: Yale University Press, 1997).

3. Jürgen Habermas, *Between Facts and Norms: Contributions to a Discourse Theory of Law and Democracy*, trans. William Rehg (Cambridge, Mass.: MIT Press, 1996), p. 94. See the entire discussion in chap. 3, "A Reconstructive Approach to Law I: The System of Rights," pp. 82–131.

4. This term has been put forward with insistence in France by Dominique Schnapper, in particular in *Community of Citizens: On the Modern Idea of Nationality*, trans. Séverine Rosée (New Brunswick, N.J.: Transaction Publishers, 1998). See the discussion in chapter 4 above.

5. See Olivier Beaud, *La Puissance de l'État* (Paris: Presses universitaires de France, 1994), whose conclusion is devoted to a very interesting confrontation between classical constitutional notions and the juridical problems of European unification.

6. We would need to devote a particular discussion to determining to what extent and in what way a performative utterance of this sort also underlies the *constative* statements chosen by the German constitutional tradition: "The German people has given itself the following Constitution" (*Das deutsche Volk hat sich diese Verfassung gegeben*), referring to the Weimar Constitution; "The German People has given itself the following Fundamental Law by virtue of its constituent power" (. . . *hat sich das Deutsche Volk kraft seiner verfassungsgebenden Gewalt dieses Grundgesetz gegeben*), referring to the *Grundgesetz* of the Federal Republic.

7. Jean-Jacques Rousseau, *Of the Social Contract*, book 1, chap. 6, in *The Social Contract and Other Later Political Writings*, ed. and trans. Victor Gourevitch (Cambridge: Cambridge University Press, 1997), p. 50.

8. G.W.F. Hegel, *Phenomenology of Spirit*, trans. A. V. Miller (Oxford: Clarendon Press, 1977), p. 110.

9. See Étienne Balibar, "Identité/Normalité," in *Nous, citoyens d'Europe: Les Frontières, l'État, le peuple* (Paris: La Découverte, 2001), pp. 57–67 [not included in the current translation].

10. Friedrich Nietzsche, "On the New Idol," in *Thus Spoke Zarathustra: A Book for All and None*, trans. Walter Kauffman (New York: Viking, 1966), p. 48.

11. The solution of such aporias of democratic representation obviously goes beyond the framework of parliamentary institutions (which does not mean that it suppresses them). The "extreme" cases are the most revealing; see Barbara Cassin's comparison of the Greek practice of amnesty with that of the Truth and Reconcilia-

tion Commission in South Africa, in "Politiques de la mémoire: Des Traitements de la haine," *Multitudes* 6 (September 2001): 177–96.

12. See, for example, Jürgen Habermas, *The Inclusion of the Other: Studies in Political Theory*, trans. Ciaran Cronin and Pablo De Greif (Cambridge, Mass.: MIT Press, 1998).

13. See G.W.F. Hegel, *Elements of the Philosophy of Right*, ed. Allen W. Wood, trans. H. B. Nisbet (Cambridge: Cambridge University Press, 1991), §100, p. 126: "The injury which is inflicted on the criminal is not only just *in itself* (and since it is just, it is at the same time his will as it is *in itself*, an existence [*Dasein*] of his freedom, *his* right); it is also a *right for the criminal himself*, that is, a right *posited* in his *existent* will, in his action. For it is implicit in his action, as that of a *rational* being, that it is universal in character, and that, by performing it, he has set up a law which he has recognized for himself in his action, and under which he may therefore be subsumed as under *his* right." An excellent commentary on the function of the dialectic of the "criminal" in the formation of Hegel's politics can be found in Axel Honneth, *The Struggle for Recognition: The Moral Grammar of Social Conflicts*, trans. Joel Anderson (Cambridge, Mass.: Polity Press, 1995).

14. This problem has arisen in France in a particularly acute way in the case of indictments of African parents for having practiced or having had practiced traditional clitoridectomy on their daughters. It is clear that we can neither accept a "culturalist" argument that would exempt African families from any sanctions against bodily violence (linked to a complete system of subjection of women), nor claim to judge them in the name of universal "human rights" whose benefits they are generally refused without admitting them to citizenship (e.g., in the form of voting rights).

15. See Habermas, *Between Facts and Norms*, pp. 512–13.

16. Herman R. van Gunsteren, *A Theory of Citizenship: Organizing Plurality in Contemporary Democracies* (Boulder, Colo.: Westview Press, 1998).

17. Karl Marx, *The Poverty of Philosophy*, ed. C. P. Dutt and V. Chattopadhyaya (New York: International Publishers, n.d.), p. 102.

18. T. H. Marshall, "Citizenship and Social Class," in *Class, Citizenship, and Social Development: Essays by T. H. Marshall* (Garden City, N.Y.: Anchor Books, 1965), pp. 65–122.

19. Jürgen Habermas, "Why Europe Needs a Constitution," *New Left Review* 11 (September–October 2001): 6.

20. Olivier Beaud, "Constitution et constitutionnalisme," in *Dictionnaire de philosophie politique*, ed. Philippe Raynaud and Stéphane Rials (Paris: Presses universitaires de France, 1996), pp. 117–26.

21. Giacomo Marramao, *Dopo il Leviatano: Individuo e comunità nella filosofia politica* (Turin: Giappichelli editore, 1995), pp. 347–59 (chap. 10, "Stato sociale: un ossimoro?").

22. The translator's index in the recent French edition (Aristote, *Les Politiques*, ed. and trans. Pierre Pellegrin [Paris: Garnier-Flammarion, 1990]), gives three prin-

cipal "meanings" of *politeia*: "constitution," "constitutional government" (i.e., the "just" form of government by the many whose perversion or deviation Aristotle calls "democracy"), and finally "political life," of which the rights of citizens are a subdivision.

23. On the potential conflict between *politeia* and *isonomia* (a term avoided by Aristotle and favored by the sophists), see in particular Christian Meier, *The Greek Discovery of Politics*, trans. David McLintock (Cambridge, Mass.: Harvard University Press, 1990). Aristotle insists at length on the deliberative competence of the mass of the people (*plēthos*). Still, despite the use of formulations such as *kratos tou dēmou* or *dēmokratia d' estin hotan ēi kurion to plēthos* ("Democracy is said to be the government of the many" [Aristotle, *The Politics and The Constitution of Athens*, ed. Stephen Everson, trans. Benjamin Jowett (Cambridge: Cambridge University Press, 1996), 1279b21, p. 72]), I do not think it would be correct to speak of "popular sovereignty," for this socially determinate mass, in opposition to the minority of the rich or the nobles, is not understood as a unified "subject" or political body as it will be in modern thought, after the invention of sovereignty by empires and monarchies. See also Claude Nicolet, ed., *Dēmokratia et Aristokratia* (Paris: Publications de la Sorbonne, 1983).

24. See H. A. Winkler, *Der lange Weg nach Westen: Deutsche Geschichte vom Ende des Alten Reiches bis zum Untergang der Weimarer Republik* (Munich: C. H. Beck Verlag, 2000).

25. We find once again here, it seems to me, what in an earlier essay I called the two "mediations" of *equaliberty*, the "communitarian" mediation and the "utilitarian" mediation. See Étienne Balibar, "'Rights of Man' and 'Rights of the Citizen,'" in *Masses, Classes, Ideas: Studies on Politics and Philosophy before and after Marx*, trans. James Swenson (New York: Routledge, 1994), pp. 39–59.

26. Étienne de la Boétie, *Slaves by Choice* (Traité de la servitude volontaire), trans. Malcolm Smith (Egham, Surrey: Runnymede, 1988).

27. See chapter 8.

28. See Robert Castel and Claudine Haroche, *Propriété privée, propriété sociale, propriété de soi: Entretiens sur la construction de l'individu moderne* (Paris: Fayard, 2001). The question of education is emblematic here, too; a particularly clear and accurate light is cast on it by the work of Amartya Sen; see his *Inequality Reexamined* (Cambridge, Mass.: Harvard University Press, 1992).

29. This should be compared with the interesting but fundamentally different proposition by Jean-Marc Ferry, *La Question de l'État européen* (Paris: Gallimard, 2000), pp. 159–61, that the "ethical substance of the postnational state" must be made up of "historical communities" that have eliminated mutual resentment, the result of injustices they have suffered in the past, by means of a symbolic "reconciliation." Ferry does not say how, within a given historical space, the communities that will take part in the reconciliation and those that will remain outside it are to be chosen (nor how the borders are to be set). In short, he poses the question of the legacy of national wars but not that of the legacy of colonization.

30. See chapter 8.

31. See Gian Enrico Rusconi, *Possiamo fare a meno di una religione civile?* (Bari: Laterza, 1999).

32. Friedrich Nietzsche, *The Gay Science*, ed. Bernard Williams, trans. Josefine Nauckhoff (Cambridge: Cambridge University Press, 2001), §344, p. 200.

Chapter 11

1. George L. Mosse, *Nationalism and Sexuality: Middle-Class Morality and Sexual Norms in Modern Europe* (Madison: University of Wisconsin Press, 1985).

2. Thomas Mann, *Reflections of a Nonpolitical Man*, trans. Walter D. Morris (New York: Frederick Ungar, 1983).

3. Thomas Mann, "Europe Beware" and "Culture and Politics," in *Order of the Day: Political Essays and Speeches of Two Decades*, trans. H. T. Lowe-Porter (New York: Alfred A. Knopf, 1942), pp. 69–82, 228–37.

4. I am especially thinking of Michel Foucault's opposing the "universal intellectual" of the past and the new "specific intellectual," which was often misunderstood. See Michel Foucault, "Truth and Power," *Essential Works of Foucault, 1954–1984*, ed. Paul Rabinow and James D. Faubion, 3 vols. (New York: New Press, 1997–99), 3: 111–33.

5. Michel Foucault, *The Order of Things: An Archaeology of the Human Sciences* (New York: Pantheon, 1971).

6. David Blankenhorn et al., "What We're Fighting For: A Letter from America," Institute for American Values, February 12, 2002. In a second Letter ("Preemption, Iraq, and Just War: A Statement of Principles," dated November 14, 2002), some of the initial signatories express their concern that the new strategic doctrine of "pre-emption" applied to the case of Iraq by the Bush administration is "inconsistent with the just war tradition" that legitimized the war in Afghanistan. Both letters are available at <http://www.americanvalues.org/html/what__ we__ are __fighting__for.html> and <http://www.americanvalues.org/html/1b__ pre-emption.html>.

7. See the subtle analysis by Sophie Body-Gendrot, *La Société américaine après le 11 septembre* (Paris: Presses de la Fondation Nationale des Sciences Politiques, 2002).

8. Bruce Ackerman, "Don't Panic!" *London Review of Books*, February 7, 2002, pp. 15–16.

9. Immanuel Wallerstein, "America and the World: The Twin Towers as Metaphor" (delivered as the Charles R. Lawrence II Memorial Lecture, Brooklyn College, December 5, 2001), *Transeuropéennes* 22 (Spring–Summer 2002): 9–29.

10. Ibid., p. 9.

11. Ibid., pp. 14–17.

12. Ibid., p. 22.

13. Ibid., p. 23.

14. Ibid., pp. 25–27.

15. "Immanuel Wallerstein on the World Movement Facing the Capitalist Domination," World Social Forum at Porto Alegre II, February 2002, available on line at <http://www.attac.org/fsm2002/indexen.html>.

16. Timothy Garton Ash, "The Peril of Too Much Power" (op-ed), *New York Times*, April 9, 2002, p. A25.

17. Edward Said, "Europe against America," *Al-Ahram Weekly*, November 14–20, 2002, available at <http://weekly.ahram.org.eg/2002/612/op2.htm>. See also Edward W. Said, *Orientalism* (New York: Pantheon, 1978), and *Culture and Imperialism* (New York: Alfred A. Knopf, 1993).

18. In September 2002, during the German electoral campaign, Chancellor Gerhard Schröder (who was to be reelected with a slim majority) declared that he would refuse any engagement of German troops in an American-led war against Iraq, even if it was endorsed by the United Nations. This led both to sharp criticism in the United States and the expression of reservations by other European governments. A radical interpretation of Schröder's intentions as paving the way for a "non-Western" Europe has been proposed by the German philosopher Peter Sloterdijk, "La différence de Schröder: La Voix de l'Europe," *Libération*, October 7, 2002, p. 9.

19. Robert Kagan, "Power and Weakness," *Policy Review* 113 (June–July 2002): 3–28.

20. Ibid., p. 3.

21. Robert Kagan, "Europe and America III: Different Philosophies of Power," *International Herald Tribune*, May 27, 2002, p. 10 (a summary of the arguments of "Power and Weakness").

22. See Mary Kaldor, *New and Old Wars: Organized Violence in a Global Era* (Stanford: Stanford University Press, 1999).

23. Resolution no. 1441 of the Security Council of the United Nations, dated November 8, 2002.

24. The Monroe Doctrine was expressed in the Message to Congress by President James Monroe dated December 2, 1823. It enunciated four principles: that the American continents were no longer to be considered open for colonization by the European powers; that the political system of the Americas was different from that of Europe; that the United States would consider any attempt on the part of the European powers to extend their system to the Western Hemisphere as dangerous to its peace and safety; and that the United States would not interfere in the internal affairs of European countries. For the text, see Richard Hofstadter, *Great Issues in American History: A Documentary Record*, vol. 1: *From the Revolution to the Civil War*, (New York: Vintage Books, 1958), pp. 244–47. It was later used to legitimize U.S. imperialist policies in Latin America as "inter-American affairs." The German conservative, later Nazi, jurist and political theorist Carl Schmitt had started very early to discuss its meaning for a new conception of international relations (see Carl Schmitt, "Völkerrrechtliche Formen des modernen Imperialismus" [1932], *Posi-*

tionen und Begriffe im Kampf mit Weimar-Genf-Versailles [Berlin: Duncker und Humblot, 1994], pp. 184–203). In 1938 he used it to legitimize German plans to create a "European Great Space" under German leadership (see Carl Schmitt, "Neutrality According to International Law and National Totality," in *Four Articles, 1931–1938*, ed. and trans. Simona Draghici (Washington, D.C.: Plutarch Press, 1999). Hitler himself borrowed the formula of a "European Monroe Doctrine" in his *Reischstagsrede* of April 28, 1939, rejecting Roosevelt's warning against an aggression of Poland by Germany. For a recent use, see Jean-Pierre Chevènement (former Socialist minister of the interior), "Pour une doctrine de Monroe européenne," *La Lettre de République Moderne* 104 (December 2000), available at <http://www.tribunes.com/tgr/JPC/Monroe%europeenne.htm>.

25. Scott L. Malcomson, *Borderlands: Nation and Empire* (Boston: Faber and Faber, 1994).

26. Thierry de Montbrial, "Europe: La Dialectique intérieur-extérieur," *Le Monde*, November 19, 2002, pp. 1, 17. See also his latest book, Thierry de Montbrial, *L'Action et le système du monde* (Paris: Presses universitaires de France, 2002).

27. Michel Foucault, "The Subject and Power," in *Essential Works of Foucault*, 3: 326–48.

28. The expression "Christian Europe," which comes from German Romanticism (see Novalis [Friedrich von Hardenberg], "Christianity or Europe: A Fragment" [1799], in *The Early Political Writings of the German Romantics*, ed. Fredrick C. Beiser [Cambridge: Cambridge University Press, 1996], pp. 61–79), is constantly used by Pope John Paul II, who, when receiving Valéry Giscard d'Estaing on October 31, 2002, urged that the coming "European Constitution" refer to the Christian values that are essential to Europe's identity. Giscard himself expressed the same idea indirectly when he argued that Turkey, as an Islamic country, could not belong to the European Union. See Arnaud Leparmentier and Laurent Zecchini, "Europe: Pour ou contre la Turquie," *Le Monde*, November 9, 2002, pp. 1–2.

29. Monique Chemillier-Gendreau, "Contre l'ordre impérial, un ordre public démocratique et universel," *Le Monde diplomatique*, December 2002, pp. 22–23. See also her recent book, *Droit international et démocratie mondiale: Les Raisons d'un échec* (Paris: Les Éditions Textuel, 2002).

30. This expression is used by historians of quite different orientation: Ernst Nolte, *Der Europäische Bürgerkrieg, 1917–1945: Nationalsozialismus und Bolschewismus*, 5th ed. (Munich: F. A. Herbig Verlag, 1997); but also E. J. Hobsbawm, *The Age of Extremes: A History of the World, 1914–1991* (New York: Vintage Books, 1996).

31. Amartya Sen, *Inequality Reexamined* (Cambridge, Mass.: Harvard University Press, 1992).

32. Machiavelli's basic idea is that the strength of the Roman Republic came from the fact—half calculated, half unintended—that the antagonism between the two great social classes (the "patricians" and the "plebeians") found an institutional

solution with the creation, after violent revolts and repressions, of the "Tribunate of the Plebs." See Niccolò Macchiavelli, *Discourses on Livy*, trans. Harvey C. Mansfield and Nathan Tarcov (Chicago: University of Chicago Press, 1996), book 1, chap. 4 ("That the Disunion of the Plebs and the Roman Senate Made That Republic Free and Powerful"), pp. 16–17.

33. Max Weber, "The Social Psychology of World Religions," in *From Max Weber: Essays in Sociology*, ed. and trans. H. H. Gerth and C. Wright Mills (New York: Oxford University Press, 1946), pp. 267–301.

34. "Expansive democracy" is a synonym for what Gramsci more often calls "hegemony," that is, a strategy of "permanent revolution" transposed within the state itself. See Antonio Gramsci, *Quaderni del carcere*, Edizione critica dell'Istituto Gramsci, ed. Valentino Gerratana, 4 vols. (Turin: Einaudi, 1975), particularly pp. 972–73, 1565–67 (see note 29 to chapter 2 above on the relations between this edition and the existing English translations of the *Prison Notebooks*). See also Claude Lefort, *The Political Forms of Modern Society: Bureaucracy, Democracy, Totalitarianism*, trans. John B. Thompson (Cambridge, Mass.: MIT Press, 1986) (many of the essays in this collection were collected in French under the title *L'Invention démocratique: Les Limites de la domination totalitaire* [Paris: Fayard, 1981]).

35. See Charter of the United Nations, chapter 1, article 1: "The Purposes of the United Nations are: 1. To maintain international peace and security, and to that end: to take effective collective measures for the prevention and removals of threats to the peace, and for the suppression of acts of aggression or other breaches of the peace, and to bring about by peaceful means, and in conformity with the principles of justice and international law, adjustment or settlement of international disputes or situations which might lead to a breach of the peace."

36. The NATO summit in Prague of November 2002 admitted new members from Eastern Europe and heard a call from President Bush to "modernize" the capabilities of the European members in order to adapt to the new type of wars that the alliance is now contemplating. "Some critics argue that, in the course of carrying out this work of political incubation, NATO has ceased to be a workable military alliance and now may be destined to wither. In fact the organization has been slowly but steadily rebuilding itself for the 21st century. The creation of a reaction force capable of deploying around the world is a significant step in the right direction. Whether NATO now becomes a force for combating terrorists and rogue states and for spreading democracy beyond Europe will depend on whether the political will for a strong trans-Atlantic partnership can be sustained, both in Washington and in Europe. Yet the power and potential of that bond ought to be evident in the two great achievements for which NATO can now be credited: first the deterrence of Soviet aggression and now the consolidation of a Europe that is peaceful and free" ([Editorial], "NATO's Success Story" *Washington Post*, November 22, 2002, p. A40).

37. See Kaldor, *New and Old Wars*, p. 111: "Precisely because the new wars are a social condition that arises as the formal political economy withers, they are

very difficult to end. Diplomatic negotiations from above fail to take into account the underlying social relations. . . . Temporary ceasefires or truces may merely legitimize new agreements or partnerships that, for the moment, suit the various factions. Peacekeeping troops sent in to monitor ceasefires which reflect the status quo may help to maintain a division of territory and to prevent the return of refugees. Economic reconstruction channeled through existing 'political authorities' may merely provide new sources of revenue as local assets dry up. As long as the power relations remain the same, sooner or later the violence will start again. Fear, hatred and predation are not recipes for long-term viable politics. Indeed, this type of war economy is perennially on the edge of exhaustion. This does not mean, however, that they will disappear of their own accord. There has to be some alternative. . . . In particular, islands of civility might offer a counterlogic to the new warfare."

38. See Charles Enderlin, *Le Rêve brisé: Histoire de l'échec du processus de paix au Proche-Orient, 1995–2002* (Paris: Fayard, 2002).

39. Giovanni Arrighi, Terence K. Hopkins, and Immanuel Wallerstein, *Anti-systemic Movements* (London: Verso, 1989). More recently, see Ramòn Grosfoguel and Ana Margarita Cervantes-Rodriguez, eds., *The Modern/Colonial/Capitalist World-System in the Twentieth Century: Global Processes, Antisystemic Movements, and the Geopolitics of Knowledge* (Westport, Conn.: Greenwood Press, 2002).

40. Samuel P. Huntington, *The Clash of Civilizations and the Remaking of World Order* (New York: Simon and Schuster, 1996). See the discussion by Bruce Robbins, "How Not to Criticise *The Clash of Civilizations*," *Transeuropéennes* 22 (Spring–Summer 2002): 31–41.

41. Olivier Christin, *La Paix de religion: L'Autonomisation de la raison politique au XVIe siècle* (Paris: Seuil, 1997).

42. A critical view of the "Euro-Mediterranean Partnership" is presented in *Critique Internationale* 18 (January 2003), special issue "Les Faces cachées du partenariat euro-méditerranéen."

43. Carl Schmitt, *The* Nomos *of the Earth in the International Law of the* Jus Publicum Europaeum, trans. G. L. Ulmen (New York: Telos Press, 2003).

44. See Germaine Tillion, *France and Algeria: Complementary Enemies*, trans. Richard Howard (New York: Alfred A. Knopf, 1961). See my commentary in Étienne Balibar, "Algeria, France: One Nation or Two?" trans. Adele Porter, in *Giving Ground: The Politics of Propinquity*, ed. Joan Copjec and Michael Sorkin (London: Verso, 1999), pp. 162–72.

45. Leparmentier and Zecchini, "Europe: Pour ou contre la Turquie."

46. As was pointed out during the discussion following this talk at the Humboldt-Universität.

47. An initial version was presented at the New School for Social Research in New York, on March 14, 2002, where I had been invited by Nancy Fraser from the Department of Political Science and Jay Bernstein from the Department of Philosophy.

48. Fredric Jameson, "The Vanishing Mediator; or, Max Weber as Storyteller,"

in *The Ideologies of Theory*, 2 vols. (Minneapolis: University of Minnesota Press, 1988), 2: 3–34 (originally published in *New German Critique* 1 [Winter 1974]: 52–89).

49. Umberto Eco, *The Search for the Perfect Language (The Making of Europe)* (Oxford: Blackwell, 1995), pp. 350–51.

50. Louis Althusser, "Philosophy and the Spontaneous Philosophy of the Scientists" (1967), in *Philosophy and the Spontaneous Philosophy of the Scientists and Other Essays*, ed. Gregory Elliott (London: Verso, 1990), p. 78.

Ackerman, Bruce, "Don't Panic!", 208–9
administration, 19, 39, 143
Africa, 219, 223, 238n.8
Albania, 4, 169
Algeria, 218, 219, 222
alien, 40, 122. *See also* foreigner; immigrant
Althusser, Louis, 19, 29, 83, 144, 173, 235
American Revolution, 137
Amin, Samir, 96
Anderson, Benedict, 130
anthropology, 19–22, 25, 40, 60, 195, 202, 240n.21, 248n.27
apartheid, 9, 65, 189; and citizenship, x, 43–45, 116, 170–72; and democracy, 113; global, 113; results of, 46; as violence of borders, 120–24
apocalypticism, 107, 111
Arendt, Hannah, 7, 8, 132, 173, 175, 189, 249n.37, 250n.48; *The Origins of Totalitarianism*, 117–18, 119, 120
Aristotle, 73, 173, 195; *Nichomachean Ethics*, 58; *Politics*, 194
Ash, Timothy Garton, 169; "The Peril of Too Much Power," 211–12
assimilation, 38, 39, 58
Assmann, Aleida, 12, 25, 26
asylum, 31, 111, 121
Austria, 63, 267n.18, 270n.48
authoritarianism, 33–34, 36, 201, 219
autonomy, 196, 197, 198, 199

Babeuf, Gracchus, 87
Balkans, 2, 3, 4, 6, 47, 121, 169, 217–18
Beaud, Olivier, 192–93, 267n.19

belonging: citizenship of, 193; to community, 72; double, 27; egalitarian vs. equitable, 144; in Esposito, 72; and human rights, 8; and identity, 25; national, 23, 220; new kinds of, 112–13; and nonbelonging, 198–99; personal vs. corporative, 144; Schnapper on, 52, 53
Beneš, Edvard, 90
blocs, rival, 10, 103, 104, 134, 166
Bobbio, Norberto, 262n.33
Bodin, Jean, 160, 183, 199, 263n.38; *Six Books of the Republic*, 141–48, 157
Boétie, Étienne de la, 196
borders, 1–10, 101, 132; and apartheid, x; in civic space, 109–10; of communism, 88; of community, 72; of democracy, 99; democratization of, 10, 49, 108–9, 113–14, 117, 176–77; determination of, 109; discriminatory function of, 113; in Esposito, 72; ethnic, 111; and exclusion, 23, 24; and foreigners, 32; as historical institutions, 108, 109; in Huntington, 231; and identity, 27, 110; lack of, 219; movement of, 109, 111; in nationalism, 23; natural, 109; as nondemocratic, 109, 117; between North and South, 104; and politics, 109, 110; in Schmitt, 140; and sovereignty, 1, 140, 157; super, 126–27; translation across, 205; and violence, 117, 124; in Vobruba, 101
Bourdieu, Pierre, 175
bourgeois, 87, 142, 143, 148
Braudel, Fernand, 7, 18
Brazil, 118
Brezhnev, Leonid, 93
Briand, Aristide, 89

Britain, 6, 14, 137, 138, 169
Bulgaria, 4
Bush, George W., 206, 213, 276n.6

capitalism, 10, 40, 82, 91, 105, 127–29, 197, 226
Castel, Robert, 60, 164–65
Chechnya, 168, 218, 228
Chemillier-Gendreau, Monique, 222
Chesneaux, Jean, 4
Chevènement, Jean-Pierre, 31, 34, 35
Chevènement law, 34, 35, 62
Christianity, 6, 86, 224–25. *See also* religion
citizen(s): active, 76; in Bodin, 142; community of, 50, 55, 61, 64, 185, 194; constitutional rights of, 192; criminal as, 188; doubling of, 195–96; as free subject, 142; immigrant as, 39–40; in nation, 21; rights of, 60, 132, 192, 195–96; in Rousseau, 151; as sovereign, 196; as sovereign subject, 198; as subject, 157; world, 201
citizenship, 155–79; active, 48; ascriptive, 182; of belonging, 193; and borders, 3–4, 6; and colonized people, 58; as common good, 61; and community, 52, 54; without community, 66, 76; constituent, 77; constituted, 77; constitution of, viii, ix, 2, 68, 156, 161–62, 182, 190, 197, 198; and democracy, 10, 77, 182, 184, 200; discrimination in, 65; *droit de cité* in, 47; and equality, 9; European, 3, 9, 43, 44, 65, 100, 116, 121, 134, 180–81; in European Union, 121–22, 161; exclusion from, 58, 59–60, 65, 76; and foreigners, 31, 32, 33, 34; future of, 198; and immigrant rights, 41; impossibility of, 156, 162; of Kosovo refugees, 4; and law, 49; and nation, viii, 43, 52; and nationality, 32, 37, 38, 149, 163, 194; political, 51, 52, 72, 163; postnational, viii, 16; as privilege, 64; in Rancière, 72; recasting of, 110; renewal of, 193–94; republican nationalist, 45; of residency, 193; rights of, 49–50, 162; social, 40, 60, 61, 163–65; in state, 182, 194; statutory, 67; substantial vs. formal, 54; supranational, viii; transnational, viii; unequal access to, 121; worksites of, 198
city-state, 18, 68, 194, 247n.16
civic space, 109–10
civil disobedience, 49
civility, 115–16, 130, 131, 132

civilization(s), 4, 5, 10, 39, 57–58, 200–201, 223, 230
civil liberties, 208
civil society, 224–25
class struggle, 18, 21, 28, 40, 84, 128–29, 152, 175, 193, 224
Cold War, 166–67
collective/collectivity, 2, 66, 148, 225–27
colonialism, 6, 7, 9, 38–42, 57–58, 151, 222–23, 249n.37. *See also* decolonization
common, 66, 119
common good, 56
common space, 42, 44, 51
communication, 20, 41, 105, 108, 131, 177–78, 205
communion, myth of, 69, 70, 75
communism, 166, 253n.15; and dominated, 86; Eastern Europe after, 93–95; end of, 78, 79, 81, 82, 93, 94, 167; in Europe, 85–89, 90; in France, 252n.10; history of, 82–83, 85–88; internal vs. external, 84–85; in Italy, 252n.9; in Nancy, 70–71; nationalism after, 93, 94–96, 98; and Nazism, 90–91; and totalitarianism, 252n.12. *See also* Marx, Karl; Marxism
communitarianism, 35, 37, 56, 64, 69, 111, 146
community, viii, 51–77; of citizens, 50, 55, 61, 64, 185, 188, 194; conflict mediation in, 230; of descent, 199; exclusion from, 23, 67, 69; of fate, 44, 131–32, 189, 199; human, 189; indivisibility of, 186; language of, 177; as nationality, 21; and nation-form, 20–21, 25; politics of, 130; primary vs. secondary, 112–13; punishment in, 188; recasting of, 110; and society, 21
conflict, 187–88, 189, 223–24, 230. *See also* class struggle; war
constitution: American, 208, 209; as balance of powers, 192; citizenship in, 58–59; democratic, 183; equivalence of sovereignty to, 153; European, ix, 162, 180–202; exception to, 136; federal, 161; foundational, 195; as fundamental law, 192; historicity of, 195; human rights under, 120; immigrant workers under, 40; material, 161, 267n.20; mixed, 224; political, 162; rights of man in, 183; in Rousseau, 151; in Schmitt, 136, 137; social rights in, 165, 268n.25; and subversion, 195; unitary, 161; use of "we" in, 185

constitution of citizenship, viii, ix, 2, 68, 156, 161–62, 182, 190, 194–95, 197, 198
cosmopolitanism, 56, 148, 173
counterrevolution, 129–30
Cournot, Antoine Augustin, 106
criminal, 139, 140, 188
culture, 8, 16, 20, 26, 60, 110, 152, 200–201, 205

Debray, Régis, 157
Debré, Jean-Louis, 31, 34, 48, 49
decision, 137, 138, 139, 142
Declaration of the Rights of Man and the Citizen, 150, 264n.46
decolonization, 7, 9, 14, 40, 57, 133, 222. *See also* colonialism
Deleuze, Gilles, 63, 129
Delors, Jacques, 160, 267n.22
democracy, 43; after communism, 80; in America, 214; antidemocratic condition of, 140; and apartheid, 113; and borders, 2; bourgeois, 92; and citizenship, 10, 182, 184; conflictual, x, 224, 225; in constitution, 183; in Eastern Europe, 80, 99, 168; equality in, 120; ethnicity in, 52; European, ix–x, 9, 134, 181; exclusion in, 8; expansive, 224, 279n.34; and foreigners, 32; Habermas on, 55, 56; human rights in, 119; and Islam, 226; in justice system, 173–74; and Kant, 7; legal/formal, 224; of market society, 98; and minorities, 8; and nationality, 24; and nation-form, 60, 149; nondemocratic condition of, 117; parliamentary, 99; in popular sovereignty, 157; in Rancière, 74, 118; reciprocity in, 185–86; representative, 187–88; and residency, 63; and rights, 63, 162; in Rousseau, 151; in Schmitt, 137; self-limitation of, 187; social, x, 91, 165; socialist, 92; social/substantial, 224; and state, 187; and United States and Europe, xi; violence in, 120; for workers, 174–76; worksites of, x, 156, 162, 172–79, 182–83
dēmos, 8, 9, 157, 158, 184. *See also* people
Derrida, Jacques, 136, 185; *Specters of Marx*, 107
Descartes, René, 74
dictatorship, 137, 140
Dietrich, Helmut, 123
difference, anthropological, 20, 240n.21, 248n.27

discrimination, 24, 37, 44, 55, 59, 64, 65, 122, 219, 224, 249n.37. *See also* racism
DOM-TOM, 39, 244n.16
droit de cité, 31, 47–48, 118, 198, 202, 243n.1
Durkheim, Émile, 20
Dutch, 6

earth, 57, 104–6, 138. *See also* world
East, 121, 172
Eastern Europe, 14, 78, 79–80, 84, 93–94, 97, 98, 99
Eco, Umberto, 177, 178, 234
economy: age categories in, 112; American, 209, 211; autonomization of, 148, 149; and Balkans, 4; communist critique of, 87; of democracy, 225; of Eastern Europe, 97, 98; European, 3, 169, 217; foreigners in, 38, 171; of nation, 17, 18, 19; parallel, 33; and politics, 147, 199–200; and sovereignty, 145, 146, 147, 159; of Soviet Union, 97; of state, 152–53; in stationary state, 106; subordination of, 157; symbolic effect of, 21; transnational, 110, 200; of violence, 130; world, 18, 21, 57, 102–3, 105–6, 160
education, 28–29, 53, 58, 159, 174, 178, 193, 197, 201–2
emancipation, 32, 59
empire, 18, 133–34
enemy, 1, 55–56, 139, 140
Engels, Friedrich, 87
English language, 177–78
English Revolution, 137
Enlightenment, 57, 159, 201
equality, 9, 59, 60, 68, 86–87, 120, 144, 182, 197
eschatology, 107–8
Esposito, Roberto, 72
ethnic cleansing. *See* genocide
ethnicity, 8, 26, 42, 52, 64, 93–95
ethnocentrism, 93–94
ethnos, 8, 9, 157, 158. *See also* people
Europe, 88, 89; and borders, 7, 168, 220; citizenship in, 3, 9, 43, 44, 65, 100, 116, 121, 134, 180–81; as closed unity, 87; democracy in, 9, 123, 134; equilibrium in, 6, 7, 138, 141; identity of, 9, 168, 169, 219, 254n.24; and international law, 209, 224; as interpreter, 235; language of, 177–78; as mediator, 214, 217, 221, 229–30,

Europe (*cont.*)
231, 232, 234; in multilateral world, 210; public opinion in, 178–79; and race/racism, 5, 44–45, 172; rival conceptions of, 166; and Russia, 218, 269n.34; in Schmitt, 136, 138; security in, 169; as translator, 234; true vs. outer, 169; and United States, x–xi, 2, 4, 211, 212, 213, 214–16, 232
European Charter of Fundamental Rights, 161
European unification: and Cold War, 166; and communism, 85, 90; contradictions in, 3; and democracy, 9; and immigrants, 44–45; and political transnationalization, viii–ix; social rights under, 165; sovereignty in, 133, 156
European Union: citizenship in, 121–22, 161; Delors on, 267n.22; domestic policy of, 220; economy of, 169; entry into, 169, 170; foreign policy of, 220; membership in, 47, 232, 267n.22; and nation-state, 14; post–Cold War influence of, 168
exception, state of, 136, 137–38, 139, 142, 199
exclusion, 9, 29, 186; in Arendt, 117; from citizenship, 58, 59–60, 65, 76; from community, 23, 67, 69; confrontation of, 76; and democracy, 8; of foreigner, 23, 24, 38, 171; of immigrants, 34, 61–65, 122; in Nancy, 69; and nationalism, 23–24; in Rancière, 72, 74; and universalism, 61
expulsion, 35–36

family, 27, 112, 123, 172
fascism, 37, 63, 89, 91, 98–99. *See also* Nazism
Ferry, Jean-Marc, 275n.29
Fischer, Joschka, 216
fiscus. *See* sovereignty: and finances
foreigner, 1, 8, 31–50; as alien, 122, 171; and constitution of citizenship, 194; control of, 111; defense of, 59; in economy, 171; as enemy, 55–56; exclusion of, 23, 24, 38; justice for, 188; in Nancy, 71; in Rancière, 74–75; representation of, 59; under RESEDA law, 62; in Schnapper, 54–55; violence against, 32–33, 34, 41, 172. *See also* immigrant
Foucault, Michel, 29, 128, 143, 144, 205, 221
Fourier, Charles, 87

France, 47, 183, 188; and Algeria, 222; clitoridectomy in, 274n.14; communism in, 252n.10; immigrants in, 31–50, 62–63, 64, 65, 170; multiculturalism in, 225; social rights in, 268n.25
Franciscanism, 86
Franklin, Julian, 145
freedom, 42, 47, 49, 59. *See also* liberty; right(s)
French Revolution, 81, 137
Freud, Sigmund, 26, 27, 196
Furet, François, 81

Gellner, Ernst, 20
Gemeinschaft, 21, 185
genocide, 4, 108, 125, 168, 218, 222. *See also* violence
Germany, 47, 90, 169, 188, 215, 216, 253n.23
Gesellschaft, 21
Giscard d'Estaing, Valéry, 232, 278n.28
globalization/globalized world, 9, 101–14, 115, 139; of culture, 205; democracy in, 225; discriminatory response to, 124; economy of, 102–3, 105–6, 160; and foreign threat, 35, 36; immigrants in, 41; life and death zones of, 126; multilateralism in, 207; as Northern point of view, 257n.11; postnationalism in, 121; racism in, 172; social conflict in, 223; sovereignty in, 153; and violence, 46, 126; workers under, 44
Gorbachev, Mikhail, 167
Gramsci, Antonio, 26, 81–82, 162, 172, 173, 224, 279n.34
Greece, 1, 2, 5
Greece, ancient, 68, 247n.16
Gunsteren, Herman R. van, 131–32, 173, 189, 198–99

Habermas, Jürgen, 74, 161, 176, 189; *Between Facts and Norms*, 183; on citizenship, 55, 56; on communication, 131; on community, 77; on constitution, 191–92; on cosmopolitanism, 136, 173
Haider, Jörg, 63, 270n.48
Hardt, Michael, 131, 133, 175
Hassner, Pierre, 55, 94
Hegel, G.W.F., 27, 28, 68, 147, 149, 152, 157, 173, 201, 265n.58; *Phenomenology of Mind*, 186

hegemony, 6, 7, 11, 26, 279n.34
Helsinki treaties, 90
Hirschmann, Albert, 34
historicity: of constitution, 195; of nation, 17; of nationalism, 11; of nation-form, 11, 12
history: and borders, 5; of communism, 85–88; comparative, 201–2; constitutional, 191; end of, 85; of nation-form, 18; of nations, 16–17; plurisecular, 6; structures in, 21
Hobbes, Thomas, 73, 130, 142, 145, 157, 160, 187, 215, 216, 263n.38; *Leviathan,* 116, 141
Hobsbawm, E. J., 94, 131
human being, 58, 59, 66, 108. *See also* anthropology; right(s): human
Hungary, 90
Huntington, Samuel: *The Clash of Civilizations,* 230, 231

identity, 8, 99; and belonging, 25; and borders, 4, 27, 110; collective, 11, 17, 24, 26, 221; common, 219; communal, 157, 158; ethnic, 64; European, 6, 9, 168, 169, 219, 254n.24; formation of, 29; multiplicity of, 27; and names, 9; national, 11, 17, 22, 23, 24, 25, 38, 220; otherness in, 223; primary vs. secondary, 25–30; univocality of, 27
ideology, 10, 17, 18, 19, 23, 25, 104
immigrant, 8, 31–50, 110, 118, 274n.14; and apartheid, 9, 170–72; control of, 111; and democratization of borders, 176–77; discrimination against, 44, 122, 219; and *droit de cité,* 47; exclusion of, 34, 61–65, 122; family of, 172; justice for, 188–89; language of, 178; law concerning, 34, 35, 48, 49, 62–63; permanent installation of, 112; recolonization of, 38–42; regularization of, 35, 45, 62, 63; repatriation of, 8; rights of, 41, 42, 121; violence against, 112; as workers, 39, 40. *See also* foreigner
imperialism, 6, 7, 19, 57, 91, 117, 119, 120, 170, 223, 234
inclusion/exclusion, x, 3, 38, 50, 54, 56
individual, x, 26, 42, 67, 144, 146, 164, 195–96, 198, 201
insurrection/revolution, 80, 81, 90, 91–93, 118, 137, 186, 187, 195, 196, 198

intervention, humanitarian, 4, 124, 125, 127, 130, 228
Iraq, 212, 215, 217, 227, 276n.6, 277n.18
Ireland, 228
Islam, 29, 225, 226
Israel, x, 213, 218–19, 229
Italy, 14, 90, 92, 252n.9, 268n.25

Jameson, Fredric, "The Vanishing Mediator," 232
Jospin, Lionel, 31, 34, 35, 47
Judaism, 225
juridical order, 136, 138, 140
jus soli, 43
justice, 35–36, 143, 144, 173–74, 188–89, 192

Kadaré, Ismail, 4
Kagan, Robert, "Power and Weakness," 215
Kaldor, Mary, 229
Kant, Immanuel, 7, 132, 183, 192, 196, 197, 215, 216
Keynes, John Maynard, 149, 152, 265n.59, 269n.36
Kosovo, 2, 4–5, 47, 168, 169
Kriegel, Blandine, 174

language, 19–20, 177–78, 234, 271n.66
law, 160; in Bodin, 142, 144; and citizenship, 49; constitution as, 192; and democracy, 173, 174, 183; education in, 174; concerning immigrants, 34, 35, 48, 49, 62–63; international, 131, 209, 224, 226; power to give, 142; in Rancière, 75; RESEDA, 34; in Rousseau, 144, 151; rule of, 150; in Schmitt, 138; in sovereignty, 142, 143; state as based on, 192
Lefort, Claude, 144, 224, 262n.34
Lenin, V. I., 7, 153
liberalism, 24, 207, 208, 214, 232
liberty, 182, 197. *See also* freedom; right(s)
Locke, John, 197
Luhmann, Niklas, 17
Luxemburg, Rosa, 7, 118, 153

Maastricht Treaty, 44, 121, 122
Macedonia, 4
Machiavelli, Niccolò, 17, 141, 223, 239n.15, 278n.32

Malberg, Raymond Carré de, 150, 261n.20
Mann, Thomas: *Betrachtungen eines Un-politischen*, 204; "Zwang zur Politik," 204
Marcou, Lilly, 98–99
market: globalized, 106–7; imperialism of, 38; labor, 29; national, 27; world as, 102; of world-economy, 18. *See also* economy
Marramao, Giacomo: *Dopo il Leviatano*, 192
Marshall, T. H., 191; "Citizenship and Social Class," 164
Marx, Karl, 18; on bourgeois revolution, 148; and collapse of communism, 80; *Communist Manifesto*, 152; on economy, 87; on end of political state, 106; on globalization, 102; on history, 191; labor in, 175; in Nancy, 70; and popular sovereignty, 149
Marxism, 7, 82, 83, 91, 131. *See also* communism
mediator, 200, 214, 217, 221, 229–31, 232, 233, 234
Middle East, 212
military, 3, 209, 211, 214–15, 227–28, 229, 242n.35. *See also* security
Mill, John Stuart, 106, 187
Milner, Jean-Claude, 76
modernity, 13, 68–69, 182, 197
monarch, 6, 145, 148. *See also* sovereign
money, 3, 145, 146, 147, 159. *See also* economy
monopoly, 19, 21, 199, 202
Montbrial, Thierry de, "Europe: La Dialecti-que intérieur-extérieur," 219–20
Montesquieu, 110
Morin, Edgar, 162
Mosse, George, 232
movement, freedom of, 47, 49, 88, 176–77
multiculturalism, 29, 111, 177, 223, 225, 230
multilateralism, 207, 210, 211, 215, 227

Nancy, Jean-Luc, 75, 250n.48; *The Inopera-tive Community*, 69–72
nation, viii, 16–17; and community, 21, 51–52; democratic, 68–69; exclusion from, 54, 61–62; indivisibility of, 150; and nationalism, 22–25; origins and ends of, 22; in Schmitt, 136; as singular, 53; sovereignty of, 7; as unity of state and people, 141

National Front, 32, 37, 122, 244n.12
nationalism, 11, 65; after communism, 93, 94–96, 98; in communism, 95, 242n.33; in Eastern Europe, 94, 97; economic planning in, 96–97; education about, 53; and exclusion, 23–24; and identity, 24; ideology of, 23; and Marxism, 91; and nation, 22–25; in Nazism, 95, 242n.33; republican, 37–38; in Schnapper, 53; and stigmatization of foreigners, 37; universalism of, 54, 56–57; violence of, 24
nationality, 22, 238n.2; absolutization of, 38; and citizenship, 32, 149, 163, 194; as community, 21; *droit de cité* in, 47, 48; dual, 47; European, 43; and foreigners, 31; immigrants and, 41; right to combine, 193; sacralization of, 38
nationals, 44, 61
national socialism, 96
national social state, 61, 68–69
nation-form, 11, 12, 16–22; assimilation in, 58; and borders, 23; as bourgeois, 57; collectivity of citizens in, 55, 56; and community, 20–21, 25; control of, 120–21; and democracy, 60; democratic face of, 149; effectivity of, 27; hegemony of, 18; institutions of, 27; military in, 242n.35; social rights in, 60–61; sovereignty of, 25; statist face of, 149; universalism in, 58; violence of, 24
nation-state, 112; belonging in, 220; colonialism of, 57; conflict mediation in, 230–31; end of, 13–16; foundation of, 195; identity in, 220; institutions of, 11; origin of, 15–16; power of, 221; and representation, 8; rights in, 118; sacred in, 20; unity of, 220; universalism in, 57, 58. *See also* state
NATO, 227, 279n.36
Nazism, 89, 90–91, 95, 99, 120, 227, 242n.33. *See also* fascism
Negri, Antonio, 131, 133, 136, 160, 175
Neo-Keynesianism, 165
Nietzsche, Friedrich, 134, 186–87; *The Gay Science*, 201
nomos, 138–39, 140
North, 14–15, 42, 104, 112, 127, 257n.11

omnipotent, impotence of, 62, 149, 153
Oslo Accords, 229
other, 36, 40, 74, 75, 223, 224

Palestinians, x, 218–19, 228, 229
Paris Commune, 89
Pasqua, Charles, 31, 34, 35, 48
people, viii, 134; and borders, 1; and civic consciousness, 2; and collective, 2; disappearance of, 160, 161; and *ethnos* vs. *demos*, 8, 9, 157, 158; as ideal, 184; new image for, 9; notion of, 8; in Rancière, 72; in Rousseau, 151; in Schmitt, 136; and sovereignty, 140–41, 195; and state, 182; and territory, 200; unavailability of, 184; unity of, 141
periphery, 1, 7, 98
Plato, 86
Poland, 91, 92
police, 3, 46, 76. *See also* security
polis. *See* city-state
politeia, 194–95, 267n.17. *See also* constitution of citizenship
politics, vii–viii; antistrategic, 225; autonomization of, 140; and borders, 109, 110; and citizenship, 51, 52; of civility, 130, 131; and class struggle, 18, 21; of community, 130; cruelty in, 115; and economy, 18, 147, 199–200; end of, 106–7, 108, 111; European, 134; of exclusion, 24; and foreigners, 24; in globalized world, 101, 102, 103, 105–6, 107; history of, 190–91, 192–94; ideology in, 25; militarization of, 209; and nation, 12, 16, 24; negativity in, 75–76; in public vs. private spheres, 112; in Rancière, 72–74; re-creation of, 111; and religion, 147; of sharing/distribution, 72–74; in society, 148; and state, 103; as subjectification, 74; transnationalization of, viii–ix; violence in, 73, 125, 128–29, 130, 131; in virtual world, 107. *See also* security
positivism, 106, 108
postcolonialism, 8, 24, 29, 39, 222, 223
postmodernism, 27, 196
postnationalism, 15; and citizenship, 16, 202; and cosmopolitical society, viii; crisis of, 65; development of, 13, 16; education in, 159; and foreign threat, 35; in globalization framework, 121; political verticality in, 196; and sovereignty, 133, 134, 161; transition toward, 12
poverty, 159, 164, 165
power, 225; constituent, 142, 157, 158, 160, 193; constituted, 160; constitutional balance of, 137, 192; and differences, 20; fis-

cal, 199; limitations of, 144–45; masculinity of, 202; monopoly of, 202; of sovereign, 142
private space, 112, 201
proletarianization, 127–28
property, 51, 60, 61, 72–73, 87, 177
Proudhon, Pierre Joseph, 68
public space, 51; in Arendt, 118; borders of, 111; control from, 147–48; European, 43; exclusion from, 42; and foreigners, 32, 33; invisibility of, 64; popular sovereignty as foundation of, 183; separateness of, 112

race: emancipation of, 59; and ethnicity, 26; and Europe, 5; exclusion by, 8, 37; of immigrants, 123; stigmatization by, 122
racism: American, 123; European, 44–45, 172; toward immigrants, 36, 63; in impotence of omnipotent, 62; in Rancière, 74–75. *See also* discrimination
Rancière, Jacques, 32, 118, 250n.50; *Disagreement*, 72–75
reciprocity, 185–86, 190, 194, 197
religion, 200; in America, 213; autonomization of, 149; in Bodin, 145–46; in civil society, 224–25; communism in, 86; comparative history of, 201–2; conflict over, 93–95; control over, 145, 147, 157; dissent in, 145–46; in education, 28; European policy toward, x; exclusion of, 29; liberation from, 159; national, 27; public vs. private interests in, 146; in Schmitt, 138; universalism in, 225
Renan, Ernst, "What Is a Nation?", 17
republicanism, 6, 33–38, 52, 76
residency, 43, 44, 48, 63, 177, 193
revolution. *See* insurrection/revolution
right(s), 34, 35; capitalist destablization of, 197; citizens', 49–50, 132, 162; collective, x; to combine nationalities, 193; democratic, 183; and foreigners' defiance, 34; founding declarations of, 58–59; human, 3, 8, 58, 117, 118–19, 132; immigrant, 36; individual, x, 198; of man, 188–89; to movement, 47, 49, 88, 176–77; natural, 146; political, 72, 118–19, 163; in Rancière, 72; of residency, 48, 63; right to have, 119, 120; social, 37, 163, 164, 172, 192, 193, 198, 199, 268n.25; in social conflict, 223; social vs. political, 41; to vote, 32; worker's, 48, 60, 163, 164

Rosanvallon, Pierre, 265n.57
Rousseau, Jean-Jacques, 17, 69, 70, 144, 149–50, 157, 160, 183, 186, 196, 197, 263n.38; *Social Contract*, 150–51
Russia, 7, 168–69, 218, 269n.34. *See also* Soviet Union

Said, Edward, 232, "Europe versus America," 212–13
sans-papiers, 31, 48–49, 118
Schengen agreement, 123
Schmitt, Carl, 7, 55, 120, 135–41, 145, 153, 157, 160, 199, 219; *Die Diktatur*, 141; *The Nomos of the Earth*, 5, 136, 138, 141, 231, 261n.16; *Political Theology*, 136, 141
Schnapper, Dominique, 77, 246n.8, 247n.16; *Community of Citizens*, 50, 52–55, 60
Schröder, Gerhard, 215, 277n.18
secularism, 138, 140, 145, 146, 159, 224
security, 43, 62, 123, 136, 169, 225–27, 228, 232. *See also* military; police
self-consciousness, 186
self-determination, 3, 66, 184, 198
semiperiphery, 96, 128
Sen, Amartya, 223, 268n.30
Senarclens, Pierre de, 124–25
September 11 attacks, 206, 207
Serbia, 3, 168
sharing/distribution, 72–74
Sieyes, Emmanuel-Joseph, 160; *What Is the Third Estate?*, 151
Sittlichkeit, 28, 30, 242n.36
socialism, 78, 87
society: civil, 148, 152; and community, 21; control of, 64; cosmopolitical, viii, 14; economic, 148; market, 98; of nation-form, 17; political, 148; transformation of, 131
South, 14–15, 39, 104, 112, 121, 128, 171, 172
South Africa, 171
sovereign, 6, 136, 137, 142, 145, 148, 150–51, 196
sovereigntism, 160, 183
sovereignty, 133–54; absolute, 144, 147; alternatives to, 133, 148; and balance of powers, 7; in Bodin, 141–48, 157; and borders, 1, 5, 6–7, 109, 140; classical representation of, 153; coherence of, 142; conceptualization of, 135; and constitu-

tion, 153; crisis of, 148, 153, 160; decomposition of, 137; democratic, 134; and equality, 196; and European Constitution, ix; in European unification, 156; external dimensions of, 157; and finances, 145, 146, 147, 152–53, 159; and foreigners, 32; genealogy of, 135; and globalization, 153; hierarchical principles of, 196; and immigrants, 36; internal dimensions of, 157–58; leap from princely to popular, 196; limitations of, 144–46; marks of, 65, 141–48, 160, 182–83, 195, 199; monarchical, 145, 196; national, 7, 25, 152, 163; and order, 142; perpetuation of, 148; popular, ix, 37, 134, 137, 145, 148–54, 157, 182, 183–90, 199, 200, 201; postnational, 161; primacy of border to, 157; recasting of, 110, 145, 147; self-limitation of, 187; spectral existence of, 185; state, 134, 152, 153, 189; and subjection, 150–51; suppression of, 141–42; over territory, 249n.37
Soviet Union, 7, 90, 92; collapse of, 103–4, 107; economic planning in, 97; end of communism in, 79, 80, 81; ethnoreligious conflict in, 94; and Europe, 89; expansionism of, 88–89; Gramsci on, 81–82; gulags of, 88; as national-socialist state, 95; normalization in, 93
Spinoza, Baruch, 137, 179, 187, 196, 197; *Theologico-Political Treatise*, 146
Spivak, Gayatri Chakravorty, 131
Stalin, Joseph, 95
state: borders of, 113–14; citizenship in, 182, 194; civil society in, 152; collapse of, 81, 98–99; communist, 81, 82, 83–84, 88; communist alternatives to, 86–87; control of flows by, 113; decentralized, 46; and democracy, 113–14, 187; development of, 20; exclusion by, 62–63, 67; fiscal power of, 199; and foreigners, 34; human rights in, 119; individual link to, 201; justice in, 192; lack of, 117–18; law of, 192; and Malberg, 150; as mediator, 200; national, 194; and national collectivity, 150; national popular, 193; national social, 61, 68–69, 127, 129, 163, 193; and nation-form, 149; nonexistence of, 157; and people, 182; personality vs. impersonality of, 137; and politics, 103; recasting of, 110; in Schmitt, 136; as social, 192; sovereignty of, 189; territorialization of, 138; unity of,

141; welfare, 112, 127, 163; work in, 40. *See also* nation-state

stereotype, 41

stigmatization, 37, 122. *See also* discrimination

Stockholm Appeal, 90

Stresemann, Gustav, 89

supranationalism, viii, 14, 133, 134, 159, 183

symbolism, 19, 21, 22, 23

taxation, 145, 146, 147, 149, 159, 200

technology, 104, 105–6, 107, 111, 129, 139, 205

Terray, Emmanuel, 42

territory, 5, 138, 143, 144, 157, 177, 200, 249n.37, 256n.6

terrorism, 208, 226, 227

Thompson, E. P., 126

Tillion, Germaine, 231

Tocqueville, Alexis de, 147, 187

topography, 116, 132

totalitarianism, 82, 119, 144, 184, 242n.33, 252n.12

trade unions, 46, 165, 174–75. *See also* worker

transindividual, 26, 186

translation, 234, 271n.66

transnationalism, viii–ix, 13, 110, 133, 176, 193, 200, 202, 222

Treaty of Westphalia, 6, 138

Turkey, 5, 232

unilateralism, 206, 207, 213

United Nations, 14, 217, 226

United States, 2, 4, 123, 171, 223, 227, 277n.18; European influence on, x–xi, 206–13, 214–16, 218–19, 220

Universal Declaration of Human Rights, 193

universalism, 15, 37, 54, 56–58, 61, 64, 188–89, 205, 206, 225

utopia, 87, 102

Vedrine, Hubert, 212

violence: of apartheid, 46; in Arendt, 117; of borders, 117; without borders, 124; in capitalism, 127–29, 226; cruelty as, 115; in democracy, 120; discriminatory, 50; for

domination, 116–17; economics of, 130; in education, 29, 159; in exclusion, 76; against foreigners, 32–33, 34, 41, 172; global, 126, 127–28, 229; against human rights, 119; in Huntington, 231; and identity, 25; against immigrants, 112, 123; legitimate, 140; of National Front, 244n.12; in politics, 73, 125, 128–29, 130, 131; possibility of, 11; in Rancière, 73; in Schmitt, 139, 140; in social conflict, 223–24; structural, 11; visibility of, 125–26

virtual, 105, 107, 125

Vobruba, Georg, "The Limits of Borders," 101

Wacquant, Loïc, 127

Wallerstein, Immanuel, 7, 18, 42, 102, 128, 153, 159, 209, 257n.19; *Race, Nation, Class,* 8

Walzer, Michael, 73

war, 138, 139, 143, 222, 230, 231, 276n.6, 277n.18. *See also* conflict

"we," use of, 185, 188, 189

Weber, Max, 224, 232

West, 4, 39, 88, 89

Western Europe, 14

Wihtol de Wenden, Catherine, 122, 172

Wilson, Woodrow, 215

Winstanley, Gerrard, 87

worker, 171; democracy for, 174–76; exclusion of, 61; foreign, 31; immigrant, 32, 39, 40, 44, 118; mobility of, 47; as nationals, 61; and proletarianization, 128, 129; recolonization of, 44; rights of, 48, 60, 163, 164; and trade unions, 46; underground, 62

world, 57, 101, 102. *See also* globalization/globalized world

World War I, 139, 169

World War II, 120

xenophobia, 32, 63, 99

Yugoslavia, former, 2, 3, 5, 6, 98, 168, 169, 217–18, 228

zones, of life and death, 126, 128, 130